Delia Despair

The
Grown-Ups
Wouldn't Like it

Adventures in several countries and many languages

Delia Despair

The
Grown-Ups
Wouldn't Like it

Adventures in several countries and many languages

MEREO
CIRENCESTER

Mereo Books

1A The Wool Market Dyer Street Cirencester Gloucestershire GL7 2PR
An imprint of Memoirs Publishing www.mereobooks.com

The grown-ups wouldn't like it: 978-1-86151-253-6

First published in Great Britain in 2014
by Mereo Books, an imprint of Memoirs Publishing

The address for Memoirs Publishing Group Limited can be found at
www.memoirspublishing.com

The Memoirs Publishing Group Ltd Reg. No. 7834348

The Memoirs Publishing Group supports both The Forest Stewardship Council® (FSC®) and
the PEFC® leading international forest-certification organisations. Our books carrying both the
FSC label and the PEFC® and are printed on FSC®-certified paper. FSC® is the only
forest-certification scheme supported by the leading environmental organisations including
Greenpeace. Our paper procurement policy can be found at
www.memoirspublishing.com/environment

Typeset in 9/12pt Bembo
by Wiltshire Associates Publisher Services Ltd. Printed and bound in Great Britain by
Printondemand-Worldwide, Peterborough PE2 6XD

To Stephen and Belinda

PART ONE

———— ❧ ————

CHAPTER ONE

For the first five years of my life I was brought up by someone my mother happened to meet on the beach. "I'm going back to Nigeria next week to rejoin my husband," she mentioned to this woman, "but I've got a baby of six months and I don't know what to do with her."

"I'll look after her for you," said the woman, whose name was Joan Priestley.

And so it came about that my sister Badger, aged five, and I went to live at Airlie House, Grand Avenue, in Hove. Joan's mother and her little boy Bretton, who was also five, lived there as well. I was a bit confused about who my mother was as I saw so little of her in my first five years: she became my Blue Mummy (I think she wore a lot of navy), Joan was my Red Mummy and I also had a Green Mummy and a White Mummy, who were probably just friends of Joan's who happened to visit.

Joan's mother was Mrs Edwards and she was a wonderful cook. She made delicious potato pie which had layers of cream between the potato, and lemon cake which had thick dark chocolate icing on top. I called her Granny Hove. I must have been a rather disagreeable baby as there are numerous photographs of me sitting in a pram with a mass of blonde curls, looking furious, and there is a nursery rhyme that was frequently quoted – "There was a little girl who had a little curl right in the middle of her forehead. When she was good she was very very good but when she was bad she was horrid!"

My very first memory is of sitting in a high chair and spitting out a prune. It landed on the green carpet that ran all over the maisonette and was much cherished both by Auntie Joan and Granny Hove, as was the polished antique furniture.

When I was about three Mummy came home and Badger and I went to stay at Granny's house in Surbiton for a short while. We had a nursemaid called Edith, whom we didn't like at all. She always smelt of TCP and if you fell over and grazed your leg she would put iodine on it and seemed to enjoy the pain this caused.

Badger and I had a toy car and it was decided that we should repaint it red with black wheels. I was to paint the red part and she was to do the black. We were really looking forward to this, but on the day we were to do it I was very naughty. I don't know what I did, but Edith sent me to bed. My curtains were drawn and all my toys were put on top of the wardrobe. "Now you're to stay in your cot and NOT to get out of bed," she said sternly.

As soon as she had gone out of the room I climbed out of my cot and peeped out of the window to see Edith painting the red bits of the car and Badger painting the black wheels, which I thought was most unfair. Not only was I being deprived of doing something I had really looked forward to but Edith was doing the best part, painting the bodywork red and letting Badger do the less agreeable part of the black wheels.

While I was out of my cot I climbed on a chair and reached up to the top of the cupboard and got a teddy bear, a gollywog and a sailor doll, all of which I played with until later when I heard Edith returning. Then I lay right on top of these toys and kept very still so that she couldn't see them. She thought it was strange that I was lying so still, but she never suspected I had disobeyed her.

We had a tortoise at this time and one day my mother and my aunt looked out of the window and saw me kicking the tortoise on its back and saying, "You silly fing, you don't do nuffing". When I saw them looking at me, I started to stroke the tortoise and say, "Nice tortoise, nice tortoise," but as soon as I thought they weren't looking I reverted to kicking it again and saying, "You silly fing, you don't do nuffing." I must have been a horrid little child. Then our mother went back to Nigeria to rejoin our father, and we went back to Hove again.

There were also some other children whom Auntie Joan Priestley looked after at Airlie House, I suppose because, like mine, their parents were abroad somewhere. Besides Bretton and Badger and me there was a little boy called Dermot and two brothers called Richard and James Van den Bergh. I was the youngest by several years, which was a great disadvantage. In the summer when we played Cowboys and Indians I was the horse that was tied up to a tree and left there. When we played Pig in the Middle I was always the very frustrated pig. When we went up on the roof and tipped snow down onto unsuspecting passers-by, I was the one that didn't realise you had to dodge back when the angry snow-bespattered victims looked up to see who had perpetrated this dastardly act. In card games I always seemed to be the Old Maid and in Monopoly I was the one who landed on Park Lane with four houses and had to pay hundreds of pounds. It was a great relief to go to jail and miss three turns, but then one of the others would interferingly pay my fine for me so that I had to go round the dreaded board again and probably land on some other equally awful place. "Right, that's Regent Street, with four houses, you owe me £1,100." I might just manage to pay this when it was my turn again and this time I would land on Mayfair. "Right, Mayfair with one hotel, that's £2,000." "But I haven't got it, Bretton…" "Never mind, you can give me all your remaining property instead." These games of Monopoly seemed to go on for days and were nearly always won by Bretton.

Living by the sea meant that we spent a lot of time on the beach. I could swim before I could walk, and my feet grew hardened to the pebbles so that I could run all over them without feeling any pain. The summers always seemed to be sunny and hot.

I learnt some curious facts of life at this time. When we were in the bath we were interested to see the differences in our anatomy. I didn't have one of those sticky-out things the boys had, which were called poufs. And women's bosoms were called pom-poms. For years I thought these were the correct names, just as No. 2 was doing your business. The cat did his business on the carpet, which was bad enough, but when my best friend's father did his business at work I was really shocked. What a shameful thing to have happened, I thought, and was it also on the carpet?

My best friend was Susie Roberts, who was only one month younger than me. She was Bretton's cousin, her mother Barbara was Joan's sister and she was very glamorous. She had once been an actress. Auntie Barbara was married to Uncle Bruce and he was very rich and lived in an enormous house in West Sussex with a long drive and royal blue carpets wall to wall. Their house was later sold to Vera Lynn. I was invited to stay there, and I slept in a big room with Susie. Next door was her brother Timothy and baby Richard was in his parents' room. We went into Auntie Barbara's room while she was breast-feeding baby Richard and I was shocked to see her pom-poms out on display.

Uncle Bruce had black hair and was very frightening. He had a terrible temper and all his children were terrified of him, especially if he was in one of his moods. Once when we were happily playing on the beach Susie told me he would make us go home, just because we were happy. When I went to stay there I blotted my copybook because I said 'damn'. I don't know why I said it, but all hell was let loose. I must have been about three.

"*What did you say?*" said Auntie Barbara, scandalised. I was standing between her and Uncle Bruce and I just remember staring up at their legs, which seemed to tower over me.

"I said, damn" I repeated.

"My God!" said Uncle Bruce, "I'm not having that child staying here in my house a minute longer." So I was despatched home in deep disgrace.

One of our greatest treats was to be taken to the cinema, but the very first films I remember were "Snow White" which had a wicked queen in it and "The Wizard of Oz" which had terrifying witches. I became obsessed with witches, I had nightmares about them and drew pictures of figures in tall hats with broomsticks. I used a hard stabbing pencil and coloured in the hats with lots of black crayon. I was convinced that some houses nearby that had black front doors and pointed pediments over the top were witches' houses and I wouldn't walk past them.

When she was nine, my sister Badger was sent away to Roedean, where she was the youngest girl. At the end of the first term she was told to bring an apron back next term, and all through the holidays she kept asking if they could go out and get this apron, but the day came to go back to school and it still hadn't been bought. People don't seem to realise how very important this sort of thing is to a small child. Poor Badger was so worried about not having an apron that she was physically sick and couldn't go back to school at the beginning of the term, and when she did go back she found half the class had forgotten all about the aprons anyway.

My mother - my Blue Mummy - came home on leave from Nigeria from time to time. She took me into Brighton and we passed a lovely toy shop in Preston Street. I asked her to buy me a toy and she said No, I couldn't have it because I had asked for it. She loved both of us children dearly but she was quite strict like that.

My mother was beautiful and she had a wonderful sense of humour. She was always taking people off and made everyone laugh, but her strong personality belied her low self-esteem, and she once said ruefully, "You should never underestimate yourself as people always take you at your own estimation." For instance, she would say she was a bad cook and then her sisters-in-law said, as if they had thought of it themselves, "Of course Eileen can't cook," which was quite untrue as she was a good - if self-effacing – cook, whose roasts were succulent and delicious. She and my father bought a house in Broadstairs, Kent where we lived for a very short time.

My father was also considered good-looking, although Badger and I couldn't see it ourselves. He looked very young for his age and later, when I went to school, the other girls took him for my brother. When we were in the house in Broadstairs I told my mother I had seen my father kissing Maud, our maid, and my mother just laughed because Maud was in her sixties and quite plain, so she didn't feel it was much of a threat. I had already developed a reputation for making up stories.

CHAPTER TWO

It was 1939 and the outbreak of war and we children were all fitted out with gas masks. They were in square cardboard boxes with a green canvas cover. We had no idea what they were for, but we had great fun putting them on and talking in funny voices as if we were under the sea.

Then the beaches in Brighton and Hove were fenced off with barbed wire and put out of bounds to the public in case the Germans landed on them. It was decided that Badger and I should leave Hove and move to our grandmother's house in Surbiton. About the same time we went there, our cousins Audrey and Jean returned from Ceylon with their mother Auntie Joan Moodey, whose husband had recently died. I don't think she minded too much about this as he had been quite unkind to her. Also there was my beloved Auntie Winnie, or Winks as she was nicknamed, whom we all adored. Granny had a lovely house called Fownhope, which was quite large and had attics with gurgling noises and bathrooms in which there stood free-standing baths with brown stains where the water tap had dripped for years.

There was a picture on the landing of a young woman named Hope with a bandage round her head, curled up and sitting on top of the world. It is a copy of a painting by Watts in the Tate Gallery. It fascinated me. What was she doing sitting there, and why was there a bandage round her head?

Granny Cooper was my mother's mother, a beautiful old lady with snow white hair. She smoked a lot and every morning a maid took her a tray with a teapot and a plate of very thin brown bread and butter, and when the maid went into the bedroom you could smell this very strong smell of smoke from the Craven A cigarettes she smoked. I felt quite envious about the brown bread and butter but we children never got any.

Granny Cooper was quite strict and we all had tasks to do. In the morning we had to lay the big dining table for breakfast. "Go and fetch the force," she said to me one day.

"The what?" I said.

"The force, the force!" she said sharply.

I went into the kitchen having no idea what I was to get. It turned out that Force was a make of cornflakes that no longer exist, having been taken over by Kelloggs. We had to put a large white cloth on the table and woe beside anyone who spilt something onto it. After the meal we had to sweep up the crumbs with a little brush into the brush and crumb tray.

After breakfast we had to go upstairs and "sit down." We didn't know what this meant at first and just went upstairs and sat down anywhere, on the chair or on the stairs. Then Granny would say, "Have you sat down today?" and it turned out she meant, had we been to the lavatory? She got quite impatient if you didn't understand what she meant first time, but really she was very kind.

She had a lovely garden where she would go and de-head the roses. The first part of the garden was lawn, surrounded by rose beds, then a little path led into the vegetable garden, which was surrounded by small box hedges. There were rows of vegetables and green glass cloches with marrows and rhubarb growing underneath. At the end of the vegetable part was the orchard with wonderful fruit trees. I especially remember the dark cherry trees and the plums, as I made myself sick eating too many and once I picked one up off the ground and put it into my mouth, unaware there was a hole in it with a wasp inside. I was stung on the tongue, which could have been dangerous, but I survived, though I did not get very much sympathy.

I enjoyed digging up tiny new potatoes in the vegetable garden, or picking raspberries and peas which were then put into a bowl and I would sit in the garden with Granny and shell them for lunch. I was horrified sometimes to find a fat white maggot inside. There were no such things as insecticides. Granny had an old gardener with white hair and a white beard. He was a dear old man and I was very fond of him. Once I met him outside in the road and we had a conversation which ended with his touching his cap and saying, "Boi-boi Miss." I repeated "Boi-boi," because I didn't want him to think I spoke any differently.

At the very end of the garden was a pond, beyond which were fields with cows in them. The pond was dark and covered with weeds and rather sinister and we were told never to go near it. Someone had drowned there, at least I think they had but maybe I made it up. However, I didn't make up the wicked uncle whom we were never allowed to mention. He was supposed to have done something really bad and we longed to know what it was. Winks said she'd tell me one day but she never did.

My cousins and I spent hours playing in the garden. We collected tiny spiders from the webs in the box hedges and kept them in a shallow box which we called our spider garden. But Badger was very frightened of spiders and soon I became frightened of them too. We were always playing jokes on one another, and one day one of the children put a dead spider on my cereal spoon at breakfast. I didn't notice it and ate it, whereupon there was a roar of laughter and they told me I had just eaten a spider. I burst into tears. Another time someone produced a glass dish with pretend raspberry jam. It was passed to me, I dug my spoon in and it was hard as nails because it wasn't real jam at all. This was disappointing and frustrating. We played games of fortune where you spun a knife and called out "This person is going to be very rich," or "This person is going to end up cleaning the lavatories at Victoria Station," which was the very worst fate we could think of.

Twice a week we had pocket money, a penny on Wednesday and a penny on Saturday. I often saved up my pennies and bought a twopenny bar of chocolate for Winks's much loved Scottie dog Macfee. He loved chocolate and would eat it all at once if he was not stopped, so one day I pushed half the chocolate bar under a tall bureau cabinet. When I went to recover it some days later there were tiny little teeth marks all round the edge. I unjustly accused my cousins of eating it but they pointed out that the teeth marks were much too small, and of course it must have been mice.

One day Macfee disappeared and was never seen again. We were all very sad and Winks was heartbroken. She said she wouldn't have minded quite so much if she had just known what had happened to him.

Granny had been born in Victorian times and was quite prudish, for instance she thought legs should not be seen so the poor canary wore cotton leggings and even the legs of the piano were hidden from view and covered with cotton. There were a lot of Cooper relations living in Surbiton. In the big house next door to Fownhope lived Grandpa's brother Uncle Harry, who was a family doctor, his wife Aunt Elaina who spoke with a funny accent as she had been born in Chile, and their children, Guy, Peter, Valerie and Tony who were all cousins to my mother and my aunts. Also in Surbiton lived Great Aunt Chattie, who had been a champion tennis player at Wimbledon and had won it five times in the late 1890s and early 1900s, and been runner-up the other times. The first time she won she rode to Wimbledon on her bicycle and her father was pruning the roses when she got back and said, "Where have you been?" She said, "I've just won Wimbledon," and he said "Oh," and went on pruning the roses. Aunt Chattie was a small bird-like woman with a beaky nose and glasses. She was stone deaf but funny, and she often made us laugh.

She was also alarmingly outspoken. She met me in the road one day and said, "Hello Delia, you get uglier every time I see you!" We used to go to her house sometimes and try to play tennis on her lawn but we had none of us inherited her talent and she told us we were "rubbish," which we were, but didn't particularly like being told so.

My mother didn't care for her very much because when she was a little girl Aunt Chattie had given her a dolls' wardrobe as a present. My mother thought this was a pretty rotten present as she had no dolls' clothes to put in it and she thought, what was the point of a dolls' wardrobe if you had nothing to put in it? So, in a fit of pique, she put Aunt Chattie's jewellery down the lavatory. Luckily it was recovered but Aunt Chattie never liked my mother after that and the feelings were entirely mutual.

Aunt Chattie's husband Uncle Alfred was a solicitor and the rest of the family thought him rather dodgy as he had speculated with all their money. Granny's husband Sam had worked on the railroad in Chile and Uncle Alfred had invested all his money on his behalf. Every time Grandpa asked how his shares were doing, Uncle Alfred was quite vague and just said they were fine. But in fact Alfred was speculating with his clients' money and when it came to the crunch he paid them back out of money belonging to his wife's relations. The result was that Granny was quite poor by the standards of those days, though she would never have dreamed of saying anything, and certainly it was all kept from Aunt Chattie.

There was another Cooper family in Surbiton, another of my grandfather's brothers called Archie, who had married his cousin Maud. They had a daughter called Nina who it was considered had married beneath her, a petty officer called Bill. They had four children who were slightly younger than we were, called Roger, Alison, Mary and Tony. We didn't think much of them – Roger thought he was a dog and spent most of his time under a table barking, and Alison was once rude to Winks who had gone round to visit them on her bicycle. Aunt Maud said to Alison, "Why is the front door open?" and she replied, "So that Winnie can go." Winks was not impressed with this.

We liked the Harry Coopers, but not the others particularly. Once my cousins and I were playing with Plasticine in the garden at Fownhope and to the irritation of the grown-ups we mixed all the colours together and made balls which we threw up into the air, shouting out "There goes Aunt Chattie!" and "There goes Aunt Maud!" We thought this was terribly funny but the grown-ups were not amused and the Plasticine, all mixed up with bits of grass and mud, was ruined.

Another of our games was with our dolls and teddies. I had two black dolls which I was particularly fond of called Topsy Turvy and Chloe, both of which had been exquisitely dressed by Granny Hove. Topsy had a yellow silk dress and Chloe had a green one, and underneath they had beautiful silk petticoats and knickers, all trimmed with lace. I also had a rubber doll called Jean, and two teddy bears called Horace and Mary Plain. We invented an amazing world in which our animals and dolls had many adventures. Stamp books which had pages of advertisements between the stamps were made into miniature passports and our dolls travelled far and wide across the sea on ships. We lived and breathed these adventures, it was our whole world. But then quite suddenly Granny Cooper said she thought we were too old for dolls, and from one day to the next we were forbidden to play with them ever again and had no more of our imaginary games. I think she thought it was unhealthy and that we were beginning to lose the difference between reality and make-believe, but I've often wondered why we didn't make more of a fuss.

Now there wasn't as much to do and we got on the grown-ups' nerves by mooching around aimlessly. We were sent for endless walks round the Recreation Ground, a most dismal place with its oblong of greyish grass and no trees or anything of interest. Every time we returned home we were told to go out again.

"What are you doing, coming back so soon? Go round the recreation ground."

"But we've been round it three times already."

"Don't be so ridiculous. You need to be out in the fresh air. Off you go."

So off we went. Reluctantly. Bored, bored with the grey grey grass and the grey grey day. Surbiton was not the most stimulating of places.

One day Audrey and Jean and I caught a bus to Kingston and went to Bentalls. This was, of course, totally forbidden, for we were hardly allowed outside the garden. We went into the cafeteria and bought Bath buns, and were having a lovely time going up the down escalators and down the up, when suddenly Aunt Elaina appeared. She said "Hello," then she must have gone back and told Granny and Winks how surprised she was that they allowed us to go into Kingston by ourselves. We were much too young, she thought. Granny and Auntie Winks were furious with us, and said we had let them down. I seemed always to be letting people down.

When it was nearly Christmas we were given half a crown each and taken to Woolworths in Surbiton to buy our Christmas presents. I bought a little bottle of poppy scent for my mother – I don't actually know what poppies smell of, if they smell at all – and a deep blue eye bath for Granny which I thought was a vase. I had no idea it was an eye bath. I didn't know you had baths for eyes. Granny roasted a goose for Christmas dinner and it was all very festive despite being at war.

Fownhope and the Harry Coopers' house next door had Italian wrought-iron gates which were soon taken away by the War Office to be used for the war effort. Granny and Winks started making elaborate preparations, which everyone had to do. They made heavy blackout curtains for all the windows so that no lights could be seen from outside and if even a tiny glimmer was visible, a warden would come knocking on the door and tell us to put the lights out. They stuck strips of brown sticky paper across all the windows so that the glass would not shatter if a bomb dropped nearby. Food became rationed and Granny pickled eggs in a bath in the cellar, which tasted horrible. Or sometimes we had scrambled dried egg, which was not too bad though it didn't actually taste of egg. The cakes had bright red cherries on top which were not real cherries but bits of turnip dyed red. I was shocked to think we were being deceived into thinking we were eating cherries when all the time it was just a bit of turnip.

It was decided that we children should no longer sleep in our bedrooms, so mattresses were put downstairs and Badger, Audrey, Jean and I slept on these. When the air-raids started and the siren went off, quite a sinister sound, we would leap up from our mattresses and go down into the torch-lit cupboard under the stairs. It was really rather exciting, lots of rugs were put on the floor and it was quite cosy. It had a funny musty smell which, when I smell it in cellars today, always brings back rather happy memories of those days. We were too young then to see the bad side of being at war.

CHAPTER THREE

Then news came that my parents' house in Broadstairs had been hit by an incendiary bomb and razed to the ground. My father's sister Margaret said we ought to come up to North Yorkshire where she lived with her family, as there was no bombing up there and it was very safe. My father liked this idea, so to Yorkshire we went. Badger was away at boarding school so there was just my mother and me, and we took the train to York. The train was packed to the hilt with servicemen.

When we reached York my mother got out of the train to buy some sandwiches and magazines, leaving me on my own. Suddenly, before she had come back, the train started off. I burst into tears. Then a tall soldier hoisted me onto his shoulders and walked along the corridor, saying "This little girl has lost her mother, has anyone seen her?" Miraculously my mother had managed to get into the very last compartment as the train started off, so we were reunited. I'm sure my mother was very grateful to the soldier for looking after me, she was always very grateful to everyone for anything.

When we got to Yorkshire my Auntie Margaret was on the platform to meet us. She was generous, pretty, very amusing and rather frivolous. She called everyone "darling". However there was a snag, as she was married to a fearsome old man called Uncle Cliff Scott-Hopkins who terrified everyone. He was years older than her. It seemed that when she was very young she and her friend Madge had decided to marry two rich old men who would presumably die and leave them all their money. However it didn't work out like that for Madge's husband became an invalid and she had to nurse him for years and years, and Uncle Cliff had no intention of dying, ever.

He and Auntie Margaret lived in a large house called Low Hall with their two children, my cousins Elizabeth and Clive, who were a little bit younger than me. Uncle Cliff kept pheasants in cages in the garden, which he thought more of than any of his family. Elizabeth and Clive were only allowed to wear gym shoes in the garden and had to creep about silently in case they disturbed the pheasants. Once, Elizabeth told me later, Uncle Cliff was furious with her because she had dropped her handkerchief in her bedroom. Uncle Cliff had terrible rows with all the tradespeople and Auntie Margaret spent much of her time going round to see them afterwards to apologise.

Auntie Margaret had found us lodgings with a Mrs Reeves in the village of Kirbymoorside, which was where she lived. I liked being with Mrs Reeves, but there wasn't enough room in her house, especially when my father suddenly appeared, having come home on leave. I didn't like my father very much because he was a total stranger and I didn't like the way he was in my mother's bedroom with the door shut. That had never happened; we had always wandered into her room when we felt like it but now we were not wanted. Another thing about my father was that he didn't much like children. He was always quoting *his* parents, who said "Children should be seen and not heard."

Every night when I said my prayers I said "God bless Mummy and Daddy and my dear little sister Badger [who was really my big sister] and please let me have a baby sister." Years later I found out that my mother had been pregnant while we were in Yorkshire and my father had made her have an abortion. This was very wrong of him because abortions were illegal in those days. Anyway, there was no chance of God answering my prayers for a baby sister and my mother seemed anxious I should not keep asking. I once said to my mother, "Me and Badger don't like being told we look like Uncle this or Auntie that. Me and Badger want to look like ourselves." But I was quite lonely as Badger was away so much and I only saw her in the holidays. Roedean had been evacuated up to Keswick, which might as well have been a million miles away.

One day somebody gave me a copy of a little magazine for children called *Sunny Stories*, and in it was the final episode of *The Enchanted Wood* by Enid Blyton. It was about a tree called the Faraway Tree which the children climbed, finding themselves in amazing lands at the top. Some of the lands were nice but then they would move on, to be followed by a land which might not be nice at all and the children would get stuck in a horrible place. It was exciting and frightening at the same time. I devoured this episode and it propelled me into a wonderful world of make-believe.

I now thought of nothing but fairies. I longed to find this tree in the enchanted wood and was convinced that one day I would come upon it. I wrote a short story about two flowers that could talk, called Buttercup and Daisy, boringly nicknamed But and Day. My next story was about a little rabbit whose mother was called Miss Bunny. Some of the little rabbit's friends came to tea and said to Miss Bunny "Why are you called *Miss* Bunny when you have a baby?" But seeing that Miss Bunny did not like the question, they did not ask any more. My mother thought this very funny because I had absolutely no idea about unmarried mothers or anything like that.

I also wrote a poem about Hitler, which I sent up to a newspaper. I was convinced they would publish it, although it was actually very very bad. It went something like, 'Aye aye yippee yippee aye, Hitler is a dirty German spy,' and continued in that vein. In due course it came back, much to my surprise and disappointment.

My mother thought it would be a good idea if I had a friend, so Auntie Margaret phoned someone she knew with a little girl the same age as me and that was how I met Margot. We became best friends at once and played together every day, usually at her house, which had a large garden. She, like me, firmly believed in fairies. We also believed in Father Christmas. I went to the shops with my mother and said, "I would like that, and that, and that." And to my amazement, all the things I told her I wanted turned up in my Christmas stocking. "But how did Father Christmas *know* I wanted these things?" I asked. I thought he must be an amazing person, and he seemed to get half the things from Woolworths. Once, when I was at Margot's house I heard my mother say to her mother, "Delia would do anything for a sweetie, she would go anywhere with anyone for a sweetie." I thought this was a perfectly reasonable thing to do and couldn't see why it was worth mentioning.

It was decided we should leave Mrs Reeves and move somewhere larger, so we moved into rooms in Town Farm in the main street of Kirbymoorside. Our landlady was Mrs Jackson, the farmer's wife. She had seven cats, all of which lived outside except a black and white one called Mary Anne who was not popular because she scratched people and kept making very smelly messes on the dun-coloured carpet. She came straight to me, however, and this endeared her and all cats to me, for evermore. When she made another mess or scratched someone I would stick up for her and try to make excuses.

Mrs Jackson had a grey cat called Greybird, but her favourite was called Whitey. She thought Whitey was wonderful and could do no wrong. I was jealous of Whitey because I felt Mary Anne was belittled by her, and one day

I did something very cruel. I picked Whitey up by her tail and swung her round and round and she scratched me all the way up my arm. Then I went inside and said to Mrs Jackson, "Look what Whitey has done!" Mrs Jackson could hardly believe her eyes, that her dear Whitey could have done such a thing. It is an awful thing to confess now, and I feel guilty about it to this day.

Mrs Jackson was very fat and wore a green overall that crossed over her vast bosom and tied in a bow at the back. She had a son called "Our Jack" who seemed to do most of the work on the farm, as I can't remember anyone else doing it. Her husband was probably dead. She took umbrage very easily but for some reason she really liked me – though she wouldn't have done if she had known what I had done to her favourite cat.

She used to come into our living room every day and give us pieces of news about the war. My mother was amused when she informed us "The Admirality announces there are no casualities." Auntie Margaret had introduced my mother to some very rich people, which made my mother feel inferior because we were so poor by comparison and could not return their hospitality. My mother had to go to Mrs Jackson and ask her most humbly if she could invite someone or other for tea. Mrs Jackson would grudgingly agree and put on a very good spread because she was an amazing cook and made wonderful cakes, but then my mother went through agonies in case the people she had invited took no notice of Mrs Jackson and did not admire her cakes. Then Mrs Jackson would take umbrage and make whistling noises under her breath and afterwards she would say, "Well! I must say, I don't think much to *them!*"

When it was my birthday Mrs Jackson made me a huge cake with the most complicated and intricately patterned icing on the top. Both she and her sister could make these astonishing and cleverly constructed cakes: they were very talented and probably won prizes.

There was no television in those days but we listened to the wireless a lot, such things as 'ITMA' with Tommy Handley or 'Much Binding in the Marsh' with Dickie Murdoch. We played endless card games, such as animal pelmanism. When I played this with my mother I always won because she was so vague and didn't concentrate. Also one of the cards of a rabbit was slightly torn on the back, so when I turned over another rabbit I was able to match it up at once. She thought this was amazingly clever of me but it was just a trick.

Once I said, "How old are you, Mummy?"

"That's none of your business," she replied.

"Would it be sixty?" I asked.

"No, it most certainly would not!" she said indignantly. She was actually about forty-three at the time.

My cousins Elizabeth and Clive were somewhat molly-coddled. This was because Auntie Margaret had previously had two babies who had died young and she was obviously fearful it would happen again. They had a nanny to look after them and they spent most of the time with her, either in the Day Nursery or the Night Nursery. Both these rooms were kept suffocatingly hot and the windows were always closed tight in case the children caught a germ, but as they were not exposed to any this could have made things worse. Certainly Clive was a very delicate little boy. Once I saw Nanny make him pee into a china mug - I hoped it would be well washed afterwards.

They didn't go to school; instead they had lessons with a governess, and it was decided I should join them. The governess's name was Miss Adams and she was a really sweet woman, who must have been quite young though she didn't seem so particularly. Sometimes we had lessons in the dining room, where we sat round the polished mahogany table on chairs with shiny, slippery leather seats. But if it was a sunny day we would go into the garden, which was much nicer. The lawn sloped a little, so if you sat with your back to the slope you were liable to fall over backwards.

Once a week we were taken to dancing class, where we met lots of rich little children with double-barrelled names like Richmond-Brown and Knightley-Smith. The girls wore pretty little dresses with pink or white net skirts while the boys looked like sissies dressed up in white satin shorts. Sometimes there would be a tea party at Low Hall, to which some of these children would come. We would sit at the table in the day nursery and there would be plates of thinly-cut sandwiches and fairy cakes with hundreds and thousands sprinkled on the top. Nanny presided over these tea parties and we always said grace before we could start to eat. One little boy objected to this, saying, "I don't say grace." I then remarked, "I only say it when I go out to tea." My mother was quite amused by this, but also embarrassed that I had let her down.

Badger and I were given pet rabbits, which we quite liked to begin with. They were called Flopsy and Mopsy. We used to have to collect dandelion leaves for them and clean out their hutch, but after a while we grew slack about this and left it for our mother to do. We thought they were rather boring because they didn't do anything, although they obviously did because in due course Flopsy had a litter of baby rabbits. I loved this and visited them several times a day, but I was told I must never touch them. Unfortunately I could not resist giving them a little stroke and the next day when I looked into their hutch they had all disappeared. When I asked my mother where they were she looked sad and said their mother had eaten them. This was a most horrifying thing and the worst of it was, it was *my* fault. Did I own up and admit what I had done? I can't remember now but probably not, I was a naughty little girl as you will see.

CHAPTER FOUR

The next time my father came home on leave my mother had to go to Liverpool to meet his boat and I was invited to Low Hall to stay the night. A bed was made up for me in the Night Nursery, but when it was time for lights out and Elizabeth and Clive settled down to go to sleep, I had other ideas. I thought it was much too boring to go to sleep, so I made them get up and pull the sheets off their beds and pretend to be ghosts. We had great fun prancing about the room until the inevitable happened and Nanny Scott-Hopkins came in. She was furious. She told Auntie Margaret I was a very bad influence and it didn't help that Clive had a nightmare in the night.

But worse was to come: on Daddy's next leave I was again invited to stay for the night while my mother went to meet him. This time I was put in Uncle Cliff's dressing room. It was a tiny little room with just a bed and a chest of drawers and a corner hanging cupboard and I don't suppose they thought I could do any harm.

"Goodnight, darling," said Auntie Margaret blithely. But once again after the light was turned out I looked around for something to do. It seemed much too early to go to bed and besides, I was wide awake. On the top of the chest of drawers was a tin with spaniels on it. I leaned over from the bed and opened the tin and inside were several chocolate biscuits. Uncle Cliff had a very sweet tooth. I ate one and it tasted so good that I ate another and then another. After that there was only one left and I thought it would be pity to leave that on its own so I ate that too.

Then I crawled down to the bottom of the bed and opened the corner cupboard. It was full of medicine bottles and pills, which were rather boring, but I did find a packet of corn plasters. I had no idea what they were for but they seemed more interesting, so I took the packet and opened it up and played with the plasters for a while. Then I put them under my pillow and went to sleep.

The next day I was sitting in the dining room with Miss Adams having lessons – Elizabeth and Clive were not there that day for some reason – when suddenly the door opened and in walked Uncle Cliff, followed by Auntie Margaret and Nanny Scott-Hopkins.

"You have been a VERY NAUGHTY LITTLE GIRL!" roared Uncle Cliff.

"Yes, you have," agreed Auntie Margaret sadly.

I was so alarmed and frightened that I slid right off my slippery leather chair until I was right under the table. The three of them bent down so that they could continue to speak to me and Uncle Cliff went on in an awful voice, "You got out of bed…"

"But I didn't!" I squeaked. "…You got out of bed and you opened my tin of chocolate biscuits and ate them all up. And then you went to my medicine cupboard and took my corn plasters."

"But I didn't get out of bed," I insisted.

"And to make matters worse, you are a liar!" shouted Uncle Cliff.

"Yes darling, because you see you left the corn plasters under the pillow so we know you did it," said Auntie Margaret very sorrowfully. She must have been wishing I wasn't her brother's child.

"You are a THIEF, A THIEF and a LIAR!" said Uncle Cliff, while Nanny Scott-Hopkins stood looking on complacently. She had always known I was a bad influence.

When they had left the room Miss Adams gently pulled me out from under the table. "But I'm *not* a liar," I told her, "because I didn't get out of bed. You see I could reach everything from the bed without getting out of it." As if that made it all right that I had taken the biscuits.

"I know dear," said Miss Adams soothingly, "I think your uncle should never have left his chocolate biscuits in the room in the first place, what did he expect?"

She thought on reflection it might be better if I went home for lunch with her and stay with her until things had cooled down a bit, so I did. She lived in a dear little cottage on the edge of a wood.

The next day was Saturday and a handsome young Army Major came and we all went off for the day and had a picnic on a hillside and picked tiny little wild strawberries and it was one of the happiest days I can remember.

Later – I do hope it wasn't because of me – Miss Adams was dismissed and we had another governess called Miss Taylor. I was told that Miss Adams was a loose and wicked woman because she was having an affair with the Major, who was married to someone else. But Miss Adams and the Major had been so happy together that day and their happiness had spilled over onto me, and I thought that if being happy was so wicked then I would rather be wicked.

There were lots of soldiers billeted in Kirbymoorside, and I was embarrassed at having to go out and be seen by them wearing brown woollen gaiters as I felt they were babyish. I tried to push the fronts of the gaiters into my buttoned shoes, hoping they would then be taken for stockings. Mrs Jackson had some soldiers billeted on her and I remember two, Metcalf and Baker, who were particularly nice to me. I played a joke on Baker one day, by giving him a trick glass of beer that you couldn't drink because the glass was double-sided with the beer inside. So when he tried to take a swig the beer just rolled up to the top of the glass and then down again, trapped inside. But Baker wasn't having any of this. He took a great bite out of the glass, broke it and drank the beer. We were amazed and relieved he didn't cut himself, but he just thought it an even funnier joke than the one I had tried to play on him.

When they left Mrs Jackson's I wanted to give them a present. I can't remember what Baker got, but I took my pocket money out of the china pig and bought Metcalf a brown teapot with yellow spots on it. He seemed touched and delighted and said he would put it in his kit bag and keep it with him always. Long afterwards I wondered if it might not have been a nuisance for him to have to lug around a large and cumbersome teapot in his kit bag, but he was much too nice to say so.

My father was in the Administrative Service in Nigeria, and eventually he became a Senior Resident. It is fashionable to disparage the Colonial Service, but they did a lot of good which will doubtless be recognised one day. All of his colleagues were good and conscientious administrators who took their jobs seriously and worked very hard. My parents kept the same staff of servants, all from the Cameroons, for some thirty years and my father took as much care of them as he did of his family - sometimes more - driving the cook's wife miles to the maternity hospital in the middle of the night and comparable things.

When the time came for the British to hand over, an old and much respected Chief came to my father and begged him not to go, saying the power would now fall into the hands of corrupt officials who would rob the people and let the country go – and so it has transpired. Only recently it has come to light that £220 billion was stolen or misused by corrupt Nigerian rulers. That old Chief knew this would happen, it was inevitable.

But years before the handover, when he was just a junior district officer, my father came home on leave to Yorkshire, telling my mother he was going to bring home all their wedding presents, so would she please meet him with two taxis as they would need these to carry everything in? However, when she arrived with the two taxis he was just wearing his hat and a rather crumpled suit.

"Where is all the luggage?" she asked.

"There isn't any," he said. "The ship was torpedoed and everything was sunk. We had to swim and all I've got is what I'm standing up in." He only had the hat because when they were swimming, someone shouted "Hey, VK, is this your hat?"

My father decided to join the Home Guard. It was winter and there was deep snow on the ground but I could pick out his footsteps in the snow because of his large feet, which turned out when he walked. He was very keen on the cinema and one day decided he wanted to go and would take me with him. The film was *Wanted for Murder* with Eric Portman and it was based on the true story of a serial murderer who went around strangling young women. My mother said it wasn't a very suitable film for a six-year old and why not go to one of the children's films currently being shown, but my father was determined to see that one and I was equally determined to go with him. "I want to go, I want to go!" I kept insisting. So we went. Eric Portman would take these young girls, one at a time of course, into a park and they would sit lovingly under a tree and then when the girl wasn't looking, he would slip his hands from around their shoulders to their necks and then strangle them. I don't remember much else except that it wasn't as frightening as *Snow White* or *The Wizard of Oz*.

I loved being in Yorkshire, I loved the farmyard with all the animals and the countryside and picnics to dear little villages like Hutton-le-Hole where there were just a few cottages and a stream ran across the main street. Besides Margot, Badger and I had made friends with other children. There were two brothers called Jonathan and Jasper; Jonathan was Badger's age and Jasper was a bit younger than me. We went to their house where they had a large garden and a tennis court and Badger played tennis with Jonathan. We also went to the sandy beaches at Whitby and Scarborough. Sometimes there was another little girl with us called Wendy, who was younger than me and very sweet. I was, however, not very kind to her because I was jealous that everyone thought she was so sweet and I made her some disgusting concoction which she drank, much to my surprise. I'm not sure it didn't have petrol in it from one of the farmyard vehicles and I feel guilty now thinking about that. I had been unkind to Whitey the cat and now to Wendy as well.

My mother wasn't really very happy in Yorkshire. She longed to have her own place and felt inadequate living at the behest of a landlady. One day she went to a party and afterwards she told Auntie Margaret, "I met someone so nice tonight, I felt so at ease with her, she didn't seem very rich like all the others, she was simple and matey and she talked to me for ages."

"Oh yes," said Auntie Margaret laughing, "That was Lady Worsley (mother of the Duchess of Kent). She's just about the richest woman in Yorkshire."

There was a handsome and charming major whom all the rich women ran after. However, he liked my mother and wanted to have an affair with her but she wouldn't. She was too loyal to my father and also to her own sex and would never have betrayed one of them. Anyway, after two years in Yorkshire we finally returned to the South.

CHAPTER FIVE

We went to Ditchling, a little village in Sussex on the edge of the downs. First of all we stayed in a house at the top of the village. There was a swallows' nest just outside our bedroom window and I loved watching the swallows flying in and out. Our landlady was a Mrs Macrae, who was very fussy. She said she would give me and Badger sixpence each to do an hour's weeding, but when the hour was up and we asked for our sixpences, she told us we hadn't done it well enough so we got nothing. She had dining chairs with leather seats and one day a slit mysteriously appeared in one of the seats, we didn't know how it had got there, and she accused us of slitting it with a knife. We were very indignant and strongly denied having done it, but maybe we did, I just don't know. And I suppose it must have been very irritating for her as she was so fussy.

Anyway we didn't stay there very long because Mummy's friend Miss Dampier, known as Damps, had recently moved from Hove and bought a cottage in East End Lane, Ditchling and she invited us to live with her. Oh, what a piece of luck that was! Damps was quite old, eccentric and delightful and I remember our time in her cottage as one of the happiest periods of my life. We were all happy with Damps, she was that sort of person. She had a Pekinese dog called Pops and a black cat called Twopence and she didn't care a damn about housework. The lavatory had a square wooden seat and was suspiciously black inside, but who cared? I certainly didn't. She made marrow and ginger jam and it all over-boiled and the cat and the dog walked in it and everywhere was sticky, but it didn't matter. She was gloriously untidy and could not have been more different from Mrs Macrae.

There was a dark blue Bristol glass bowl on the window sill in the hall and portraits of her ancestors on the walls and piles of books everywhere. She had a sweet wild garden full of birds and fruit trees. One of them was a quince tree which grew delicious quinces. Next door lived the Farjeons, Herbert and Eleanor, a brother and sister who were both writers. They had written books and I wanted to write books too. I went down East End Lane to the little stationers and bought exercise books to write stories in. Badger was reading the Chalet School books which were very fat and I boasted that one day I would write books as fat as those. I bought a large exercise book and started a novel called "THE AWFUL TRUTH" but as I didn't know what the Awful Truth was, it didn't progress very far.

There was a black cat with kittens in the bakery in the main street and I went down every day to visit them. It was warm and sunny in the shop and the baker welcomed me and gave me sugary buns straight out of the oven.

From time to time a young man called Mountenay Welcome came to see Damps. She was very good to him and let him keep a bike and all sorts of stuff that he collected in her garage. His fingernails were always black with oil. He wasn't what some people called "the full shilling", not that it mattered, but he was rather a bore about his bike, which was of no interest to us. It seemed he was the son of Sir Henry Welcome and Syrie Maugham, wife of Somerset, and was sitting on a fortune which was held in trust. I told my mother we mustn't be too nice to Damps or she would leave Mountenay to us in her will. In later years he came to visit us in Hove and he wrote letters to us at school in large childish handwriting. The Trust never told him about his fortune and dissuaded him from ever getting married so that he would not inherit it, but apparently he married a nurse at the hospital where he lived and I am glad to think he did finally get the money he was entitled to, and sucks to them.

I had a friend called Josephine Phillips whose mother was a friend of my mother's, and we often met for picnics at Lodge Hill. Through Josephine I became very interested in wild birds and we spent a lot of time bird watching and climbing nut trees where we would sit all afternoon, eating nuts that were not quite ripe and having tummy aches afterwards, but it was worth it. I spent my pocket money on bird books, some of which I never read all the way through as they were too technical and complicated.

Josephine went to a school in the village run by the Misses Dumbrell and it was decided I should go there. At lunchtime the older sister, Miss Edith, who was thin and stern, sat at one end of the dining table and Miss Mary, the plump one, sat at the other end. There was always rice pudding at Miss Edith's end of the table and she would ask the children, "Would you like some of my pudding or Miss Mary's?" and everyone said, "Miss Mary's," and Miss Edith looked more and more depressed as the time went on. I'm surprised she didn't give up on the rice pudding, as nobody liked it and only ever chose it out of politeness.

My form mistress was called Miss Knowles. She was a good teacher but very sarcastic, and she had a rule that you could only go to the lavatory in the ten-minute break half way through the morning. Unfortunately you could not always get to the lavatory, as the little boys at the school always got there first. One day I did not manage to get there in the ten minutes and wanted desperately to go but knew I was not allowed to ask. I went through agonies and finally cried out "Please Miss Knowles, could I be excused?" But it was too late: I had wet my knickers and there was a puddle on the floor. I was ashamed and mortified, especially when Miss Knowles tied a red band onto the back of my chair so that no one else would sit on it.

At the end of the day I walked home across the fields with two other girls, one of whom said to the other one, "Have you heard the story of the little girl who couldn't wait?"

"No," said the other one in a sing-song voice.

"Well," said Margaret gleefully, "It was like this." And the awful story was repeated, slowly and with emphasis.

I rushed in to tell my mother and said I was not going to go to school the next day, but she said it would be much worse the day after if I didn't go in. My sister remembers that afterwards Josephine's mother went to see the Misses Dumbrell and complained and Miss Knowles was forced to give up this sadistic rule - which someone who had been to the school later told me had caused scores of children to wet the floor - but it was too late for me. The whole humiliating episode had a lasting effect for the rest of my life. I was then seven years old.

CHAPTER SIX

After a while my mother decided she wanted to go back to Hove, so we said goodbye to our dear friend Damps and rented a house in Shirley Drive. We had a sweet woman called Mrs Marshall who came to do the housework, and a grumpy gardener. He was only allowed to use the outside lavatory and had his tea from a special enamel mug, I don't know whether our mother thought that we would catch something, but no one else was allowed to use it. She bought some tomato plants and asked him to plant them in the greenhouse, and was amused afterwards to hear him muttering, "I don't know what the bloody woman wants me to do with these bloody tomato plants."

I was sent as a day girl to the Convent of the Sacred Heart in Hove. It was considered a very good school: my mother's friend Esme Glen had sent her daughter Maureen there. She was a Catholic of course, but another of my mother's friends had sent her daughter Pauleen there too and they were Protestants. As it was war time, all the boarders had been evacuated up to Shropshire so only the day girls and one or two small boys were left. Children can be very cruel, as I had learnt to my cost at Dumbrells.

The day I arrived one of the older girls said to me, "Is there anyone here you don't like the look of?" I looked round the room and saw a girl with a white spotty face and greasy black hair scraped back from her face. "I don't like the look of her very much," I said. It was the right answer, and the girls who had spoken to me looked triumphant.

"That's Barbara Leek," they said. "Nobody likes her, *and* she smells."

Poor Barbara lived with some aged aunts who didn't wash her clothes very often, but she was a really nice girl whom I came to like. She collected birds' eggs and so did I. We didn't get them out of nests, we bought them and swopped those we had two of.

26

Once she told me of a shop in Brighton where I could get an ostrich egg for half a crown. I saved up and went with Badger, who was home from school for the holidays. It was a mean little shop in a mean little street in a slummy part of Brighton. A little old man told us the ostrich eggs were on the top shelf and he would have to get a stepladder to get them down and could we please come back in half an hour. We said we could but as soon as we got out of the shop, Badger said "We're not going back *there!*"

"But we must go back," I said, "The old man is getting the egg down from the top shelf especially!"

"I don't care," she said, "We're never going back there again, ever."

And we never did. I have always felt guilty about it, thinking of the little old man getting the ostrich egg down from the top shelf and waiting and waiting for us to come and collect it. As for Barbara Leek, I heard later she had become a nun.

The Catholic religion was a great mystery to me. I did not know the words of the prayers so I just chanted what they sounded like. Thus the second part of the 'Hail Mary' went 'Holy Mary, Mother of God, de dah de dah de dah de dah de dah.' When we knelt in front of the altar I had been told I must not look or I would be struck blind. I covered my face with my fingers and peeped through them and when I found I hadn't been struck blind after all, I peeped a bit more. There was a funny little cabinet called a tabernacle which had an ornate gilded door, but you couldn't see what was behind the door. Sometimes when they prayed, nuns would prostrate themselves right down on the floor, also the postulants and those taking Holy Communion. On certain festivals there was a procession all around the convent grounds and in the chapel. There was one in honour of Our Lady and we each had to hold a white flower, but when I told my mother this she was reluctant to buy one. It had to be a large white chrysanthemum and these were very expensive. She didn't at first understand that it was ESSENTIAL for me to have it. But she did buy me one in the end.

We developed a craze for autograph books. Most people did a drawing or wrote a verse. I gave my book to one of the nuns and she wrote in it:

"Little dabs of powder,
Little dabs of paint
Make a little lady
Exactly what she ain't."

The moral of this was totally lost on me, as at the age of eight I had no idea what it meant.

The form prize was a tiny little turquoise prayer book which I greatly coveted. Eventually I won it, but the gilt wore off the gingerbread somewhat when Betty Veil objected, saying what would I want with a Roman Catholic prayer book when I was only a Protestant?

I was the only Protestant in a class of five pupils and our form mistress was a nun called Mother Lilley who made a big fuss of me. English was my best subject and she encouraged me constantly. I still have the exercise book in which I wrote about Saint Teresa and underneath she put "You ought to write 'A Child's Life of Saint Teresa'". I also wrote an adventure story (which owed a lot to Enid Blyton) and went on for pages and pages. She, having probably never read any Enid Blyton, wrote an enthusiastic appraisal, saying 'We look forward to the next instalment.' We had to learn chunks of the Catechism by heart, and nine verses of the New Testament every night. Before long I could recite most of the Gospel according to St Luke entirely by heart and some of the other Gospels as well. We learnt Latin and French and because I was the brightest in my class – not difficult, there being only five of us – *and* a Protestant, I was given practically one-to-one teaching. I was the star pupil.

Then once again I blotted my copybook. It was my second year and we were all going through rather a vulgar stage, influenced by a naughty but funny girl called Pamela. We had been learning about Pages who went on to become Squires and eventually ending up as Knights. We were asked to write an essay entitled 'Memories of an Old Knight' and I drew a picture of a small page peeing onto the curtains in the corner of a room. It was quite graphic, you couldn't mistake what was going on. Anyway, I passed this note to my neighbour and it went round the class – about ten of us by that time – in the middle of prep. It caused titters of amusement. Finally the last girl to see it tore it up and put it in the waste paper bin, whereupon the nun taking the prep asked what she had just torn up. She said, "Nothing," but the nun said, "Bring the pieces of paper to me." The girl gathered up the torn paper and the nun then pieced them together and was horrified to see what it depicted.

"Who drew this?" she said.

"I did," I answered.

It was a very bad and wicked thing to have done and my mother was called up to the convent to be interviewed by Reverend Mother. My mother and she walked around the convent grounds together. "If the Angel Gabriel himself had told me Delia could have done such a thing I would not have believed it," said Reverend Mother. "I shall have to consider whether she can stay here or not."

My mother was mortified and went home deeply depressed that her little girl was depraved and on the road to Eternal Damnation. She saw our old friend Damps and told her all about it. Damps said, "Oh but my dear I think that was rather clever of her," which cheered my mother immensely. Reverend Mother thought about my sinful act and all the nuns prayed for my soul and in the end it was decided I had been under the influence of the wicked Pamela, and I was allowed to stay.

CHAPTER SEVEN

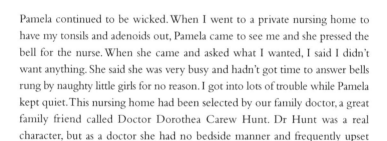

Pamela continued to be wicked. When I went to a private nursing home to have my tonsils and adenoids out, Pamela came to see me and she pressed the bell for the nurse. When she came and asked what I wanted, I said I didn't want anything. She said she was very busy and hadn't got time to answer bells rung by naughty little girls for no reason. I got into lots of trouble while Pamela kept quiet. This nursing home had been selected by our family doctor, a great family friend called Doctor Dorothea Carew Hunt. Dr Hunt was a real character, but as a doctor she had no bedside manner and frequently upset patients by saying, "There's nothing wrong with you, you're just being a nuisance to your family, now get up!"

On the other hand many other patients were devoted to her and that included my family. When I went to have my tonsils and adenoids out I arrived in the nursing home in the evening and was very surprised to have the operation the next morning. I had assumed there would be several days before the operation and several days after it. I was put in a room with three other patients, all elderly. One of them said she didn't like to see hospital beds (though she didn't mind her own) and in consequence my bed and the beds of the other two were curtained off. This meant two of us were in constant darkness. The food was strange too; this woman would be given a boiled egg or a junket, would take one mouthful and leave the rest. It was then passed on to me. Dr Hunt heard about this and was furious. She said she didn't expect any of her patients to be given someone else's half-eaten food and she had a terrible row with the Matron about it. "I shall never be able to use that nursing home again, now," she told my mother.

Because my throat was sore after the operation I was given chocolates and lots of grapes, a great luxury in those days. Badger and Bretton came to visit me and ate quite a lot of them and also did my jigsaw puzzles, but I didn't blame them as it is very boring visiting someone in a nursing home and there's nothing much to do once you've said hello. My mother made home-made ice cream which she brought in a thermos flask and which got better and better the more she practised making it. Best of all was her coffee ice cream, made with Nestles' Condensed Milk and, I suppose, coffee. I've never tasted any ice cream as delicious as that. She and Doctor Hunt used to play tennis together right into their seventies, serving under-arm but quite fast and pretty lethal.

Once Doctor Hunt came to tea and talked to my mother about not being married. I was kneeling on the floor behind the sofa, reading – and listening – and heard her say wistfully, "I always thought that some day my prince would come on his white charger but he never did." I think he would have been quite unnerved by her if he had come, but it must have been sad for her that he didn't.

I had a tabby kitten called Twinkle, who grew into a large and rather unattractive cat who was quite capable of giving you a nasty scratch. However, I loved him dearly. Twinkle no longer seemed a suitable name and he was always known as The Cat. One day he caught a mouse but it wasn't quite dead, so I put it in my satchel and took it to school, where I thought it stood a better chance of survival. However, I forgot about it and when we were about to have prayers I opened the satchel to get out my hymn book and the mouse promptly leapt out and raced across the floor. Most of the nuns screamed and some jumped up on their chairs, which we thought was very funny.

One day I walked up the Droveway to the Post Office and some other little shops to get some things for my mother. While I was there the air raid warning sounded and the postmistress said I had better not leave, but should wait till my father or mother came to fetch me home. There was a man in the post office with a large hooked nose and he said to me, "Where do you live, little girl?" I said, "Shirley Drive." "Oh I live quite near there," said he, "I'll take you home. Which way do you usually go?" "Down the Droveway," I said. "Oh well, I live in Mallory Road so we'll go down Onslow Road," he said, and when the all-clear sounded, off we went together.

He then said, "Why don't you come home with me, and my housekeeper will give you a lovely tea?" but I had been feeling more and more uneasy about him and at this point I suddenly ran away very fast down the road, darted into another driveway and hid by the side of someone's garage.

"Come back, come back!" he shouted, thundering down the road. I waited till he had gone and all was quiet, then I crept out of my hiding place and ran all the way home. I told my parents all about it – but they didn't believe me! They thought I had made it up. I thought it was extraordinary that all these years they had told me never to go off with a strange man and now when a horrible man with a hooked nose had tried to abduct me they didn't believe it. I was quite indignant.

"I could have been murdered," I said. "I am sure there was no such person as the housekeeper who was going to give me a lovely tea. I was about to be murdered by this hook-nosed man and you don't seem to care." But they only laughed at me. It was most unfair, I thought. I'll admit that I did sometimes make things up but this really and truly happened.

Sometimes my cousins Audrey and Jean came to stay with us in Hove, where there was always lots to do. If it wasn't warm enough to go on the beach there was Louis Tussaud's waxworks, not as good as Madame Tussaud's in London but quite fun for us, especially the Chamber of Horrors with people being tortured and lots of rather unrealistic blood everywhere, and the Hall of Mirrors in which you saw yourself as tremendously tall with long spindly legs or short and fat with a funny round face. There were two piers, the Palace Pier and the West Pier, and I had my caricature drawn by a man on the Palace Pier which I didn't like because it wasn't very flattering. Everyone else thought it was terribly funny. "It's not a bit like me," I grumbled, "Just because my teeth stick out a bit... and anyway I haven't got a double chin." "But it's the image of you," they laughed.

Also on the pier were slot machines where you put in your penny and looked at 'The Haunted House' and 'What the butler saw.' We put pennies into the telescope but instead of searching the horizon for ships we swung it round to look into the windows of the Regency houses on the sea front, hoping to see people undressing or having a bath or something equally riveting. We invented a secret society in which we studied lovers. If we saw a young couple arm in arm going into the park we would follow them at a distance and write notes about them in a notebook. We never saw them do anything except walk around a bit and perhaps sit under a tree. My cousin Jean told me about sex and I was shocked. "My parents would never do *that*," I said flatly.

Sometimes we went to the Royal Pavilion, which was built by the Prince Regent, later King George IV. There was a long queue of people who had paid to see a scandalous painting hidden by a curtain, as it was not considered suitable for children. Everyone wanted to see it and we especially wanted to see it because we were not allowed to. Today the curtain has been stripped away and anyone who wants can see it, with the result that nobody wants to. It depicts an obese and nearly naked Prince Regent raping the Spirit of Brighton in the form of a young maiden. It hangs on one wall of the tea room and nobody gives it a second glance.

My best friend at school was called Marigold and we saw each other often; either she would come to tea with me or I would go to tea with her. She didn't have a father and lived with her mother and her aunt. She was a very nice, sensible little girl of whom my mother much approved (which she didn't always). Then one day when I had been invited to tea with her, my mother said I couldn't go. She said Marigold could come to tea with me but I wasn't to go to her house again.

"Why not?" I demanded. She then told me that Marigold's mother and her aunt had been caught stealing and had gone to prison. This was a dreadful shock. I sat on the stairs for the rest of the afternoon and into the evening when it was quite dark, thinking about Marigold's mother and aunt who had been stealing and were now in prison, and I thought that it was just not possible because they were Grown-ups and I knew them and they were very nice and people you knew as well as I knew them didn't steal and get sent to prison. And besides, what would happen to Marigold with no one to look after her?

In the event the nuns took Marigold and she lived in the convent. At least, I think that's what happened – I didn't see Marigold after that.

At home I had another friend called Jill, known as Silly Jilly Willie, who really preferred Badger. She lived opposite us in Shirley Drive and would cross over the road and ring our bell and ask if Badger could come out to play. My mother would say that Badger was at school, and Jill would say, "Oh well, can Delia play then?" "I'm just the reserve," I grumbled. So we would play together, bouncing balls endlessly and hitting them against the garage door.

Despite her nickname, Jill was a very clever girl who went to St Mary's Hall. We went to Sunday School every week, the best part of which was collecting colourful stamps which we could stick in special albums. Getting the stamps was the only reason for going as far as I was concerned. Then Jill became interested in different religions and wanted me to accompany her to different 'churches'. One was in a club-house and we sat on wicker chairs at glass topped tables and had orangeade out of paper cups. There was nothing very religious about it, and if I had been tempted to change my religion it would definitely have been to the Catholics.

Because of the war and air raids and being so often woken up in the middle of the night, I went through a period of not being able to sleep. The more I worried about this the less it would happen and I began to dread night-times. I would lie in bed hour after hour and think I was the only person in the whole world who was still awake. If I heard a sole aeroplane fly overhead I'd be comforted by the thought that at least the pilot was awake. He and I must be the only people in the whole world who were.

Sometimes my mother and Badger took me for long walks to try and tire me out. We walked up Shirley Drive, through a little copse and right onto the downs. It took ages and then we had to come all the way back again. These long walks did work but they took so long and tired all of us out, not just me so we didn't do them very often, and my sleeplessness continued. I took to writing little notes saying "Please God, let me go to sleep tonight, I live in the house with the yellow hedge," and throwing them out of the window. I thought they would go straight up to Heaven and was horrified one day years later when I found one of these notes in the top drawer of my mother's dressing table. It appeared that neighbours had found dozens of them in their gardens and had returned them to my mother. Oh, the embarrassment of knowing that this private, if one-sided, correspondence between God and me was known to all the neighbours!

Once when my mother had to go away, I was asked to stay the night at Silly Jilly Willie's house and as usual I couldn't get to sleep. I lay awake with mounting panic, listening to their grandfather clock chiming every quarter of an hour, until finally Jill's mother, a very kindly woman, actually went to the trouble of stopping the clock. I must have been a real pain in the neck, but they never said a word.

Besides Sunday School stamps, I also collected postage stamps. My father encouraged me greatly in this, sending me stamps from Nigeria including first day cover ones, and some that he bought in mint condition, joined on to others that had been franked by the post office. He said these would be very valuable one day. To increase my collection I bought packets of assorted stamps, which is not really the right way to collect, it is considered cheating, but as I didn't know anyone apart from my father who would write to me from abroad it was the only thing to do if I wanted to increase my collection. It certainly taught me quite a lot about geography. I would kneel on the floor in my bedroom and spend hours sorting out the stamps I had bought into piles according to which country they belonged to. Then my mother would come along and say, "Tidy up your room at once!" and I would say, "But I can't at the moment."

"Why can't you?"

"Because I've just spent all morning trying to sort out my stamps."

But that was no excuse – I would have to put them all back in the cigar box I kept them in, where they got muddled up again. It was disheartening and eventually put me off collecting stamps.

I was untidy and my mother was constantly having to tell me to do things and I always said, "I'm going to."

"You always say you're going to."

"Well I *am* going to."

"But *when?*" she said, "*When* are you going to?"

I would avoid this question and go and lie in the long grass in the garden where I could not be seen, and read a book. There The Cat would join me, making high leaps in the long grass and giving my hiding place away to my mother.

My mother and Badger and I walked up the Droveway to catch the bus into Brighton, which only went every twenty minutes. We didn't have a car and anyway my mother couldn't drive. She and Badger walked in front chatting away nineteen to the dozen and I walked behind, feeling grumpy. Then I said, "There goes the bally bus!" At once they turned round and my mother said, "*What* did you just say?" "I said, there goes the bally bus." "Oh," she said lamely. She had thought I'd said bloody.

She was cross with me one day because I had eaten all the apples and she said I was greedy. I felt hurt and angry, so I made her an apple pie bed to pay her back for being cross. When she came into her bedroom and saw I had made her bed she was touched and delighted and said "Delia, how sweet of you!" I then felt dreadful.

"Actually," I said in a small voice, "It's an apple pie bed."

"Oh, how funny," she said, disappointed and not thinking it was funny at all. I was racked with guilt but it was too late, I couldn't think of anything I could do to make up.

My mother had a very strong personality but she was also a mixture. Besides her sense of humour and talent for making everyone laugh, she was also very emotional and would take things in the news to heart to such a degree that if, for instance, she read of someone whose child had been killed or maimed in an accident she would lie awake half the night thinking and grieving over it. She got very angry with people who stared at children with cerebral palsy or anything like that, which, being ignorant, they did in those days. Thank goodness they are more enlightened and kinder now.

My mother could play the piano by ear and was apt to go and sit down at the piano and start to play quite suddenly when she was in the middle of dusting a room. She could play anything after only hearing it once and somehow knew instinctively how the accompaniment should go. She was very vague and would go upstairs and put her fountain pen in the bed and a hot water bottle in her desk. Once she was reading me a story and she said, "Pale blue and rather faded…." I said, "Is that what it says in the book?"

"Oh no!" she laughed, "I was thinking of your pyjamas."

When she was young she was run over by a horse and cart. Another time she was riding her bicycle along a dark road one night when suddenly a man leapt out of the woods nearby. "Oh thank goodness you're here," she said, "I was feeling quite nervous on my own. Now we can go together." And they did.

Her mother – my Granny Cooper – got quite impatient with her at times, saying she was thoroughly irresponsible. Nor was she impressed with our mother's piano playing as she herself played beautifully, but read the music instead of playing by ear, which she said was the purist way. Granny also played the violin.

Because they were so poor our mother lost her nerve when she was invited to stay with her rich friends Ailsa and Dick Rawlinson. They were going to a ball at the Savoy and my mother was embarrassed because their maid unpacked her suitcase and saw all her much darned clothes as she put them away in a cupboard, and she was further embarrassed because she had no jewellery to wear with her ball gown. Ailsa said, "For goodness sake, why didn't you ask me? I could have lent you something."

Because of the war and the food rationing our mother always thought people were just being polite when they offered us sweets or biscuits, so before accepting anything like that we had to look over to her for permission. There was a special ritual which went like this: someone would say, "Have a chocolate," and you had to say, "No thank you," and then they would say, "Oh, go on," and you would say, "Are you sure?" and they would say, "Yes of course," and then you would look at our mother and if she nodded approval you could take it. The reverse of this situation was when people came to tea and you offered them a plate of cakes and you would be praying they wouldn't take the chocolate one, and when they picked it up and said, "Can I really have this?" you had to say, "Yes, of course". It worked both ways.

Our mother didn't believe in praising us, she thought it seemed conceit on her part and would make us too big for our boots. Nor did she like other mothers who 'thought all their geese were swans'. One woman she knew was always going on about her daughter who was such a wonderful little dancer, an Anna Pavlova in the making. And her son was a little Winston Churchill. Our mother had no time for this at all. A Jewish couple came to live next door and my mother didn't much like the look of them, they were hugely fat and had to have double-width deck chairs in their garden. They had very vulgar pink net curtains at all their windows. A plumber told us they had a bath with a false bottom in it with goldfish swimming around and my mother said the goldfish must have heart attacks every time the couple got into the bath.

There was quite a lot of anti-semitism in Brighton at that time, partly because there were queues for food in all the shops but Jews often knew someone and would go to the top of the queue and get all the best stuff. Anyway, one day I met the Jewish lady next door and she was very friendly and said, "Give your mother these tomatoes."

"Oh, thank you!" I said gratefully.

"And tell your mother to come in and have a nice glass of sherry wine with me."

"All right, I will," I said.

I went into our house and said, "The lady next door has given you these tomatoes."

"Oh dear," my mother said. "and she wants you to go in and have a nice glass of sherry-wine with her. Will you go?"

"Well, I don't know about that."

"Oh, you must go, you must" I pleaded. "Do go and have a nice glass of sherry-wine, you'll enjoy it, I know you will." But she never did go. Auntie Joan Priestley wasn't like my mother, she had several good Jewish friends. Personally I couldn't see what the problem was.

In the house next door but one lived Mr Seymour Howard and his immensely fat wife Edith. Mr Howard was tall and distinguished-looking and one day he became Lord Mayor of London. Edith was a bit of a problem as she mostly sat in a chair all day with her feet up. She was immensely kind, though. Mr Howard got two Swiss au pair girls in to look after Edith – and people did say they looked after him as well. I had no idea what they meant. He didn't seem to me as if he needed looking after.

A new magazine came out called *Cats and Kittens* and one day I wrote a letter about The Cat and sent it to the Editor. To my amazement and great delight she wrote saying she wanted to publish it and would pay me five shillings. She also wanted a photograph of me with The Cat, so it was arranged I would take him to a studio where the two of us would have our Polyfoto taken. My mother's cousin Valerie Cooper was staying with us at the time and she agreed to take me. With the greatest difficulty we managed to get The Cat into a picnic basket and we waited for a No. 51 bus which went into the town. We sat down on the bus and Valerie had the basket on her lap. The Cat objected very much to the indignity of being put into the picnic basket and miaowed loudly. Suddenly someone said, "Oh look, something's coming out of the basket!" and a long, seemingly endless stream of liquid came out all over Valerie's new skirt. She never forgot this and I'm not surprised, for it did stink, and she didn't even like cats, but at least we got the Polyfotos done. I sent them off to the editor, whose name was Grace Cox-Ife, and one was published with my letter. I told her my views on cats and she included them in an article called "Our Younger Readers". Thus started a correspondence between us that went on for quite a long time and only ended when the assistant editor wrote to tell me that sadly, Grace Cox-Ife had died. I was very upset, as she had become a real friend.

CHAPTER EIGHT

In the spring term of 1945 all the boarders who had been evacuated up to Shropshire returned to the convent. We day girls didn't like this at all as we had been the kingpins and now our noses were put out of joint. They took over and treated us with disdain. There was snow on the ground and there was a great snowball fight between the boarders and the day girls, which they won hands down.

This was my last term at the convent. I had been there for about two years and it was decided I should be sent to Roedean, like Badger. There would be a reduction in the fees because of my father being abroad. I had to do an entrance exam, which I did in bed as I had some infectious disease at the time. (I assume my exam papers did not carry the germs of the disease and pass it on to someone else but we probably didn't think of that.)

In due course we heard that I had passed the exam and started to collect the things I needed for school. I had Auntie Margaret's trunk with her initials HMJ inscribed on it. She and her sister, my Auntie Hazel had both been at Roedean, after the First World War. A lot of my uniform was handed down from Badger and she in turn had had things handed down from other people so some of my clothes were about tenth hand. All of them had to be marked with Cash's name tapes and my mother spent hours sewing these into every item. I had my name stitched on in red which looked very smart.

I started in the summer term of 1945, when I was ten years old. We all got on the train known as the 'School Special' from Euston to Carlisle. Everyone seemed very excited to see each other and to be going back to school. I was to be in the Junior House, known as the Prep, which in Keswick where the school had been evacuated, was in the Millfield Hotel. Badger was in the senior school at the Keswick Hotel, across the river from us. It had been arranged that I should sleep in a room in a house called Shu-le-Crow with four others including Judy Harris, the niece of my mother's great friend, Lilian Sparks. Judy, Pat, Jane and Elin were all in the form above me and it was good of them to put up with me, a new girl and younger than they. I suppose that as it had been arranged between Judy's mother and mine poor Judy had no choice in the matter, but she and her friends were all very kind and I was extremely lucky to be with them. Nevertheless, I was desperately homesick. I couldn't understand why everyone liked the Lake District so much. I hated it. I hated the constant rain and the bleak hills that seemed to engulf us and the dry stone walls which seemed so alien to me. I wrote letters home and on the back of each envelope drew a picture of the train that was to take us home at the end of the term. But that was thirteen weeks away, a lifetime. And then after the holidays we would be back again for another thirteen weeks, and so it would go on for years and years.

I was in the Lower Third. Our house mistress was Miss Leigh, known as Tilda. She was tall and thin with a deep voice and very short cropped grey hair, cut like a man's. She was strict and instilled terror into most of the girls in her charge. I had met her years before when Badger had started school aged nine, and I was then four. We had had tea with her in her sitting room. She was enchanted by me then, I had blonde curls and we shared the same birthday. She had looked forward to my coming to school, expecting to see this dear little curly-haired child who looked her in the eye and chatted away, unafraid and not the least in awe. Instead here was this miserable little white-faced creature who was clearly terrified of her. I was, understandably, a great disappointment.

And once again the sleeplessness continued. Every night I lay in bed wide awake, hour after hour. The mistress in charge of Shu-le-Crow was Miss Holroyd, who was young and pretty and very kind. She taught the piano and was engaged to a handsome Lieutenant in the Navy. One night I had earache and a temperature and she asked her fiancé, the dashing Lieutenant Hart, to carry me over to the sick room in the Millfield Hotel. That evening in our room we had all been discussing what we most wished for and I had wished for a midnight ride and I thought it a great coincidence that my wish had come true. But unknown to me Tilda had written to my parents and said they might have to take me away from Roedean as I was becoming too much of a problem, what with my sleeplessness and earache and everything else.

In due course the earache went away and I was fortunately allowed to return to Shu-le-Crow and the very kindly Miss Holroyd, who said, "Now my dear, if you can't get to sleep, come along and knock on my door and I'll give you some cocoa. That will help." It did – years later I heard that she had put some sleeping draught in and it mercifully did the trick. It made me sleep and gradually I got back into the habit of sleeping. How lucky I was to have her to help me. I can't imagine what my parents would have done and where I would have gone had I suddenly been bundled back to them.

Tilda wrote and told my parents I had at last settled down and had made friends with a girl of "good farming stock." This was Rosemary Day, always known as Fuzz because of her wild, unruly dark hair. Our friendship was to last a lifetime.

That summer term there was great rejoicing when the war in Europe came to an end. Huge bonfires were lighted on all the hills and mountains around Keswick. We in the Prep were not allowed to join in as the Upper School were doing, but we could watch from our bedroom windows. People thronged the streets, singing and cheering. There were Union Jacks and bunting everywhere. My mother sent me red, white and blue ribbon and I fastened it round the necks of Horace and Mary Plain, my much-loved teddy bears. We had a day's holiday – as a matter of fact we often had holidays on those rare days when it wasn't raining - and went for a picnic to a wooded promontory called Friar's Crag, and to a hill called Latrigg. Badger's house, No 3, went for a walk round the lake as her housemistress didn't like climbing mountains. Fuzz and I went off on our own and she jumped fearlessly from crag to crag, urging me on with cries of "Come *on* D, don't be so feeble!" which I undoubtedly was. We crossed the river by way of the swing bridge and joined in prayers of thanksgiving with the Upper School.

We went to church on Sundays and were told that we could either go to Crosthwaite, which was quite a long walk, or if we thought we might not last out the walk and the service without wanting to go to the lavatory, we should opt for the nearer St John's in Keswick. My experience at Dumbrell's School prompted me to opt for St John's. It might not have been so exciting as Crosthwaite but it was comforting for all like-minded pupils to know we wouldn't have the worry of wondering if we would be able to 'hold out' – and I think it was eminently sensible of the mistress in charge to give us the option.

In the holidays I went to Surbiton, to Granny Cooper's house. Fownhope had been bombed and they had moved to 28 St Matthew's Avenue. It was much smaller than Fownhope and not nearly as nice, I thought the garden very boring but the house itself must have been reasonably large as it had an attic and beyond the kitchen was a pantry and a scullery and a larder. Today those sorts of rooms would have been knocked into one and made into a smart utility room. The house was right beside St Matthew's Church and on Sundays you could hear nothing but bells, bells, bells. I liked to hear them.

Not long after they moved, Granny Cooper died. I was very sad about this as she was my favourite Granny, and although she was so poor she always sent me postal orders for half a crown for Christmas and my birthday, which must have been quite a sacrifice. After she died, Winks ran the house, doing the housekeeping and the cooking. I had a room at the top of the house in the attic, with a brass bedstead and cobwebby cupboards under the eaves. There was a bathroom next door which wasn't used and you could always hear a gurgling noise from the bath. Audrey and Jean went to day schools in Surbiton and their mother, Auntie Joan Moodey, was jealous that Badger and I were at boarding school. She might not have been if she had known how much I hated it. Auntie Joan was a difficult person as she was jealous of everything, especially of Winks. She once jogged Winks's arm when she was pouring out tea and Winks was scalded with the boiling liquid. She was also very nosy and would read personal letters if she found them lying around. I once found her nosing around in my bedroom, looking at my most private things, and she found a letter my mother had written to Winks in which she read some very unflattering things about herself. Winks said it was her own fault, she shouldn't have been reading other people's letters and what did she expect?

By this time Winks had a new Scottie dog called MacDuff and my mother's little dachshund Mr Chips was also there. Chips was always cold and covered himself up in a smelly blanket. Whenever Auntie Joan Moodey passed his basket, he always growled and sometimes showed his teeth in a snarl and she said, "Nasty dog you are." But I had seen her kick him one day, so it was not surprising he didn't like her. I didn't like her either, except when she took us to the pictures. Chips was not the only one who was cold at 28 St Matthew's Avenue, for it seemed to be a really cold house. Of course there was no central heating and we would sit so close to the fire that our legs would get red and mottled and Audrey and Jean got terrible chilblains. They always wore sleeveless gloves but they still got chilblains. At night when we were sitting round the fire we dreaded having to leave it and go up to our cold, cold bedrooms. I would lie in my bed with my legs curled up in a ball, not daring to stretch them down into the icy depths below. We didn't have hot water bottles until we were much older.

Audrey, Jean and I had private French lessons in the holidays with a Miss Cecilia Bortwick, a funny old woman who always wore layers and layers of clothes. We were fascinated to watch her take off her coat, her crocheted yellow woollen hat, her crocheted yellow woollen scarf and then about three different puce or purple cardigans, leaving the fourth on over her skirt and jumper. She then spoke to us in French. It was mostly things like, "What did you do in the holidays?" which wasn't very interesting as what we mostly did was listen to her speaking to us in French. But she was so well-meaning you couldn't hurt her feelings by saying that.

Winks had lots of friends in Surbiton who invited us children to tea. People never invited anyone for lunch or dinner in those days, it was always tea, which is an easy and rather cosy meal to prepare, and I have often regretted it is not in fashion now. Also you didn't have to provide wine, which was expensive and considered a bit fast. So we went to tea with Miss Harum and Miss Fry, who had apparently looked after me when I was small and whom I considered rather nice, and Miss Fowler and Miss Harrison, who asked us to tea in the old people's home they jointly ran. One of the inmates of the old people's home was an old man with a wooden leg which stuck straight out in front of him and I was horrified to see Chips walk up to this, sniff it and then lift his leg against it. Once more a stream of liquid issued forth onto the carpet. We were hugely embarrassed and just pretended it wasn't happening, and I'm not sure Miss Fowler or Miss Harrison or any of the staff saw.

CHAPTER NINE

The next term, the Michaelmas term, was our last in Keswick. I was put in a room called Cat Bells with three other girls. All the rooms were called names after lakes or mountains. We therefore had Helvellyn, Skiddaw, Scawfell, Derwentwater and Windermere, to name a few. The three other girls in my room were Hilary, Pamela and Jane Bowman. It was Jane Bowman's first term and she was as homesick as I was, if not more so. She was also mercilessly teased by Hilary and Pamela. She had a set of nature books of which she was inordinately proud. One day Hilary threw them out of the window and they got rain-sodden and covered with mud. This must have been the last straw: Jane ran away, only to be discovered and brought back by Miss Walters, or Wally, as the matron was known.

Wally was a scraggy, spotty- faced woman with greasy black hair swept up on top of her head and secured with combs. Nobody liked her, but many managed to keep in her good books for it is unwise to fall out with the matron. Matrons have a lot of power in a girls' boarding school. We were having a maths lesson with Tilda in one of the Nissen huts where we had lessons when Wally entered, dragging behind her the bedraggled Jane. She was carrying a spotted handkerchief on a stick over her shoulder like Dick Whittington. "Look what I found under the bridge near Penrith," said Wally in triumph (What, not who.) That was about ten miles away, so it was quite amazing for Jane to have got that far.

She told me about it afterwards. She had nearly reached Penrith when suddenly she realised that Wally was behind her, shouting to passers-by, "Stop that girl!" Someone put out an arm, barring her way, and the next thing she felt the hot breath of Wally on her neck. She was then dragged all the way back to Keswick.

I think Tilda was less in sympathy with Wally than with Jane. She said, "That will do, Miss Walters," and Jane was taken away and put in the sick room in the dark. I visited her there often when I thought I could do so without being seen. There was nothing wrong with Jane at all, yet she was kept in bed in the dark by herself with nothing to read and nothing to do for a whole week. It was not long before she ran away again, and this time she succeeded, disguised in her school cloak as an old woman. She managed to get on a train to Leeds near where her parents lived, and this time she was not sent back. Well done, Jane, I thought. But I missed her, and often wondered what happened to her afterwards. Yet she could never have been as unhappy as she was that term in Keswick.

With Jane gone, Hilary and Pam turned on me. I was a bit deaf with the constant aftermath of earache, so I was fair game. They talked very quietly and if I said, "What did you say?" they would chant in unison, "We don't repeat twice!" I cried under my pillow, hoping they would not hear.

I was also picked on by Wally, who took a vicious delight in the little cruelties she could inflict on those she disliked. One of the highlights of our week was House Reading, when we sat on the deep pile green carpet in Tilda's comfortable drawing room while she read to us. It was usually Dickens - I remember 'Nicholas Nickleby'. But if you had mending to do, you could not go to House Reading until it was finished. I always had mending; not only was my uniform very worn but my socks always seemed to have large holes in them, so time after time I was on the mending list along with - while she was there - Jane Bowman. We would hurry to try and finish the mending before the end of House Reading but when we took our efforts up to Wally for inspection she invariably said they would not do. "Do you call this a darn?" she said. She would then get her scissors and cut the darns out, making the holes larger than ever. I never did find out what happened to Nicholas Nickleby.

Another of Wally's tricks was to put you down on the parcels list. Being on the parcels list was the greatest excitement. It was put up on the notice board in the morning and you thought of nothing else all day until it was time to go to Matron's room and open your parcel. For me, having a parcel was a rare event, so when my name was on the list one time I looked forward to opening it all morning, only to be told by Wally that it was a mistake.

And then there was the occasion of the birthday party. Anyone who had a birthday was allowed a cake and they could choose about ten people they wanted to come to their party. A list was put up on the board and a plan of the table with their name at the top and their best friends on either side and the people they wanted least – but still wanted – at the bottom. I was at someone's party and as usual Wally hovered around, hoping for some cake as she was a greedy woman. I said under my breath but so that the others could hear, "She's a greedy pig." She must have heard something but not all and said, "What did you say?"

"Nothing," I said.

"Oh yes, you did – *what did you say?*"

"Nothing," I repeated. I could afford to be brave with all my friends around me.

"Right, we'll see about this. Come with me."

I got up from the birthday table and followed her upstairs and into her bedroom. It was small, airless and claustrophobic. There were religious pictures all over the walls.

"Now," she said, her face so close to mine I could see the blackheads around her nose and a black bristle on her chin. "What did you say?"

"She's a….." I mumbled.

"She's a what?"

"She's a…." I couldn't say it. Then she hit me hard across the face so that I fell over backwards onto the shiny satin eiderdown on her bed.

"A greedy pig."

Her anger mixed with triumph on hearing this was awful to behold and was to cause me much further misery during my time in Keswick. I wrote in a notebook that the two people I hated most in the world were Wally and Auntie Joan Moodey. I've often wondered if the latter read this on one of her sorties into the most private things in my attic bedroom.

Back at school I got earache and was put in the sick room. After a couple of days the earache went away, but I was kept in bed for over a week with the curtains drawn and nothing to do, no books to read, just one, a religious book of Wally's that I found eminently depressing. I'd rather have had the Bible – at least that had some amusing stories in it. Every day Wally would come into the sickroom and take my temperature. Then she would look at the thermometer for an eternity while I waited, hoping against hope I would be allowed to get up.

"Can I get up today, please, *please* can I get up?"

And each day she would reply after a long pause, "Not today, my dear."

Eventually I was allowed up but alas, the earache returned a couple of days later. I wept silently in the cloakroom and pretended it wasn't there, but in the end I had to go and tell Wally and back I went into the sick room. My sister Badger came over to visit me with a friend who said to her, "But Johnny, your sister looks so *miserable*!" Afterwards Tilda told my parents that Wally had been a most unsuitable matron but that it was hard to get people of the right type because of the war.

It wasn't all bad in Keswick, even for me. I remember once being very hungry after lights out and creeping down to the kitchen. Mrs Taylor the cook welcomed me and gave me a pancake filled with golden syrup. I enjoyed that more than anything, for most of the food we had was not very good. We used to queue up in front of a hatch from the kitchen and a little round woman called Mrs Postlethwaite, known as Possy, would serve out our food with her bare hands, porridge or cabbage or mashed swede. This was surprising, yet no one was surprised, we just accepted it.

The food for the Upper School in the Keswick Hotel was just as bad and the beds in the dormitories were so close together that one girl got tuberculosis, which caused quite a scandal. It was said that the owners of the hotel made a fortune out of the school being there and were able to retire when we all left. Nevertheless most people remember their time in Keswick with much affection. Certainly in the upper school it was a very free and easy life, the discipline was relaxed and both staff and girls enjoyed being in the countryside. Yes, it was beautiful - what a shame I didn't appreciate it then.

CHAPTER TEN

In the spring term of 1946 we returned to Roedean School in Brighton. The Junior School was some distance away from the Upper School. We slept in dormitories with coloured curtains over each cubicle. The dormitories were called less imaginative names than the rooms in Keswick; we had Blue, Green, Rose, and Terracotta. There were bells over each bed with a little plaque saying "If you need a mistress in the night, ring the bell." The school had been taken over during the war by the Navy and when we returned we found that all the bells were broken. This was a great joke, often to be repeated.

We had a new matron now called Miss Cook who was much nicer than Wally. She had been in Brighton before the war and remembered my sister Badger with affection, so that was good for me at first, but after a while she went off me. I was untidy and my hair was a mess, unlike the neat plaits some girls managed. Fuzz's hair was curly too but somehow it didn't look as bad as mine. My clothes always seemed to need mending because of being passed on by other people. I was embarrassed to discover that my navy blue knickers were a slightly different shade of navy blue from others, and this also applied to my coat and skirt which we wore to chapel on Sundays. It was my sister Badger's last term and she was a prefect. I was very proud of this, as to have a sister in the upper school who was a prefect gave you a certain amount of kudos. The junior house marched in a crocodile to the school chapel and there was my sister standing on duty in the cloisters. I was delighted, and called out "Hello, Badger!" and she said, "No talking there!" She always took her duties very seriously and her conscience would not let her make any exceptions to the rule of not talking in the cloisters.

We were all given small patches of garden and Fuzz and I shared one of these. We planted things in it but they didn't seem to grow. The ground seemed

48

hard and full of little stones and however many you took away there were always lots left. Nobody's gardens really flourished and eventually we got bored and let the weeds take over.

In the grounds at the back of the school were disused air raid shelters and we were told on no account to go near these as some of their roofs had caved in and were unsafe. On fine days we went down to the Roedean beach via a tunnel that went right through the cliff. The tunnel had been blocked up in the war in case German spies used it to get into the country, which we thought would have been quite interesting. The beach wasn't very good because it had lots of sharp rocks covered with barnacles and all the girls who paddled there came out with bleeding arms and legs.

I showed some of the girls in my dormitory the copy of 'Cats and Kittens' in which my letter was printed, and Christine said she didn't believe it was me who had written it. She said there must be hundreds of Delia Despairs in the world. She was a catty girl and we avoided her and her friends, who could be very spiteful. Bullying still went on at school and Valerie was expelled for shutting a younger girl in the disused air raid shelter we had been warned not to go near. She had also shut her into a wooden chest, where she nearly suffocated. I escaped most of the bullying but when I was in Terra Cotta dormitory someone chased me with a spider and everyone joined in until Lizzie Whitehouse said, "Stop it, all of you. She really doesn't like it." I was grateful to Lizzie for evermore. She also said my mother's photograph looked nicer than anyone else's mother. At half term Lizzie came back to school with ringworm, which she had caught off animals on her parents' farm in Devon. Her long blonde hair had to be shaved off and people avoided her in case they caught it too.

One Sunday Fuzz and I went for a walk and as we climbed up over the downs behind the Junior House we suddenly came upon a couple making love. They were much too intent to notice us.

"What *are* they doing?" I asked in amazement.

"They're mating, of course," said Fuzz, matter-of-factly. Having been brought up on a farm she knew all about such things.

I was sent to the sanatorium, which was very different from the sick room in Keswick. There were nice nurses working in the San and often there were others girls to talk to, and you could read all the books you wanted and do puzzles and play games so that you often didn't want to leave. The only thing was, when I was playing my flutina, Sister came along and took it away, saying,

"We don't have flutes in Sans." I can't say I blame her as I was not very good at it and made an awful noise.

While I was in the San Elaine Cameron caught poliomyelitis and everyone was in quarantine except the three girls in the San who had not been in contact with her. It was then decided we three should be sent home. I was delighted and so was my mother, at first. Every time the telephone rang I said, "Was it the school? Have I got to go back?" But they didn't phone and I stayed at home for the rest of the term. My mother wasn't that pleased and thought it was a bit of a nerve that they never refunded any of the school fees.

Before I had left the convent one of the nuns told me I should interrogate the staff at my new school and ask them why they said in the Lord's Prayer, 'I believe in the Holy Catholic church' when as Protestants, they clearly didn't. There were other things too I was supposed to ask and try to catch them out, and sure enough, in loyalty to the convent, I blindly went through the list. Of course our scripture mistress had answers to everything and must have found me very irritating.

When I had started at Roedean my standard was high, I had learnt Latin for two years as well as French and had had such excellent teaching that I was way ahead for my age, but after a year at Roedean I fell back and was run of the mill. The only subject I was any good at was English. We had a wonderful red-haired Irish mistress called Miss Mortimer who encouraged us to write freely in our essays, spilling out all our innermost thoughts. My friend Melanie Harmsworth and I took this to heart and spilled out with abandon. I came out with all sorts of wild excesses about my family, which they would not have been pleased about had they known their little eccentricities were being broadcast to the entire form.

My grandmother came to take me out; this was Granny Despair, my father's mother, whom Badger and I didn't much like. She was always going on about her poor heart which was supposedly weak, but when one of the heart specialists told her there was nothing wrong with it she was furious and said she was never going to see *him* again. She was very embarrassing, she wore a funny orange hat and had a slight moustache and what was worse, she came to chapel and sat in the visitors' gallery so that everyone could see her. She took me to a cinema which was showing a film about Princesses Elizabeth and Margaret Rose. There was also a nature film about caterpillars – whoever wanted to see that? - but the main feature, the one I really wanted to see, was a romantic drama with James Mason and Margaret Lockwood. This was something Granny did not think suitable, so we went out right in the middle of a long, passionate kiss, causing a lot of noise and sighing from people in the audience whose feet we tripped over. I walked out slowly and with many backward glances, but it was no good.

"Why, *why* did we have to go out, Granny?"

"It wasn't suitable, dear."

"But I *liked* it!"

"Don't be silly, dear."

I told Granny I was very hungry but she didn't take any notice and just said, "You're a *big* girl!"

Once Badger and I hinted to her about a wooden pencil box with rabbits painted on it that I wanted desperately. We kept bringing the conversation back to this pencil box, but to no avail. We were not sure if she was a bit deaf or a bit dim.

Sometimes Winks would come and take me out and I loved every minute of my days with her, and dreaded going back in the evening. It could be pouring with rain but she'd trek all the way on the train from Surbiton and then out to the school on the bus and I'd wait at the window until I saw her dear figure in a rather drab brown coat and hat, coming across the grass. It must have been difficult to think of things to do on a rainy day out from school if you had no car and not a lot of money. We went window shopping and then to Fullers and had walnut layer cake with thick white sugary icing on top, or to Lyons for Bath buns and margarine.

When Fuzz's parents came to take her out she would sometimes ask me to go too. They came in a car instead of on a bus. They were quite rich and stayed at the Grand Hotel or the Metropole. These seemed very splendid to me, the height of luxury. My family would never have gone to such places as these, not in a million years. When I went to Surbiton for the holidays Winks took me to the Mascot, a funny little café where you could have lunch for three shillings and sixpence.

When we were in Hove we heard you could have very good practically free meal at the British Restaurant which was in the Town Hall. My mother took me there and we sat at trestle tables with loads of other people who were shovelling stew and mashed potato into their mouths as fast as they could. She obviously didn't think much of it, because we only went once. When my father was home on leave he sometimes took us to the Old Steine in Brighton, to

51

Jimmy's, an ornate Victorian restaurant with lots of gilt everywhere and waiters dressed up in dinner jackets. You were not supposed to go to Jimmy's if you were under twelve. My parents took no notice, but I was racked with guilt in case I was spotted there and arrested.

In the Easter holidays I was invited to stay with Fuzz. My mother took me on the bus as far as Tunbridge Wells and Fuzz's mother met us there. She was short and quite stout. We went to the cinema and I was very impressed that we sat in the four and sixpenny seats, up in the circle. We normally went in the one and nines or occasionally the two and threes, never anything as dear as that.

After the cinema Mrs Day drove us back to their farm at Marden in her big car. The house was called Spitzbrook, a huge Victorian house with a conservatory and even a room just for playing snooker. Fuzz's father played snooker after supper with her uncles. He was a huge man, both big and tall with very shaggy dark eyebrows. He could get very angry, especially with her older brother Edward, who was considered rather wild, but he was especially kind and gentle with me. I shared a bedroom with Fuzz and we had a bathroom all to ourselves and luxurious peach linen sheets. At home we had white cotton ones which had machine darns as they had been mended many times and Winks had had to put them 'sides to middle'. At Fuzz's house we had porridge or Grape Nuts for breakfast with thick yellow cream from the farm, and there were bacon and eggs in a silver dish on the sideboard. Fuzz's garden had a lake in it with a rowing boat and swans, and there was a tennis court and a croquet lawn.

On the Thursday before Easter we went into the woods and picked primroses and tied bunches of them onto a stick with string. Then we took them to the village church and decorated all the window sills with the primroses and daffodils. After church on Easter Sunday there was an Easter egg hunt in the garden, and after that we went into the sitting room and Edward came in and played Ink Spots records on the radiogram.

On Easter Monday we went to a point to point meeting and Fuzz's mother packed a splendid picnic lunch which she laid out on a table with a white cloth and silver cutlery. It was a bit chilly and she gave us a glass of cherry brandy before lunch, then she gave us a pound each and we went off to put our bets on at the Tote. Lunch was slices of chicken and ham and salad and fruit salad in a screw topped jar with more of their thick yellow cream. We stood and watched the races, standing on a hay wagon belonging to one of

Fuzz's uncles. We drank more cherry brandy and everyone was very jolly.

One afternoon Mrs Day went into the village of Marden to visit some poor people who lived in a cottage there. She took soup in a wide-topped thermos flask and eggs and butter and cream. We went straight into a dark little parlour and there was a family with raggedy children and a big bed in one corner with an old woman lying ill in it, and they all seemed very pleased to see Mrs Day and the basket of goodies. That same evening we all went off to the theatre in London and afterwards out to dinner in a grand restaurant.

At the end of my visit we drove into Tunbridge Wells and my mother met us there and took us both back to Hove on the bus for a return visit. It was all so different, and I was worried Fuzz would not enjoy herself, but she loved it, I suppose just because it *was* different. Badger took us to Zetlands, a lovely tea room in the Old Steine in Brighton where chocolate and coffee éclairs cost a shilling each. Fuzz ate and ate and then said wearily, "I really don't think I can manage any more," because she thought Badger had paid for the whole plate.

We went on the pier and to the beach and the Hippodrome and the Royal Pavilion and the usual things we always did when guests came to stay. We got the overseas *Daily Mirror*, which I loved because of the strip cartoons about Jane and Garth. The story lines were very exciting and I couldn't wait to see the next instalment so when it arrived I snatched it up, but Badger said I must let Fuzz see it first because she was the guest.

In the summer term Fuzz's parents sent her boxes of fruit from the farm. She had Cox's orange pippins and sweet dark cherries which she would hand out to her friends. We played a game in which you lay on your back on your bed and tried to cram as many cherries into your mouth as possible. The most anyone managed was twenty-four – quite a feat.

My father sometimes sent me wooden boxes of dried bananas from Nigeria. These were delicious but an acquired taste. Chips, our dachshund, acquired this taste and we saw him with his belly practically touching the floor, having eaten about three pounds of the heavy-weighing fruits. Normally Chips, being a miniature dachshund, was quite thin. Once when Audrey, Jean and I had taken him out for a walk we were stopped by an old lady who was scandalised at his thinness and said she could see his ribs and that he must be half starved. We were shocked at this accusation and explained that he was a miniature and supposed to be like that, and it was much healthier to be thin than fat. Fat dachshunds got paralysis of the back legs and had to be put down.

Back at school it was our last term in the Prep and we had to decide which house we wanted to go into in the Upper School. I was of course going into Number Three where my sister and my aunts had been, and Fuzz elected to go with me. That term she and I shared a two-room which had rose-patterned curtains. We lay in bed at night and looked for faces tucked in amongst the roses in the curtains. "I can see a face in the left hand corner at the bottom."

"Where? I can't see it!"

"It's a girl's face – you *must* be able to see it!"

But neither of us could see the faces the other one saw.

We decided that if we could only get her brother Edward and my sister Badger to meet, they would immediately fall in love, so at the end of the term we concocted a meeting between them. We insisted they should come up and see our bedroom and then, when they were both inside, we rushed out and shut the door. They were together in the room for about three minutes but instead of falling in love they decided they didn't like each other at all. It was a great disappointment.

CHAPTER ELEVEN

It was exciting to go into the Upper School in the Michaelmas term of 1947. Fuzz and I shared a two-room on the upper floor of Number 3 House, known as Heaven (though I don't recall the lower floor being called Hell). I was quite glad to get away from Miss Cook, the matron in the Prep, and now we had a new matron who actually liked me – for the first time in my life I was liked by a school matron, which I think was largely due to her liking my sister. Her name was Miss McCulloch and she was nick-named the Muck, and her sister, logically enough, was the Mess. Our house-mistress was a Scotswoman called Miss Will. She had black hair going grey at the temple and she wore a lot of crimson lipstick which came off on her teacup. She also smoked and left lipstick-stained cigarette stubs in her saucer. She wasn't particularly popular with the girls as she was so fussy about unimportant things, but my parents liked her. Once they invited her to dinner and my father gave her rather too much to drink and she became squiffy and giggled a lot and fell over at one point and they said I should never mention this to anyone at school – and I never have, until now.

We had all our lessons in the main school house and we did our prep and slept and had all our meals in Number 3. People said how boring that our houses should be called 1, 2, 3 and 4, and it does seem unimaginative. In the Junior House we had been divided into groups, named after famous women. Fuzz was in Nightingale and I was in Austen. There were two other groups called Fry and Siddons. It is obvious why Nightingale and Austen were famous but I was a bit vague about the others. I think Fry was something to do with prisons, but I never really knew what Siddons did.

As in the Junior House, we seemed always to be hungry. I had started to write a diary (very mundane it appears now) and for several years food figured in it with the greatest regularity. We sat at tables which were rearranged about every three weeks and for tea there were scrum tables where you could sit where you liked. At tea also we were allowed to have bread and jam as much as we liked. We provided the jam ourselves, or sometimes we'd have peanut butter or tins of Golden Syrup, which we liked to mix up with the butter and make into a gooey mess. At breakfast we'd have fried bread with our bacon and we liked to spread this with marmalade, which was surprisingly good. Every day our table would move on to the next one and when it got to the Servers' Table we spent the whole meal serving the rest of the dining room and ate our own afterwards when everyone else had gone. If you were serving you invariably got more food so it was a great treat to serve, especially if you liked what was on the menu. Treacle pudding was especially good but sod's law meant that it was more often semolina or tapioca - frogs' eyes, we called it, and thought it was disgusting.

I went to Winks's house in Surbiton for the Christmas holidays and Winks and Aunt Chattie took us to see "Little Red Riding Hood" in Wimbledon. And around this time I started saving up for a canoe. I was desperately keen to have a canoe but no one else seemed as keen that I should have one. Daddy thought it would be dangerous. Then I saw an advertisement in the Daily Mirror for some plans to make a canoe. You had to send a postal order for seven and sixpence to someone called "Percy", The Daily Mirror, London to get these plans. I sent off my seven and six and everyone thought I was mad and that I'd never see my 7s 6d again, but in due course the plans arrived. They were immensely complicated but a friend of Daddy, a colleague of his, thought it might be possible to have it made in Nigeria, so I posted the plans out to my parents.

The holidays ended and I had to get ready for going back to school. *"Going back is weighing on my mind,"* I wrote on 13th January 1948. *"Its thought dreaded me all morning."* But once I was back it wasn't so bad. There were compensations such as films: "The Last Chance" (*very sad, everyone cried*) and listening to "Dick Barton, Special Agent" on the wireless in the Girls' Drawing Room. One night Fuzz and I, getting quite beauty conscious, curled our hair, which Muck thought a great joke. The next day I wrote *"Hair came out nicely. Parcel from Winks, skirt and jumper, 4 choc wafers, bible. School is quite a nice place now which is saying something."* On the 30th January I wrote *"Today Ghandi popped off at 12 noon."* Fuzz and I thought this was hilarious – not that Gandhi had died, for we hardly knew who he was, but the facetious way of describing it.

As the 14th February – St Valentine's Day – approached I wondered if it was going to be yet another big let-down – or would this be the year I'd get a romantic communication from an unknown admirer? I had lived in hopes of this ever since I found out it was the day in the year most eagerly awaited by English schoolgirls. The day when reputations were made or ruined, when the prestige rose or fell and when your wildly exaggerated account of an encounter with a boy in your road was proved to be – alas – wildly exaggerated. There were avid discussions for days beforehand.

"Janet Wilde's expecting eight valentines this year."

"You're joking!"

"No, honestly."

"D'you think you'll get any, Delia Despair?"

I answered mysteriously that I wasn't sure. There were some girls in my class, even at thirteen, who got three or four each. They were what the grown-ups I knew would have described as precocious or a bit fast. I don't think they were really fast, just prettier than the rest of us. They went to parties in the Xmas holidays and met all sorts of exciting boys. It also helped that they had trendy mothers who bought them trendy clothes that did something for them. The clothes I had were hand-me-downs from my sister and cousins. I even had a bathing dress that my mother had knitted for me. What could possibly be worse than a hand-knitted bathing suit? How I longed for one of those elasticated ones that other girls were wearing.

The first teenage party I went to was Fancy Dress given by Auntie Lilian. The great problem was, what to wear? It was finally decided I should go as Lord Woolton's Appeal. I was dressed in a white tennis dress with posters sewn on it with "Lord Woolton's Appeal" painted on in shiny crimson paint. I had no idea either who Lord Woolton was or for what he was appealing. Certainly I was not appealing.

The other teenaged girls had lovely fancy dresses their mothers had hired for them from some smart fancy dress shop, and looked as pretty as a picture, dressed up as Snow White or Little Bo Peep. I wanted to crawl into a hole in the ground in my horrid white tennis dress with the posters stuck on it and the paint looking as if it were still wet – maybe it *was* still wet - so that no one wanted to risk coming anywhere near me. We danced, somewhat awkwardly, and the spotty boys held me as far away as possible in case the crimson paint came off on their suits. "*Boys were rottern dancers*" I wrote savagely in my diary.

Things did not get any better. For my first grown-up party I had to wear my grandmother's rose-bestrewn taffeta housecoat because it was wartime and there were not enough coupons to buy me a dress. No wonder none of the boys there fancied me. Nevertheless, I looked forward to St Valentine's Day as eagerly as anyone. After all, you never knew what secret passions might not be burning in some unknown (to me) boy's breast. I mean – I thought – surely I must have an unknown admirer somewhere. The world's big enough, isn't it, there are enough people aren't there, millions, surely it's not asking much to have just one (thinnish) unknown admirer? The trouble was they were obviously determined to remain unknown. "Someone, somewhere is waiting for you," said the GPO. But my unsent message went unheeded.

That spring term the staff did a play called Noah which was not a good choice. When we saw all the mistresses dressed up as animals in the ark we shrieked with laughter. Seeing them as monkeys or camels or giraffes was more than we could handle, and despite the approving entry in my diary *"Staff play awfully good, all about staff crawling about,"* our reaction went down very badly as the play was not supposed to be funny at all and it was considered shocking that we had laughed. We were in deep disgrace. Mademoiselle Lavauden, known as The Lav, wrote a critique of the play in the school magazine in which she said, "To appreciate the play one must have either a most innocent heart or extreme literary sophistication… it is practically beyond the grasp of an audience of 13-15 year old schoolgirls, who are at that specially awkward and insensitive stage of development… the piece was too complex for the comprehension of the young audience, who, in this particular case, revealed itself very unworthy of the grandeur of the theme represented."

But really, what did they expect?

We were doing *Macbeth* with Miss Woodcock, (known as Peahen) and when we came to the part where Lady Macbeth says *"I would…. have pluck'd my nipple from his boneless gums,"* I asked guilelessly, "What is a nipple?" Peahen went bright red in the face and somehow evaded the question which I'm sure she must have thought I'd asked deliberately to embarrass her. But I really didn't know what it was. I think I'd progressed from calling those parts of the anatomy pom-poms, now calling them bosoms instead, and Winks sometimes mentioned bust-bodices or said someone was large in the bust, but we never ever said the word "breasts" - that was much too risqué.

CHAPTER TWELVE

Extracts from the Diary of a Roedean Girl, aged 13

1st Jan 1948   *Resolved not to bite my nails.*

4th Jan   *Went to tea with Miss Fowler and Miss Harrison. Chips and Mackie came and behaved very badly. They lifted their legs and had dog fights. Jolly good tea.*

5th Jan   *Winks promised to tell us a dirty story when we're grown-up* (But by that time she had forgotten what it was).

10th Jan   *Our party went off well. The food was good. We played Murder, Yes and No, and Blow Football. The girls were quite a nice crowd.* (I don't suppose there were any boys as we didn't know any).

11th Jan   *Went to church. Read book. Pat came to tea and we all ate full to bursting. Getting ready for school.*

13th Jan   *Winks packed my trunk. Said goodbye to Aunt Chattie. Went out to tea with Winks and Jean and to see "Singapore".*

14th Jan   *In afternoon went back, great excitement at Victoria. Got a carriage with others. Sleeping in a 2-room with Fuzz in Middle.*

16th Jan   *Jolly nice scrum table, sitting next to Di quite chatty.*

19th Jan   *Monday, depression as usual. Backs and Feet. Wonk and Pam, me and Hal had a good joke at supper.*

20th Jan   *Never felt so cold in all my life as when playing goal. Horrible drizzle and no gloves. Missed evening lessons but no posture or flat feet, whopee!*

21st Jan   *Gym, couldn't do a handstand. Horrid games. Decided to try a cure for biting nails so as to win prize from Winks. It is bitter almons.*

22nd Jan	*Felt pleased with my Bambi model in Art, it is going to be grilled today.*
23rd Jan	*Tried nails idea, worked fairly well. Had letter from Mummy, enclosed Princess Liz's photo. More coming, hurah!*
24th Jan	*Saturday at last! Sweets though I only got 2oz and Jill got none.*
26th Jan	*Went to the dentist with Wonk, nothing doing. 2 men stared at us. In Piano Lesson Bacon is helping me to conquer sight-reading.*
31st Jan	*Saturday at last. 6oz of sweets, ate them all. Walk on the Undercliff, got soaked by big waves.*
6th Feb	*Horrid lessons. Consider I wrote a <u>wonderful</u> poem! Very moving. 84 lines!*

When I look at that poem now I think I was deluding myself, for it wasn't really wonderful and didn't scan at all. But it was quite sad, about a fox that gets hunted and killed by the hounds.

Foxy Tradgedy

T'was a bitter April morning and the wind was very chill
And the Master blew a warning to his huntsmen on the hill
A horn that broke the silence, that rent the cold still air
And it echoed down the woods and lanes and reached the foxes' lair.
Then Mother Fox grew cold with fright for she had heard the horn
And Fox had been away all night and now t'was long past dawn.
The foxcubs looked with loving trust to the opening of the cave
Their dinner always came that way, brought by their father, brave.
But on that day they hoped in vain, no meal for them was on the way
For soon would end their father's reign, he could not live another day.
And now he ran, that practised thief, A hen lay in his jaws.
Fox of foxes, this their chief, he'd taught them cunning, made their laws.
But as he ran back with his prize he heard the yapping of the hounds
He set off down beside the stream, running with great leaps and bounds.
He had great faith in all his tricks, he had no cause for fear,
He turned and saw the leading hounds, the horses in the rear.
But as he turned his luck turned too, down on his left foreleg he fell
It hurt him now when fast he ran and he saw it had begun to swell.

And soon he saw that the hounds were gaining, but he must keep on, he must!
For t'was he the foxes' leader, in him had they placed their trust.
He felt so tired and weary now, he forgot his cunning tricks
He longed to lie down in his restful cave and to feel those tender licks.
And still those dreadful hounds were gaining, but he could not stop, not now
For he thought of his wife and his four small cubs and he could not let them down
So as he went he wondered if he'd ever get back home
For his body seemed to sag so and his mouth was full of foam
And his ears were cut and bleeding and his eyes were dull and sore
And his lovely coat was matted and he guessed what lay in store.
Yet his valiant spirits flagged not, and with determined air
He kept on, kept on running till he thought he couldn't care.
And oh, how his leg was throbbing and he looked round with eyes of despair
To the first of the bloodthirsty bloodhounds and he knew it was rather too near.
He had now passed through miles of country and the sun had come up in the sky
And the brave little fox felt so weary but he held up his tail still more high.
Then quickly he turned round and faced them and stared with defiance at his foe
And a burst of morning sunlight set the men's red coats aglow.
And they marvelled at that little fox there as he stood and he faced them at bay
And his eyes had grown suddenly brighter for he felt he was barring their way.
But then came the time when he realised that he could hold out no more,
And he sighed once again, a little sigh, and *down* on him then, the hounds bore.
Long after the hunt was over, the vixen came out and she saw
That the hunt had been successful and *her* fox would come back no more.

7th Feb 1948	*Saturday! Sweets! Matches! Free time! House Dancing! Dick Barton! Sewing! Can eat our tea as long as we like! Had a jolly good time. Won matches. (Pity sweets disappeared down the little red lane before tea.)*
9th Feb	*Rottern post. Change of staves. Rottern staves* (Staves were staff, we had to "sit up" to them and make conversation at meal times. I'm sure some of them thought it was just as boring to sit next to us.)
11th Feb	*Had a valentine! Either from Tim or Bretton. Clues on back, probably Bretton.* (Probably not!)
12th Feb	*Felt so hungry.*

13th Feb   *Starved almost.*

14th Feb   *Jill, Fuzz, Coll and I went for a wonderful walk to Ovingdean. Explored church, gathered violets.*(We always seemed to be gathering violets – maybe that's why you never see any nowadays.)

26th Feb   *The Queen came! I took a snap of her car going to St Dunstan's. Fancy, the Queen!*

28th Feb   *Saturday! Sweets went too quick. Hansel and Grettel disappointing. We sat on bus in Civilisation. Very hungry – ice creams floating around.*

(They may have been floating around but I'm sure we didn't get any. Hansel and Grettel was an opera at the Dome in Brighton, and although I thought it disappointing, it was great to be outside school in Civilisation, as we called it.

We went to lots of concerts at the Dome where it was mostly the Halle Orchestra conducted by Sir John Barbirolli, and heard many famous musicians including the violinist Ginette Neveu, the pianists Solomon, Myra Hess and Denis Matthews and the contraltos Kathleen Ferrier and Kirstine Flagstad. I am sure we did not appreciate this at the time.)

29th Feb   *Fuzz went out and got a wireless – super! Civilisation.*

1st March   *Listened to "Monday Night at Eight" with Dickie Murdoch on Fuzz's wireless, wizard!*

3rd March   *All wirelesses confiscated.* (They didn't last long).

6th March   *Saturday! Sweets, 23 toffees, rather monotonous taste. Guide party fun, ate as much as possible.*

7th March   *Went out with Uncle Teddy (jolly nice) and Auntie Hazel, Auntie Margaret, Clive and Granny. Went to a wizzed hotel in Rottingdean, once belonged to smugglers. Went down to the cellar with Clive. Had my fortune told. My fortune is to change for the better, that's good. Clive jolly nice.*

(Uncle Teddy was the husband of Auntie Hazel and he was considered rather a failure in the family as he didn't have much of a job, but I liked him. He was mad about cricket and would jump up and down with excitement when there was a Test Match being played).

8th March   *Monday again – O week, fly! fly! fly! Got a second class.*

(Mondays were awful for me because our marks were read out by the Head Mistress and I dreaded it all week. I was bottom of the A division and it was excruciatingly depressing if I got less than a 2nd Class – the average of all your marks added together. A Second class was in the seventies and was the highest I could ever hope for. To get less than a Second was letting down the rest of your form. The others in the A division were all very clever and easily got 1st Class which was in the eighties, or above.)

9th March   *Photos back, hurrah, they're super! One of the Queen's car.*

(The fact that you couldn't actually see it was the Queen inside the car seems to have escaped me.)

10th March   *Nearly did a handstand in Gym, did feel pleased.*

(Fuzz had broken her arm doing a handstand when we were in the Junior House and I never had the courage to do that extra flip over. Again, I was the only one in the class who couldn't do it.)

12th March   *We all started reading "The Scarlet Pimpernel" 1267 pages. DID a handstand in Gym! Ship was bucked.*

(The Ship was our gym mistress whom I liked. She was very jolly hockey sticks and used to call us by our surnames, shouting "Knickers, (Rachel Nickerson) Run like a rabbit!"

14th March   *Sermon rottern.*

18th March   *Disapointed in my fawn, it's horrid.*

(This was something I was making in Art. It was supposed to be sitting looking back over its shoulder. I envisaged it being a noble-looking animal and much nicer than it turned out).

20th March   *Grand National won by Sheila's Cottage. Kept in by Distilled Woman.*

(This was a mistress who taught chemistry and whom we didn't think much of.)

21st March   *Went out with Winks. Granny we could not get away from. Winks brought dates and biscuits and jam so sweet of her. Ate merangs and éclairs and ices galore and felt grown-up.*

22nd March   *Midnight Feast. There were biscuits, dates and horlicks tablets. Also jellys that got upset.*

23rd March   *Feeling excited. Last hairwash. 5 more baths. Read Scarlet Pimpernel hard.*

26th March   *Good Friday. Went walk and picked violets.*

27th March   *Cambridge won Boat Race.*

28th March   *Three more days. Easter Sunday. Chapel looked simply heavenly.*

29th March   *Monday. 2 more days. Could hardly work, in fact didn't much.*

30th March   *1 more day. PACKED. Not much lessons. S. Burdett's party.*

31st March   *Last Day! This time tomorrow, so excited. Rushed everywhere doing everything. Extra sewing, finished skarf.*

1st April   *Went home on School Special. Met Winks at Victoria. Spent day in London, borght clothes.*

2nd April   *Wonderful to be home among my own things.*

9th April   *Borght a Guide Book to Switzerland.*

                   (It had maps and plans of all the cities and everyone thought I was mad because there was no chance of my going to Switzerland in the foreseeable future.)

                   Went to see "The Four Feathers" one of the best films I've ever seen. Ralph Richardson terribly good. To do with the war.

11th April   *Went to cemetery on bicycles.*

12th April   *Awful dog fight, Audrey bit.* (I think Audrey got bitten rather than bit). *Went to Pack Hams for tea, and then "The Best Years of our Lives." Bankruptsy is at hand. Ways and means to make money??????*

13th April   *Went into Surbiton. May have sold bus. Aunt Chat came, she is a scream.*

14th April   *Bus didn't sell, nor ornaments. Rottern!*

15th April   *Winks said she'd buy bus.*

                   (That was the nice thing about Winks, for after all, what did she want with a toy wooden bus? She only bought it to give me a bit of money. She was a really sweet person – she had very blue eyes and snow white hair which people said had turned white overnight when she was only twenty-one because someone she had loved had been killed in the First World War, but she never talked about it, nor did we ever ask. She was not pretty like my mother or Auntie Joan, but we all loved her dearly.)

20th April   *Went to LONDON! Borght dress for Audrey and airtex shirts and a glass pig for Coll. Went to Madame Toussards, saw Heath. Liked the Chamber of Horrors. Went to Lyons Corner House for tea, very posh! There was a band. Went on tube trains and saw many new look dresses. Felt wonderful.*

21st April   *Went to ask Miss Fry to tea on bike.*

22nd April   *Had my first tennis coaching lesson with Mr Johnson. He was very nice. He has holes in his vest. He plays awfully well.*

23rd April   *Had my second coaching lesson. Did quite well really.*

24th April   *Went to Cemetary.* (I don't quite know why we were always going to the cemetery). *Miss Fry came to tea. Made cake. She was nice..*

26th April   *Had 3rd tennis lesson. Didn't do as well.*

27th April   *Went to have last lesson. Found I'd missed it. He gave me balls. Well, goodbye to Mr Johnson! I packed my trunk.*

28th April   *In the evening went to the club night of the "Arcadians" in my pink silk dress. Had my hair done. Jolly good play. Afterwards refreshments, Jean and I went pushing around to get cakes. We were excited.*

(The Arcadians were an amateur dramatic club in Surbiton. Our mother's cousin Tony Cooper usually played the leading man, he was good looking and very amusing. Badger and I thought we would have married him any time he asked us but alas, he was gay, though no one ever talked about that – probably didn't even know. My pink silk dress was my best, it had white spots on that you could pull off – and I did all the time. I'm surprised there were any left on it in the end.)

29th April   *Went back to school, felt sick. Sleeping in Colony – wizard! - with Fuzz and Lizzie Grant who is very nice.*

(Colony was a group of three rooms away from the others, on our own and was considered a good place to be).

4th May   *Decided I smell a little owing to having had no bath since Thursday. That will do the trick.*

(Well I certainly hope it did).

6th May   *Went to a secluded spot in Spiders* (a copse of thin, spidery trees – hardly any trees would grow at Roedean, it was much too windy) *with Colleen and Jacky. Coll told us the story of her romance with Colin. It sounds marvellous, like a story with her as heroine. But then Coll will always be the heroine of any story.*

           (My friend Colleen was clever, pretty, could dance like a ballet dancer, could sing beautifully and was grown-up and sensible whereas we others were rather silly.)

8th May   *Went to the Philharmonic Orchestra conducted by Victor Sabata. It was wonderful, I shall always remember it.*

18th May   *Received a blow about my canoe at last. I half expected it really but it came as a shock. My dreams, my hopes and fears are realised and confirmed at last and are crashed to the ground. I am very, very disapointed.*

           (My parents had written to say it was not possible to make the canoe in Nigeria after all because the plans were too complicated. I think really there was never any chance they would have let me have it.)

22nd May   *What does it feel like, the last day of being 13? Well let me tell you, wonderful. Everyone was bagging things for me. There were lots of letters, Fuzz is keeping them for me, and hard and knobbly, exciting parcels. The eve of being 14 – farewell 13!*

23rd May   *My birthday at long last – I was 14! Everyone rushed in and gave me some wizard things, Coll gave me a smashing turquoise blue thin scarf with D on it, Joyce gave me a scrubbing brush* (maybe the bath hadn't done the trick after all) *Jacky a box of notepaper, Jill an expensive bottle of scent, Soup a book, Felix a book, Hal a pencil and rubber, cards galore. Went out with Auntie Joan Priestley, had lovely time reading in front of fire and eating and listening to wireless.*

24th May   *Empire Day. £1 and sweets from Granny, 2/6 Auntie Joan, 5/- A.D. 10/- Auntie Hazel = £4.13.6!! What shall I get? Great problem.*

25th May   *I may play Macbeth! Me, Coll or Melly. I <u>hope</u> it's me! Curry as Lady Mac.*

26th May   *Said Macbeth. Curry and Lodgy come into the race now, and I went out a bit. Jacky gave me helpful critisism of my book. She likes it very much. I'm so glad, my life depends on it.*

27th May   *EMPIRE DAY HOLIDAY! Went to Ashdowne Forest, went with Fuzz, Hamish, Hal, Felix, Juliet, Sashby, Soup, Libs, Grant and Jean. Ate wizard lunch, took lots of photos, caught beetles. Sat in clearing by log hut. Climbed tree. Went to Peartree farm for tea. Wizz place, very old. Had smashing tea in barn with Hal, Felix, Fuzz and Hamish.*

29th May   *Had my birthday tea! No candles but everyone said it was wizz and it was!*

13th June *Was the only one in the form with a third class, felt most depressed.*

17th June *Acted Macbeth again, 3rd time running. I do hope I play him....*

18th June *Wrote scripture plays. I feel excited when I think of Mummy, Daddy and Badger coming home – quite soon now.*

21st June *Felt dissy. After a sleepless night woke with earache and packed off to San. Jean is here, I wish I could see her. Had different impressions of the San. Nurse is nice. Ear ached quite a bit. Hope I get some letters. Felt a bit lonely.*

22nd June *Felt better, had head swathed in bandages. Saw Jean, was so pleased, she is next door. Did puzzle, did it next door with Lizzie Ham and Jean. Had good food though not enough. Finished "Beau Geste" Played Halma, made card houses and bombed them with Halma. Hope I've got a 2nd class. Began to read "Joyful Surprise" by Baroness Orcsy. Felt pleased being with Jean and Lizzie. The maid in the San is dotty.*

23rd June *Rather hoped I would stay in San today but didn't. Went in the middle of doing exciting puzzle and reading a Baroness Orcsy. Poor Lizzie Ham being left. Everyone has been very nice, tigging me things. But I got a shock, had nearly a weak Pass and I did so want a 2nd class.*

5th July   *Badger's birthday, awful exams! Badger was 19. Had Arithmetic and Latin which was simply foul, also Eng Lit, not too bad.*

8th July   *Went out with M, D and A. Had strawberry splits. Gave me Medieran dolls and sweets. Mummy has grown quite fat and Anne quite thin but both look very nice.*

10th July *School sports. Was disapointed because there was no running. Won nothing. Wrote play. They said I brightened up the evening, made everyone laugh.*

11th July *Went out with Anne, we went to Jimmy's for lunch and I had Scotch Broth and Salmon Mayonaise and then Strawberry Soufle Tart. Then we went home. Oh, it's good to be home..*

15th July *Read Baroness Orcsy's novel "Will o' the Wisp", it was wizz. I wrote a modern version of "Macbeth."*

21st July *I am in A division next term. Such a relief! Was fetched home. We have a new car, it is a Ford and jolly nice.*

25th July *Took tea on beach and bathed twice. Bretton was there, also A.J. Pauline and her cousin Christine. I am going to make a bird table, start tomorrow.*

26th July *We went shopping and bourght me a lovely New Look Horrockses dress. I feel grown-up in it.*

28th July *Went riding on Charlie this time.*

29th July *THE CAT CAME HOME!* (He had been staying with Josephine). *At least, we brought him home. We went to Fittleworth in the car and fetched him but the main problem is Would The Cat settle down?*

30th July *I settled The Cat down at home and locked all the doors. Then we went out and took Badger to Bidi's and Mum and I ate ices.*

1st Aug *Went riding, rode Fudge. She is sweet and willing but trots too fast.*

3rd Aug *Went riding, rode Charlie. He is nice but eats grass too much. A little boy on Mulberry was funny and nice. Went and bathed at the King Alfred swimming baths. Had lunch there, goose and jelly. Went to Bramber and saw museum.* One of the items was a kitten with two heads, which was a horrifying sight and one I have never forgotten. *Then Jean and I climbed Devil's Dyke. My, what a climb! We were tired and just gobbled our tea. The climb looked much better than it was. The Cat got lost and was found.*

5th Aug *Jean and I went on the pier. We had our fortunes told. Then the rain came down and we got drenched, just in our cotton frocks.*

8th Aug *Went for a long walk with Jean over the downs, through a wood, valley drive, cabbage hill, hill brow. Picked wild raspberries and flowers.*

9th Aug *Monday. We borrowed Monopoly and I won with Regent St, Piccadilly etc. then we took some photos. I got a marvellous one of The Cat, also of the downs. We went to the Old Wheel in Reigate, Audrey came. Winks brought Chips..*

10th Aug   *I rode Charlie. Learnt a lot but not how to mount. I felt a fool. We played Monopoly and I won £20,000.*

11th Aug   *I went riding again. I had practised mounting on the bed and it was better. Audrey and I went to see "Spring in Park Lane," very good.*

13th Aug   *It is Friday 13th today! Our bonfire caught fire and had to be put out with buckets. Played tennis, Pauline, Badger, Audrey and me.*

14th Aug   *Borght choc ices. Went on beach with Badger. I had no cap.*

19th Aug   *Mummy lost her gold watch and accused the window cleaner. What a to-do! Then she found it. I went to Hazeldenes and borght stuff to make my bird table. It was a job! Nails wouldn't go in. I forsee an argument. Granny came.*

20th Aug   *Friday. Badger and I went to London and went shopping. I borght a glass dog for Fuzz. We had a jolly good lunch at Marshalls. Oh, how I long to be grown-up!*

21st Aug   *Toby came. He is very nice and easy and Badger likes him. We went to see "Dr Angelist" on the pier with Pauline. It was a very dark and rainy night, and I had that eerie feeling as we strode along.*

22nd Aug   *Sunday. Toby, Badger, Chips and me went for a walk. We climbed on the breakwater. The sea roared and pounded far, far below. We went to see "So Evil my Love" with Ann Todd and Ray Milland. Good acting but not a film I would choose to see again.*

23rd Aug   *I went riding and cantered for two minutes by myself on Star who was sweet and it was all right. A day to remember. Daddy, Badger, Toby and me went on the downs with our tea. I felt squashed.*

25th Aug   *I went riding and cantered on Fudge. The wind was in our faces as we went over the hill. She said, "You've come on now!" Just what I've been hoping for. I made the tea and some strange sandwiches. We walked in the park and picked blackberries in the sun.*

26th Aug   *Went to Jimmy's for dinner but I felt awkward and embarrassed. The menu was in French. I did not enjoy it greatly.*

27th Aug   *Went on beach with Susy. She is a sport. We met a beastly man. After a lot of fuss I stayed to lunch (Orange Chiffon Pie) and then Susy, Richard and me sent to see "Dick Barton, Special Agent" quite good.*

29th Aug	*Did stamps. Made and painted bird table. Went on beach. Went to tea on the Howards' yacht, it is smashing. I rather wish I was a sailor.*

29th Aug *Did stamps. Made and painted bird table. Went on beach. Went to tea on the Howards' yacht, it is smashing. I rather wish I was a sailor.*

30th Aug *I cantered on Star quite a long way, but bounced up and down.* (I had reached the age when I needed a bra, and was deeply embarrassed. I told Mummy and eventually she bought me two Kayser Bondor bras). *I sat up in a tree with a book and read. You can see the riding place from there. Jumped down with one knee straight and felt a twinge of pain. Had tea in the garden.*

31st Aug *Toby went back to London and Badger was sad.*

1st Sept *I have Water on the Knee. My knee throbbed.*

2nd Sept *Stayed in bed on new mattress. Had The Cat and wireless and read Women's Journals. The aunts came. The Cat remained all night. Badger did my nails.*

3rd Sept *In morning I rested again and read mags. Went to fetch Josephine. She is very nice.*

6th Sept *I banged Badger's finger in the car door!* (It hurt her very much and I felt awful). *Took Susy out to Jimmy's, then went to see "The Wilmslow Boy" with Robert Donat who I like. Borght a puzzle for Badger but it is too babish. She starts work tomorrow.*

9th Sept *Everything went wrong today. Lost fountain pen. Spilt paint on dress. Broke bathroom basin! Chrumps! Got things ready for school. Bird table looks wizz with food on it.*

10th Sept *Went to see "The Red Shoes" with Moyra Shearer and Robert Helpmann. A marvellous film but sad. Dinner afterwards in the Ship restuarant.*

11th Sept *We went shopping again, Mum gave me some lovely fur gloves and other things, wizzard.*

12th Sept *The Lurcotts came in the evening. We had cock tails and all sorts of drinks.* (I thought cock tails were the tails of cocks) .

13th Sept *Had lunch with Granny. She was in a very great hurry* (Probably fed up with being with us). *Then went riding. Cantered on Fudge, a very dashing canter.*

15th Sept *Went riding for the last time. Rode Fudge. A nice ride. Cantered about. John says I'll be in the club soon.* (Not sure what John meant by that…) *Went to see Ivor Novello's "Perchance to Dream" with him in it. Marvellous music. My last night in this wizzard bed. Oh dear.*

16th Sept   *Finished packing. Borght wizzard suitcase. Packed for Surbiton. Went to lunch at Boots Restuarant. Made some fudge, it turned into toffee. Did everything, climbed tree, saw The Cat, went up in loft. At last went back to school. Boo. Sleeping with Fuzz in Heaven.* (That was the top floor, nothing like Heaven.) *Nice room. Felt sick.*

19th Sept   *I got advice about Robert Donat from Eileen and Joan* (As I had a crush on him.)

20th Sept   *Monday. My lofas came, they are simply smashing and fit beautifully.*

21st Sept   *I was sorry to find my lacrosse is worse and I cannot find my stick. Was overjoyed to find there is to be a film at the end of the week – "The Young Mr Pitt" with ROBERT DONAT!!!!!!!*

24th Sept   *Had a rottern morning. Piano lesson. Played lacrosse, received a compliment and an insult. Roll on tomorrow!*

25th Sept   *TODAY at last! Dressed up in my New Look dress and Lofas. "The Young Mr Pitt" with Robert, John Mills and Phyllis. What a film, what a team! Cocky and I are writing play for Hallowe'en.*

26th Sept   *Badger, Richard A and Daddy came. I may go to the wedding, whopee!*

Went to Rottingdean, ate ices with Fuzz. Still nuts about Robert Donat.

Went to Soup's party.

27th Sept   *Keep thinking about Robert Donat, in the bath.*

28th Sept   *Decided on our play for Hallowe'en, Cocky and me are producing it.*

30th Sept   *Awful lessons. Found time to write to Robert Donat.*

2nd Oct   <u>*Day of Wedding*</u>*!!! Peter v. Valerie. Mum and Dad came, felt ungrateful about having my hair set but was pleased though I didn't seem it. Saw The Cat! Wore SILK STOCKINGS, lofas, pink silk dress, carnations. Jean and Audrey looked nice. Wizz journey up in car. Valerie looked lovely. Gorgeous wedding. Took photos in Marquee. Saw lots of people. Ate masses of cakes. Peter is nice. Saw Mac, James etc. Wizz ard flowers. Loved every minute.*

4th Oct   *Got a shock to find I'd only got a Pass this week. It was that 0 for Maths. I must do better next week.*

5th Oct   *Got more bad marks, 4 for French, 3 for Latin, 4 for Algebra – feel depressed. Have to take marks to the Will in house-reading. Corks! What can I do now?*

6th Oct	*Determined to get better marks today and thank God, I got 8 for English and 8+ for Biol but blot, 4 for Geom.*

6th Oct — *Determined to get better marks today and thank God, I got 8 for English and 8+ for Biol but blot, 4 for Geom.*

7th Oct — *Not had a letter from Robert Donat yet, when <u>will</u> it come?*

8th Oct — *Foul lessons in morning. Cocky and I began our play. Have great expectations and ambitions.*

11th Oct — *Was in Agony about marks – Agony. Surely I should have had a Pass but gosh just thank God, had a 3rd. So releved no one has any idea. Cannot play games for a week owing to crack on head, so pleased!*

12th Oct — *Got some better marks today, 9 for French and two sixes for Latin. Must get second class next week. But – only 2 for Geography. Wrote more of play.*

14th Oct — *Managed to finish play and rehearsal went off very well. Everyone kept order and was keen.*

15th Oct — *Friday. How I loathe Fridays, at least the mornings. Got 2½ in a Chemi Test, no hope now of my longed for Second. Very busy arranging rehearsals.*

16th Oct — *Photo of Robert Donat came back, quite good consid.*

17th Oct — *Went out! Richard Adams was there, he is very jolly and quite a sport, we ate most of the time, The Cat recognised me. Made fudge which was wizzard. Ate cakes with Fuzz in bed.*

18th Oct — *So pleased to find I'd got a Second Class!!*

21st Oct — *Getting near the weekend. Lots of rehearsals. Our song isn't very good. I do hope it's OK.*

23rd Oct — *Prize giving, we were squashed in the gallery. Some reporters were there I hope I am one some day. Mum and Dad came but not Badger. We went to the Regent and saw "The Wistful Widow" with Abott and Costello and after we had fish and chips and jelly.*

24th Oct — *Daddy and Badger came to chapel then we all went out. Went on bumper cars with Badger, It was wizzard, we did enjoy it and I drove very fiercely. Then we went home and I got scratched horribly by The Cat.*

25th Oct — *Thank goodness! I have a Second Class again, so releved, it makes the day better.*

27th Oct   *Had rehearsal before breakfast which was better than usual. In the afternoon we had a proper dress rehearsal. It was better, specially Sashby.*

28th Oct   *More rehearsals. Grant is doing fine and bringing bottles. Had parcel with maustaches in it. They are dears to remember.*

30th Oct   *HALLOWE'EN at last! Today is the day. Worked hard at posters all morning. Dress rehearsal in the music wing went off badly. But finale of Land of Hope and Glory was good and the maustaches looked wizzard. In the end it wasn't as good as it might have been but they laughed a lot and said it was funny.*

31st Oct   *Felt extremely flat but the Russell said I have the makings of an actress! The other plays and things were very good specially the VI.*

1st Nov   *Was dreading Monday, thinking I'd get a 3rd class - and I was right. We had a serious talk in our room and Felix told us many things about Life.* (Felix was in the form above us so knew all about Life.)

2nd Nov   *Played goal in a vile game. Got one on the jaw. Felt weak, watery and thoroughly depressed. In the end told Muck and went to the sickroom. I spent a restful evening, dozing and dreaming.*

3rd Nov   *Still felt sick and had a cold. Read "Murder must advertise" by Dorothy L Sayers. Hal, Fuzz, Sashby sent me notes and cheered me up. Felt very hungry in the afternoon and never ate so fast. May get up tomorrow.*

4th Nov   *Did get up, rejoicing..*

10th Nov   *VI form conference. Lots of Boys and Girls here. Brighton Coledge best, Vandeen worst. Picniced on terrace.*

11th Nov   *Fuzz's birthday, Fuzz was 15. Such a crowd, and wizzard presents, photo frames, scarves etc. I gave her the glass dog. Her ma came down.*

13th Nov   *Fuzz's birthday party. Wizard cakes, crackers and balloons. Prepared for feast after midnight.*

14th Nov   *Royal Baby is born. M & D came to chapel. The Will is letting me stay out for supper, jolly nice of her. Winks was there and Badger, Bretton, and Auntie Joan P came. Played the piano and they said I'd improved. Lovely evening with fire and crumpets. I felt very sad.*

15th Nov   *Monday again. I loathe Mondays. I dread Marks. But I got a Second..*

17th Nov   *Today is the day Robert Donat is going to be in "Curtain Up", so excited.*

18th Nov *Had sewing. Have decided to make a rust woolen skirt with wide waist band and a zip. Decided to make toffee but Will said no. Caught making butter balls.*

19th Nov *Had horrid lessons. Started Graphs. Admirable essay for History I hope I've writ. Horrid P.L.*

20th Nov *Princess Liz and Phil's anniversary. Saw "The Overlanders" it was really wonderful. The herds of cattle stampeding and going over the cliff. I did enjoy it*

23rd Nov *Had hair wash and my hair looked dreadful.*

24th Nov *I felt rather depressed. I was looking forward to tomorrow and the casting of "Emma." Mr Knightly! That sounds good and exciting. (D. Despair as Knightly in EMMA!) What castles in the air, what foolishness.*

25th Nov *Thursday. Casting. The Will cast me as Mr Woodhouse and I wanted to be Mr Knightly. The Will asked who was the best actor for Emma and everyone said me!! I was very pleased but I am too tall. Grant wanted to be Mr Knightly and I went through agonies. But she gave up in the end. Joyce and I went through the most gorgeous scenes. (I have got the book that the real Mr Knightly used).* (I doubt that.)

29th Nov *HOLIDAY MONDAY! Went to Rottingdean. Had coffee at Highcliffe with Fuzz. Hal and Felix. Plan to do it again when we are grown-up. Next year. Lovely coffee and cream and choc sundae.*

2nd Dec *Got a shock in sewing. The woman said would I give up my idea of making a skirt and not do dressmaking, but Embroidery? I'd loathe to!*

3rd Dec *Friday but I wasn't dreading it so much. No P.L. but Chemi test made up for it. I got 4. Brilliant. 9 out of 40 for Geometry. Also brilliant.*

4th Dec *This is a great day for Fuzz. She was confirmed. Fuzz is now very holey.*

8th Dec *Felt iritatated To add to it the Prep went and got a germ and we could not go to their play.*

9th Dec *Getting nearer the end of term! I am so excited when I think of Xmas shopping. What shall I get Badger?*

10th Dec *Melly invited me to her party on Jan 8th. Oh, I do hope I can go! Last Chemi. Watched bubbles burst into flames.*

11th Dec   *CONCERT. Celibidach was conducting. He has showy, greasy hair. Not as good as Sabata but very good seats, lay back enthralled as always.*

14th Dec   *Packing today – will I get everything in? I did, thank goodness. Did lots of odd jobs. Patmac has set us lots of prose translations. Oh fiddlededee to Patmac! Uproarious evening, crackers and ginger, we got quite drunk – Sabo, Stella, Cherry, Eileen and me.*

15th Dec   *Wednesday. School Dancing and Speech. Oh, I'm excited! Mucked around, doing desks and all the last minute jobs. For once I think I'm ready! Fuzz went early and poor Hal was very sick.*

16th Dec   *WENT HOME on School Special, hurrah! Got a carriage with 9 others, Felix, Fiona, Juliet, Joyce, Jean, Jill P, Joan, Grant, Sheila and me.*

17th Dec   *Woke up in Surbiton! Wonderful feeling. Mrs Joy Rossiter is quite nice but very loud.* (She was a P.G.) *Unpacked trunk.*

18th Dec   *Did a lot of shopping. Borght 10/- worth of cards. Audrey and Badger went off to their dance with the naval cadets! Mary H came back to tea, (she is much improved).*

22nd Dec   *Badger went up to London again. They seem to have had a wizzard time. In the afternoon I went to Kingston with Jean and borght presents – Badger and parcels. Depressed because I am broke, as always.*

23rd Dec   *Stayed in and read book: "The fourth Mystery Book" – very exciting. Just did that all afternoon in front of the fire. Lots of presents started to arrive (well, two).*

24th Dec   *Today is Christmas Eve. Tomorrow is Christmas Day. Lots of carol singers. Did up all my presents. Will wear my new frock.*

25th Dec   *Christmas Day at last. Wizzard stocking, Little Chris Mouse. Had Agatha Christie, "The Murder of Roger Ackroyd". Belmont came down plus 10/- (I take back what I said about him being mean!) Wizzard supper and then – presents! Whopee, money, books and maybe fur boots??*

26th Dec   *Boxing Day. We got up when we felt like it and spent the day writing thank-you letters and feeling ill with cake. I hope I may have the fur boots! Had a glass pig, lots of books and scent, and writing paper.*

27th Dec   *We went to Aunt Chattie's and saw "Cinderella" with Buttons by Jack Hulbert.*

28th Dec *Winks says I may go to the party, whoopee! Took dogs to see Miss Bortwick.*

30th Dec *Borght a file to write stories in. After a lot of fuss went to Kingston and cinema with A & J. Smarties were borght and shopping. Didn't go to Aunt Chattie's.*

31st Dec *Last day of the Year. Went to LONDON! Looked everywhere for snow boots as my Xmas gift from M & D, at last got some just write, quite the nicest pair in London! Also got a wizzard book about Switzerland and SOCKS. And finally to top it all, heard Robert Donat call the New Year in – terrific!*

Although this diary for the year 1948 is so mundane, it certainly gives a flavour of our lives at school and at home both in Hove and Surbiton. We had a happy childhood, and what strikes me now is that we always seemed to be going to the cinema - but of course in those days there was no television.

CHAPTER THIRTEEN

And so with the start of 1949 life carried on in much the same way, and I continued to alternate between being elated and happy one moment and deeply depressed the next. It strikes me now how very young we were for our age, compared with the girls of today. We spent our time longing to be grown-up because then, we felt, we would achieve our true happiness. We thought quite a lot about boys but didn't really meet any and would not have known how to behave if we had. At school the only man we saw was the games man, who was blonde and quite good-looking but he always seemed to be miles away in the cricket pavilion.

The first man I fell in love with was Robert Donat. I had to keep this from my parents as they would have thought it very silly. I envied Fuzz who had subscriptions to two weekly papers called "Film Fun" and "Radio Fun". They were comics really and featured people like Max Miller, who was a bit before our time, but they were enormous fun to read. In contrast my parents, who would not have approved of *Film Fun* and *Radio Fun*, paid for me to receive *The Children's Newspaper*, which was deadly dull. It had no pictures in it and only had articles on boring things like collecting coins. I suppose some people didn't think them boring, but I certainly did. I also took a magazine on Wild Birds, but though I was interested in birds the magazine palled after a time.

My New Year Resolutions in 1949 were: 1) *Will not bite nails* (Obviously the 'Bitter Almons' hadn't worked) 2) *Will be scrupulous and careful with money* (that didn't last long) and 3) *Will be sensible* (that didn't last long either. I don't think New Year Resolutions ever do.)

After Christmas Aunt Chattie took us to the pantomime in Wimbledon. Going to the pantomime with Aunt Chattie was an annual event and this time it was *Jack and the Beanstalk*. We continued to see the maiden ladies of Winks's acquaintance. We had a "dainty" tea with Miss Harum. We also had tea with Miss Fowler and Miss Harrison, with Miss Bortwick who taught us French conversation, and Miss Fry who had looked after me when I was small and was "rather nice". I imagine all these ladies suffered from the same thing as Winks, that the eligible men they might have married had been killed in World War One.

I had lunch with Granny which was "so-so" and Auntie Hazel took me to a film with Greer Garson and we went on the top of a bus all round London with me saying loudly, and much to her embarrassment: "Oh, look, Regent Street, I bought that, *and* Bond Street. Oh there's Park Lane, I had a hotel on that, and on Mayfair."

Did not go to Melly's Party after all. I don't know why not but imagine it must have been the logistics of getting me there and back, for we didn't have a car, Winks didn't drive and we went everywhere by bus or train. Instead of the party I went to see "Sleeping Car to Trieste" with David Tomlinson which I thought "*a most refreshing murder.*" I finished my Agatha Christie but "*the murderer wasn't satisfactory.*" On the 11th January I went to buy "*necessary things for school*", in other words sanitary towels. I bought three packets and put them in my bicycle basket, but it was pouring with rain and when I came out of a shop with jam was horrified to see my bicycle had fallen over and the packets had burst open and sanitary towels were swimming around in the gutter. What is more, several men picked them up for me – what could be more embarrassing than that?

On the 12th January I went back to school. Winks went with me and took me to the dentist. I wrote, "*It was a very windy day and he told me my mouth would soon be very windy what with all my holes.*" He also decided that my teeth stuck out so he made a plate for me which I christened Mrs Crab. It was rather uncomfortable so I didn't wear it as much as I should have done, and was always losing it. Miss Will would announce at supper time, "Delia has lost Mrs Crab again, would you all keep an eye open for it?" They did and invariably it would be found.

Our dentist was a tall Jewish man called Mr Middleborough. He was extremely charming to patients and always shook you warmly by the hand, but he could be quite sharp with his nurse, and I felt sorry for her when she couldn't find some instrument he wanted and was treated to his sarcasm. There was no such thing as the National Health and his fees were quite high. When

Badger got married he gave her a free appointment as a wedding present, which must have been the funniest present she received.

That term Fuzz and I were delighted to find we were sleeping in a 4-room with Hal and Felix. We had a lot of fun in that room, and many of our other friends gravitated to it and joined in long, intriguing discussions on Life. We played fortune telling. On the 29th Jan the fortune teller told me I would go on a journey. This was a fairly safe bet for a fortune teller, as everyone is bound to go on a journey at some time, but this didn't strike us. We often wondered what it would be like to have a boyfriend and how it would feel to be kissed, which we had seen so often in films. We would press our lips onto a tiny jar of Lipsyl and imagine that was what it would be like – but then one girl came back having been kissed in the holidays, and said it was nothing like that.

On the 22nd January I got an unofficial invitation to a dance from John Filmer, who was a distant cousin. He had a younger brother called Bill, and they were practically the only boys we knew. They were rather a strange family. Their mother, Betty Filmer invited us to tea and we went over there from Surbiton – Badger, Audrey, Jean and I. All I can remember about the tea party was that there was an uncut cake on a plate and Bill said, "Can we cut that cake, Mother? Or is it just for show?" It had probably been on show a few times as it was rather stale. John used to send me cryptic notes with riddles in and clues as to their meaning. I think it was probably he who had sent me a valentine in 1948 with indecipherable clues on the back, and not either Bretton or Tim.

28th Jan   *Awful lesson with Nokey.*

Nokey was Miss O'Kelly, who took Division 3 for Maths. She was Irish and had flaming red hair when young, but when we knew her it was completely white. She was greatly feared as she had a terrible temper. One day I was late for her lesson and when she asked why, I said "There's no reason." She was pleased with this reply and said I was the most honest girl in the class because I had not made up some silly excuse. (Probably because I hadn't thought of one.) After that everyone caught on and when asked why they were late would say, "There's no reason," so that excuse didn't work any more, not for me or for anyone and we would get a rocket.

2nd Feb	*Got our exam time table. Crumbs. Badger and Sheila came down and took me out. They cheered me up a lot about the cloud that is coming over us.* (The cloud was Exams).
12th Feb	*Just sat and read, a most relaxible day.*
23rd Feb	*Exams awful. Have to do Geog again. Bottom.*

We started playing "cricket" in the sermon. What happened was this: The person on the end of the row was "in" first. Every time the vicar said "and" that was a run and if he said "but" you were out and the next person was in. We listened to the sermon most attentively and "buts" caused eruptions of silent laughter. It is surprising how often the word "but" occurs in the average sermon.

Fuzz's brother Edward had learnt to fly and on 13th March he said he would fly over the school and drop an orange so we'd know it was him. We all waited for him in our room. He came but did not drop an orange. Later he won the King's Air Race.

15th March *Very good sermon. He talked about all the sins we commit. He asked us to pray for the people we hated. I prayed for Tiddle. (*That was Miss Middleton who taught us Geography, probably my worst subject. In one exam I finished off by writing "*Merino sheep are found in —- no time to finish.*" Tiddle saw through that one. I must have been naïve to think she wouldn't.)

21st March *Had a nice little discussion about a pantomime we might do in the next Christmas term. I could be an Ugly Sister and Sashby the Man in Black.*

26th March *Boat Race – Oxford won by 4 feet. Grand National, I picked two horses but neither was mentioned. Russian Hero won, Raymond was second and Royal Mount third.*

We packed to go home for the Easter holidays on 29th March. I could never get everything into my trunk, partly because of Horace, my very large teddy bear, who always stuck up. I had to jump up and down on the lid of the trunk to close it. The 30th March was our last day. We had lessons, cleaned out our desks in the Junior Prep Room, had speech – *an awful lot of gabble from the Horrobin (*our headmistress). *A VERY TIRING DAY.*

31st March	*Went home, yippee. Civilisation. I've got such plans for when I get home.*
	I got off at Clapham, Winks met me. Report not very good but still. I had a long talk with Badger, she is In the World and implied that she MIGHT be in love with Richard Angeloni - corks. Would I like him for a brother-in-law? I never thought before.
	Badger, having spent a year in Nigeria with our parents, had met lots of people and many of them had fallen in love with her. Richard Angeloni was just one of them, he was an ADO to my father.
1st April	*It is distressing to find I have no clothes and look awful and fat in what I have. We went to Kingston and I borght a New Look tartan dress with frills.*
2nd April	*I am worried. Does it really suit me? Last year I wouldn't have cared less about clothes. All of a sudden we seem to have grown-up.*
3rd April	*A fuss about church* (probably because we didn't want to go) *but we went in the end. It's so nice to sit in front of the fire and have tea with Winks and Badger.*
4th April	*Winks and I went to London to try our luck for a coat and skirt. In the end we went to Dickins and Jones and got one for £6.17s. Very nice, young browny tweed. I look quite different.*
9th April	*Marrietta came down to play tennis with Badger.* (She was one of Badger's friends from Nigeria. Much later, her daughter Clare was to become Badger's god daughter). *I put on my coat and skirt and met her and Badger for tea. She is very nice and thought I was very grown-up! Me of all people! It is extraordinary.*
12th April	*Toby's wedding to which Badger went.* (Toby had always said he was going to marry a very rich girl, and he did – she came from New Zealand. I am not sure if he was really in love with her.) *Audrey, Jean and Auntie Joan went to London, and Winks and I were left in peace.*
13th April	*Decided to get an evening dress. I was so excited, went to Bentalls in Kingston and got the first one I tried on. It is pale blue water taffeta - a sort of turquoise blue - with a gathered bodice, puffed off the shoulder sleeves and a full skirt. I was thrilled.*

14th April   *Went to stay with Fuzz! Badger and Winks saw me off. Borght Black
Magic chocolates for Fuzz's mother. I had to stand on the train, very
hot and packed like sardines. Thrilled to see Fuzz and drive to
Spitzbrook, her home. Lovely tea and supper. Saw lots of lambs.*

It was always great fun and a real treat to stay at Spitzbrook. On the first day
we cycled over to see Fiona, a girl from school who lived nearby, passing
through narrow Kent lanes bordered with fruit trees. We had a picnic with
Fiona in the woods, which were carpeted with primroses. Later we had dinner
at the Royal Star Hotel in Maidstone and went to a show called "Painted
Sparrow." The following day we got two lambs and called them Horace and
Mary Plain after my teddy bears, and I took lots of photographs of the lambs
and Ranger, Fuzz's golden retriever. Then we picked daffodils and decorated
the church, and after that we went to a point to point. There were crowds of
people. At first I backed losers and was fed up, but then I had three winners
and won 13/9d out of 10/-, which seemed a lot. Fuzz said we would back
horses on the Tote, not on the bookies. Mrs Day marked her card and asked
us to put the bets on for her. We had a *wizzard* picnic lunch and tea and then
a wonderful dinner with the Highwoods, who lived at a house called
Brandenbury. The parents were Fuzz's Uncle Sid and Auntie Joyce, whom Fuzz
secretly called Soppy Sid and Jealous Joyce. Auntie Joyce was Fuzz's mother's
sister. Their daughter Margaret was at school with us and they had an older
son Tony, whom I described as *quite nice.* We had a lovely drive home by
moonlight.

The next day was Easter Sunday, and we had a great Easter Egg hunt in
the garden. I hid the Black Magic chocolates I had bought for Fuzz's mother.
We then went to the Easter service. We thought the window we had decorated
looked especially lovely. All at Brandenbury came back for drinks and we had
a drink called the Spitzbrook Special, which probably contained a lot of gin
and maybe Cherry Brandy, which was Mrs Day's favourite tipple. I wore my
new Horrockses dress. In the afternoon there was a tennis party to which
everyone came, and we all wore whites. I played with Betty and Peter, whom
I thought *not very nice,* and afterwards we bathed in the lake. We had dinner
with the Grown-ups.

On Easter Monday there was another point to point. I was afraid I would
lose what I had won on Saturday but I needn't have worried, for I backed five
winners. There was no tote that day and Fuzz's Uncle Jim was the bookie.

Then we went back to Spitzbrook and played tennis, Margaret and me against Fuzz and Tony. I didn't record who won but no doubt it was them. We young ones had supper together and I decided Tony was *wizzard*, especially later on when we discussed school and I sat next to him on the sofa and we watched television and his hand closed over mine. That did it – I was in love!

On the Tuesday we set to work in the daffodil fields. Mrs Day looked after this part of the farm, and when the daffodils were out she employed loads of people from the surrounding villages and we all picked daffodils till there were none left. It was very hot. I picked the lovely flowers, thinking of Tony, and was delighted to earn 5/- We filled 52 boxes with twelve dozen daffodils in each at a shilling a bunch. In the afternoon we had tea in the hammock on the lawn, then we had baths, supper and watched television in our dressing gowns. This was a great treat, for hardly anyone had television at that time. My family certainly didn't have it, though my parents got it many years later while Wimbledon was on.

On Wednesday I packed my case to go home. It was a dreadful squash. After picking flowers for Winks and saying goodbye to everyone, I was taken to London by Fuzz and her mother, who very kindly bought me some silk stockings for my birthday. Ruefully I wrote, *Well, goodbye to luxury, farm, cream, furniture, Spitzbrook and Tony.* It was always wonderful to stay there.

23rd April   *The day of John Filmer's party. Jean and me went to Kingston and round all the old antique shops to find some turquoise beads but no luck so I wore pearls instead. There were great preparations for the party – baths, hair brushing, then we got all dressed up and went off in state in a private hire car. John is very small. Lots of quite nice boys, two from Winchester. One, David Reid was quite nice. Badger went with one all evening. I met a real drip. My dress was simply smashing. I did enjoy it and did quite well considering.*

25th April   *Read The Murder of Roger Ackroyd and was horrified to find the murderer was I. I'll never trust anyone again.*

27th April   *I put on my coat and skirt and went in a bus to London all by myself. Auntie Hazel met me and we went and had lunch with Granny who gave me a shilling. Auntie Hazel took me to see St Pauls. It is enormous and very awe inspiring and made me feel small.*

1ˢᵗ May   *Badger and I went over to Hurlingham and met Michael and Gill Gould and their parents, all very nice. A lovely club. We played a game and won. Pity Michael wears specs..*

3ʳᵈ May   *Winks got a letter from Mummy and it said I may FLY over to Nigeria in the summer hols – oh I hope so. Had passport photos taken – so happy and thrilled. I shall have some new cloths and meet people and what an experience it will be! I went up to London with Winks and borght a blue satin bathing dress.*

4ᵗʰ May   *I was much shocked and depressed to discover that Soup (Sue Pettman) also likes Tony. I might have guessed it. I beleive there is something between them but I hope not. His sister Margaret gave me a photo of him.*

8ᵗʰ May   *We had letter writing. Soup has written to Tony! I told her everything and much passed between us.*

12ᵗʰ May   *We signalled to a submarine with the electric light and they signalled back!*

13ᵗʰ May   *Had vacsination. Soup had a letter from Tony. I have decided I may give up Tony as she will see him more than me and anyway I might meet someone in Nigeria. I hope so.*

14ᵗʰ May   *We went on the downs and put on cream and tried to get brown but not much luck. Vacsination doesn't feel.*

15ᵗʰ May   *I am going to London to have yellow fever vacsination, how SMASHING. Coming back on Tuesday evening.*

16ᵗʰ May   *Curled my hair, packed case and Groves took me to the station. Funny travelling companions. Had injection, then went round London trying to get a horrockses dress but finally got a striped gingham with a square neck. I fancy myself in it no end, as Fuzz would say. Had a good tea at Dickins and Jones. Lovely to be home and to see Winks.*

17ᵗʰ May   *Went up to London, had lunch and tea at Fullers. Met Badger, she and Winks put me on a train. I had a sore throat and felt rottern but did enjoy being in civilisation. The school taxi didn't turn up so I took another one and was swindled.*

19ᵗʰ May   *Hal and I skipped choir practise and Hal and I ate a tin of blackcurrant purree. Our throats improved greatly afterwards. Did not return spoons.*

20th May   *Empire Day Picnic. Wizzard. We went right over the downs to Pevensey Castle. A lovely picnic lunch. We went in the dungeon and over the moat and to Drucilla's for tea. My leg aches dreadfully and when I came back I felt very cold and not hungry. Had asprins and went to bed.*

21st May   *Had splitting headache and felt so dissy, Muck called me and took my temp and sent me off to the San. Well whatever happens I must be back by tomorrow, Auntie Joan P is taking me out. My leg looks very red and raw. As Nurse says, "What a mess!" Nurse is very nice, so is June but Sister is stern and not so nice. Soup, Joan and Smouha are here.*

22nd May   *So I am going to be here after all. Wept a few tears. Did puzzles and read Lord Peter Wimsey in "Trouble at the Bellona Club." Felix and Gordon came in for a chat. They are going to bump Horace (my large teddy bear). I must be brave about tomorrow. My leg does hurt and after all other people have done much worse things and I shall be 15. It must be better next year.*

23rd May   *I was 15. Well I must say it's sad to be in the San, still Joan and Pat came in and pulled my hair. And Soup gave me a lovely card. They are going back today, oh lucky things. It didn't feel like my birthday till the Will came over with lots and lots of parcels.....*

24th May   *My leg feels better now though it is still red. I can go back tomorrow. Went down to the play room with Jean from Number Four. We through our pie down the lavatory.*

27th May   *Miss Tanner came and we gave her a big welcome (she was a past and very popular headmistress). I must say she looks very fat and rather like Mrs Roosevelt.*

29th May   *Was horrified and VERY upset to find The CAT died last week. How awful, how can I bear it? But I shall see him in Heaven and I have a scar he gave me.*

31st May   *Cherry borrowed my loafers. She showed Maureen and me a book on Physiology. I am the Picnick type.*

3rd June   *Bruce Woodcock v Freddie Mills, very exciting. Jacky lay disgusted under the bedclothes tossing and turning in agony. Bruce won.*

4th June   *Nimbus won the Derby. Photo finish between Armour Drake and Swallow Tail.*

7th June	*French Reading Competition, I was terribly nervous. Grieve coached me. It was very close. Lots of people in the Upper IV went in for it but none of us did anything. Gladys Wright won. The Judges were 2 men, very stern.*
10th June	*Macaroni cheese and Art. I'm bored stiff with clay.*
11th June	*Had some stingy little boiled sweets and only a quarter too.*
1st July	*EXAMS! Chemi tomorrow, I felt fairly confident as I'm not taking Chemi for SC and anyway I think I know it.*
2nd July	*But I didn't! It was foul. I don't like to even think about Geography, I'll probably get 6% or something like that. Badger came and fetched me. Marvellous lunch of peas, strawberry soufflé and cider. We took a picnic tea on the beach and Badger coached me in Biol.*
4th July	*At last this horrible day has dawned. As usual I revised at 6 a.m. but my heart sank as I went into the Geog exam. I felt cold and stiff and everyone was writing away and I was in the depths of misery. Then Biol, I did not finish and went and did a wrong diagram.*
5th July	*Badger's birthday – she was 20. I sent her a telegram.*
6th July	*I must say I didn't mind the Latin but made a muck of the French. At lunch EXAMS ENDED! What an overflowing relief. I hardly like to read a normal book, it's wonderful.*
18th July	*My last day at school in the Lower V.*
19th July	*Finally I got away. Everyone said goodbye and was very envious. All done – nothing left – no more school. I was so happy in the train. Winks met me and we spent the day in London and met Granny and Badger for tea at Fullers. I borght some wizzard red shoes, pyjamas, bras, pants, tennis shorts and a mack with a hood.*
21st July	*Wizzard to be home. Valerie and Nina are both expectant. (Your telling me!)*
22nd July	*So excited, at last it's come. One of the most important days in my life. I ate Quells and was not sick. The start of a great adventure.*

CHAPTER FOURTEEN

Naomi Trevor-Williams and I flew to Kano, Nigeria on 22nd July 1949. Naomi was a girl whose parents were in Nigeria, as mine were, and we were among the first schoolchildren to go out by air in the holidays. Up until that time people had only travelled by ship, so it was considered quite innovative. Certainly it was my first time ever to leave the country, let alone to fly.

Winks and Badger came to see us off at Blackheath. Winks expected me to be nervous but I wasn't a bit as I had no idea what to expect. When the aircraft started to taxi I thought it was going so fast we would take off any moment and was surprised when we came to an abrupt halt. A few minutes later we set off again faster, and this time rose into the air like a bird. In fact our aeroplane was called a York Speedbird.

We were very excited. It was spacious and comfy inside. There were two small boys besides us, and some babies. In front of each passenger was a sick bag and it was expected that we would be sick. I had taken Kwells; whether that had an effect I don't know but I wasn't – however, when much later on everyone else was being sick and the air hostess came round and said they had run out of sick bags and could she have mine, I was suddenly alarmed at the thought of not having it and said I would prefer to hang onto it, if she didn't mind.

Naomi was seventeen, two years older than me. She was at Cheltenham Ladies' College and Badger and I were surprised to see her saying a tearful farewell to the headmistress who came to see her off at the airport. I was never so fond of my headmistress that I would have hugged her and shed tears on saying goodbye, but it seemed that Naomi didn't go home to an aunt or other relative at the end of the term, but stayed on at school in the care of the headmistress, who had become a mother figure for her. She probably loved the headmistress more than her own mother, which is quite sad when you come to think of it. It is rather like the children in the heart-breaking stories by Kipling and Saki, whose parents were in India for years and years so that they never saw them. They were like orphans and were shipped off to strangers, "aunties" for the holidays. These "aunties" were often unkind to them, and the stories are a reflection of their own unhappy experiences. Badger and I were so lucky to have Winks, or sometimes Auntie Joan Priestley and Granny Hove to look after us.

At 12.30 a.m. we landed at Tripoli. We were surprised at how warm the night air was. Tripoli was pretty with all the lights and I bought some postcards of it, but of course we couldn't see much, so we just got out and walked around the tiny airport till it was time to get back into the plane.

The night seemed very long and we didn't get much sleep. I did drop off once and when I looked out I thought I could see the ripples of the sea below. The Captain came round and I asked him if it was the sea and he said no, it was the Arabian desert. He was very nice, he sat down beside me and we had a long chat.

At seven-thirty a.m. we arrived at Kano and once again when we got out of the plane it was a surprise to be greeted by a blast of hot air. Everything looked very vivid, the green grass, the red poinsettias, the blue shirts of the African airport staff. Being in Africa was a Technicolor world after living in a black and white one.

On arrival we were met by Desmond and Diana Milling, the Commissioner of Police and his wife. They were friends of Naomi's parents who were also in the police service. It was intended that they should put us on a connecting flight to Enugu, but due to strikes the plane was cancelled and we had to stay in Kano for a week. Not that we minded, for we had a wonderful week. It was all very new and exciting. The Millings were kindness itself and took us around everywhere, first of all to their home for breakfast. They had a dear little baby boy called John, a toddler really. Then they took us into Kano and we went round the European shops and afterwards to the Catering Rest House, which was like a hotel. There we had a suite and a nice young boy to look after us. We unpacked and were fetched and taken back to dinner with the Millings, and later they took us round Kano by night. Naomi ordered tea for us in the morning at half past six and on subsequent mornings we decided that was too early and asked our boy if we could have it later, say at seven – but he did not understand – he could only say yes – so we had to have it at half past six throughout the week.

Meals were taken in the main part of the Catering Rest House. We met a nice man at lunch and another who said he knew me, which was funny because I didn't know him. I wrote, *"They are in hydes and skins, whatever that means."* The next day I felt ill and Diana was very kind to me. She said she thought I had a touch of malaria. Later Hydes and Skins and his friend came over, and I was pleased because they seemed so concerned, and the malaria miraculously melted away.

The next day the Millings took us round Kano market, which was enormous, colourful and buzzing with life. It seemed to go on and on in every direction. "We'll go in single file," said Diana, holding little John tightly by the hand, "and we must stick together as we don't want anyone to get lost." We could see that could easily happen.

The market stalls seemed to sell everything imaginable, all sorts of strange fruits and vegetables, beans and pulses, meat and fish, pots and pans, colourful materials of every description. The people seemed very poor, and most of them wore long flowing white robes as they were Mohammedans of the Hausa tribe who mainly inhabited the North. Beyond Kano was the desert. I was intrigued to see flies buzzing around everywhere, on the meat and the fish, even going into the eyes and mouths of the children, who luckily seemed oblivious. I would have hated to have flies flying into my mouth. I decided that Kano was the most amazing and interesting city I had ever seen. (Not that I had seen any outside England, but looking back I still think it is the most fascinating city in the world.)

During our week in Kano, the Sallah took place – this is the yearly procession of the Emir on his social visit to the British Resident. It was an important and festive occasion which we felt very privileged to witness. The people in the procession rode on horses and circled round in front of a vast crowd. There were many stunts to amuse the crowd, including men walking tall on stilts. At last the Emir came dressed all in white in an open carriage under an umbrella and surrounded by native police.

We saw Hydes and Skins and his friend again: we watched them play tennis, not very well which was a comfort, and at dinner we arranged it so that they would come to our table. They did and we were exhilarated. We went to a film and they were there too. We saw them again at breakfast and *"they seemed to find us a great sauce of amusement."* I wondered why. They probably thought us young and very silly. In the evening we dressed up in our best things but alas, they went out early – though Sandy did say good evening.

We met other people while we were in Kano, some who were friends of the Millings, someone else who was a friend of my Uncle Tommy, and who like he, had a Romanian wife, some people called Brown who knew my father, an American couple, a woman who we played tennis with and not very well, some nursing sisters and a woman who knew my mother. But all paled into insignificance compared with Hydes and Skins.

On our last day we looked for them at lunch but were acutely disappointed to find they'd gone! *Goodbye, Hydes and Skins,* I wrote sadly. The next morning we got up very early and finished our packing. Then Diana Milling and little John arrived to take us to the airport and see us off. We left Kano with mixed feelings, for we had enjoyed our week so much. It had been fun staying at the Catering Rest House and being independent and everyone, especially the Millings, had been very kind. At the same time we both looked forward to seeing our parents again.

It was a smaller plane this time and the flight was very bumpy, but we enjoyed that, we thought it was fun. It stopped at Kaduna and Jos and finally Enugu in the south east of Nigeria, where my mother and father were waiting. I was delighted to see them again. We had lunch in Enugu, then said goodbye to Naomi and her parents and drove to Onitsha where my father was stationed. I thought it was *a marvellous place,* but everything about Nigeria seemed marvellous to me. The Residency was a large colonial house with a porch at the front and a verandah that ran all the way round with arched doorways. There were lizards constantly running up and down the walls. The bedrooms above had balconies. I was introduced to the servants, known as the boys, who were kind and welcoming. The head boy was called Steven and he was tall and solemn and very dignified. The second head was Fuhru and he was fat and jolly with a good sense of humour. There was also a chauffeur and six others who did various things, including cooking and gardening and the laundry. They came from the Cameroons and had been with my father since his arrival in Nigeria in 1926. My mother got on well with them but would rather have had women working for her, as she thought she could have had more fun and jokes with women.

The dogs were adorable: there was Daisy, a bull terrier who was rough and lovable, and Feet, a sweet little dachshund very much like Chips, so called because he was born feet first. My bedroom was huge and there was a mosquito net over my bed. From the balcony I had an extensive view of the garden and distant hills. My parents gave a dinner party on my first evening and I wore my striped dress. *There were lovely candle lights on the dinner table and sweets in little silver dishes.* We had a delicious palm wine stew which was like nothing I had ever eaten before. Afterwards we all sat and talked and I was bitten to pieces by mosquitoes. People said that was because I was newly arrived in the country and they liked fresh meat. They said I should wear high leather mosquito boots which some of the other women were wearing. I went to bed very tired and enjoyed the sensation of lying cosily under the mosquito net.

The next day a furious letter came for my father from a man called Bill Sherley: it appeared that my father had stuck his nose in and sent a telegram bitterly complaining that his precious daughter was stranded in Kano, and the Millings were deeply hurt. "After all the Millings did for your daughter and her friend," wrote Bill Sherley, "for their care and kindness ensuring that the girls were *not* stranded, you have shown the most appalling ingratitude and insensitivity…" and so it went on. My father was indignant and felt the letter was totally unjustified, but I was shocked and annoyed that he should have interfered in this way and upset our dear friends Desmond and Diana Milling, who had been so kind and looked after us so well. I felt that this episode marred my whole visit. My mother understood and tried to make amends by sending the Millings a present and a letter of thanks and I too wrote, but they didn't reply and I always wondered what they thought and hoped they had been mollified.

A few days later my father went on tour, which he did very frequently, and we went with him. We went to a village called Udi. I loved our little house in the bush on the edge of a ravine. The lavatory was just a tin bucket with sand to cover. We stayed there several days during which time my mother and I played tennis and met one or two people who came to our house or asked us to theirs. The Trevor Williamses came over for dinner and I was delighted to see Naomi again and have a good old chat. She too was upset about the Bill Sherley episode but she and her parents agreed he had gone over the top.

While we were in Udi I took the dogs for long walks and one morning I nearly got lost. It was lovely countryside with hills and rivers that I couldn't cross and I was afraid of encountering snakes. After a few days I was quite glad to get back to the luxuries of Onitsha – though even there, we had no mod cons such as electricity. We had oil lamps and at night the moths and flies clustered round the lamps and would plop into your soup bowl just as you were about to take a mouthful. The bacon and the butter always tasted rancid and chocolate went white and tasted different from English chocolate. And if you had any sweets in your bedroom, even if they were in tins as they usually were, there would be columns of ants coming up the walls and across the floor to try and get at them. Someone told me a grisly story about an army of red ants fighting with an army of white ants and a man decided to intervene, so he poured boiling water over the white ants so that the red ants won. And a few days later several armies of white ants came from miles around and they found the house of this man and climbed his walls and entered his bedroom and in the morning his servants found just a heap of dust where his body had lain. On hearing this story I resolved not to intervene between any ants and to let them have whatever they damn well wanted.

I met a couple called John and Isla Mann – unbelievably she had been called Isla White before her marriage, her parents must have had a sense of humour but maybe she didn't appreciate it as it was forever a talking point. My mother asked someone called Dorothy Perkins if she would coach me in Maths and she gave me lessons and lots of homework, Arithmetic and Algebra. I thought I had done rather well but years later I met her again and she said, "Oh dear, I'm afraid you didn't have much idea about Maths, did you?" Slightly taken aback I said, "No, I suppose not," so she obviously thought I was worse than *I* thought I was. I must have been an unsatisfactory pupil, and although I always found it a mystery I did manage to get a Pass in Maths, probably thanks to her coaching.

But I really loved our life in Nigeria. It was the rainy season and every morning the rain came down like water in a power shower, and great puddles filled the red mud roads. Then unexpectedly it stopped, the sun came out and before long all the puddles had dried up. I went for long walks over the hills with the dogs. It was lonely but fascinating, Africa at its most superb and how it intrigued me!

One day I got lost by a pool and it was very dark and I thought I could hear crocodiles, though it was probably just my imagination. I walked up a long gloomy lane hoping to run into a rather nice forestry officer called Jimmy Jackson. I pictured him rescuing me from the crocodiles and carrying me home. My father had to visit several outlying stations in each of which was a District Officer and an Assistant District Officer, known as DOs and ADOs. My mother and I always went too and the boys set up house for us, it was rather like camping. The first of these out-stations was Nsukka where the DO was Bud Savoury. The first night we went to dinner with him and his wife Phyllis who had a laugh like a witch. She read people's hands and she read mine. They had a mud house with a grass roof set amidst magnificent scenery. I took the dogs for a long walk in the bush and came across a circle of Africans playing the drums and dancing round a fire, with the witch doctor, adorned with white paint and frightening to look at, in the middle of the circle. This, I felt, was the true Africa. I thought Phyllis Savoury with her witch's laugh might have been there too but of course that was absurd.

We returned to Onitsha and to a sparkling social life of a kind I had never experienced before. Every day there were tennis parties at the Club or lunch and dinner parties or visits to the cinema. I met a lot of people, including a DO called Dennis Gibbs who I thought very handsome; he came to dinner and we played battleships. There was also a lonely Frenchman who had only been in Africa for three weeks. I talked to him a lot and we played tennis. There was an open club night and I danced with him and with Dennis and some others and came home at 3.20 am.

My parents drove me up a steep hill in the rain and mist to Enugu and we stayed in a catering rest house where, to my delight Naomi Trevor Williams was also staying with her parents. There was a Club open night and I wore my blue taffeta. A dark Irishman fell for Naomi and his friend danced a lot with me. We stayed till 4 am.

We also saw Toby Lewis again and his wife Jean. She was the rich wife from New Zealand, very pretty as well as rich, so I expect he was pleased his plan had worked out so well. While in Enugu we met the Walls family, Elizabeth, Rachel and Edward, who had come out to Nigeria on the same scheme as Naomi and me, and we went for walks with them. I went to stay with Hilary and Ray Bridges and their little boy Robert at Agulu in their house on a hill with lovely views. I slept in the dining room, and that night saw my first really big spider. It was over the doorway and when I moved to go through it ran down the wall like lightning.

Hilary and I made fudge and one day we changed into shorts and went down to the lake, surrounded by palms and bushes. We got into a boat which overturned and the next minute were floundering about in the water, to the amazement and great amusement of the Africans. They stood on the banks of the lake shouting "Crocodile!" and falling about with laughter. I think they were only teasing but we didn't take any chances and plunged out onto the bank as quickly as we could. I got very sunburnt on the water as the sun was so strong even though it appeared to be hidden behind thick clouds.

On our return I was shown round the Convent of the Holy Rosary. It was very interesting and the nuns were so nice – Mother Bernard and Sister Patrick Mack and the others. The children were sweet and very polite. My parents thought the Catholics in Nigeria were much better missionaries than the C of E, who tended to be narrow-minded and po-faced. Also they didn't really do very much other than try to convert people, which was a bit of a cheek. The Catholics, on the other hand, ran schools and hospitals and worked very hard. Then again, my mother thought the nuns were much harder working than the priests. The priests had a jolly good time, she thought, drinking whisky half the time. But at least they *were* jolly, which was more than you could say for the C of E lot.

The last village we stayed in was Awgu, where Dennis Gibbs was stationed. He had a small one-storey house with a thatched roof and a pretty garden with a view of the hills. I wrote:

Sept 8th   *I am longing to get there but mustn't expect too much. (There wasn't much to expect!) Awgu is quite the prettiest of all the places. Dennis met us and lent me his camp bed. It is very comfy. We went to dinner with him and I wore my blue silk. Quite a pleasant dinner in his sweet little house.*

Sept 9th   *Dennis popped over several times in the morning and chatted. Tennis was off worse luck because of the rain so I went for a walk with the two D's. We saw the prison and went everywhere on the station but they would talk shop all the time. In the evening Dennis came to dinner. We played battleships (the return battle) and won again.*

Sept 10th   *It is nearly over and rather disappointing too. Yet I don't know what I expected. I would have liked to walk with him without Daddy being there… well at least I have some photos to remind me.*

As we drove away in the car my father said, "I wonder if Dennis would make Badger's heart flutter a little?" My mother thought maybe he would. I sat in the back of the car saying nothing, but thinking he made *my* heart flutter a lot. They were oblivious of this, as I suppose girls of fifteen weren't expected to fall in love. He was the first person I had ever really fallen for, sadly unrequited.

I felt sad that my visit to Nigeria was now nearly over. I had a leaving party which was a great success, then did my packing. I went to the Club and said au revoir to the lonely Frenchman and goodbye to all the others I had met there. The next day I said goodbye to the boys, not forgetting Daisy and Feet, and we started off on the long journey to Lagos. We went across the Niger in a ferry and had a picnic lunch in Benin Province. That place had a sinister reputation but I didn't see anything sinister. The next day we called in to see my parents' old friends the Roseveres in Ibadan, reaching Lagos in the evening. I wrote: *What a city! It's different to everything I've seen so far.*

Sept 17   *Went all round seeing the sights. Met the Lady Governor. I had a bathe in a pool with some sissy boys, then to the very smart Ikoyi Club.*

Sept 18   *What an awful flap. I lost my yellow fever certificate just as everything was packed. Luckily it was OK and I didn't have to show it. Saw the Williams – Naomi was sweet and so pleased to see me and I to see her.*

We settled into the plane and the Walls children got in at Kano. In the night we landed at Tripoli and we four went together and walked in the moonlight with all the lights. Goodbye Nigeria, goodbye Tripoli, I'll never ever forget this trip.

CHAPTER FIFTEEN

On 21st September 1949 I went back to school for the autumn term. We were all in the Upper Fifth now and felt very grown-up, although we were still obsessed with food. But it made all the difference to be able to stay up till 9.30. At first I was upset to find I had been down-graded and was in Upper Vb instead of a, but it turned out much better as there wasn't the pressure to get good marks all the time. The girls in B and Beta were on the same level, they were much more relaxed and seemed to enjoy life in a way that was new to me.

The headmistress still came round the classrooms to read out our marks at the beginning of the week but she didn't expect much from us and I no longer dreaded Monday mornings. I was not letting down my form if I only got a Third Class or a Pass, for that's what everyone got in B and Beta. I had found my level. We had Nokey (Miss O'Kelly) for our form mistress, and were taught English by Miss Godfray, known as Minnie Ha-Ha (from Hiawatha). She always wore purple and was considered eccentric but I really enjoyed my English lessons with her. She wrote about me, "She should write well but must beware of exclamation marks and dashes. She must get out of the habit and cultivate a better style." Quite right – but I never have! She always said, "Amn't I right?" instead of "Aren't I?" which she considered incorrect. She said, "Up with this I will not put," and deplored split infinitives and people saying they were "intrigued" by anything. "An intrigue is the secret planning of something illicit," she told us.

She would hate the present habit of saying "I so am this," or "you so are that." She would also hate the frequent use of "hopefully". Thus it would be quite wrong and abhorrent to say, "Hopefully I am going to pass all my exams," or "Hopefully we are going to win the match." You could travel hopefully but not much else.

One day at lunch she was sitting at the head of our table and when the plates were piled she noticed that someone had left some fat from a lamb chop on the side of their plate. "Who left that fat?" she asked.

"I did," I said.

"That's a disgrace," she said, "Starving children in Africa would be pleased to have that."

The top plate from the pile was taken off with the now cold and congealed length of fat on it and given to me with the first knife and fork that came to hand. "Now you will eat up all that fat," said she.

"I could post it out to the starving children in Africa," I offered, hopefully (and that *is* the right way to say it).

"Don't be insolent. You will not get up from the table until you have eaten it all up."

So I stayed there till tea time, when someone kindly gave me a glass of water and a hunk of bread to swallow it down with.

Fuzz and I had a new piano teacher called Miss Dunlop, whom we both liked enormously. She was young and very understanding, and made me want to work as hard as possible. I wrote, *"She has given me a piece of Grieg to learn, much better than boring old Shubert."* Poor old Schubert, he was sadly unappreciated. We had a new history teacher whom we also did not appreciate. I did not record her name – luckily – but wrote unkindly, *"History still as dull as ever. She seems to be going backwards instead of on. She is cracked anyway."*

That term we became worried about the atom bomb. The people at my table discussed the atom bomb endlessly, it was a *"shadow that loomed above us,"* and we thought we might be blown up any minute. "I do hope Heaven won't be too crowded," said Jean Pentreath, much to our amusement.

On Sunday afternoons we foregathered in someone's bedroom and listened to the afternoon play on the wireless. There was *Brief Encounter*, which was 'romantic and so very pitiful' and *Goodbye Mr Chips* with my dear Robert Donat. I read *Jalna* and *Whiteoaks* by Mazo de la Roche when really I should have been reading *Great Expectations*. There was so much work to be done before our exams next summer, but it didn't stop us spending a lot of time on our costumes for Hallowe'en. Felix was going as a Roundabout. I decided to go as a Christmas Pudding – quite apt as I weighed 10 stone 4. I got a sheet from the sewing cupboard as sauce, and painted the pudding part with brown and yellow powder paint from the Art Room. My friends helped me with it: Fuzz and I went to some workmen to ask for some wire to make a frame. *The men were very nice but we felt like convicts.* (I don't know why we should feel like convicts.) Hal helped me to stretch the pudding part over the wire frame, and we painted spots for the currants. I had a parcel from Winks with *"holly and 2 pairs of navy blue knickers."* The Hallowe'en party was *wizzard* and some of the fancy dresses were *awfully good.* Felix won a prize for her Roundabout.

28th Oct	*This is Ginette Neveu's last day for this evening news comes of her tragic crash in the Air France liner "Gone for a Burton."*
2nd Nov	*Letter from Mummy telling me that little Feet is dead. Oh how very very sad, I could not control my tears. Kept thinking of him and what he was like.*
6th Nov	*This is Remembrance Sunday and I thought about the war.*
9th Nov	*Revised Latin till I was sick to death of it. Caesar. How I loathe him.*
11th Nov	*Fuzz was 16! Fuzz is a big girl now. I gave her a lovely chiffon scarf and she had the most wizzard bag, only rather too smart for the likes of me. Felt quite like suicyde after Latin Unseen and Geometry.*
22nd Nov	*Today is the day of the Verse Speaking Competition. I was very nervous and unsure of myself but he was very nice. I had shampoo and indigestion and Latin and then Chris told me, "Good luck, you're in!" I never expected it and was petrefied. Me in the finals with 8 others. We sat like statues and longed for it to be over. In front of the whole school we had to get up, what a terrible experience. My legs were shaking like a jelly. Mr Compton said, "These few girls have been through a great ordeal, it's not an easy thing to get up and face your school and say a poem." Your telling me! Jos won, Phillida was 2nd and Hamish 3rd. I'm very glad, they did really well.*
29th Nov	*Mock School Cert Exams start! Nina called us into the GDR and told us we must do a play for Miss Russell's Leaving Party.*
1st Dec	*Got up early and went down for the play rehearsal. It is Chinese. I am the Property Man and he seems to say Quack Quack most of the time but is very funny. Biology exam. It wasn't bad but I made a mess of it and did a lot of foolish things. Still, Miss Dunlop said, "Exams aren't the most important things in life you know, even S.C." That is comforting and I wish I could believe it.*

2nd Dec   *I felt so fed up I went through the Music Wing window and danced with the VI form.*

3rd Dec   *Did history before breakfast, lunch and again in the evening for 2 hours. I am sick of Robert Walpole and George III.*

4th Dec   *Had Art, had to stand for 2 ½ hours but I felt quite pleased with it. A winter's evening. I did a house lit up between the trees.*

7th Dec   *It seems queer to write Christmas cards. Hal and I found very cheap ones at Woolworths for tuppence halfpenny each. Cocky and I have got to write a poem for the Russell's leaving.*

9th Dec   *Thought of a verse for the poem. Hal is reading "Young Renny."*

10th Dec   *Had Art back. I felt disgusted with mine, I only got 36% and she said, "This resembles a rather nasty Christmas card!" A bit much especially when I thought it was so good too! I felt very hurt, more than with the other results. Oh well never mind. Next time I will put some more people in.*

13th Dec   *Told Cocky my idea for the poem. She agrees. We spent much time composing verses.*

16th Dec   *Felix's birthday. I gave her 2 hankies. We had two rehearsals for the play and then after a hurried supper we stood waiting in the wings in Chinese costume. Hurrah, they laughed and the Poem too was a great success. I was very relieved. The Russell was sweet and gave a lovely speech and we all cheered and sang For She's a Jolly Good Fellow and it was very sad.*

17th Dec   *Now it's all over but I think it was a great success – had many congratulations.*

19th Dec   *GOING HOME. Said goodbye to all the Number 3 staff. Packed and the others came out of House Dancing and saw me off in a taxi. The flat is wizzard but what a pity Kemptown is behind.*

20th Dec   *The only thing about the flat is, the front room stinks to heaven of old ladies.*

21st Dec   *This is my shopping day. Mum gave me £1 and it was depressing because it went so quickly. I had my lunch at Lions.*

23rd Dec   *I have now posted all the parcels I mean to send. I hope everyone will be pleased. This Christmas has cost me £2 so far, I haven't yet finished getting Badger's and Mummy's things. I can't quite decide what to get. Badger came early and we went shopping in Palmeira Stores and afterwards Mummy and I had tea at Orange House. They are all fat there because they eat so much.*

25th Dec   *Christmas Day, hurrah! We opened our stockings at breakfast and parcels after. I have some lovely things, books, bath salts, a china pig and £4. Late for church. Went to Courtlands Hotel for lunch and tea, and more parcels when we got back. What a wonderful Christmas!*

26th Dec   *Spent a lot of time writing thank you letters, what a fag. Then Badger and I went for a walk on top of the cliffs and had a long talk. I enjoy these heart to hearts.*

27th Dec   *Went to the theatre to see "The Cocktail Party" by TS Elliot. I fear it was a bit too deep for me.*

28th Dec   *We went up to the old house and collected some more things from the loft. I do wish we were still living there.*

31st Dec   *This is the last day of the year. I went out and borght a loose leaf album for my Nigerian photos and saw a dreadful man like Archie in "The Shop at Sly Corner". In the afternoon I borght a wizzard pair of brown shoes with laces and square toes, I hope they will be comfy. And then we went to see Robert Donat in "The Cure for Love."*

CHAPTER SIXTEEN

Most of 1950 was spent in working for, and worrying about, School Certificate, which we took in the summer. I spent much of my time in the depths of despair, and wrote *"If Hell is a mental state surely I am in it now."* I could not understand Biology, and Maths was a hit or miss affair. You had to show the workings out of a sum and if they went on and on endlessly you more or less knew you were on the wrong track, but there was nothing to be done about it. If only we had had calculators, how much easier it would have been!

Anyway, life wasn't all misery. There was a General Election, which was narrowly won by Labour. At school we had a mock election, which was fun. We had to vote for the person who had put up the best argument, and this was the communist candidate. Along with Colleen, Hal and Juliet, I was now in the senior choir, and was proud to sit up in the choir stalls and look down on the rest of the school below. We felt very grown-up and there was certainly no more playing cricket in the sermons. Instead we spent a lot of time rehearsing anthems.

I was not allowed to play games, for it seemed I had developed water on the knee and had to go to the Sussex Hospital in Brighton for treatment. I was not allowed to go on my own and had to be escorted either by Muck, the matron, or Trower, the under-matron, in a taxi. This must have been as much of a bore for them as it became for me, for although I was pleased to go into Civilisation it began to grow tedious after a while. I had my treatment with a young man called Mr Palmer, whom I tried to imbue with romance, but really there was not a vestige of romance in him. He was just a boring little man in glasses.

On Friday 17th March I was reading a book and found I had missed chapel, which was a cardinal sin. I was terrified and crouched in hiding in our room, but luckily it was St Patrick's Day and Nokey, our Irish form mistress and very much a Catholic, forgave me. *Oh, I blessed her with all my heart, what a stroke of luck!*

In the Easter holidays my father bought a Jowett Javelin car, which we thought very sporty. My mother would say, "Can we go for a run in the car?" and my father would willingly agree, for 'runs' in the country were delightful, with hardly anything else on the road. We took friends out for picnics and picked primroses and violets.

On Easter Monday we went to Plumpton Races. My father gave us ten shillings each and we lost the lot and it rained dismally but I still recorded it as *"great fun."* On the 16th of April I went out with my friend Mary Reid and we planned to go out in a canoe but *"alas for our plans - the family poured water on the whole project. If only they knew how much it means to me to go out in a canoe! I was bitterly disappointed. How I envy people who can go when and where they want. But what's the use? Instead Mary and I wasted a lot of money on the Palace Pier."*

Later that holiday we drove over to Maidenhead to visit Elizabeth and Clive, whom I thought were *"great kids."* Like my grandmother, Auntie Margaret was always moving house and I decided this was the loveliest house yet. As usual we spent a lot of time at the cinema and films we saw included the much-acclaimed Italian film *Bicycle Thieves,* also *Morning Departure* and *They were not Divided* with Edward Underdown, an actor who reminded me of Dennis Gibbs.

In the summer term I saw him again:

13th May   *Did some work but didn't get it all done because at 1 o'clock the Will said to me, "Badger has come to take you out." I went outside and found who but DENNIS in the car. I was thrilled, he was simply wizzard. We went to the Albion for lunch and after bathed in the sea. Mum has made a bathing dress for me.* (I hate to think what that was like.) *We had strawberries and icecream for tea and then he took me back to school very fast in his wizzard red sports car with the roof down. Fuzz and Hal were very pleased (they were watching out of our bedroom window) and so was I – I loved it, all day I was so very happy.*

The 23rd of May was my sixteenth birthday. My parents gave me £5 to buy a watch which I got on June 3rd. It was *"Marvellous, Swiss, small and round with a brown strap and cost £6.3s."*

On the 17th June Fuzz's brother Edward won the King's Cup Air Race, which was a great triumph for him as he was an amateur and quite unknown. We listened on the radio and were excited and proud when at the last minute he appeared out of nowhere in his little aeroplane, beating all the crack opposition to come in first. Later he was awarded the cup and Fuzz and all her family were photographed with the King and Queen.

After months and weeks and hours spent revising, School Certificate started on the 3rd July. I had a letter from Naomi wishing me luck. The first one was English Lit which was *not as nice as I'd hoped it would be but I wrote 14 sides. The French Unseen was much better than expected but Biology was much worse.* In Art the plant we had to draw was the foxglove and *mine looked most peculiar.* On the 6th we had History. I woke at quarter to five and the previous night till quarter to eleven. *Felt horribly nervous before the exam and when I went in I thought it was horrible. The Hand* (our teacher) *didn't like it either. It was all right if you'd learned it.....* Every morning Hal and I woke at five or six o'clock for last minute revision. Fuzz thought we were mad, and probably we were. This was to be Fuzz's last term and she wasn't too worried, not like Hal and me. We spent hours on Caesar and the Gallic wars. I was *pretty depressed about Biol, but resigned to my fate whatever it is.* The second Biology was the last exam, on the 12th and it was *lousy! I need never have revised anything at all. Oh but it is wonderful to be free of exams, just to think we need wake at 5 a.m. no longer. I just can't believe all our troubles are over. M says sit back and relax now till September, because it's no use crying over spilt milk. How utterly wonderful the relief is: to lie in bed and do nothing! We were hysterical in our laughter.*

Summer holidays in Brighton were always good and 1950 was no exception. I saw a lot of Mary and Frances Reid until, sadly, they went to Kenya. My cousin Jean came to stay, then Audrey and then Susan Bayly. Susan had a very heavy suitcase, I noticed. She talked a lot and was most amusing and we thoroughly enjoyed having her. We went down to the Palace Pier and mingled with the day trippers and she remarked, "Isn't it funny that common people have such common faces?" This was because they went bright red in the sun, and had ice cream dribbling down their chins and the middle-aged men wore vests and knotted handkerchiefs over their heads. They had paunches and tattooed arms and the women had deep ugly red marks where they had sat in deck chairs and caught the sun. English people should not go out in the midday sun, they do not look attractive as do the darker-skinned Latin races. Brighton was full of French and Italian and Spanish people who were tanned and glamorous in well-cut clothes but unfortunately the English don't seem to learn from them and don't have the knack of dressing well.

Badger went on holiday to the Pyrenees with her friend Sheila Scott, which was quite unusual, for English people didn't go abroad on holiday much in those days. Apart from going to Nigeria, Badger had probably never been abroad before, and certainly I had not, so it was quite lucky for us to live by the sea where there was so much to do.

Badger and I bathed every day and one day we were nearly drowned, being foolish enough to go when the red danger flag was out, just because we didn't want to break our record of bathing every single day of the holidays. It was very rough with huge waves, then came a really enormous wave like a mountain which swept us right out and a strong undercurrent prevented us from getting back in, and after a while we were exhausted. When I saw that Badger had managed to get back I wanted to cry out to her, "Come back, don't leave me!" But then I thought there was no point in both of us being drowned. In a few minutes I was able to get back in as well, but a man bathing on a beach further along was not so lucky, and he drowned. We told our mother, but she didn't seem to take it very seriously. I thought it ironic that my parents had been so adamant I could not go out in a canoe, yet the day we nearly drowned she thought nothing of it.

It was nice having Badger at home as she was still on holiday from her job with the Red Cross. We went for walks and had long conversations about everything under the sun. I told her all my worries and she told me all hers. Once when we were deep in conversation a man stopped us and said to me, "Don't worry, it may never happen." Perhaps my face had a worried expression in repose, like our mother's. We once passed her when we were on a bus and she was looking quite cross but I don't think she was really, it was just her natural worried expression. I wished I had a naturally happy expression and practised walking around with a little smile on my face – no doubt looking rather loopy.

Badger joined a little tennis club in Kemptown. It was a brilliant club because it didn't have many members, so it didn't matter if you didn't have anyone to play with, you just went along and the first four to get there started to play. This was good because as she had been at a boarding school (and I still was) we didn't know that many people in Brighton and Hove to play with, and it was good to belong to a really friendly little club, not like the Grasshoppers in the Drive which was rather snooty – and also, I regret to say, anti-Semitic. It had NJ written into its rules which meant No Jews. That is quite disgraceful in these days of political correctness. Badger and I once saw a poster advertising a dance for the All Blacks and we said, "What a very good idea, how sensible!" It sounds as if we were racist but it was just an attitude that prevailed at the time.

Anyway, at this little tennis club Badger met a young man called John Harland who was tall and good-looking and our mother thought eminently suitable for Badger. On the 27th August she met *a new one, Michael Pope, not too bad*. But I didn't really think much of him. On the 3rd September I wrote, *I do wish she would see more of John Harland, he is so nice. If only Richard Angeloni would come home or something would happen.*

On Saturday, 9th September Josephine came on her motor bike to stay. We talked and talked and ate sweets and had so much for supper I was nearly ill. We went to the theatre on the pier and saw fireworks afterwards. The next day we went into Rottingdean and had coffee. It was so nice having her I didn't want her to go, but she could only stay for the weekend as she was working on the Monday.

That day I got my School Certificate results and found I had Credits in English Language, English Literature, History and Latin, and Passes in Maths, French, Biology and Art. At first I was bitterly disappointed I hadn't got Matric, for which you needed five credits, but in the end I was quite pleased. Later I was upset to hear that Fuzz had failed. *It is very depressing and I feel so terribly sorry for her. It is perhaps fortunate that she has left.* I heard also that Pat Smouha had failed and was very sad, knowing how hard she had worked. It seemed most unfair.

CHAPTER SEVENTEEN

Our tenancy at 164 Marine Parade was now coming to an end and I was *very sad to think it is my last night in this dear little flat*. My mother was soon to go back to Nigeria and Badger and I were to go to Winks's house in Surbiton. On the 20th September I said goodbye to my mother's friends Mrs Langton and Mrs Gilling, and went back to school. I was sharing a room with Hal, facing the sea front. I was delighted to hear that she had got Matric with eight credits, and many others in A division also did brilliantly and got distinctions, including Colleen. We were now in the Lower Sixth and looked forward to doing subjects in which we were interested for a change. I was taking English Literature, European Literature, Modern Literature, History of Painting, Architecture, Art, British Government, Modern History and French. I was also having Music and Elocution. It was decided I should re-take Maths to try and get a credit and thus Matric (but in the end it was a waste of time because I just got another Pass). Gordon and Colleen were taking Cookery and Gordon was also taking Philosophy and Economics, which was taught by an eccentric mistress nicknamed the Lioness.

Gordon learnt that the moon is made of cheese. "How come?" we asked.

"Well," she said, "Do you accept that the moon is *either* made of cheese, or it is *not* made of cheese?"

"Yes, all right, we can accept that."

"Well," she said, "It has been proved that it is *not* made of cheese, therefore it *is* made of cheese."

So that was Philosophy, we thought. Interesting.

We had moved out of the JPR (Junior Prep Room) into the SPR (Senior Prep Room) which was marvellous for those of us lucky enough selected to be in it. It was a cosy room with desks round in a circle. The windows looked out onto the sea and there were easy chairs on which we sat and drank cocoa and toasted crumpets by the fire and had long, interesting discussions putting the world to rights. I became friends with two very clever girls in the Third Year Sixth, Tatiana Miller and Susan Grigor-Taylor, both of whom I liked and admired greatly. We discussed writing a play for Hallowe'en and I thought of an idea about Roedean in the 30th Century being an Advisory Bureau for the Not So Bright, perched precariously on the edge of a cliff. This idea was taken up with enthusiasm. The play was called "Malice Aforethought" and ended with Roedean falling into the sea. It was a skit on Shakespeare and other poets: Grigor and Tatiana wrote the funniest lines but I was invited to contribute and spent many enjoyable hours having tea in Grigor's study and helping to write it. We thought it was hilarious but when we performed it at Hallowe'en Miss Will failed to see the funny side and was shocked.

I had long conversations with Grigor and she was a great influence: she introduced me to George Orwell whom she had discovered long before he was famous for *Animal Farm* and *1984*. The first one of his I read was *Coming up for Air*, followed by *The Road to Wigan Pier*. Grigor persuaded me to enter for the Cope Cornford Essay competition, which was flattering, though I wasn't really in that league. I did enter but did not do well; the examiner wrote that it was 'Disconnected and immature.' I felt discouraged but Minnie said the Judge had enjoyed reading it because it was 'alive,' which was something I suppose. Grigor won it, which was well deserved as she was particularly brilliant.

In October, because I had said I wanted to be a journalist, I was given the minutes to keep in VI Current Events. I was delighted about this and considered it a great honour. In Art Pat Illingworth from Number Two house, nicknamed Ti, and I were making a model theatre. This was an ambitious project which took up a lot of time – so ambitious I don't think we ever finished it. I also joined the Literary Society, known as the Lit Soc. That year we were doing *Romeo and Juliet* for the colour play. I had hoped for a good part, but our elocution mistress, who was also producing the play, was in Number One House and all the best parts went to the girls in Number One. I was just a servant.

At the end of our first term in the Lower Sixth, Hal and I were supposed to be leaving, but in the end my parents decided I should stay for the full year. I was very sad to think that next term there would be no Hal, no Grigor and no Penty. Grigor had applied to Oxford University but in the end she went to Girton, Cambridge. She said she would see me in the holidays as she lived at

East Horsley, which was not too far from Surbiton. Hal, however, lived in Hexham, Northumberland and it was hard to see how we would be able to meet very often in the future.

On the 12th December I was told I'd been made a Sub-Prefect, along with Gordon, Juliet, Jackie and Di Kew. At first I couldn't believe it and thought it must be a joke, but it was true. Not that it was *so* special, for every other person in the Lower Sixth was made a Sub (and I'm sure Sashby, Colleen and Joyce must have been made Subs at the beginning of the year.) Now being made a full Prefect – as Badger had been – was really prestigious. And her friend Martha Hamilton had not only been Head of the House, but Head Girl of the whole school. It's interesting that some people have what it takes and some don't. Anyway I got my report and opened it and read it and it was the best I'd ever had – so that was something.

On the 15th December we broke up for the Christmas holidays. It had snowed the previous night and our train was delayed for an hour but Winks, reliable as always, was there to meet me. I don't think I appreciated how good she was. We had lunch at Fullers and did some shopping in Harrods before returning to Surbiton. 28 St Matthews Avenue had always been a cold house and now with snow on the ground it was absolutely freezing – it was the coldest night for ages and I could not sleep. The next day we went to Kingston to get some fur-lined boots for Audrey and Jean, and I got gloves for Winks's Christmas present.

Auntie Joan Moodey had become impossible to live with and in order that she should have a place of her own, the house had been divided into two flats. She had the first floor and Winks was on the ground floor. I slept in the attic which was also Winks's part. This was a much better arrangement and Auntie Joan was a different person. Winks had a new fire which was lovely and gave out lots of heat. You no longer had to sit right on top of it to get warm.

The next day Audrey and Jean started working at the Post Office, which took on extra people to help with the Christmas mail. They seemed to quite enjoy it and were pleased to make a bit of money. Two young Canadians arrived to stay with Winks as paying guests: these were Christine and Lionel Lawrence. Christine was seventeen and Lionel was fifteen. I liked them enormously, they were very talkative and grown-up and fun to be with. Christine and Laurence had a habit of answering "Negative" which I thought the height of sophistication – but also rather rude. Hence when Winks asked Christine if she would like a cup of coffee or a second helping and she answered "Negative," I was filled with admiration, but at the same time I would never have dared to answer in the same way.

Grigor rang up and asked me to come over for her young brother's birthday party in East Horsley. I went on the train, getting hopelessly lost but eventually I got there and joined in feeding lots of hungry six-year-old boys with tomato sandwiches and sausage rolls. It was hectic but hilarious. After they had gone home the family asked me to stay for supper in the kitchen, and I enjoyed myself immensely with them. They were delightfully vague and untidy and there seemed to be piles of books stacked up everywhere, which befitted the house of a professor.

21st Dec   *The others wanted to go to London and although I can't really afford it I wanted to go too. We took a train up and spent the morning in Harrods. I bought two lemon soaps and a book. Lots of Oxfordy people there, I could never have coped working in the book department. Lunch at Fullers, then decided to see a film. I was a bit depressed at first but 4/7d paid for the show as well so it was worth it in the end.*

22nd Dec   *Sat in front of the fire with Lionel and Christine and played cards because we could not be bothered to go out but in the afternoon we had to. I have so many presents to get and so little time – but money is the biggest drawback. I owe Badger heaps and could shop so easily with heaps of money…*

On the 23rd December I went into Surbiton for last-minute shopping with Christine and Lionel Lawrence. Winks gave me ten shillings and I took them out for lunch *but horrors, it was the Christmas menu and cost five shillings and sixpence each! We had a la carte, all the cheapest things but it was still expensive.* I did not record how we paid for it and whether we had to do the washing up. On Christmas Day I wrote *My first ever Christmas without a stocking but Badger gave me a little cow bell and that made up for it a lot.* Badger also gave me some Goya face powder and a lipstick, my first ever. *Sweet of her.* Winks gave me Canasta. Dinner was *excellent and uproarious.*

27th Dec   *Decided to go to London tomorrow. Rang Liesl, she asked me to tea about 4 pm. Felt uneasy about London and Winks didn't seem keen and there was the question of Audrey and Jean. How I wished for Badger's wise counsel.*

28th Dec   *Wore my duck-egg blue dress and new lipstick and went up to London by train.* (I don't know who I was meeting) *Went to Madame Tussauds first and then to Derry and Toms but the roof garden was closed and lunch looked too expensive so we parted company.* (But who was we and why was I uneasy about meeting them?) *I had lunch at Lyons for tenpence with awful companions, then I found Liesl's flat and had a very good tea. Uncle Tommy came back and we had a long chat and sherry. He took me to a milk bar and we had coffee, then I caught my train back.*

29th Dec   *Winks was in a bad mood, even Christine and Lionel noticed it. She said, "Have you got lipstick on?" I said I had and she told me to take it off and not wear it again until I am seventeen. I was not annoyed but most astounded and hurt. She is very old-fashioned and I never put much on. Well never mind, I shall always be miles behind the others so why worry.*

30th Dec   *I bought lots of new clothes.*

31st Dec   *Badger and I discussed J. She is so catty these days, I can't think what's come over her.*

1st Jan 1951   *At 2 am after seeing in the New Year with the Moodeys,* (Lionel called them those strange dames) *Lionel and Christine and I crept out of the house and went for a long walk all over Surbiton. It was such fun and we watched a party going on through a window. We came back and had cocoa and went to bed at 3 a.m. Winks brought us breakfast in bed and we did not get up till 12. I put on my cherry suit for Bertram Mills' circus. Went up, us three and Audrey.* (Badger was staying away having been to a New Year's Eve party) *It was wonderful, especially the lions, elephants, dogs and trapeze.*

4th January   *Heard that Daddy had been awarded the OBE, very thrilled. Aunt Chattie took us to a pantomime, "Queen of Hearts" which I enjoyed very much apart from Muffin the Mule. I wore my cherry suit.* (That seemed to get a hammering). *The snow is beginning to go. We had supper in the kitchen off one plate.*

On the 5th January I smoked my first cigarette and felt dizzy afterwards. On the 7th I persuaded L and C not to go to the flicks because of Miss Fry's cake and Winks was preparing a little party for her. Grigor rang and asked me to a party on Tuesday night. Winks said I could go and I went on the 9th. It was such fun but the time went too quickly. There were *very good dancers, not so good conversationalists.* I can just imagine what it was – "Where do you go to school? Did you take School Cert last summer? Do you live near here?" and then silence while we tried to think what to say next. I left the party at 12.30 and had a lovely drive home. *Winks was a dear the whole time and brought me breakfast in bed next day and I got up at 12.* On the 11th I wrote *Got 3 wizzard pink vests and 2 peach celanese petticoats.* Now I can't think of anything more ghastly. How could I possibly have thought them wizzard?

I went up to London to stay with Uncle Tommy and Aunt Liesl and had *a marvellous supper of ravioli!* Uncle Tommy took me round the *Daily Herald,* where he worked. He said the journalists on the *Herald* were more conservative than those on the *Times.* It was most interesting, I did enjoy it and found them all very nice. It was so kind of Uncle T.

13th Jan	*Christine, Audrey and Jean went early up to London and Lionel and I went after lunch by bus. We ate half an apple each and counted women in red hats and men with red hair. Popped into a news theatre and saw 'Seagulls over Sorrento' for a second time, just as funny. Went home together and had fun and larks.*
14th Jan	*Badger played Canasta with us before supper and she and Lionel won. We went upstairs and played the piano for ages and then had coco cola. Lionel dressed up as a woman, it was screamingly funny.*
16th Jan	*Our last day and I don't mind admitting I felt extremely sad. I do hope we see them again. The hols have flown. Oh dear.*

The next day we went up to London and saw Lionel and Christine off from King's Cross on the Flying Scotsman, as he was going back to Loretto. It had been such fun having them with us and it was very sad to say goodbye. We never did see them again. Later, on the 18th January, I went back to school.

This term I was in a single room, and felt a bit lonely without Fuzz, Hal, Felix or Gordon, because for some reason a lot of people did not return to school till the following week. Cocky and Joyce came back on the 22nd, Joan on the 23rd and Felix, Coll and Jacky on the 24th, so, I wrote *things are looking up.* I had been recommended for solo singing lessons. My father was none too pleased to have to pay extra for these as the school fees had gone up to an outrageous four hundred pounds a year. He grumbled a lot about this especially as I was also having private elocution, but my mother persuaded him to let me have them. There was a lot of tedious technique to learn, breathing etc. but I enjoyed them and liked my teacher, a dear little woman called Miss Bingham.

6ʰ Feb   *Began a poem called "The Pond" and spent half the night writing it.*

The Pond
Black with evil shadows gleaming
Chok'd with weeds and slimy seeming
Dark with ruthless malice scheming
Is the silent Pond.

Streaks of eerie moonlight seeping
Twixt the trees, their vigil keeping
Light the water, slowly creeping
O'er the silent Pond.

My brother drown'd there long ago:
The currents suck'd him down below,
And o'er his body waters flow
The waters of the Pond.

Now again, and oft when thinking
I see my brother slowly sinking
Suck'd in by the rushes, slinking
Round the cursed Pond.
And still the lonely wind moans drear
And vultures swoop and hover near
The evil water lurking there –
How I fear the Pond!

15ʰ Feb   *Planned to go to Rottingdean again on Saturday. The trouble is money.*
The trouble always is money – with me anyway. Five shillings ought
to do it at a pinch, if I cut out tea 6d.

17ᵗʰ Feb   *Gordon, Juliet, Sashby and I went into Rottingdean and shopped, then had crumpets and coffee at the Highcliffe and most delicious eggs, bacon and chips all fried and cream walnut cake at Ann's Pantry. <u>Most delicious except that I overdrew and had to borrow. Walked back by the sea with Juliet. The sea was glorious and it was a wonderful evening and I felt very happy.</u>*

For now that we were Subs we could go into Rottingdean by ourselves, which we did at the weekend. The Highcliffe Café was right at the end of the village on the edge of the cliff with large plate glass windows overlooking the sea. Alas, it has gone from there long since, though it was a marvellous site for a café. Ann's Pantry has also gone. I remember thinking I had never tasted anything quite so good as the Welsh Rarebit we had there with poached eggs on top. It is no wonder we put on weight and my grandmother continued to say, "You're such a *big* girl!"

18th Feb   *Grigor came down for the staff play, she came into the SPR and talked for ages, then we had the Lit Soc meeting which I dreaded. She came to it and what should be my joy but that my contribution 'The Pond' was chosen to go in both. Grigor voted for it what's more AND I was elected onto the Committee. Felt so very proud.*

But my elation did not last. It should have done because I was doing all the subjects I really loved and the freedom of being in the Sixth after all the years of constraint was stimulating. The long discussions we had in the SPR, Sashby and I and the others, were exhilarating in the extreme, but it was all too late. We didn't want to be at school any more.

1st March   *Found out I'm to lose my place in the SPR and go down to the JPR again. It's very depressing, and I seem to have so many essays to write. One is 'Can a Satirist be a great poet?' another 'All education is for citizenship' and yet another 'Should our Civilisation die?' The latest, 'Is the freedom of the Press worth having?' I haven't thought about that but sometimes − it's an awful thought but sometimes I wonder if Life is worth living − it goes on and on. What are we all struggling for? But I guess that's an ungrateful thing to think…*

On the 11th March some of the choir were chosen to go up to sing as part of the chorus for the St Matthew Passion at the Royal Albert Hall. I asked Badger if she could get accommodation for us at her club in London for Colleen, Cocky and myself, and she said she would try. We were very excited, and we packed and caught the train up to London the day before. Badger had booked theatre tickets for us for a play called 'Penny for a Song' and afterwards we had supper at the Chicken Inn in Piccadilly. The next day we went to the Royal Albert Hall and I gasped when I saw it, it was so magnificent. The organ was tremendous, the whole performance wonderful and we were not bad either. (Winks listened to it on the wireless and said she'd enjoyed it very much, though I can't imagine she had really). Afterwards I could not find Badger anywhere and felt quite unhappy at the thought of not seeing her to say goodbye, but in the end we met up and she took us to the Grosvenor Hotel for coffee before we caught our train back to Brighton.

On the 17th March, along with Colleen and Sashby and some others, I was confirmed by the Bishop of Lewes. He was very nice indeed and gave a marvellous address. I felt quite chokey. Fuzz gave me a prayer book which was so sweet of her and I was very touched. Winks came down for it and I showed her round the school, then she took me out and we bought *The Oxford Book of Christian Verse* and another book of poetry.

At the end of the term we got our reports. Mine might have been worse but was not as good as the last one by a long chalk. Felix, Rachel, Wonk and Rosemary Brett were made prefects and Lizzie Grant a Sub. Wonk was Veronica Chevalier, who was destined to die tragically in the terrible train crash a couple of years on. How lucky we don't know what is to happen to us in the future. We spent many hours telling one another's fortunes but we wouldn't really have wanted to know.

In the Easter holidays I went to another of Grigor's parties. As always it was terrific fun. There were charades, wonderful refreshments and then Scottish dancing. Some very nice people gave me a lift home at 1.30 am. Two days later I went to London with Audrey and Jean and we went to see John Clements and Kay Hammond in Shaw's *Man and Superman*. which was marvellous. We queued up for seats in the gallery and while we were in the queue there was a thunderstorm with thunder and lightning and hailstones. Two violinists played to us and a man recited Donne. I thought I would never forget it.

I continued to have long and absorbing talks with Badger. I arranged with

Miss Bortwick to have some more French lessons which I suppose Winks paid for. Miss B was really more keen to give them than I was to receive them but nevertheless I reckoned my French did improve a little. Good old Cecilia, I thought. Jean and I went to tea with Miss Harum. It was very nice of her but we were a little bored. Winks and I met Badger at the Tolworth Odeon and saw *The Dark Man*, with Edward Underdown. He was my new pin-up as he looked like Dennis Gibbs.

Badger and I went to stay a weekend with Auntie Margaret and Uncle Cliff in Shiplake. We went on the train from Paddington and were met by Elizabeth and Clive in the pouring rain. They had a lovely house and garden and I thought how nice it would be to live by a river and see boats and herons and ducks and moorhens all day long. You could just sit on the bank and watch. The next day we took a picnic lunch to Oxford, where I was delighted by the number of old bookshops selling books and antique maps. We went round St John's College, which was impressive and interesting, and altogether there was such a wonderful sense of history in Oxford that I immediately wanted to live there too. "You can't live here as well as Shiplake," Clive pointed out. "It would have to be one or the other."

Later on Badger, Elizabeth, Clive and I went to the flicks and saw *Walk Softly, Stranger* with Joseph Cotton and Valli and then *Secret Fury* with Claudette Colbert. There were usually double features in those days and often both films were equally good. The performances were continuous and you could walk in at any time and then, because you didn't know what was going on, you would see it round and stay on a bit longer. Sometimes with Audrey and Jean we would see it round twice but on this occasion Elizabeth and Clive said, "This is where we came in," and we went out immediately.

Next morning Auntie Margaret kindly brought Badger and me breakfast in bed and a pile of magazines. "Don't worry about getting up, darlings," she said, "Stay in bed as long as you like." We took her at her word and didn't come down until lunchtime and Uncle Cliff was shocked and disgusted. For lunch there were strawberries and cream and he said to Auntie Margaret, "Really my dear, you give such ridiculously large helpings! Why, anyone who could eat all that" he indicated my bowl of strawberries, "would be a GREEDY HOG!" This was a dilemma for me: should I eat them all or not? I did and was marked out as a Greedy Hog for ever more. In the afternoon we went to see the two uncles who were *both very nice, much nicer than Uncle Cliff.*

Uncle Cliff continued to give us angst, and every time we saw him we did something to upset him. Once my mother was staying in the house, having brought Mr Chips, our dachshund. This unreliable little dog then did its business on the stairs. "Luckily," my mother said, "it was pick-upable," so she picked it up and didn't think Uncle Cliff saw. Badger too blotted her copybook by talking too loudly and, so Uncle Cliff said, disturbed an egg-bound budgerigar. I don't know what talking did to the budgerigar but Uncle Cliff literally jumped up and down, incandescent with rage.

"Do you know Phyllis Court?" asked Clive with a chuckle. "No, who is she?" we asked. They roared with laughter as it was a long-standing joke: Phyllis Court was not a person but a beautiful club right on the river bank at Henley. We went there and had *a very good tea indeed*. Apart from my being a Greedy Hog, it had been a thoroughly enjoyable visit and we returned to 28 St Matthews Avenue sated with antiquity and good food.

One fine day Jean and I decided to walk to Reigate, which was some sixteen miles away. We packed our lunch, put on our oldest clothes and set off on the expedition as if we were about to climb Everest. The countryside around Reigate Hill was beautiful. We had lunch in a lovely field where the cows were so curious they came right up close and stood round in a circle all the time we were eating. "It's quite embarrassing," I said. "Do you think they expect us to give them something?" We arrived in Reigate at about half past four, footsore and weary, and had an expensive tea at The Old Wheel before taking the bus back home. Next day our feet were covered in blisters but we felt we had achieved something and it had been worthwhile.

The next expedition for Jean and me was to Kew Gardens, but we didn't walk there as it was too far. We packed our lunch and tea and spent all day lying in the sun by the Old Pond. We watched the birds and gave them names: Seala and Parson and Francis and Manda and Midget and Mosquito. Then we came home on the bus.

One day I met Fuzz at Harrods and we went to Fortes for lunch and got four and sixpenny seats for *The Holly and the Ivy* which was on at The Duchess - *A marvellous play, well worth seeing*. Fuzz was just the same, very matey and great fun. Another day I met Gordon looking very smart in grey and black. We went to Lyons Corner House and then saw *The Little Hut* with David Tomlinson which was *screamingly funny*.

*27th April   Went up to London in my coat and skirt and court shoes and had lunch
               with Badger at Judith Ann's, then met Auntie Hazel at the Carlton
               and saw 'The Tales of Hoffmann' which was magnificent and fantastic
               with incredible scenery. We had tea at Fullers and later dinner with
               Auntie Hazel and Uncle Teddy in their flat.*

What strikes me is how very good our relations all were about asking us out
– I don't know if they were making a special effort because our parents were
abroad or what. Auntie Hazel was very social in those days and gave frequent
dinner parties for her interesting theatrical and artistic friends, and she tried
out new dishes on Badger and me which we didn't mind at all. She didn't like
housework which she thought very bourgeois and we were interested to note
that her bath mat was really grubby looking, almost black in fact. "If ever you
notice my bath mat looks like that," said Badger, "Will you tell me?" I promised
I would and asked her to do the same.

Uncle Teddy was a dear. He was tremendously interested in sport, especially
cricket, and if there was a match on he would insist on listening to the
commentary on the wireless and would literally jump up and down with
excitement. He had low self-esteem and considered himself tremendously
lucky to have married a Despair girl, an intellectual and an Old Roedeanian
to boot. Auntie Hazel let him think so and basked in his admiration with a
little self-satisfied smile on her face. Sometimes he would tickle her and she
would giggle and say, "Oh Teddy, what are you doing?" but whereas we were
embarrassed for her, she obviously enjoyed it. This was strange because she was
very keen on doing 'the right thing' and was devoid of emotion.

I needed to go to the dentist so I caught the bus down to Brighton. It was a
very hot day, there was that blinding white light you get in Brighton. I went
to Airlie House to have lunch with Granny Hove and found to my delight it
was Susy's birthday and she was there with Auntie Barbara and Richard.

Later I had to go and see Mr Middleborough and had a miserable time while
he drilled remorselessly into my fillings. There was no such thing as having an
injection, you just had to grin and bear it. I would fix my eye on a tree outside
the window and stare fixedly at a particular leaf until the drilling stopped.

Badger went to a dance with John Harland and Audrey tried her luck
with the WRNS. That didn't work out so she tried to get into the Police but
they said she was too young and would have to wait till she was twenty. Uncle

Alfred had told me he wanted me to write a story as he had a friend who was a publisher. I spent quite a lot of the holidays writing but I don't seem to have finished it. What a wasted opportunity. I read a lot, including some short stories by Peter Fleming (brother of the later more famous Ian).

They are good but very sinister indeed. I think he must have been rather a peculiar man to invent and imagine stories like these.

I met Grigor in Bentalls in Kingston and we had coffee and nut sundaes, then lunch at Packhams, followed by a film with Tyrone Power and Susan Hayward – *Rawhide*, which was definitely a better class of cowboy. When I went to cowboy films with Audrey and Jean we always took the mickey and waited for the same old scenery to come round again and for the cowboys to keep riding round the same rocks. Grigor was great fun to be with and we got on well. Little did I know she was destined to be killed in a car crash in her first term at Cambridge. Yes, it is so lucky we don't know what is to happen to us in the future.

I went up in the attic to pack for school and to repack things in an old black trunk for Hove as we would be going back there in the summer. While I was poking around I found a photograph of Granny Cooper when she was young. *How very beautiful she was, and grandfather too* – (not that he was beautiful of course.) The story was that she had lived with her parents, the Davenports, at Bramhall Hall in Cheshire and had eloped to marry our grandfather in South America when she was only sixteen. She had arrived off the boat with her wedding dress and all her trousseau and Grandfather was waiting for her and said, "Oh, there's no time for that," and she never even got to wear it. If that is true and I'm not sure it was, it was practically grounds for divorce.

So I went back to school for my last term. I was fed up to find I was sleeping in a *back* room and had no view of the sea. That was one of the things that made life worth living. However my knee was much better and I was able to play tennis again for the first time in two years, and quite often Felix, who was now a Prefect, would invite me to tea in the study she shared with Hamish, which was a compensation.

On the 23rd May I was seventeen. Crowds of sixth formers came in when the bell went and gave me the best presents I had ever had: books, a fruit knife, soap, perfume, bath salts, rose lotion and hankies. Fuzz sent me a powder compact and Hal a necklace. I also had lots of cards and money – nine pounds altogether. And Badger sent me a glorious historical map of England and

Scotland which was part of her birthday present to me. I was delighted with this and thought it was *wizzard and frightfully decent of her.*

I was lucky too because we went on the Empire Day Picnic on my birthday. We went to Arundel on a special sixth form bus and had a picnic lunch near Swan Lake. We went round the castle and later had tea at 'The Warming Pan'. When we got back we played tennis and won. It had been a good day, and the next one was good too, for the Lit Soc were taken to a Young Vic production of *The Merchant of Venice* which we loved, at the little Dolphin Theatre in Brighton. In Current Events we had debates which were stimulating and fun.

On the 26th it was ORA which was Old Roedeanians' day and Fuzz came down for it. It was lovely to see her, and she brought me some flowers. Winks also came down to bring my birthday cake. I still remember that cake, which was an iced sponge with pineapple and cream. It was so incredibly sweet of her to trek all the way to Brighton lugging a large cake and I thought the Will very mean and unimaginative because she would not allow Winks to take me out. Luckily Winks's visit was not wasted as she was able to spend the afternoon with Granny Hove, but two days later I wrote *I feel suddenly fed up with school, with all the rules and regulations that are so unnecessary. How very petty is school life!*

It was a pity because it could have been so rewarding. I went with my friends from Number Two house, Melly and Pecker and Ti, on several architectural expeditions: We went to the Regency squares in Brighton and the Royal Pavilion which I had been to many times but had never before appreciated the architecture. I was inspired to buy a book on architecture by Bannister-Fletcher which cost £2.12s.6d *but is simply heavenly. It has masses of photographs, diagrams and plans, is beautifully bound and will last me all my life.*

The next expedition was to Sompting church, very quaint with its strange and unique Anglo-Saxon tower. There is no other like it in England. While there we made little sketches and talked to an old man about heraldry, and then had a lovely picnic supper.

The next expedition was to Poynings, a sweet little church at the foot of the downs which my family sometimes went to in the holidays. It had been used as a refuge from wolves before the advent of Christianity, so the dear old vicar told us. He was about ninety and conducted the entire service single-handed, even playing the organ with one finger. He gave the most interesting sermons, not about religion at all but about the history of the church which suited me. I wasn't very religious myself though more so than my mother who,

I was shocked to learn, thought the stories in the Old Testament were not true. I had not considered that possibility and it sounded rather blasphemous not to believe in them. With the same group who were studying History of Painting we went up to London, first to the National Gallery where we saw many Old Masters, mostly religious, then to the Tate to see Impressionist and modern paintings which I liked much better.

We also went to a wonderful concert at the Dome and heard Sir John Barbirolli conducting the Halle Orchestra, and to *The Winter's Tale* with John Gielgud, Diana Wynyard, Flora Robson and Virginia McKenna. I wrote *Words can't express my rapture. I wept, heart-broken at the end of Act I. The whole play was perfect in every way and Joan, Sashby and I were overcome with intense joy and enchantment.* This now seems a trifle –more than a trifle - hysterical and over the top but I think we were lucky to see that play with such a cast.

Miss Bingham told me I was probably going to sing the solo in an anthem on July 1st which filled me with a mixture of pride and terror. I knew my voice was not a patch on Colleen's, hers was a pure and beautiful voice. Like me she had solo singing lessons with Miss Bingham and also private fencing lessons. Besides being talented and clever at so many things Colleen could dance. She had learnt ballet as a young girl and her role model was the beautiful red-haired ballerina Moira Shearer, who had danced so wonderfully in *The Red Shoes*. Colleen was very graceful and was the only girl in the class who danced with her whole body, right to her finger tips. The rest of us were like heffalumps by comparison.

Half term came and as usual it was great to be home for the long weekend. Audrey, Jean and I went to see *Tom Brown's School Days*. Badger was also off and it was wonderful seeing and talking to her again. She showed me Richard Angeloni's letters, and I was hurt on her behalf by one tactless sentence of his but I didn't record what it was. On the Monday we went up to London to see the Festival of Britain on the south bank. It was wonderful, yet much of the technical part was above my head. I changed into my school uniform in a lavatory on Waterloo Station, and went back to school. The next day I wrote: *Lord! What an anticlimax school is.*

Then, on 20th June I had to sing my solo to Miss Bacon alone, after choir practice. I was relieved to find how my voice filled the chapel and that I was not too breathless. A week later I sang it with the choir. I was very nervous and the first time it was awful. The second time it was a bit better, and several Number Three Upper Fifth loyally said they liked it, though someone in

Number Two wasn't very nice to me. Colleen very kindly said she would go through it with me and she did a few days later. That helped a lot. Miss Mason, my piano teacher suggested ways of controlling nervousness, such as taking deep breaths. On the 1st July I wrote, *At last it's arrived, this much dreaded day. Woke at 4.30 feeling sick. The practice wasn't bad, the third time I sang it well. Then it was the real thing. I took deep breaths and suddenly I felt almost OK. I sang it, not as well as the third time but better than the second. Miss Bacon said it was the best of any of them and I was congratulated by 40 people (though not by G!) It is such a relief now it is over.*

By the end of the term I couldn't wait to leave. I had my last piano lesson and my last art lesson and the last of the Englishes. Nokey was in a very good temper. Either she quite liked us or she was pleased to see the back of us. There was a party for the choir and Miss Bacon gave us raspberries and cream. That was so nice of her and I felt rather emotional. Later that night I read *Regency Buck* by Georgette Heyer in a lavatory on my corridor till 12.30 am. Next day I took back all the books I had borrowed from the Reference Library, said the first goodbyes and had a sale of my uniform tops, which surprisingly sold quite well considering they were tenth hand.

There was a tradition that you had to do something daring before you left school. People did things like having a midnight swim or going into Brighton at midnight or roller skating down the main corridor. One girl climbed up the clock tower and hung a pair of knickers over the clock. Felix and I rang the chapel bell. Also my friends Melly and Pecker in Number Two and I in Number Three devised what we thought a very funny plan. There was to be an important staff meeting in the reference library and we hid lots of alarm clocks behind the books, all timed to go off at a quarter to nine in the middle of the meeting. The next morning we wondered what had happened and waited with increasing apprehension as not a word was said.

Then it began to filter through from some of the younger members of staff. It seemed all the clocks had gone off at different times (it would have been difficult to set them accurately) interrupting the meeting and causing chaos. Most of the staff did not see the funny side and were simply furious, particularly the house mistresses in Two and Three which housed the ring leaders, Melly, Pecker and myself. Also in disgrace were Sashby, Juliet and Gordon in Number 3. Apparently various members of staff rushed to the bookshelves and tore out the books, throwing the alarm clocks to the floor in a rage. Some of the clocks had labels on the back, cheekily saying 'Please return to Number 2' which was certainly not going to happen. Instead all the clocks were confiscated, we had to own up to our part and write letters of apology to every member of staff.

I worded my letter carefully, not saying I was sorry for having done it but sorry if they had been upset by it. I still think they over-reacted, for it was really very innocent and much safer than most of the other dares. Girls going into Brighton at night could have been murdered, those who went swimming could have drowned and anyone climbing the clock tower could have fallen off and been killed. All we had done was cause a bit of disruption (much-welcomed disruption, said some of the younger staff who found the meetings tedious). Our house mistresses however, were incandescent with rage. Miss Lloyd Williams in Number Two was so incensed she told Melly and Pecker to leave and not return as she never wanted to see them again. Miss Will stopped short of that but when, three days later my parents arrived to fetch me, I told them I was in disgrace and to drive off without speaking to her. And thus my time at Roedean ended.

CHAPTER EIGHTEEN

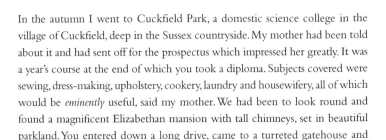

In the autumn I went to Cuckfield Park, a domestic science college in the village of Cuckfield, deep in the Sussex countryside. My mother had been told about it and had sent off for the prospectus which impressed her greatly. It was a year's course at the end of which you took a diploma. Subjects covered were sewing, dress-making, upholstery, cookery, laundry and housewifery, all of which would be *eminently* useful, said my mother. We had been to look round and found a magnificent Elizabethan mansion with tall chimneys, set in beautiful parkland. You entered down a long drive, came to a turreted gatehouse and then to the house itself. It was run by the Misses Black and France.

My parents drove me there on a Saturday evening at the beginning of the term. I was nervous that the girls would be very sophisticated and smart but found them friendly and nice, especially my room-mate Sally Pearson, whom I liked immediately. She was outgoing and funny. She had been to a small but fashionable school called Southover near Lewes, although her home was in the Yorkshire countryside. She liked to go hunting and could exactly imitate the sound of the huntsman's horn, which she did frequently when feeling particularly happy and buoyant. Her great hero was Churchill. Our bedroom faced the front of the house and had oak panelled walls with roses carved into them. Having been told that the house was haunted and contained secret rooms we spent a lot of time pressing the centre of various carved roses, hoping a panel would roll back to reveal a hidden chamber, but though we kept trying we never found anything.

Our first full day at Cuckfield Park was Sunday, a more or less free day in which to settle in. First we had to do some housework and after this we went to church, then Sally and I, Ann Herbert and two others explored the village of Cuckfield. After tea we walked to Haywards Heath, quite a long walk but enjoyable with virtually no traffic on the road. I thought Cuckfield Park was lovely and the girls were delightful and that I was going to enjoy my year there. I went to bed very happy.

There were about sixty girls most of whom were new together, and we were divided into three groups. Sally and I were in the same one, the Bs. Our first lesson in the morning was dressmaking with a sweet-faced woman called Mrs Hilder. She told us we were to make a skirt for which we had provided the material, but first we had to make the pattern. I realised that the rust-coloured material with a check in it which my mother and I had chosen was too thick, it would have made a better car rug than a skirt.

In the afternoon we had cookery with Miss Wilson, who seemed very efficient. She was sharp and thin-faced with glasses, and was not, I thought, someone to mess around with. She was to take us for laundry as well, so it would be advisable to stay in her good books. We made pancakes, which were quite nice and were eaten by the rest of the school at supper. It had been quite a good first day.

The next day we had sewing with Miss Thornton. We had to cut out a pair of pants for a baby. In the afternoon was upholstery, in which we had to nail some webbing across a plain pine stool. On the third day we had cookery when we learnt to make shortcrust pastry, then came housewifery with Miss France. On the fourth day we had sewing again, then first aid and on the fifth day, laundry. That was awful, just washing. I hadn't realised you needed lessons in how to wash a shirt or an item of underwear. After laundry came another session of dressmaking which seemed to be very slow-going. Interspersed between the lessons was a lot of theory. Every subject had theory and we wrote endless notes in hard-backed red notebooks. We also had a lot of prep to do. Each day seemed less likeable than the one before, and Friday was the worst. We had now got through the first week and it seemed to have gone very slowly, but it was the pattern for the weeks ahead.

Every morning before the beginning of lessons we had to do the cleaning. We did all the cleaning of the house, as there was no one else to do it. There was a rota and we cleaned every room in the house in turn, giving it either a daily or a weekly clean. We even cleaned the commode in Miss Black's bedroom and the drains, having to put our hands right down into the drain and pull out the slimy gunge that came from the potato peeling machine. We were not allowed to use any of the preparations that make life easier, and there was no such thing as spray-on furniture polish. We had to make our own out of beeswax and turpentine.

The meals were also cooked by us, whichever group had a cooking lesson would make the lunch or the supper. We would make our own individual jug of chocolate sauce and pour it into the communal one which would be served up for the next meal. Once I poured my jug of gravy into the chocolate sauce by mistake but no one seemed to notice.

The food was very plain indeed, very basic. We had such things as rissoles and Russian fish pie, meat roll which was mince covered in suet, or lentil cutlets. Preparing the suet made me feel sick, it was not like the stuff you get in packets today. I did not enjoy cooking those but enjoyed eating them less. We also took it in turns to do the washing up, scrubbing out a seemingly endless pile of blackened, greasy pans.

I was beginning to think that domestic science was not really my cup of tea. Both Sally and I found the sewing hard going, we laboured over the baby's pants and frequently had to undo the stitching and do it over again. The more we did this the grubbier they became. Dressmaking was a mystery. We couldn't understand where to place the pieces of pattern we had made and were terrified of cutting out in case we cut the wrong bits. Because we couldn't understand we spent much of the lesson waiting for Mrs Hilder to come round and tell us what to do next.

On the 4th October I wrote *Took lots of beastly notes and had a miserable upholstery lesson in which my stool seemed to be ill-fated. Everything went wrong. Had first aid in the evening and poor Sally had a miserable attack of asthma and a thoroughly bad night. A most depressing day.*

Cookery was all right but we seemed to work slower than some of the others and got left behind. Then we would get the sharp side of Miss Wilson's tongue. She could be very sarcastic. On the 30th October I wrote that we had had housewifery and she had been beastly to Sally and that I was worried for her. Poor Phil Fox too got into trouble. *I don't like Willie now as much as I did.* I liked her even less on 23rd November when we had laundry and she was in a bad mood and *went for me like anything.* In fact other than Miss France and Mrs Hilder, we thought most of the staff were a strange lot. The only things I really enjoyed doing were the extra lessons I had in elocution and music. I had a young and pretty piano teacher called Miss Eyre, who was herself a fine concert pianist. One day she invited me to a recital she was giving in Cuckfield at the large house intriguingly called Burnt House where she lived with her parents on the edge of the village. There were refreshments and I met her brother Richard whom I thought *bumptious but very nice with blue eyes.*

There were two things that made Cuckfield Park bearable: one was the companionship of the girls, who were a particularly nice crowd. We all got on well and there didn't seem to be any bitchiness, which must be quite unusual in a group of girls living together. We shared in one another's successes and misfortunes, rejoicing in the one and commiserating in the other, knowing we would always have support and a shoulder to cry on if needed. The other thing was the house itself and the garden. I came to love it. After the bleakness of Roedean I really appreciated living in the countryside surrounded by ancient great trees and the lake which lay beyond the garden and the long walks and the picnics and the bicycle rides we took down quiet lanes.

On the night of Hallowe'en we went into the Girls' Common Room. All the lights were turned out and we sat in the firelight while Miss France told us stories of ghosts at Cuckfield. She was a good story teller and we were enthralled. She told us that in the time of Queen Elizabeth I the Catholic family who had lived at Cuckfield Park had hidden a priest in a secret chamber. Then suddenly they heard the Queen's soldiers arriving so they left in a great hurry forgetting about the priest, and nobody knew he was there. About a hundred years later someone accidentally found the entrance to the chamber. "They pressed a part of the panelling, the door swung back and out fell the skeleton of the priest," said Miss France with relish. We shivered and drew nearer to the fire.

Another story was that of a young bride whose husband was cruel to her. She was desperate to get away from him but she could not escape. Eventually she had a baby and was so unhappy that she drowned herself and the baby in the lake. "To this day her ghost haunts the passages here," said Miss France with satisfaction.

We roasted chestnuts in the fire while she told us about the avenue of lime trees, and said that every time a member of the family was about to die there would be a thunderstorm and one of the trees would come crashing to the ground. "And now," she said, *"There is only one tree left standing."* We went upstairs to bed with a mixture of excitement and horror. Sally and I thought of trying once again to find the entrance to the priest's secret chamber in the panelling of our bedroom but then we thought we didn't really want to in case his skeleton was still there and fell out on top of us.

We had to go to church at least once on a Sunday, either for early communion or matins. We were allowed to go out for the day provided we had asked permission on the preceding Thursday, but we had to return in the evening. I often took other girls home including Sally, Flick and a French girl called Christine Lennad. We were permitted two or three long weekends a term when we could go home from Friday evening till Sunday. Except when my father was home and we had a car, I would either get home with a lift from one of the other girls' parents or by taxi or train from Haywards Heath. The fact that you had a five-mile walk to the station didn't seem to be a problem. However you were not allowed to go if you were behind hand with the work. The year's syllabus was the *raison d'etre* of the principals. Getting through it and passing all the exams was the most important thing in the world, and we soon learnt how hard we would have to work to do it.

In the middle of November Miss Black and Miss France came round to examine the baby's pants we had been working on in sewing. I was terrified. They said I was very slow but 'quite a nice sewer' (fortunately pronounced like 'mower,' not 'fewer'). They said I would have to sew in the front hall from six till seven every night, along with Flick, Judy Gay, Di Blackburn and Evelyn Aspinall.

On the 3rd December we learnt that Benjy had been run over, which was very upsetting especially for Miss Black and Miss France who wept bitterly. He was their pet spaniel.

We broke up on the 8th December and Jean Paterson and I went home in a taxi.

Auntie Lilian Sparks invited us to a dance she was giving on 10th January for her son Alexander and I started making an evening dress for it. My mother had brought me a roll of apple-green lawn from Nigeria and I began on the 3rd January but didn't make much progress: I needed more material and had to go out and buy some more, and it didn't quite match. Also I wasn't very confident about it. *It may look pretty when it's finished if it doesn't look home-made and makes me look fat,* I wrote not too hopefully.

The day before the dance was terrible. The dress wasn't finished, and my mother tried to help but it all went wrong. She became worried and irritable and I more and more despondent. It was cold in the dining room because the fire was dying, the room looked untidy and sordid with sewing and bits of cotton and pins everywhere. By eleven o'clock we knew it was no good and gave up. "I'm fed up with messing about with this *bloody* dress, why don't we go out and buy one?" said my mother, much to my relief and gratitude. So the next morning we went off and found a beautiful strapless lemon taffeta and net dress at Plummers, which made me look quite thin. We got a sweet necklace to go with it and gold shoes and I was delighted. Then we went up to London to the hotel where we were staying, and I got changed and went to the dance feeling nervous and excited. *I had lots of nice partners but some were very high brow and I was out of my depth and one foxy looking fellow I didn't like at all. During the meal I felt a bone in my bodice curve outwards, much to my embarrassment. However it turned out all right later (or rather turned in). We drank red wine and champagne and there were speeches, first Mr Sparks, then Grandfather, both a bit starchy and finally Alexander, and his was easily the best. It was original, amusing and witty. After dinner I went downstairs to powder my nose. Coming down the large staircase I was glad of the banisters as I felt quite far away after the champagne. When I got back to the ballroom our foxy friend came up and there followed a series of very unpleasant dances which I hated. I tried not to dance well and to make myself even more boring than usual. At last we mutually parted and I sank with relief into a chair and prayed he would not come back. Then after a few dances with Anda and some others, a very nice but shy young man came up and we danced and then had some drinks. He was at Emanuel College, Cambridge and I found him delightfully easy and interesting to talk to. We spent the rest of the evening together including the last dance. Afterwards we sang Auld Lang Syne. It had been a wonderful evening and I was ecstatic. When we got back to the hotel I was still feeling excited and my feet hurt but I didn't mind. The yellow dress had brought me luck, it was the best dance I had ever been to and it was with great tranquillity I slipped into the cool sheets and went to sleep. The next day we got up late, left the lovely hotel and went home again.*

We went back for the spring term on the 26th January 1952. It was snowing and the lakes were frozen over. I found I was sleeping in a four-room with Ann Herbert, Elizabeth Aglionby and Lily Sansom. Lily was the daughter of Odette Churchill and one day she invited me to lunch at their beautiful house on Camden Hill. I was rather intimidated by Odette who was supremely confident and remote, and I felt sorry for Lily having such a cold mother.

During sewing on the 6th February we were shocked to hear of the King's death. We could scarcely believe it and were very sad. Now Princess Elizabeth would have to fly home and be Queen. Everyone was talking about it, the papers were full of it and nothing else.

The next day after supper we listened to Churchill's speech. On the Sunday Sally and Jean and I went to matins, a lovely service. *After lunch we went for a long walk, partly on the other side of the lake which is where I've longed to go, and by the waterfall and part of the lane and through the marshes. A dear old woman gave us* *tea at the cottage on the way to Ansty. She was just like Mrs Tiggy Winkle. On the 13th all of our room overslept and woke only at quarter to. We were late for breakfast and both B and F were <u>livid</u>. We were all separated and I had to move my bed to Room 4. On Friday we moved back to our room. Miss Black went for me because I was late for housework. After lunch we listened to the broadcast of the King's funeral service and afterwards went to a service in Cuckfield and then Chris Lennad and I went for a walk all over the bog, jumping streams. We saw lots of cows and she told me a lot about herself. I never realised how different a life French girls lead.*

Miss Wilson (or Willie as we called her) seemed to be in a bad temper most of the time. On 19th February we made lemon meringue pie and *it was rather fun apart from all the bad temper on Willie's part.* On the 26th we made apple charlotte, sausages and mash. *She in a foul temper but fortunately mine turned out quite well.* We had a lot of cookery tests for which you had a list of things to make and you had to complete them all in the three hours you were allowed, which was quite hair-raising. You made out an Order of Work first and then went into it like entering a race.

We were very excited that term, as there was to be a dance and we were each to invite a partner. I didn't know who to ask, but eventually decided on Bill Filmer whom I had met again in the holidays and thought *quite* nice and even quite good-looking – certainly better than his older brother John. I wrote to invite him but he didn't reply for ages and by the time he accepted there were no rooms to be had in Cuckfield. In the end I managed to book him one at the Haworth in Haywards Heath but it was 15s 6d, which seemed exorbitant, still I felt sure it would be worth it. I built up a romantic picture of Bill in which he became more good-looking and charming by the minute. With pleasurable anticipation I imagined how it would be, how we would fall into each other's arms and dance into the sunset. After tea on the day before the dance, Liz Aglionby and I went into Haywards Heath and had our hair done, and after supper we all ironed our dresses and paraded up and down the passage.

At last it was the day of the dance. Bill arrived in the middle of high tea and oh – what a disappointment! How could I ever have thought him good looking? He was shorter than I remembered and very ordinary. He must have thought the same about me as I didn't see him at all, not once. Luckily I met three boys I liked much better, especially Mrs Hilder's nephew who was in the Navy. The dance was great fun and Pat was the Belle of the Ball. The next day we all talked about it and discussed it endlessly and said how nice everyone had looked in their dresses. Then we felt a little flat with nothing to look forward to except the theory exam and the blouses we were to make and no more weekends out.

26th March	*We had a dress parade. Black wasn't very nice about mine but France was quite. Cookery, it was a foul lesson. Willie in such a temper.*
27th March	*Finished my curtain – next will be a cushion. Last home nursing, how I dislike Miss Dengate..*
28th March	*After supper went to Women's Institute production of 'Much Ado about Nothing' with Miss Dengate as Beatrice – it was ghastly.*
1st April	*Had a very hectic cookery lesson. Willie in a bad temper as usual.*

On the 5th April we went home for the holidays. A couple of days later Jean Paterson and I caught a bus back to Cuckfield to fetch our bicycles. We were riding them back and decided to go to Bolney, though it was twelve miles out of our way. There we picked primroses and found a lovely spot for our picnic lunch. After this we felt rather tired so were delighted when a large Carr's biscuit lorry stopped and gave us a lift, bikes and all, as far as Dyke Road in Brighton. We thought it very decent of him. I sat on a biscuit tin feeling on top of the world.

Back at home and anxious to show off what I had learned, I decided to make an orange cake, but alas, it was a complete disaster. The mixture wouldn't rise, the icing would run and the filling tasted of fat instead of orange. Next I made an apple pie and put salt into it instead of sugar. I didn't seem to be doing very well, but unabashed, I decided we should clean the house ourselves as Mrs Marshall, our dear daily, was unable to come in. I duly made out a rota to last over five weeks. The first day my mother cleaned the drawing room, Badger cleaned the hall and stairs and I cleaned the dining room. However I finished my room long before they did theirs and they were disgruntled.

"How did you manage to finish so quickly?" asked my mother suspiciously. "You must have skimped on it."

"I certainly did not," I said indignantly.

Housework is a difficult thing to judge because unless it is absolutely filthy it doesn't look much different when you have finished. Years later I met someone who said she never cleaned her house at all because after four years it didn't get any worse. I thought that was a marvellous philosophy.

People were always saying things to me: Commenting on my untidy curly hair, Winks said, "Delia you look as if you've been through a hedge backwards!"

Miss France said, "Delia Despair, you'll be late for your own funeral!"

Daddy said, "Why do you *always* have to argue? You are the most argumentative person I've ever met."

We had just had an argument about Bing Crosby and Frank Sinatra. He said Bing Crosby was the better singer and I said Frank Sinatra was. Daddy regarded Frank Sinatra as rather fast, a newcomer and an upstart. He said scornfully, "Frank *Sinatra?* Better than Bing Crosby? Absolutely *not!*"

"Well, I think he is," said I stubbornly.

"Really, Delia, you are the most argumentative person I've ever met!"

"Perhaps you haven't met many, then."

"That is cheeky. No, you're quite wrong. Bing Crosby is far, far better than Frank *Sinatra!* Bing Crosby is in a class of his own."

"But why can't I have a different opinion from you?"

"Because you're wrong, Delia. Wrong, wrong, wrong!"

There was a similar argument about Fred Astaire and Gene Kelly.

"You mean to tell me you think Gene *Kelly* is a better dancer than Fred Astaire? Why, there's no comparison."

"I don't happen to agree."

"Really, you are the most argumentative person I've *ever* met!"

And so on. I wonder if he enjoyed these arguments – but no, I just think he was totally exasperated.

My mother had an obsession about washing behind your ears. Except that she didn't say ears, she said years.

"Delia, have you washed behind your years?"

"Yes. Well- not exactly. Anyway, it's not years, it's eears."

"That's what I said."

"No, you said years."

(Really, you are the most argumentative person we have ever met!)

"Well anyway, will you please go upstairs *now* and wash behind your eeears!"

The holidays passed uneventfully. I went to stay with Susy, and Uncle Bruce was in quite a good mood for a change. Tim was there and so was Richard. Susy and I went to see *King Lear,* which was marvellous – it was fun, just the two of us, but I hoped I wouldn't be asked to stay there again. On Easter Sunday Aunt Elaina and Peter and Tony Cooper were coming to lunch and tea and I made gingerbread and some pastry to cover a plum tart. There was too much fat in it and it wouldn't roll out. It cracked and split and stuck to everything. When I finally put it on the tart it broke and all fell in and I had to delve down among the plums to recover all the bits. I pummelled them and kneaded and squeezed them together until they turned into a sort of dirty greyish mass which I plastered over the plums and bunged in the oven. Aunt Elaina said, "What delicious pastry! Did you *really* make it? *And* the gingerbread?"

On the 15th April I wrote *Went to bed with Somerset Maugham.* (That would have been a first - I meant his short stories). Elizabeth and Clive came to stay, and we went to the cinema, the theatre and on the pier where we had our fortunes told. Mine was "You will go abroad and will be whirled into a passionate romance." *Fancy that,* I wrote.

We went to see *Singin' in the Rain* with Gene Kelly, and a man at Lilley and Skinners said I had very bad feet, which was a bit of a cheek. You can say your own feet are bad, or criticise your own family, but you don't expect someone else to. Badger went out with lots of different boyfriends and I decided I would like Julian best for my brother-in-law, and John Harland second.

On the 10th May I went back to Cuckfield for the summer term. As requested, Ann Herbert and Sally and I were in the 7-room with Pat, Pam, Phil and Molly, all of whom were vivacious and fun. It was a large sunny room on the side of the house facing the lake. I found I liked Cuckfield much better this term. The weather was good and we spent lots of free time going for long walks, bike rides, picnics in the woods and playing tennis. Meal times were great fun as the lively and amusing Pat, Pam and Phil were at the same table and we laughed a lot. I really enjoyed living in such a magnificent Elizabethan house and being able to wander through the gardens and parkland. We could walk anywhere except the other side of the lake, which for some reason was forbidden, and of course we wanted to go there all the more. We would look longingly out of the windows onto the other side of the lake and think how enticing it looked. But we also had to work very hard as the exam time drew nearer. There were frequent cookery tests; in one we had to make a meat pie, fish and chips, cauliflower au gratin and steamed custard (my steamed custard turned out horribly). The preparation for the test was most important, it took two hours but we could not have got through without it.

That year, 1952, Badger and I were invited to the 4th of June at Eton. We met on the London train and went to her club, where we changed into our new dresses and hats, then Auntie Hazel drove us to Eton and we had a wonderful picnic lunch sitting in the sun with Elizabeth, and Auntie Margaret shrieking "Darlings, you look *lovely!*" - and of course Clive who was at school there, looking embarrassed and standing apart, pretending he had nothing to do with us. I don't think I looked particularly lovely but Badger looked sweet in her little red hat. The whole point of the 4th June is the cricket match against Harrow but this is of minor importance to the girls who like to walk around and show off their hats and dresses. I imitated the upper class accent of someone I heard saying "Have you seen Mothah or Fathah? I've looked hyah, thah and everywhah and they are just nowhah!" One year my father told us with much disgust that some girls had been overheard to say, "Oh look – aren't there some little boys over there playing cricket?"

Anyway, after our picnic lunch we walked about, I saw one or two people I knew, looked round the school and my new court shoes nearly killed me. Later we changed and sat on the bank and had supper and watched the procession of boats and glorious fireworks. We got back to Badger's club after midnight and the next day I returned to Cuckfield *with a heavy suitcase and a heavy heart*. That was a bit melodramatic for I got over it quickly enough and enjoyed telling everyone all about it.

We now revised in earnest for the exams, sitting somewhere in the garden, on the swing seat or beside the lake or sometimes in the gatehouse. All too soon the Theory exam was upon us. On the day I woke at 5.30 am and revised all the notes I had taken at the last minute, but there was no need, it turned out to be a waste of time. Still, it was a great relief when the exam was over, and Ann and I went into Cuckfield and bought lots of ice creams for everyone in Room 7.

Two weeks later we had the practical exams which were like the tests we had done all year and were now the real thing. Probably because we had done so many practice tests we found the exams not too bad. All the things we had made - often so laboriously, with tears and sweat, having to sit in the front hall and not being allowed out till they were finished – were laid out for the examiner to look at and duly admire. There was the upholstered stool, the cushion, the curtain, a skirt, a blouse, a dress, baby's pants, a slip and a smock. The day after we finished, Elspeth and I got up at 6 am, crossed over the grassy bridge and onto the forbidden side of the lake and went for a long walk. We were not seen and it was worth the risk. We were free from care and the early mist was rising, leaving behind the beginnings of a beautiful day.

A week before we broke up there was the parents' day. We helped France to set the chairs out on the rose-lawn. The parents arrived after lunch, for me it was my mother and Badger as my father was still in Nigeria. They saw the display of all our work, and then there was a very good tea with everything home made and no disastrous orange cake that wouldn't rise or grey pastry that fell to pieces. I pointed out all the girls and my mother thought Pat Pears was the prettiest and how clever to have a dress that so exactly matched her hyacinth blue eyes. Finally there was the dress parade, after which they all went home, presumably thinking what an excellent establishment Cuckfield Park was and how very useful their daughters were going to be.

All that was left now was the end of term entertainment which was to be performed on the last night by each of the three groups in turn. The Bs decided to do a series of skits, Flick and I wrote one based on Aladdin, Pat wrote one on Ascot Day from 'My Fair Lady' and I wrote a poem called 'Cookery Test'.

COOKERY TEST

It's nine o'clock, am I ready to start?
There's the rice for the curry, the jam for the tart.
Great Scott, I've forgotten the cheese for the straws
And the apples are peeled but they still have their cores.
My methods, I'm sure are confused or forgotten,
And let's hope the eggs for the salad aren't rotten.
Must pick up the currants I dropped on the floor -
Thank goodness, I've done it and nobody saw!
Half a gill milk – oh well, water will do,
(No one'll notice the colour of roux!)
Beat out the lumps – but oh dear they're still there –
Quick, put on the lid, the examiner's near!

Should arrowroot go thick and lumpy like this?
What happened last time, must be something remiss.
The table's untidy, the floor's such a mess,
The milk's boiled away and I couldn't care less.
Some pastry left over – the pig bucket, quick -

Nobody saw me, but oh, what a brick!
Already the others are miles ahead,
I've done the cake, but it's the omelette I dread.
What's this? It's the jam that was meant for the sauce,
A pudding without it's a stodgy third course.
Sniff, sniff – I smell burning… now what can that be?
Oh the scones! Why does everything happen to me?
Ovencloth idiot, (not tea-towel) now steady,
Take care – but good heavens, is break here already?
The time's getting on and I'm half an hour late –
The grapefruit's inside's in a horrible state –
The pin from the raised pie has vanished from sight –
Let's hope no one finds it at dinner tonight!
Oh dear, I've forgotten the oven again,
The smoke will be flooding the kitchen, that's plain.
The chocolate biscuits are nothing but cinders.
Would I be wise if I opened the winders?
The bread hasn't risen and oh what a riddle,
The gingerbread's got a large split in the middle.
I wonder if those boiled potatoes are cooked,
They're hard, yet it seems ages since last I looked.
The jam's overboiling, the jelly won't jell –
And Minnie has eaten the kippers as well.
The fried fish is soggy and I'm all behind –
Keep your thumbs crossed the old girl doesn't mind.
Well really, if that isn't just the last straw
The Blanquette of Veal's all over the floor!
Who cares that the cheese straws have burnt to a frazzle
After this morning I'll go on the razzle
For some things are burnt to bits, others are raw,
And everything she'll judge "Decidedly poor!"
I'm half an hour late but I've finished somehow,
Well, no more use worrying, it's much too late now.
"How d'you get on?" a whisper comes terse,
"Oh, not too badly – it might have been worse!"

We had a lot of rehearsals that didn't go too well, but the actual performance was a triumph. Nothing went wrong, everyone loved 'Ascot Day' and 'Cookery Test' and thought the B's were the best. We went to bed flushed with success. The next day came the last minute packing and goodbyes and Ann Herbert and I drove off in her car. It was the end of another chapter.

CHAPTER NINETEEN

In August I went to Switzerland. It was a country I had always longed to go to ever since reading about Mary Plain, who lived in the bear pits in Berne. The trouble was it was a very expensive country and my father couldn't afford to send me there for very long. I wrote and begged him to let me go and told him how I would put my savings towards it and eventually he agreed I could go for five months, after which I was to go to the Triangle Secretarial College.

Some girls I knew, including Susie, were going to Swiss finishing schools but I didn't want to do that even had we been able to afford the extortionate fees. At first we hoped I might be accepted at Lausanne University but they wouldn't take me for such a short period. In the end it was decided I should go to l'Ecole de Commerce. I had no idea what it would entail but was glad to be accepted somewhere – anywhere.

A friend of my mother's called Margaret Smith found the family where I was to stay. She had lots of friends in Switzerland and said it was important to go to a nice family. She gave my mother the addresses of several families and we wrote to them all and decided Madame Galland sounded the nicest. She was Swedish and had been married to a Swiss doctor, but he had died when her children were quite young and she had taken in students ever since.

We went to Lloyds' Bank and arranged for £50 to be deposited in an account in my name on the first of each month and I was to live on that, pay my board and lodging and fees and all expenses. My mother arranged for my passage with Thomas Cook's and on Sunday the 24th August I went to Folkestone and said goodbye to dear Mummy, Winks and Badger. They were very worried that I would lose my documents or have them stolen so I had my passport, money and tickets put into a pouch which was tied with tapes round my waist under my coat. This proved most inconvenient as it was such a palaver every time I needed to get to it. I got on the ferry and my mother shouted, "Have you got your passport?"

"I think so," I said, suddenly doubtful.

As the boat moved slowly away I delved under my coat and started to untie the tapes and search feverishly in the little pouch. "I can't find it!" I cried in panic. I saw the alarm on their faces as the expanse of sea widened between us and then they got smaller and smaller until they were out of sight. Then I sat down and put everything out on the deck and found it – luckily.

When we got to Boulogne I took the train to Gare du Nord, Paris, where I would have a wait of five hours and have to change stations. My mother had been very worried about this, so she had paid Thomas Cook's to arrange for an agent to stay with me all the time and escort me across Paris to Gare de Lyon, but when I got to the Paris office of Thomas Cook's, the agents were all sitting around smoking with their feet up on the desks and none of them had any intention of staying with me every moment of the five hours. And really, who could blame them, what a bore it must have seemed - but I was annoyed because my mother had paid a vast sum for them to do just that and I hated the thought of her being cheated.

I didn't mind a bit about being alone in Paris. I did as they suggested and walked across the bridge over the Seine and had a good meal in a little café. It grew dark and I wandered around for a bit, then went back to the station and the men from Cook's told me to wait in the waiting room. Eventually one of them came and took me to Gare de Lyon and saw me onto the right train.

Then came a long journey overnight. My fellow traveller was a charming Frenchman named Paul who looked, I thought, like the British actor Derek Farr. He was the most perfect companion: he could speak a little English and as there was no one else in the compartment and it was getting late, we put our feet up and stretched out on the seats opposite one another and went to sleep.

At some point in the early hours I got up and went to the loo. The next moment the train came to a shuddering halt, there was a lot of noise and shouting and banging. Then the door of the loo was forced open and I was shocked to see a whole lot of customs officials demanding something, I didn't know what. I returned to my compartment and Paul kindly explained to them that I was English and told me I should show them my passport. This happened again when we got to the border and again he helped me and explained what was going on.

Daylight came and I was astonished to see high snow-capped mountains on either side. When I eventually wrote and told my parents about the journey and how nice and protective Paul had been, they didn't seem to understand at all and were only horrified that I had spent the night in a train with a strange Frenchman. "What were you thinking of? Anything could have happened," wrote my father.

"Well, it didn't," I wrote back. "He protected me from all the customs and excise people. And anyway, what was I supposed to do if he was in the same carriage as me? It's a free country, you can travel where you want."

"You should have got out," persisted my father, "And got into a carriage where there were ladies sitting."

How ridiculous – what a fusspot he was, I thought. Why, I wouldn't have missed the excitement of the journey for anything.

When I got to Lausanne I took a taxi to Madame Galland's house at 10 Chemin du Grand Praz, which was above Lausanne and almost, but not quite, outside it in a village called Chailly, which was nearer the mountains. Madame Galland was a charming woman, not young, very serious and eminently respectable. She had a son called Denys who was married and lived in Geneva, a daughter, Ariane, who was engaged to Jean-Marie, and a younger son, Bertil, who was at the university. I loved her house, which was tall and narrow and very French-looking. I was taken up to the top of the house and shown into a room facing the back of the house. We had lunch in the rather shambolic garden which I found delightful and so different from English gardens, and I met Bertil, who was tall and blonde and very good-looking, and Ion Collas, the handsome dark-haired son of the Greek ambassador in Lausanne. There was also a pretty Swedish girl called Christina who had been doing a holiday course at the university and who would be leaving that week, and Olivier, a little French boy who would also be leaving.

Lunch consisted of a meat and potato dish followed by delicious peaches, which attracted wasps. A wasp came buzzing round my plate and I said, "Go away," and Bertil said, "I'm afraid they don't understand English," and everyone laughed. After tea he invited me to his fascinating room in the basement, which contained a large desk and a good many easy chairs and books piled up everywhere. In one corner of the room was a stove, so it was warm and cosy. After supper he invited me to his room again, and some of his student friends arrived and we sat around drinking coffee and I was in a seventh heaven. What amazing luck, I thought, to be here in Switzerland in the company of this glorious Adonis who was so kind and so charming to me.

The next day I walked down to the lake, which was very beautiful with the mountains in the background, but when I got back I was dismayed to learn from Delphina, the little maid, that Bertil had gone away and would not be back till Saturday. It was then Tuesday – how would I last till Saturday without seeing him?

I felt quite lonely in the next few days as there were no more students in the house and I was on my own. I sat in Madame Galland's salon and played *The Moonlight Sonata* on her piano, which was the only thing I could play. I wished Bertil would come back and that when he did he would like me for myself and was not just being kind. Everyone was kind yet I wished someone – anyone - would ask me to go for a walk or just talk to me.

Ion and Christina went out together the night before she left to go back to Sweden. They were both sad that she was leaving as they had been having a bit of a fling. I was sorry too, as I had liked her. Once we were down in the basement together, hanging up our washing in the laundry room and I thought how beautiful her underwear was and felt ashamed that mine was not more glamorous.

When Christina had gone back to Sweden, Ion invited me to his room to listen to a concert on his wireless. Afterwards the English news came on and he asked me to stay and interpret things for him. He, like Bertil, was at the university and was studying politics. He had a map of the world on his wall and when Turkey was mentioned on the news, he told me to point out Turkey on the map. I stared at the map for ages and couldn't see it anywhere.

"Do you mean to say you don't know where Turkey is?" he asked in amazement. I blushed and mumbled that of course I knew, I'd just forgotten for the moment. That didn't fool him, but although I was so stupid and ignorant he seemed to like me for some reason. He asked me if I would read a book with him; it was called *I Chose Freedom* by Victor Kravchenco, and it was about a Russian who had decided to give up being a communist. We would benefit mutually from this reading, he said, as I would explain any English he did not understand, and he would explain to me the politics.

That week, before any of the other students arrived, he and I went for long walks around Lausanne, either down to the lake or through the forest and up to the hills. In the meadows there were wild flowers and cows grazing, dark brown cows with black on top as if they had been in the oven and someone had forgotten to take them out. They had sweet faces with soft eyes and long lashes and bells around their necks. When we went into Lausanne itself Ion knew all sorts of short cuts which didn't seem like short cuts at all, as they involved going down lots of steep stairways and then up even steeper ones. If we felt hungry we stopped and bought peaches which were cheap and delicious.

I was now in love with Ion as well as with Bertil, and couldn't decide which one I liked best. Bertil was charming and Ion was fascinating and funny and charismatic.

When I wrote and told my parents all about everything – well, not *quite* everything – I received a great long lecture from my father. "I'm not sure I like the sound of all these long walks you are taking, nor do I like to think of you going into the bedrooms of young men," he wrote. "Young men are very hot-blooded and one thing can lead to another." If only they would, I thought. I was longing to be seduced either by Bertil or by Ion, I didn't really mind which.

At meal times we were served by Delphina, the little Italian maid. Most of the dishes were Swiss or Italian and contained meat and potatoes, liberally spiced with herbs. They were delicious, if rather similar to one another. When I had finished my plate, Madame asked me if I would like some more and I said, "Merci," and then the dish was taken away and offered to someone else. Ion said, "You wanted some more, didn't you? You shouldn't have said 'Merci,' that means '*No* thank you.' There was a student staying here once and he kept being asked if he wanted some more and he kept saying 'Merci' and he couldn't understand why he never got any. In the end he said in desperation, "Merci, merci, *merci!*" and then it occurred to everyone what he meant."

I made other mistakes; for instance when Delphina put down a plate in front of me I would say, "Merci," and she would say "Pas de quoi." I soon caught on to this and when I passed a dish to Bertil and he said, "Merci," I said "Pas de quoi," as Delphina had done. Bertil and Madame Galland then frowned and said I should not say that. "But why not, Delphina always says it?" I said. "Delphina doesn't speak very good French," they explained. "Pas de quoi is – how would you say? *Common.*"

However, my worst mistake was all Ion's fault. He told me mischievously that when I was annoyed about something I should say, "Merde!" This was the equivalent of "Bother!" said he. So one day at lunch I knocked over my water glass and exclaimed, "Merde!" and Madame Galland looked deeply shocked and scandalised. "That is a very bad swear word," she said, "The worst thing you could say!" Then she noticed Ion laughing and said, "Ion, I believe you have taught this to Delia – you are a very bad boy!"

Within a week a German girl called Claudia (pronounced like cow, not claw) von something arrived from Bavaria, with her mother. She was very tall with dark curly hair and a sweet smile like Jean Simmons, the actress. I liked her at once. She was to have a room on the first floor, next to Madame Galland's, a big room looking down onto the lake.

The next day the English girl arrived, also accompanied by her mother (no adventures for them on the train, then). Her name was Gillian Lloyd and she was rather sharp-tongued and full of annoying common sense. I didn't like her as much as Claudia. Gillian was to have my room at the back, so I moved out and for several nights went into the room Christina had had, on the top floor next to Ion's facing the front and with a wonderful view. I would stand at the window and look at the mountains and the lake for half an hour at a time. Sometimes there was distant lightning over the mountains, lighting up the night sky. The mountains were always different, sometimes blue, sometimes purple, sometimes clear and bold – a sign of bad weather – and sometimes faint and mysterious, rising out of the mist. I wished I could stay in this room, but it belonged to an American lady called Joyce who was studying the guitar under Segovia. She was away but would be coming back, so Madame Galland told me I would be moving to a room in a chalet a short distance away. "You can return to the house for meals," she told me.

I packed my trunk and Ion carried it over to the chalet. I had a very comfortable room facing the lake but it was on the ground floor and you couldn't see much because of the houses in the way. The owner of the chalet was a nice old woman who didn't speak a word of English. She gave me a bunch of keys as there were three doors which had to be constantly locked. I might go into the garden for the briefest moment and when I got back I found the doors had all been relocked. I'm not sure what she was afraid of as there was no crime in Switzerland, it must have been the safest country in the world. But she was a pleasant landlady, she made my bed for me every day and put a tin hot water bottle in it at night. She kept a bowl of apples for me on the table, and it was like a fairy bowl for however many apples I ate it was never empty, and was constantly replenished.

Tuesday the 2nd September was my first day at l'Ecole de Commerce and I was very nervous, not knowing what to expect. The other two girls were going to l'Ecole des Jeunes Filles, but not until the next day. Bertil still had not returned. My journey to the college took over half an hour as it was in Chauderon, on the other side of Lausanne. I found myself in a class of fifteen, all aged seventeen to twenty and all Swiss-German except an Italian boy aged fourteen and myself. We were to have twenty hours of French a week, four hours of *comptabilité* or book-keeping and banking, four hours of commercial arithmetic and two hours of *dactylographie* or typing. That was great fun, but the professor who taught French grammar was very sarcastic and I dreaded him asking me anything. On the first day he asked each of us to tell him something about ourselves. When it came to my turn I said, "Je suis Anglais," and he said, "Non! C'est impossible!" Then he made us go up and write things on the blackboard and he yelled so much that we would get a shock and break the chalk making a terrible squeak and then – what an outburst there would be.

He liked to quote Shakespeare whenever it was my turn and would say "Orrible, orrible, oh most orrible!" every time I spoke. I soon realised that I was pretty dumb, but luckily the others were as bad as me and some of the boys were worse. They were all very nice and included me in everything, which was decent of them.

I had found book-keeping bad enough in English, but in French it was a thousand times worse. Luckily the professor who taught it was charming and thought it a huge joke. He would read out long paragraphs in French, pausing now and then to explain in German. Then the little Italian boy and I would have to go up separately and he would attempt to explain in practically non-existent English and we would go away and do an exercise and the Italian boy and I would compare notes while the professor would watch us and roar with laughter.

Ion helped me with Comptabilitie and always explained my preps to me when I got home. I didn't enjoy Arithmetic much and was very surprised when our teacher said, "The English seem to understand Arithmetic very quickly." How Nokey and Division 3 at Roedean would have laughed.

One day I had to get up and give a ten-minute lecture about Brighton. I drew its position on a crude map on the blackboard. Ion had helped me with it the night before and had begged me to say at the end, 'The English are still a very seafaring people, as were their glorious ancestors.' I said this but didn't have the nerve to say 'glorious'. But the class seemed to like the lecture and thought my English accent very funny.

Every day we went off to our various schools. I had to be at mine by eight o'clock most mornings, which was quite hard as I never knew when the tram was coming and kept missing it. I would leave the chalet and dash over to Madame Galland's house and help myself to *café au lait* and then run down the road for the tram, eating a piece of delicious brown bread and butter and Swiss cherry jam on the way. We all came home for lunch. Claudia and Gillian decided they were not learning as much French as I was because the girls all spoke English to one another at l'Ecole des Jeunes Filles. This also applied to the various finishing schools. Susy Roberts was at one called Mon Fertile, which she hated. We soon realised how lucky we were to be at Madame Galland's, for there were two girls called Harriet and Jenny in Gillian and Claudia's school who were miserable where they were staying. They did not like their *pension*, were terrified of their Madame, and as they were the only students staying there they had to sit with her in the evenings and ask her for permission to go anywhere at all. Gillian and I went to visit them one day and they were frightened all the time we were there and kept running outside to see if Madame was back from town and had heard us.

My father need not have attached so much importance to my visiting the rooms of young men, because we all went into one another's rooms all the time. It was the way of life at 10 Chemin du Grand Praz. The others had wirelesses, which I did not. Wirelesses were much prized and the others constantly invited me in to do my homework or read or write letters and listen to concerts at the same time. Classical music was very important to us and we went to concerts at the Cathedral, a lot of which were free to students, and were lucky enough to hear all sorts of eminent people playing, including the pianists Solomon, Denis Matthews, Myra Hess, Eileen Joyce and Robert Casadesus. I also heard Kathleen Ferrier and Kirstine Flagstad.

After these concerts we would adjourn to one of the cafés to drink hot chocolate or coffee, for which Lausanne was renowned. The Dome café was the most fabulous but we went to others, such as the Vaudois. The only snag was the expense. Coffee and hot chocolate were very expensive, but then everything was in Switzerland. People used to laugh at the English and say how bad their food was, to which I replied, "At least it's affordable. I would sometimes rather have a cup of bad coffee I could afford than no coffee at all."

All of the students at Madame Galland's were hard up. Sometimes Claudia and I tried walking all the way to school instead of taking the tram, but our shoe leather wore out more quickly and shoe repairs were expensive and we ended up not saving anything. We learnt to buy cooking chocolate from the grocery stores instead of the wonderful but expensive Swiss chocolate. And the only thing in the beauty line we girls could afford was nail varnish. We went to a glossy pharmacy and bought little bottles of gleaming jewel coloured nail varnish – which made us feel good but sadly looked nicer in the bottles than on our somewhat scruffy nails.

Soon Joyce, the American lady, came back and reclaimed her room. She liked to sit down and talk for three quarters of an hour at a stretch about herself and all her troubles, for she was unhappily married. But mostly she would say things like, "I nearly died when Hugh (the professor) said, 'Joyce, I've never had such a brilliant pupil as you!'" Then she would tell us that for a long time her parents forbade her to take up music "but at long last they gave in for they realised there was something there, some genius they had not suspected."

"Genius, my foot!" said Gillian in disgust.

Madame Galland had two Swedish ladies staying with her, and she suggested we should all go to the Wine Festival at Morges, a little town on the lake, fairly near to Lausanne. "When the grapes have been picked," she explained, "and the first wine has been made for the year, there is a big festival in this little town and people from all over Canton de Vaud come to help with the celebrations." So we girls went with her and her friends on the train.

Hardly anyone had cars in those days, nor even scooters, so anywhere you went was a mammoth excursion. First of all there was a big procession: there were forty carts drawn by horses, each with a scene relating to the vineyards and wine-making made out of flowers. Each cart represented a village or a band of people and they were all dressed up in national costume. There were many children taking part and between the carts marched bands from different places playing and people singing and dancing. It was very colourful. On the carts were little Swiss chalets made out of flowers, and there were swans and gardens and merry-go-rounds. The procession went all around the town past streets lined with people, ending up on the road by the lake where we were standing.

Afterwards there was a loudspeaker announcement that the big confetti fight was about to start. Along the roads were piled big wooden boxes which I first thought were grapes but they contained confetti, masses and masses of it. Everyone bought packets of it and many had their pockets filled to the brim and everyone threw it in great handfuls. It got everywhere, in our hair, mouths, eyes, in our shoes, behind our collars and inside our clothes. Bertil had warned me to wear a dress with a closed collar. I didn't believe him and wore one with a V-neck, but he was right. We all threw confetti and soon the streets were covered and you could not see the ground. A policeman threw a whole lot down my neck and I retaliated and threw some down his. An English policeman would have been very surprised!

We all enjoyed it, it was like a snowball fight but not so cold. We walked through the crowds that were surging all over the roads and there was much noise and jollity. Claudia told us it was like the Carnival at Münich and she gave Gillian and me a pressing invitation to come and stay with her while it was on and meet all her friends. We finally came to a little café where we sat down in the late afternoon sunshine and drank Mout, a thirst-quenching drink made of crushed grapes, and then of course we had some of the famous wine.

In October Hardy Regli, a Suisse-Allemand friend of Margaret Smith's rang up and said he was passing through Lausanne on a business trip the next day and that if I liked to go with him I would be able to see quite a lot of the Rhône valley. I thought it was very kind of him and jumped at the chance, for travel in Swizerland was very expensive. So we met the next day at the Metropole café. Hardy Regli was the 'beautiful skier' Margaret Smith had talked about, who lived at Andermatt. He was older than I had expected, probably in his thirties, spoke English well and enough French to get by.

We set out over the hills to the east of Lausanne, passing through Lutry and Cully to Vevey. Here we stopped and had coffee and then he went to see a business colleague and I wandered down to the lake and sat in the sun and watched an old man feeding some tame sparrows from his hand, and some white swans struggling with black swans for crusts of bread children were throwing to them. Then Hardy came back and we drove along the side of the lake, through Montreux and Chillon, from where you could see the fantastic Dents du Midi, mountain peaks that really did look like teeth. From Chillon we went to Leysin and then to Aigle, where we stopped to see another man, then on again to St Maurice, then over the Rhône and into the next county, Canton de Valais.

The scenery, always beautiful was very varied: around Lausanne were the lake, the hills, the forest, Jura. Where the lake ended at Chillon it was flatter, boundless, more like a national park. Valais was different again – wild and more mountainous, dominated by the river and the rocks and the great tall pines and the waterfalls.

At Martigny we were to part company; he was going on through a pass through the mountains, returning next day, while I was to buy a train ticket back to Lausanne. But he found that the pass was almost blocked with snow and impossible to drive through until morning, so he decided to drive back to Vevey and spend the night with a friend, and I only had to take the train back to Lausanne from there.

On the Friday my class were taken on an all-day excursion into the mountains above Lausanne, much to the envy of Claudia and Gillian. Madame

Galland gave me a picnic lunch and I met Ninine, a German girl who had recently joined my class, and coincidentally knew Claudia as they both came from the same part of Bavaria. One of the French professors took us up through the Jorat, the forest covering the hills behind Lausanne. It was very beautiful there with all the trees changing colour, though some people said it was lovely in spring too, when the blossom was out. We climbed up to a little shack where we made a fire and ate some of our lunch, then on up to a small *auberge* called Chalet à Gobelet from which there was a magnificent view. It was such a good idea, I thought, that you could go into little mountain *auberges* and eat your own food there and nobody minded.

We finished our lunch, then someone put on a gramophone record and we danced. After lunch we walked on again until five o'clock when we reached a little village and went into the local inn there, which was very jolly. We had some wine and sang Swiss folk songs and did not get back to Lausanne until half past seven, having walked about twenty miles.

At the weekend Gillian and I decided to make an excursion to the Château de Chillon but we missed the boat, so instead we went on the lake in a rowing boat. Then we went to the cathedral and climbed to the top of the tower, but it was all spoilt when two workmen in blue overalls came up to us and started to talk and wanted us to have supper with them. Then one of them tried to kiss me, and we were both horrified and escaped from them at once, tripping down the steps of the tower in our haste to get away.

When we got back to Madame Galland's we told them all a tall story, that we had taken the boat across the lake, and a man had fallen overboard on the way over, and when we got to the Château de Chillon we had got stuck in the dungeon. To our surprise everyone swallowed the story hook, line and sinker. I told them we had made it up and Bertil said he'd never believe me again - but what imagination!

On the following Saturday I asked Gillian, "What about going to the Château de Chillon?" but she said she had lost interest and didn't care whether she saw it or not. In the end I managed to persuade Claudia to come with me. We caught the boat from Pully and went across the lake in the autumn sunshine. We thought the Château was wonderful, romantic like a fairy tale but Bertil said later it was just a chi-chi castle for a second-rate English poet to write about. Byron – second-rate? I couldn't believe what I was hearing. I read 'The Prisoner of Chillon' aloud to them and Ion said I read it beautifully and Bertil admitted grudgingly that perhaps it wasn't such a bad poem. Some of his friends came round and there was a fierce debate about whether French literature was better than English or not. We were losing the argument, but then Ion stepped in and said English literature would win with Shakespeare alone.

One day Gillian and I discovered that Somerset Maugham was in Lausanne in hospital after an operation. "We must go and see him!" I said excitedly, for he was one of my heroes. So we went out and bought some beautiful peaches and very expensive grapes which they kindly put into a little basket, and then we took a tram to the hospital where we believed him to be. It was a beautiful modern hospital, quite different from anything we had in England. The doorman told us he was in room 39, so we crept up the stairs and searched along the corridors. There were lots of nurses and men in white coats around but nobody stopped us or asked us what we were doing - we could have been going to murder him for all they knew. Instead they seemed amused.

Eventually one of the men showed us in which part of the hospital he was, and we climbed and climbed many, many stairs, until on the top floor at the very end of the corridor we found room 39. We hovered outside until a nurse came by and we told her we were two English girls who had brought some fruit for Mr Somerset Maugham. She went into the room and in a moment came out and said Mr Maugham says "Merci beaucoup, beaucoup." He was very touched and would like to see us, she said, but we were not to approach too near.

So we went into the enormous room and stood near the door and far away on the other side by the window we saw a very old man sitting up in bed. It was Somerset Maugham. He put up his hand and gave us a little wave and then the nurse ushered us out. We went home to Madame Galland's and told everyone, exaggerating a little. We had sat by the bed and talked to him for at least ten minutes, we said.

The others were impressed. "What did he say to you?" they asked.

"Oh, you know," we said vaguely, "This and that. He asked us how things were in England."

"But you don't know how things are, do you?" said Bertil. "You haven't been there lately."

"No, but he didn't know that."

"Why did he say 'merci beaucoup, beaucoup' if he knew you were English?"

"He didn't know *at first*. He only knew afterwards."

"But you said you'd told the nurse!"

"Well – well, she obviously hadn't told him. Anyway what does it matter?"

But obviously our tall story about the Château de Chillon had made Bertil suspicious and he was disinclined to believe us.

Joyce came in one day and told us she was planning to leave Madame Galland's and find an apartment in town. "When I go, you should have my room," she said. "You must ask Madame Galland if you can have it." Meantime, Madame told us an English boy called Hensley Nankeville would soon be coming to join us. She added that she had received two astonishing letters from the boy's mother, the first of which said, "Hensley has some nice new woollen underwear, I hope you will see it is properly aired when it comes back from the laundry," while the second said, "Hensley must *not* stay up late, bed at nine every night!" Madame found this amusing but extraordinary, considering Hensley was eighteen years old. I thought in a way it was rather bad luck that Madame Galland should have told us, as he would have no idea we were all laughing about it before he had even joined us and I knew Ion and Bertil would tease him mercilessly.

In due course Hensley arrived. He was really rather funny, though nice too I thought - but not at all the image of an Englishman that Gillian and I wanted to promote. He was tall with fair hair and a faint fair moustache, more like a bit of fluff on his upper lip, and he was always blushing, like a girl. He also had an unfortunate lisp and not much sense of humour.

Much to my delight, Madame Galland asked me if I would like to move into Joyce's room, saying Hensley could have my room in the chalet. I packed my trunk and Bertil carried it over to the house for me. Luckily Hensley didn't seem to mind being in the chalet. He said, "Sleeping in the chalet is wearly wather convenient because I can wun for the twam evwy morning." He was doing a course in modern French at the university and going to Oxford the following October.

About this time Delphina, the little Italian maid, left, which was sad. She had found the work too hard, and I was not surprised. She had to clean the house, make the beds, tidy the rooms, cook meals for six, eight or ten people and do all the washing of the bed linen. Madame Galland helped her, but even so it was a lot of work. When Delphina left, there was no one for about a week and we girls would help when we got in from school. Bertil was amazing and always went into the kitchen first and put on an apron and started washing up. When we had finished drying the china and putting it away he would say, "Go now," and finish by scouring out the great greasy pots and pans himself.

Hensley helped quite a lot – his mother had trained him well – but Ion was not good in the house. He helped occasionally and it always was an occasion. Once when Claudia and I were washing up with Bertil he apologised that we should have to do it, and said a new maid would be coming very soon. She arrived, a shy little Italian called Bruna.

CHAPTER TWENTY

My mother was very upset because Badger had taken a basement flat in the Old Brompton Road. "A *basement!*" she complained, "There will be rats as likely as not and she will get tuberculosis. It will be a rat-infested hovel." I thought she was letting her imagination run away with her a bit to call it a rat-infested hovel!

Then Badger wrote to me with some very sad news: Grigor had been killed in a motor accident while at Cambridge. She had been travelling in a car with three friends at night and the car had gone off the road and crashed. I could hardly believe it. What a waste of a marvellous human being. She was the most brilliant Roedeanian of her generation. She was also original and funny and I had been so lucky to have her for a friend. I thought sadly of her clever though happy-go-lucky parents, her comfortable shabby house and the two little brothers and wondered how it would all change without her. Writing to the Grigor-Taylors was one of the hardest letters to write, because what could you say? And I felt especially awful as I'd meant to write her a long letter for ages and ages and I never did in the end.

Bertil and his older sister Ariane came to me one day and said that Marie-Lise, a friend of Ariane, wanted to know if I would give her English lessons. She would either pay me, they said, or she would give me French lessons in exchange. I opted for the latter, as I did not feel I could take money from a friend of the family when I had no idea how to teach. I had never taught anyone anything in my life. However it was easier than I had imagined, as Marie-Lise had a very good book called *Brush up your English* which was purely conversation in the form of a play about a modern London family. It was rather amusing and much easier than the usual stiff French and English grammars. Once when I was at the convent my mother had bought me a similar sort of

French book about a young married couple discussing their wedding presents. I thought it was fun and took it to school to show the nun who taught French, but she pronounced it "very vulgar", which was a bit deflating. Marie-Lise was a quick pupil and got on well. For my part I had lessons in conversation and pronunciation which was very satisfactory for us both.

Bertil had his 21ˢᵗ birthday on the first day of his exams, but luckily 20 is coming of age in Switzerland. Madame Galland made a special nut cake which she said was customary to eat for breakfast. Gillian and I between us gave him a large chocolate monkey with a mug of beer and two little pink pigs made of marzipan. That day there was a bazaar and Madame Galland was asked to have a sweet stall, so the day before we were all busy making different kinds of fudge, caramel and nut toffee, which we divided up and put into little bags of coloured cellophane paper. We had our lunch and tea at the bazaar and helped her to sell them. She was very pleased to make 250 francs just on this stall alone.

I received a warm congratulatory letter from Miss Black and Miss France to say I had got a first class diploma. My parents were very pleased, but I thought it was more luck than ability. We also got our half term marks from l'Ecole de Commerce, which were sent to Madame Galland: I got 9 for Comptabilité, 9 for Arithmetic, 7 for Dactylographie and 6 for French. That was the subject I was meant to be learning and I had got my worst mark for it, which would not please the parents. I was allowed to give up Arithmetic as it didn't seem to be much use and I could then concentrate more on French.

Exactly a week after Bertil finished his written exams he got the results and to everyone's shock, found he had failed. Poor Bertil, and poor Madame Galland, who had so desperately wanted him to pass. It was the second time he had failed and everyone said it was the French professor who didn't like him and who had failed him by one mark. Two years of time and money wasted and Bertil having no idea what he could do next. After two months of pretty well studying all day he said he wasn't going to attempt the exam a third time with the knowledge that the professor might quite easily fail him again.

That night there was much despondency in the Galland household, and we all rather dreaded going in to supper. Ariane had red eyes as if she had been weeping and Madame Galland was silent and full of despair. Then Bertil came in and was very jolly, cracking jokes as if nothing had happened, and we all played up. After that he went round trying to find a job, but without success as he had no certificates to qualify him for anything. In the end he decided to do another course in Science and Geography, lasting 2-3 years and not very satisfactory. It was very sad for Madame Galland. Ion told me she had suffered a great deal in her life and had always been very brave and Bertil was the apple of her eye.

"There won't be much for her to look forward to when Ariane marries and Bertil may leave Switzerland altogether," he said.

Ion said, "Do you like the Swiss people?"

"Yes," I said, "Do you?"

"No, I hate them!"

He said he thought they were narrow-minded and cold-blooded and mean and thrifty and self-satisfied. "Of course, I don't mean the Galland family," he said. "In any case they are half Swedish." But Bertil visited Sweden and came back disillusioned. He didn't like the Swedes either; for some reason they had failed to be won over by his charm and good looks. I still liked Bertil, but now I thought I liked Ion more. However, my feelings for both of them were unrequited. Sometimes I thought Ion was on the verge of falling in love with me but I was kidding myself. It was only friendship.

One Sunday I met Susy, who was at a finishing school called Mon Fertile, at Morges. We couldn't do much as the weather was awful, but we had lunch of grapes and then went to a film and later peeped in to the British and American club which was terrible, full of very old people playing bridge, frowsty and dull. So we had tea at a little café and then I saw her off on her train. She told me she had enjoyed herself more that day than during her whole stay in Switzerland. I felt sad because we had done so little, but she just loved being free as I was and not tied to a school party.

She told me she hated Mon Fertile and was depressed with the work and the other girls and having to be herded together all the time. In the winter they would be going up into the mountains to ski, and she thought she would like it better then. We arranged to meet again in a fortnight's time and I resolved to think of an excursion we could make if the weather was good.

When I woke up the next day it had snowed in the night, and there was thick snow everywhere with more to come. The view from my window was magnificent, the tall pine trees, the roofs of the houses and the church tower all coated with snow, and everything silent and white.

During the following days the children went to school carrying their sledges on their backs and riding down the hills. They wore coats made of rabbit fur with high collars and little fur caps. They all had sledges which were cheap, well-made, light and fast. We got to know many of the children on the same little road as us, and exchanged snowballs with them most days. I was glad to have my fur boots. I wrote to my parents, "I am so happy here and so lucky. I thank you again and again for giving me this chance."

One night when Claudia had met some German friends and gone to a ball, Bertil suggested that Hensley, Gill and I might like to see the low life of Lausanne. So we followed him into the lower part of the town, down small staircases and through narrow cobbled streets and once, as a short cut, through a house, until we reached a night club called La Grappe d'Or. Bertil told us that, as it was about the only place with a really Parisian atmosphere, quite a lot of people came to relive memories of Paris. Bertil ordered wine and was brought three bottles, all of which he tasted. The one he chose had cobwebs all round it, and it was thrust into a pail of iced water.

Hensley behaved very badly, we thought. A glass was poured out for him but he refused to drink it, just sat stiffly with his knees together looking shocked and glum. So bad was his attitude that one of the comedians in the cabaret asked him why he wasn't laughing and apologised for not being funny. Gillian and I were ashamed. At last Hensley got up, took his mackintosh and went out, not having offered to help Bertil pay or anything. The atmosphere lightened after his departure but the next day I ticked him off and told him I thought he had behaved very rudely.

Susy and I met twice more before she departed with her school to the mountains: the first time we went to Montherond, a little village high above Lausanne where there was an abbey. Bertil said it looked especially beautiful in the snow and so it did. We took a picnic lunch with us of chocolate, biscuits and tangerines and went up by a little bus. After seeing the abbey we set off to walk but it was so cold we returned to the *auberge* in the village. Inside we had the parlour to ourselves and there was a great roaring wood fire. We ordered hot chocolate, which tasted wonderful after the cold, and I discovered that the chocolate we had brought with us, which had been melting in the bus, had now frozen solid like ice cream.

Susy was still very depressed about her school: she felt she wasn't learning much French because the girls were so self-conscious about talking to each other. The staff were difficult and critical and they never met any other French people to talk to. I tried to comfort her. "But I'm sure it will be better when you go up in the mountains," I said. And so it was: she wrote happily to tell me that she loved skiing and it was quite different living up in the mountains.

Claudia had her nineteenth birthday and she had a little party to which Harriet and Jenny came. Madame Galland made a delicious cake and a drink with rum and lemon in it and then we all played games and told jokes. Bertil and Ion knew a lot which they wouldn't tell for fear of shocking Hensley, who in any case departed at twenty past nine. Everyone was quite unkind to poor Hensley. If someone said something funny, Ion would say, "Why, good heavens, Hensley laughed! Look everybody, Hensley's *laughing!*" Every time he disappeared to the little cloakroom next to the front door, everyone would chant on his return, "We know where *you've* been!" He never knew what to do or what to make of anything and would blush and stutter and insist on telling the girls tedious jokes which made everyone yawn. He asked me for my home address which was flattering in a hopeless sort of way and I felt reasonably safe in giving it to him, as he lived in Cheltenham.

Bertil made us all a cheese fondue. First he rubbed garlic round a pan, then he added Gruyere cheese and cooked it very slowly in white wine until it thickened. Then it was placed on the table over a flame and we all gathered round the table and dipped chunks of bread into it, drinking Kirsch at the same time. "If anyone drops their bread into the pot they will have to pay for the next round," said Bertil. "At least, you would have to if we were in an auberge."

It gradually grew more and more thick and sticky and it became a game to see who could keep on eating for longest. "It's good, isn't it? Don't you think it is good?" said Bertil. We all agreed that it was delicious, but Madame Galland said hers was much better. She dropped out first, then Claudia, then me, then Gill, then Ion, then Francois a friend of Bertil's, then Hensley and Bertil finished last, tied with his friend Alec.

In November Claudia and I joined the University Choir, which met for an hour on Monday and Friday evenings. There were about thirty sopranos, altos, tenors and basses. We thought the tenors sounded rather odd. The conductor was a great character, he was about seventy, full of vitality with snow-white hair. Claudia and I were sopranos and were practising Handel's Alleluia Chorus, which was sung at the Christmas service on the 22nd December, sitting up in the gallery of the cathedral. We also sang the Sanctus and Gloria from Handel's Messe. It was sad for Claudia because she had returned to Germany for Christmas and missed it. Afterwards we repaired to the Café Vaudois, where long tables were laid out with a buffet supper. The choir sat at one table decorated with Christmas tree sprays and candles. Whilst we ate and drank the whole of the University Orchestra played and then we sang French songs and the rest of the students joined in. I met Francois, one of Bertil's friends who later took me home.

There was to be a concert in the following May with the Orchestre de la Suisse Romande and we were already practising for it, although unfortunately neither Claudia nor I would be there for it, as I was leaving in January and Claudia in the spring. Meanwhile we continued to go to all the concerts we could, mainly at the Cathedral with Ernest Ansermet conducting the Orchestre de la Suisse Romande. After a concert we invariably met up with Gillian and Ion and Bertil and ended up in the Dome Café.

As Christmas approached I began shopping in earnest but was discouraged that everything was so expensive. I was very pleased with my present for Badger, which was a silk scarf of many colours. After getting that I didn't have much money for anything else. My parents had asked me if I needed more money but I was so conscious that they could not really afford it that I said no.

Madame Galland had talked of taking a chalet in the mountains at Christmas when we would be able to ski, but she decided not to as there were not enough of us staying. Then Bertil very kindly invited Gillian and me to join him and some friends in a chalet at Le Sepey, owned by his friend Alec. We went up into the mountains, Gillian and I and six boys, friends of Bertil. There was Alec, whose parents owned the chalet, Bertil, two brothers called Jacques and Danny, who were cousins of Alec, and two Belgian friends of Bertil, Luc and another Jacques. Gillian and I were a bit depressed that we were not allowed to take suitcases – instead we were lent rucksacks and had to carry everything on our backs, plus our skis.

The little chalet was very pretty. It was called La Mossette, and was painted white with green shutters. It was furnished simply with red check curtains at the windows and several comfy armchairs and two divans. There were bookshelves filled with books, some of them English, and unframed pictures on the walls. Every time a bottle of wine was finished it was hung by a hook from the ceiling. There was a dresser filled with blue china and several bowls of fruit and nuts and a writing table and a cuckoo clock which hadstopped at half-past six thirty years before when Alec's grandfather had bought the chalet. It was isolated but in a beautiful place surrounded by mountains and rivers.

Le Sepey was not a fashionable resort and there were no ski lifts and no tourists there. There were two bedrooms in one of which Gillian and I slept, with two of the boys in the other. The other four boys slept downstairs in the living room. Everyday the boys did the cooking and Gillian and I did the washing up and tidying of the chalet. Our meals were usually macaroni cheese unless the Belgians, who were more inventive, did the cooking. We had to boil all our water and fetch milk, eggs, butter and bread from one of the little peasant cottages nearby.

We led the most abnormal life I'd ever known. We would be woken up by the sound of sleigh bells of horses driving sledges through the snow, then we'd get up at about eleven, and have brunch, then a siesta, then ski all afternoon and evening. We would walk up the mountain road for about one and a half hours and then ski down. Then we'd lie on the sofas and go to sleep or listen to classical music or someone would read aloud or we'd play a game. Supper was any time between seven and eleven. At about midnight we'd go luging by the light of the moon until about two-thirty when we made up our beds and went to sleep.

Luging down the mountain road was very exciting. The boys would string two luges together and the one in front would lie on his tummy and steer, and because the road was so steep and so icy we would go very fast. I went on a luge driven by Danny, with his brother Jacques behind me. It was exhilarating travelling at such speed, careering round corners, first leaning left and then right and always going ahead. Luckily, late at night, we saw no cars on the road. The fact it was so dangerous made it all the more exciting.

I have to say this was the best holiday I ever had – and not only that, for some reason Danny took a fancy to me. He was tender and gentle. Wonders would never cease, for the first time in my life I was in love and it was reciprocated. Nothing happened of course. It lasted a week, then he went off to Strasbourg to study law and I never saw him again.

On the 16th January 1953 I too, with great sadness, said goodbye to Madame Galland and Bertil and Ion and Claudia and Gillian and all my friends in Lausanne, and returned to England. At last I had grown-up.

PART TWO

---◆---

WORSE THAN USELESS
CHAPTER ONE

I loved Switzerland so much and if I have one regret in my life, it was that my father did not allowed me to stay on there after my five months was up. Madame Galland's house and the students who lived there had become such friends and the way of life was everything I could have envisaged or wanted. I never asked him if he would let me stay a bit longer for I knew he would never agree, so it was pointless even to ask. I therefore returned to England in January in order to commence, of all the dreariest things, a shorthand and typing course at the Triangle Secretarial College, as had been ordained for me. I was allowed to choose this place as it had a course in Journalism, which was what I most wanted to do, otherwise I would probably have followed Badger's footsteps to Mrs Hosters' establishment which I knew she had hated.

I didn't exactly *hate* the Triangle, it was just the most boring thing I could imagine. First of all I had to find somewhere to live. My old friend Josephine was staying at the Devonshire Street Club (situated – surprisingly - in Devonshire Street) and she had booked me in there to share a room. Every day we went to a Lyons café to eat – but after five weeks the Club closed, so I moved to Beaufort Gardens, where my Aunt Margaret's best friend Madge Harland had a house in which she let rooms. As I mentioned earlier, Aunt Margaret and Madge had years before decided to marry rich old men in the hope that they would soon die and leave all their money to their wives, but it didn't work out like that as Madge Harland's husband became a chronic invalid and she had to nurse him for years, while Uncle Cliff was an unbearable old tartar who seemed to live for ever. Eventually Madge's husband did die and did leave her all his money, so she had a large house in Yorkshire plus her house in Beaufort Gardens which was certainly worth a penny or two.

My room was a tiny bed-sit at the top of the house, which I christened The Matchbox – but I was delighted she could fit me in at all, as all her other rooms were taken. I had a bed, a dressing table and armchair, and a two-bar electric fire on which you could boil an egg if you turned it on its side. This is supposed to be rather dangerous, maybe even illegal, but it worked out quite well. Unfortunately my room was on the wrong side of the street, and never got the afternoon sun which streamed wastefully into the bathroom half a floor down. When I got home from the Triangle I would therefore go and sit in the bathroom on the sunlit lavatory with a book.

Shorthand and typing is unbelievably tedious. Our shorthand teacher was a fat woman with glasses called Miss Jones who liked to speak in a sort of Franglais-cum-Italiano with a purposely dreadful English accent. She would say "I am very agitato about your shorthando." I think she thought she was very funny, but after a while it wore a bit thin. Often, too, she was in a terrible mood and then there were no jokes whatsoever.

The journalism course, which was meant to be the best bit, turned out to be just one hour a week, which I thought was a bit of a swiz. However the college was in South Molton Street in the heart of the West End, so that made it a little less unbearable. My friends and I had sandwich lunches every day, though sometimes we splashed out and went to Selfridges. Once I had gooseberry cream there, it was marked "1/11, Delicious" which I thought a bit of an exaggeration. Then we'd go window shopping, mostly to M & S, deciding what we would buy if we only had some money, for none of us had, and what we did have seemed to disappear far too quickly.

Pat Pears, who had been with me at Cuckfield Park, had started at the Triangle at the same time as me and she and Jill Massey and I often went back to her father's flat in Dolphin Square, where we spent many amusing evenings.

These were the years when we talked endlessly about love.

"Are you in love?" Pat would ask, and we didn't have to say, as Prince Charles was to say, "Whatever love means", because we knew exactly what it meant. We were all going out with men, some of whom we wanted to avoid and others whom we liked too much, so there were always problems. They were married or they didn't want to settle down yet or they were Jewish

(Jewish mothers never approved of Gentile girls, however gentle). Pat said that if she hadn't gone to bed with anyone by the time she was twenty-eight she would have a jolly good affair. We didn't go to bed with people because there was no such thing as the pill and we were scared of getting pregnant. Besides it had been rammed down our throats that 'nice girls didn't.' I was staying with Fuzz once when her mother told her if she should ever get pregnant without being married, that would be IT. She would be banished, never to darken the doorstep again. It was a very scary thought, especially as Fuzz's doorstep was so particularly super. The house was spacious and the bedrooms had en-suite bathrooms and the sheets were peach-coloured linen, not boring white sides-to-middle cotton, like in our house. The grounds of Fuzz's house were extensive and there was a lake with a boat tied up and a tennis court. It would not be worth risking banishment and never again being allowed to darken that doorstep.

Fuzz's mother used to read romances by someone called Ethel M Dell that contained sizzling passages about love, and men breathing heavily and tearing the thin black silk off girls' shoulders. I thought wistfully it would be rather nice to have thin black silk on my shoulders, whether or not it was torn off.

We had been invited to a dance in Richmond, and I decided to wear my yellow taffeta and net evening dress. Somehow I always felt that dress brought me luck, but the beginning of the evening was not very promising. I found myself dancing with a dreary collection of miserable spotty-faced partners who were smug and pleased with themselves, despite the spots.

Then suddenly the door opened and in swept a tall, very good-looking young Scotsman, with a flourish and a swirl of his splendid tartan kilt. It would be hard to imagine a more different partner from those I had danced with previously. He seemed cut on a different scale altogether. He was tall, strong and sturdy with wavy brown hair and a gentle, dreamy look in his blue eyes. But what appealed to me most was his zest for life. He was delighted with everything, the party, the music, the food and most of all – surprisingly - with me. I was very flattered that this good-looking young man, whose name was Gerald, had chosen me of all the girls at the party; not only that but he seemed to consider it the greatest piece of luck. His enthusiasm was naïve perhaps, but refreshing. There was none of the blasé boredom about him. It was like the enchanted evening of the song: the handsome stranger who took one look across the crowded room and it was enough.

Gerald had eyes for no one else. He danced with no one else, holding me firmly but carefully like some cherished possession he did not intend to let go.

Between dances we sat close together on a deep sofa in the sitting-out room and he talked of his beloved Highlands where he had been born and brought up, of walks over the purple heather-covered hills, of descending steep-sided valleys for a dip in an ice-cold loch below, of climbing the rocky mountains, wild and rugged, and seeing golden eagles circling and soaring high above their eyries on isolated, mist-enshrouded peaks.

He even began to quote the poems of Robert Burns. I listened spellbound, for although it was mostly incomprehensible to me I was aware of the depth of feeling and the romance of it. He was very romantic, telling me how glad he was he'd found me and how he longed to take me home with him and show me the beauties of the Highlands.

Later on in a Paul Jones I found myself dancing briefly with one of my former partners. He seemed piqued. "You've no time for any of us now that Prince Charming has arrived," he chided me, but I simply shrugged and was glad to be reclaimed by the gallant Scotsman.

In no time at all it was half-past three and my aunt came to say that the car that had been ordered to fetch us home had arrived. I went upstairs to fetch my coat and in the flurry of people leaving and saying goodbye to our hosts, I missed seeing my Scotsman to say goodbye.

The very next day I was down in Hove for my three-week summer holiday. Sometime after, Mrs Harland told me my Scot had come round to Beaufort Gardens with red roses for me, and she hadn't known what to do. She had asked Badger, who had said not to say anything to me as I might be upset - so it was a lovely episode that just fizzled out. I never saw Gerald again.

Soon after that, while I was still at the Triangle, I was introduced to a very handsome young man called Guy. His father was an Indian maharajah, but he was separated from Guy's mother, who lived in Haslemere. Guy had been at Marlborough and was extremely debonair and sophisticated with a wonderful sense of humour. Today he would be described as 'cool'. He would phone me up and very casually invite me out. At first it was only about once a week on a Tuesday, then more frequently, but I never knew when the next time would be. I always had to wait for him to phone me because that was how it was in those days. You had to wait for the man to phone you, however agonising that was, however many wasted evenings you spent beside the phone, waiting and hoping. It is much easier for girls today being able to take the initiative without being thought pushy. Besides, I had far too much pride to contact him.

Guy had a job, not a very good one, at Austin's in the car showroom where he attempted to sell cars, but he was too laid-back, too languid and lazy and didn't sell many. He shared a flat in Egerton Gardens, South Kensington, and he was always very charming and always walked me home to Beaufort Gardens after a date. He liked passing the car showrooms in Knightsbridge and South Kensington and we'd spend ages looking at all the cars and deciding which we'd buy if we had any money. He took me on the river and to the Oxford and Cambridge boat race and to Lords to watch the cricket or to watch him play rugger or squash. There were many cold and wintry afternoons when other girlfriends and I shivered as we watched rugger matches with mysterious scoring we none of us understood. Every time it got exciting they seemed to stop abruptly and go into a scrum.

I was taken to see huge fat men, one called Big Daddy, wrestling at the Albert Hall, which was funny and not to be taken seriously. We met for drinks in Guy's favourite pubs, one near the Triangle at the end of South Molton Street, another in South Kensington, or sometimes to a funny little club in Beaufort Gardens called the Corkscrew Club, where it was very dark and full of cigarette smoke. Or we'd have dinner and then go on to dance somewhere afterwards.

Going out with Guy gave me a certain amount of kudos at the Triangle as not many of the girls had boyfriends. One very pretty girl called Adele used to question me every week and say, "When are you seeing Guy again?" and I'd say "On Tuesday." And there'd be a glint of admiration in her eye.

When I was six months into my shorthand and typing course, a friend of my sister's asked me if I would take her place for a week, working for a doctor while she was on holiday. I agreed and went to the address she had given me, an enormous house in The Boltons where the very richest people lived, including Douglas Fairbanks Junior. I felt quite overawed as I stood on the top step outside the grand front door and waited for the door to be opened, which it eventually was by the cook. The doctor had a private practice, he was good-looking, reasonably young and very smooth with a beautiful wife and several young children. Besides the cook they had a daily and a live-in-nanny. I am not sure what his wife did. She was so beautiful she probably didn't need to do anything.

I was shown into a room adjoining his consulting room and told to sit at the desk. Doctor C came into the room, gave me a charming smile and a pile of letters to type on beautiful thick cream headed writing paper with his address engraved at the top. I took a long time with these letters but after only six months at the Triangle I was still pretty hopeless at typing and made horrendous mistakes in all of them. After a while he came into the room to see how I was getting on. The charming smile faded when he had a look.

"These won't do at all," he said. "I can't send out letters like these!"

"Can't you?" I said sadly.

"Of course I can't. Surely you can see that? You'll have to do them again."

His wife came in. "We're going to have lunch now, are you ready darling?"

"Yes," he said somewhat wearily.

"And this is?" she said, looking at me.

"Delia," I said apologetically, "I'm just here while Val is on holiday…"

"Well come and join us," she said.

We went into their dining room and sat down on red striped chairs at a mahogany table. The cook brought in a dish of home-made lasagne and a bowl of salad. "Would you like some wine?" asked Mrs C. I said I would, but was worried in case it went to my head and made me make more mistakes than ever.

They didn't talk much at lunch, he hardly said a word. She, I thought, was smart, sophisticated and hard. I felt nervous. I put some salad on my plate with the lasagne, then noticed they had put theirs on a special plate on its own. I started eating the lasagne with a knife and fork, then noticed they were only using their forks. Dr C was so silent then and on subsequent days that I began to think that perhaps the marriage was not altogether happy. She seemed so capable and efficient and could be charming – or else a bitch. Altogether it was quite an uncomfortable meal.

After lunch I started on the pile of letters, but my next efforts were no better than the first. I stared miserably out of the window looking onto the garden, where the doctor's children were playing with the nanny in the sunshine. I took to crumpling the letters up and throwing them into the waste paper basket. Soon it was full to the brim with paper balls. That was a bad mistake, because anyone who entered the room could see at once the evidence of my inefficiency. When I realised this that day and on subsequent days, I took to placing them noiselessly face down in a drawer of the desk, reminding myself to remove them when I left.

Besides the letters, I had to answer the telephone. This was a very complicated machine, which I never mastered. You had to pick it up when it rang and say, "Dr C's surgery. Can I help you?" They would then say who they were, but I was never to put them through to Doctor C. No, I had to ask them to hold on, and press a button which put them on hold while I told Dr C, and he decided if he wanted to speak to them or not. Quite often it was Not. If I pressed the right button the caller could not hear the conversation I had with Dr C, but another button meant we could all hear one another. Well, one day I got a call and told Dr C that Lady S was on the line.

"Not that old cow," he said, "Tell her I'm out."

Alas, I had pressed the wrong button.

An indignant voice said, "I heard that – and I can assure you, Doctor C, I shall *not* be dealing with you again. Good day to you!"

"Oh, Christ!" said Doctor C savagely, "Thanks a bunch, Delia, you really are worse than useless!"

"Well I'm sorry," I began, "but you did say she was an old cow."

"A very profitable old cow as it happens – one of my most profitable patients. And anyway it's none of your business – and never, ever do that again!"

Every day while I worked for the doctor, Guy rang me up; the first night we went to see *Innocents in Paris* at the Metro Victoria, then out to eat at The Escape. The next day he rang to ask when we could arrange to play tennis. The third day he rang and said he would meet me at South Ken. We had coffee, then went back to his flat to join Badger and Peter and some of his other friends. The fourth day he rang me, speaking in a funny voice and pretending to be a patient. I was cross when I realised it was really him but then we laughed and Doctor C came in while I was laughing and looked at the waste paper basket full of his expensive cream engraved writing paper balls and thought I was worse than useless all over again. I asked the doctor if he wanted me to come in on the fifth day and surprisingly he said yes.

Guy rang and asked me to stay up in London and have supper with him instead of going home. I was delighted to get my first pay cheque from the doctor and Guy and I spent it on wine, which was not cheap in those days and was quite a treat.

It was the summer holidays and I would not be going back to the Triangle until the autumn. I went home to my parents in Hove and had a lazy summer when the sun seemed always to be shining. We spent days on the beach, taking picnics and swimming in the sea. There were many people to stay, some who were on leave from Nigeria. My mother made them very welcome, cooking them endless delicious meals. We took them into the country for picnics, to the theatre or the cinema, to the Royal Pavilion, the Aquarium or Louis Tussaud's waxworks. They enjoyed themselves so much that one or two of them just wouldn't go. One stayed for seven weeks, without any idea he might be overstaying his welcome.

I had now met a young man called Tim who started taking me out. He was a tea taster, and his first present to me was a packet of very special Indian tea. As I hated Indian tea, it was totally wasted on me. My mother invited him to tea with us and he probably didn't think much of the tea he got with us, either.

He told us he had started to learn the violin and my mother was very scornful on hearing this. She herself had learned the violin and her mother (my granny) had made her give it up as she said my mother wasn't good enough. My mother was very critical of Tim, starting to learn the violin when he was grown-up, as she didn't believe he'd be any good either. One day he brought a poem he had written for me, entitled "The Alpine Queen." It was a horrendously bad poem and I'm afraid we all laughed unkindly over it, and I thought I'd never live it down.

I was nineteen and Auntie Margaret gave me a delightful early 21st birthday present: it was a Siamese kitten. I called him Pym after the Siamese princess who had been at Cuckfield with me. He was perfectly sweet and very affectionate. He didn't have the elongated wedge-shaped face that you see in Siamese cats these days, his face was round and he was cuddly and had very blue eyes. After a short time he got on splendidly with Mr Chips, our dachshund, and we always took the two of them out in the car with us, where they behaved beautifully. Pym was admired by everyone we met.

Badger and I bought the material for our new evening dresses – mine was turquoise brocade and hers was rose slipper satin. We had them made up at Hanningtons. Guy asked me to go in a party with him to Hatchetts and my evening dress would not be ready in time, so I bought a blouse to go with my black quilted skirt: it was duck egg blue taffeta brocade with a square neck and large puffy sleeves – very chic my Mother and I thought. The next day I went up to London and at 9.30 pm Guy fetched me and we all went to the Public Schools club for drinks and then on to dinner and dance at La Ronde. We danced there till 3.30 am but I did not get to bed till half past five.

On the 2nd October it was the 21st dance for Susan Sparks, the daughter of Uncle Cedric and Auntie Lilian, who were my parents' greatest friends. We all drove down to Weybridge, where they lived in a big house with a long drive. There were lights all the way up the drive on the evening of the dance. I changed for the dance in their room and Uncle Cedric said I was another beauty like my mother – which was flattering, but I did not believe it. The dance was fun and I spent all evening with a corn merchant called Steve who was nice enough and danced well, but of course it was not like being with Guy. The dance ended late and we got home just before 6 am, so when my parents went shopping in the car the next day I didn't go with them.

At 1 pm a police car came and a police officer told me there had been a car accident and my parents were in hospital, badly injured. It seemed they had been coming up Shirley Drive when someone came out of Hove Park Road, which is a side road, and hit them. My mother was found lying half in and half out of the car with her head on the road. She had a broken skull, and my father had cracked ribs.

At first I couldn't take it in. Our neighbours, the Websters, were very sympathetic, and Peter and Guy came down to Hove and were tremendously kind and supportive. They drove me to the hospital and I was shocked to see how strange and different my mother looked.

Then we took Guy round Brighton and showed him the lanes. Back at the house Peter went into the sitting room and slept with the cat and dog on his lap, and Guy helped me to make the supper and he was so sweet and understanding and tender with me. He got the animals their food and we had coffee round the fire and I put Scheherazade on the gramophone.

At half past ten he and Peter drove back to London and I was alone, but not for long, for next day Winks and Badger came down, and Auntie Joan P and Bretton, and the Websters continued to phone up and offer help. Guy had promised to phone the Triangle and 33 Beaufort Gardens for me to tell them about the accident and that I would not be returning for the time being.

Gradually my parents got better and came out of hospital, to recuperate under the care of Winks and myself. In the event I stayed in Hove another ten days, not returning till the 12th October.

The next morning Guy rang and asked me to go round to the flat in the evening. When the time came I dressed very carefully in a new black jersey dress with a polo neck and an elasticated waist, which the girls at the Triangle said looked terrific. I hoped Guy would think so too, and set off to walk to Egerton Gardens. He had a friend there called John who wore a bowler hat and seemed rather smug and hoity-toity though, I wrote in my diary, he looked quite nice. We had supper at Lyons Corner House and afterwards went to the cinema to see *The Man Between,* which was good but rather sad.

John said goodbye and departed and I was miserable, because I thought it was over with Guy. I had such low self-esteem I was always thinking it was over with Guy. But then we went back to the flat for coffee and he did admire my new dress. And afterwards he kissed me very passionately for a long time on the floor on a Persian rug.

Guy and I went out for about ten months. In my diary I nicknamed him Monsieur le Philanderer, hoping I would prove to be mistaken and that one day we would laugh about it together. That did not happen. I think he was quite fond of me, but he was not madly in love, as I was. He took me to the Guinea Pig dance at the Café de Paris on a Monday night which ended at half past two, then he took me home and was again very passionate. He came into the house – though I wouldn't allow him upstairs – and we stayed in the hall smooching till quarter to four. For me it was a wonderful night, but because he did not phone me until the Thursday I was in the depths of despair.

It was only two days – two days! – but by the Wednesday I felt suicidal and it was the most miserable evening of my life. I could not sleep a wink that night and wept till my tears were exhausted. Why hadn't he phoned? How could anyone make me so unhappy? On Thursday morning I had no idea how I managed to get up and go to the Triangle. I was sure it must be over with Guy, and I felt as if my life had ended.

That evening I spent with Pat, telling her everything. She was very sweet and consoled me. When I got back to Beaufort Gardens, Mrs Harland told me Guy had phoned, having no idea of the misery he had caused. We went out the following week as usual, but I was now wary of him, waiting to be hurt all over again. Still, things carried on and I'm sure he had no idea of what he had put me through.

But after Peter, my sister's boy-friend with whom he shared his flat, told him he should stop seeing me unless he was serious - because otherwise I was going to be very hurt - our relationship came to an end. He was only twenty-one and had no thoughts of marriage at that time. Besides, he had no money. He was a rolling stone – I think it was he himself who said that.

Soon after Peter told him he should stop seeing me, I went to the flat with Badger and Peter, and he was on the balcony, watching out for us, but once inside the flat he hardly looked at me – except once, for a very long time. Meanwhile I tried hard to be natural, but I was feeling dead inside. For the first time he did not see me home. When we left the flat later, I looked up and saw him standing on the balcony watching us go and looking very sad. I could see the light of his cigarette as he stood watching us till we were out of sight.

I was heart-broken. I had been expecting it to end, yet I couldn't believe that he wouldn't be phoning me any more.

I saw a lot of my Triangle friends, many of whom had now left – Pat, Jill, Jane, Joanna and Brenda. All of them were kind and did their best to console me. We had meals out and went to lots of plays and films including *Genevieve* and *La Ronde*. We also had suppers at Pat's flat in Dolphin Square. There was a new and amusing young Swedish inmate called Glen at Beaufort Gardens, destined to be one of my dearest friends, and there were other young men who took me out, so I should have been happy enough – but wasn't.

I continued my shorthand and typing course at the Triangle and left eventually on 13th November 1953 with the minimum speeds of 100 words per minute in shorthand and 44 in typing. I was never destined to be a top flight secretary. When I said my goodbyes to the staff they were surprisingly nice to me, and the principal wrote a rather stunning – and astonishing - testimonial saying I was a particularly charming girl with whom to deal. Maybe she wrote that about everyone. Anyway. she did not add, as Doctor C had told me back in the summer, that I was Worse than Useless.

A young man called Mick had invited me to a grand Ball at Cambridge. There were a lot of preparations for this Ball, lots of discussions about the dress I should wear, and the pearls, and the velvet cloak with satin lining and fur collar. My mother and Winks and everyone thought I was very lucky to be going, but I was not enthused. On the day of the Ball I went to the Cavalry Club to meet Nigel Pemberton, who was to drive his girlfriend and myself down to Cambridge. Nigel was very rich and had a superb car in which we drove with the hood down. His girlfriend was called Adele and she was very beautiful, but nice. Often, I had found, people who were very beautiful were not very nice, but she was. (Equally people who looked awful often were.) Mick met us and took me to the hotel where I was to stay for two nights. We had dinner at Nigel's rooms with champagne and roast pheasant, then went on to the Ball. It was quite pleasant in some ways, but I danced all night with Mick and most of the time I thought of Guy.

Pam Malthouse, whom I had met at Cuckfield Park, was there and the two of us met up for quite a few long sessions in the ladies' loo, where we commiserated with each other, as neither was with the partner of our dreams. I was only slightly mollified to notice that many men were staring at me, both that night and the following day.

The next morning I got up late and Mick came round to fetch me at eleven and we went out for coffee. After lunch he showed me round Cambridge. Although I wasn't enjoying being with Mick, I thought Cambridge was lovely – how I myself would have liked to go there instead of taking a boring secretarial course in shorthand and typing. But my parents would not have considered it. Apart from the expense it was unnecessary, they thought, for a girl to have a degree, which would probably be wasted when she got married. Besides, I was probably not clever enough.

Mick took me round the mellowed ochre yellow stone colleges and then back to his digs where we chatted and I thought about Guy, though I had intended not to. Poor Mick, what a dead loss I must have been and what a disappointment. Later we had tea at the Copper Dive, then supper at the GSU and in the evening we went to a fearfully depressing play called *Ariadne*. By night time I was in a pit of misery. "Oh Monsieur le Philanderer," I thought melodramatically, "Where are you in this abyss where there is only darkness?" I felt disloyal to Mick who was trying so hard to give me a good time.

I met Mick the next day after breakfast, having packed, and he insisted on escorting me by train up to London, which was quite unnecessary but very kind of him. We sat and read newspapers and I looked out of the window and thought about Guy and dreamed…

When we got to London we lunched at the Sloane Grill and I remembered how Guy and I had dinner there the third time we met. It had been exciting then, and I had thought it would never come to an end.

CHAPTER TWO

I was now looking for a job. The first one I was offered was at a place called World Power Conference and it appeared to be so dull I could not bear to accept it. Instead I signed on at Ackroyds Agency, and eventually they sent me to Simpkin Marshall's the book exporters in the Marylebone Road, where I was offered a temporary job at £6 10s a week. I was asked to start then and there for a nice little man called Mr Harwood – he pronounced it Arwood. "I'm Mr Arwood," he said. He looked like Jack Warner.

I was in an office with him, Doreen, a schoolteacher, Nina, an American and a very good-looking man from somewhere in Eastern Europe. Mr Harwood, and indeed everyone else, was very kind and helpful and I was pleased to find my typing speed quickly increased. The bonus of working in a book exporters was the discount we got on buying books. I bought three volumes of the short stories of Somerset Maugham, whose sparse writing style I greatly admired. They were 15 shillings each, the discounted amount, which was still far more than I could afford. Winks kindly gave me Volume 2.

I also bought eight navy blue cloth-bound volumes of Everyman's Encyclopedia at 14 shillings each. Later I bought three more volumes, a later edition in emerald green, but it was unfortunate that volume 8 went from JES to MAP and volume 9, the first of the emerald green edition, from MUR to PHL so there was a gap from MAP to MUR and it is surprising how many things fall between these two. Besides, I afterwards bitterly regretted not getting the twelfth and final volume, as the eleventh ended at TAP and I was never able to complete the set.

On the Thursday I was offered a permanent job at Simpkin Marshalls, but decided against as I still wanted to be a Journalist – though my Uncle Tommy told me journalism would be very hard and the women were bitches, competitive and tough as old boots. I didn't listen to Uncle Tommy and when Miss Jenkins from the Triangle wrote to tell me of a job at the *Tatler* as secretary to the Social Editor, at £6 10s a week, no Sats, I was delighted. It was just the sort of job I wanted, or thought I wanted – be careful what you wish for!

Mr Arwood was very kind and let me have two hours off for the interview, but it was not with the Editor herself, only with the Sub Editor, who was very young and seemed to lose interest when she found out I'd had no experience. On the Friday I received the not unexpected letter of rejection. The following Monday, 7th December, I went back to Ackroyds, who said there was another temporary assignment going at Simpkin Marshalls. This time I found myself in a small office working for the Sales Manager, a Scot called Mr Mackenzie, who called me Lassie. Also in the office was a blonde lady in her forties called Mrs Minet. She had a sweet face. They both seemed very nice and friendly.

Mr Mackenzie sat at a huge desk on which reposed a large photograph of, I assumed, his wife, rising out of a sort of mist. He must love her very much, I thought, to have this large face in front of him all day long. He dictated very fast - it seemed like 200 words a minute and I had only just got my 100 - lots of long letters which, much to my alarm, I found I could not read back. It was a nightmare. I tried to guess what the gaps might be but invariably guessed wrong. "Och, that'll nae do Lassie," said Mr Mackenzie. But he was nice about it and I soon realised I must always read back my shorthand straight away while the words were fresh in my mind.

So we went on for a week, then on the Friday Mr Mackenzie dictated all afternoon and my notebook was full. "Ne'er mind," he said, "You can leave typing them till Monday." Just as well, I thought, seeing it was then six o'clock and I had a train to catch. My mother cooked delicious suppers and could not understand that sometimes you could not get away on time at the end of the day. I should have taken the notebook home to read through but I didn't and alas, on the Monday I couldn't read any of them. Mr Mackenzie was *not* best pleased. He more or less had to rewrite all he had dictated on the Friday. I was still Worse than Useless.

"Don't worry, you're not the only one," said Jill. She told me about a girl who had been a temp somewhere and was given a whole lot of dictation in the morning. She found she couldn't read it, so she went out to lunch at one and never went back. At least I wasn't that bad – at least I went back to face the music. And I really liked Mr Mackenzie and Mrs Minet, they were very sweet, even though he continued to dictate so fast.

Then, on the 15th December '53, I received notification from the Triangle of a job in the Woman's Department of the *Daily Telegraph*. I rang up straight away and was given an appointment for that evening, so after work I took a taxi to their offices in Fleet Street. There I met Evelyn Garrett, the Editor of the Woman's Page, an eager, hyperactive little woman with her hair scraped back in a bun, Winefride Jackson, the cool and elegant Fashion Editor, Beryl Thomson, Head of Features, and Jill and Rosemary, two secretaries, one of whom was leaving and whom I was to replace. The job was Correspondence Secretary, and involved answering readers' correspondence. I would have to draft my own letters. The salary was £6 18s a week, 9.30 to 5.30, no Saturdays, three weeks' holiday a year and a really nice office.

They were all extremely charming and after asking me to write a couple of letters, Miss Garrett told me I was exactly what they were looking for and offered me the job on the spot. It was not to start until the 11th January 1954 so that Jill, the secretary who was leaving, could work out her notice. Miss Garrett and the others were really flattering and seemed to think I was the bee's knees, so – subject to a letter of confirmation – it was in the bag. At least I thought it was. I was thrilled – I would be working on the prestigious *Daily Telegraph*, no more shorthand and being unable to read it back, and maybe - though they hadn't said so – a chance to break into journalism proper, which is what I had always wanted.

I rushed back to 33 Beaufort Gardens and told Mrs Harland and Glen and she opened a bottle of champagne. I made a few phone calls and then we all celebrated my immense good fortune.

The next day I went to Simpkin Marshalls at half past eight, as I was going to have lunch with Uncle Tommy and wanted an extra half hour. At 12.19 I duly set off for the Dog and Duck in Frith Street, where we had a very good lunch of curried eggs, steak, fruit salad and wine. Lots of wine. I was horrified to find the time had slipped by so fast that it was quarter past two already. I rushed back to the office to find Mr Mackenzie in a very good mood - in fact he seemed more amused than angry.

That afternoon I was puzzling over some gaps in my notebook, thinking how lucky I was that I would not be having to do shorthand for much longer. One letter had taken a whole hour to take down, it was to Doctor Bloch – bloody Doctor Bloch, I called him. I had come to the office early that day, at half past eight, because of bloody Doctor Bloch.

"Are you all right there, Lassie?" said Mr Mackenzie. Mrs Minet had left the room and there were just the two of us. He rose from his desk and came behind my chair, leaning over to point out what the words should be. The next moment he was groping me, his hands all over my black polo-necked sweater. I was in a panic, not knowing what to do but too polite to tell him not to do it.

In the days that followed I tried desperately not to hesitate over my notebook so that he had no excuse to come over, but whenever Mrs Minet left the room he would get up from his desk and come across, asking me if I was all right and groping my breasts.. And every time I was too shy, too polite to ask him to stop. I wonder how many girls had to put up with this sort of thing at that time? He would certainly not get away with it nowadays.

When he was out of the room I told Mrs Minet. "I did wonder," she said. "That's the trouble with him, that's why we keep having to have temps all the time – he can't keep a secretary for long."

"But what about his wife?" I asked. "Whatever would she think?"

"I can't imagine," said Mrs Minet.

I was telling a friend about this episode recently. "But why did you put up with it?" she said, "Why didn't you slap his face?"

"But I couldn't have done that," I said, "I was much too shy to do anything. Besides, I was only going to be there a short time. I got on really well with Mrs Minet and enjoyed the job - and apart from this one thing I liked him too. He was a nice man."

"Not that nice!" she said. "You should have reported him and then walked out. He should have been sacked."

"But then his wife would have found out and maybe it would have broken up their marriage. It's not as if he raped me."

I stayed at Simpkin Marshalls for five weeks altogether, which took us over Christmas. As usual I left everything till the last moment and had not started the Christmas shopping till the 19th, nor Christmas cards till the 20th. Friends of my parents from Nigeria came to tea, a father and son; they were nice but Badger and I were rude and dashed on with our Xmas cards. I wondered whether to send one to Guy but decided to wait and see if he would send me one.

I had found a beautiful book on Italy for Mummy but it was two guineas and I was not sure I could afford it. In the end I did splash out on it, as Italy was very special to her. She had been to school in Florence and had a love affair with the place – and maybe also with someone, maybe her first proper affair, but she never talked about that.

Back in London, the last few days before Christmas were fun: there was lots going on, Felix gave a super party, and I went out with different people, some of whom I liked and others not particularly but of course, no one like Guy. On the 22nd we made up a party and went carol singing in a big group starting from Egerton Gardens. We went round the back of Knightsbridge and to Belgrave Square and were invited in for drinks by some of the people whose houses we went to. Guy was in the group, also his brother Bunny and a friend of his from Oxford called Paddy who took me to coffee afterwards and then back to Beaufort Gardens. He was nice and I wondered what Guy thought, seeing Paddy and me together. Would he be regretful, even slightly? Guy was with Moyra and Jenny, neither of whom, I knew, interested him in that way.

Glen was becoming a good friend. There was no romance but we had long chats late into the night on every subject under the sun. He was a very unusual young man, original, very funny and kind, but he did have fits of depression. Perhaps, looking back, he was bipolar. He liked talking to me and we went out for lots of meals. He wanted to teach me Swedish and we did start, though I didn't see much point in it. What would be the use of my learning Swedish?

Also living at Beaufort Gardens were cousins of Glen's, John and Rosamund Clark and the four of us sometimes went out for dinner. Rosamund was nice but none of us girls liked John, he was tiresomely randy and apt to catch us under the mistletoe. He seemed to have no idea that his attentions were unwelcome.

On Christmas Eve I gave my Christmas presents to Glen and Mrs Harland, dates and biscuits for him and a plant and some perfume for her. Then I packed and Glen and I shared a taxi to Victoria. On arriving home I found Christmas cards awaiting me, including one from Guy: I went out immediately to post him one and then to a cocktail party at the Dockings who lived up the road.

On Christmas morning Badger and I opened our stockings, for Mummy so enjoyed filling these and said she always would, even if we were ninety. At 12 we went down to Airlie House to exchange presents with Granny Hove, Joan and Bretton, then after lunch came the Queen's speech, which was, of course, non-negotiable. In the evening we changed and went to the Dudley Hotel for dinner, which was very good. Looking back, I wonder if it really was very good. Hotel food is not the same as home cooking – but I don't ever remember my mother cooking a turkey.

I did not go back to work on Monday 28th December as I had a streaming cold and my mother made me stay in bed, but on Tuesday I arrived in London to discover Badger had been urgently trying to get hold of me. I had never replied to the letter from the *Daily Telegraph* offering me the job. "How could you have been so stupid?" said Badger. They had tried to phone me at Beaufort Gardens and Mrs Harland had then phoned Badger and she said I'd better jolly well phone them pretty damn quick, as there was another applicant for the job they liked just as much as me, if not more. I had been so complacent, thinking the job was in the bag, but it most certainly was not. I had not really understood you were supposed to reply. So I phoned them and apologised and luckily they were all right about it, but I so nearly lost the opportunity through being too casual.

On New Year's Eve Guy's brother Bunny rang up and asked me to go out to supper at Dino's and then to a party at his flat in Weymouth Street. Lots of people I knew, including Felix, were there and it was a good party, chiefly memorable because at one time a lighted candle set fire to a curtain. The next moment the window was a sheet of flame. Some people screamed, while others, like me, stood rooted to the spot and did nothing. At once two young men sprang to action and put out the flames. I have always wondered what I would do in an emergency and now realise I would be useless, but at least I had the excuse of being a girl, not like some of the young men who also had done nothing and must have felt ashamed. Guy was not at the party. He was in Haslemere with his mother that night and it seemed strange to be with his brother Bunny and not with him.

In fact Guy did telephone me early in January and asked me to go out with him the next day. We went to a restaurant in Kensington and then to a film called *Mogambo* with Clark Gable and Ava Gardner. Afterwards we had coffee – and that was that. Then on the 24th February he phoned again and asked me to have lunch with him the next day. I felt sick with excitement. I left the office at quarter past twelve and we met at the Kardoma on the top floor. I think he enjoyed our lunch – we both did. We talked about many things but not about us, of course not. He was nice and friendly, no more, and even asked for my telephone number at the *Daily Telegraph,* but I did not expect him to phone me, for by now I had accepted that our affair – if you could call it that – was over. Unquestioningly, irretrievably over.

CHAPTER THREE

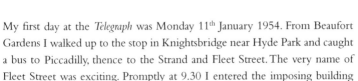

My first day at the *Telegraph* was Monday 11th January 1954. From Beaufort Gardens I walked up to the stop in Knightsbridge near Hyde Park and caught a bus to Piccadilly, thence to the Strand and Fleet Street. The very name of Fleet Street was exciting. Promptly at 9.30 I entered the imposing building and took the lift up to the Woman's Department on the 4th floor, to be greeted by Rosemary, Miss Garrett's secretary. She was tall and elegant, dressed in black with rows of pearls.

There were two offices in our department with an inter-communicating door. Miss Garrett sat in the larger office with Rosemary. Also in this office sat the Features and Junior Editor, Beryl Thomson, the Fashion Editor, Winefride Jackson, and the Cookery Editor, Claire Butler. In my office were Wendy Peterson, the Chief Sub Editor, Alice Hope, who wrote news and general features, and a young trainee journalist called Felicity Brown. Felicity had not been there long and her letter of application had said something like "You'd better employ me at once because I'm brilliant, you'll wonder how you ever managed without me". I thought this was wonderful, I would never have dared write such a letter, and it had greatly appealed to Evelyn Garrett, the Editor, who had instantly given her a job.

None of the journalists came in until eleven o'clock, so Rosemary and I had an hour and a half on our own, but as there were seven telephones to answer, often all ringing at the same time, we did not have much time to sort things out. Rosemary showed me what I was to do. First there was a huge pile of post to open and sort. The quantity of post depended on what had appeared in the paper the day before. It represented the reaction of our readers, hence if they found a particular article of interest, there could be hundreds and hundreds of letters the next day. In that hour and a half we rushed from desk to desk, answering – in my case, trying to answer – all the telephones, and in between we would start sorting the post. At eleven or after, the journalists would start to drift in, breezy and important.

Just as I was trying to make a start on the post, I was called upon to make the tea. This involved carrying a tray of assorted mugs up to the ladies' washroom on the floor above, washing them up and then bringing them down again to make tea for whoever wanted it. The cups were always dirty and often had great lipstick marks all over them, and were filled with cigarette stubs and ash from the smokers. There didn't seem to be any Fairy Liquid or anything like that and it took me quite a while to wash them, then I'd carry them carefully down the flight of stairs to our office and make the tea.

"Oh Delia – no tea for me, I prefer coffee."

"But there doesn't seem to be any coffee…"

"You can get it at the kiosk up the street."

"Delia, I think this milk might be sour, did you get the fresh from Reception?"

"Oh I'm sorry, I didn't know I had to do that."

"Good heavens girl, no wonder it's sour, it must have been here since Friday!"

"I'm sorry." (Rosemary, why didn't you tell me about the milk?)

I took the lift down to Reception and picked up the milk. Then I settled down at my desk to make a start on the post.

"Delia, could you be a sweetie and get me some cigarettes?"

"Cigarettes?"

"Yes. You can get them at the kiosk up the street."

Into the lift and down to the Ground Floor. Cigarettes are quite expensive. I hope she'll give me the money… back again, up in the lift to the 4th floor. Now at last to make a start on the post.

"Could you answer that phone, Delia, it's been ringing for ages."

"Delia, dear heart, I'd kill for another cup of tea – could you be an angel?"

"Oh yes, Delia – and perhaps another cup of coffee for little me? You are a star!"

The star was beginning to feel distinctly grumpy by now – with all these errands to run, it seemed impossible for me to get my work done.

"Is it always like this?" I said to Rosemary as we passed one another in a dash to answer the telephones.

"Yes – always," she said with the suspicion of a laugh.

The post was interesting. The letters were addressed to various specialist journalists but they didn't have time to answer them so it was left to me. I had to make up the answers I thought they might give.

"Dear Winefride Jackson," said one, "My daughter is getting married in June and I don't know what to wear. I've seen an outfit in emerald green but I am quite large and my friends and family tell me I should stick to navy blue or black. What would you advise?"

"I would definitely go for the emerald green," advised Delia Despair, aged nineteen and clueless. I signed the letter Winefride Jackson, the Fashion Editor.

A panicky woman rang up to say she was making the coarse-cut marmalade in yesterday's *Telegraph* and it was all over-boiling.

"What shall I do?" she said.

"Turn the gas off," I said.

"Oh I see," she said, "but it does say to boil rapidly and that's what I'm doing."

"Put it in a larger pan," I said.

"I haven't got a larger pan."

"Well then, put it in two smaller pans."

"Yes I see," she said.

She rang me back shortly to say it hadn't set.

"That's because you didn't use a larger pan," I said.

"But I didn't have a larger pan and *you* told me to use two smaller ones," she complained.

"Well, it was only a *suggestion*. That was all it was, just a *suggestion*, to try and help you out. I can't help it if it didn't work, can I?"

(And don't blame me, it's not my fault your bloody marmalade won't bloody well set.)

Every day there were more and more letters to answer. Many of them just wanted tear sheets of recipes that had appeared in the paper. It was easy to answer those, but many others wanted advice of all sorts – how they should manage on their inadequate house-keeping, what they should wear, how they should they make their bosoms look larger or their bottoms smaller. I had no idea, but I took a lot of trouble in trying to help them.

Some of the letters were angry. One day a horrible dripping parcel was delivered to our office. I opened it and discovered a piece of putrid meat, swarming with maggots. Attached to it was a letter from a woman who was angered by a recipe we had published for Steak Au Poivre. "See what sort of a dish you can make with *this!*" she wrote bitterly. I am not sure what her point was, whether she was so poor she could not afford to buy steak, or maybe she had no refrigerator.

At first there was a honeymoon period with the Editor, Evelyn Garrett. She thought I was wonderful – at first. "Do you write?" she asked me.

"That's what I want to do," I said.

Beryl Thomson scowled at me. She cornered me in the office and said in a low tone, "I don't approve of secretaries who've been to swanky schools and then think they can side-step their way into journalism. I had to do it the hard way. I went to a comprehensive, then joined our local paper in Leeds when I was sixteen. I was the office girl. I had to work my way up, and it was hard graft, very hard. So don't you imagine you can come swanning in here sucking up to Evelyn Garrett and get straight into journalism, because you've got another think coming."

"I'm sorry, I didn't mean –" I began.

"Oh yes? Not much!" said Beryl.

"Delia, my dear " said Evelyn Garrett. "You go to lots of smart social events, don't you? You went to Lords for the Eton and Harrow match, now tell me – what was the latest fashion trend? What were the ladies wearing?"

But I was very unobservant and hadn't really noticed.

"They wore dresses with a vee at the back and the front," I said cautiously.

"A Double Vee," said Miss G, excitedly. "Winefride? Did you hear that? A Double Vee, we must do a feature on that."

Winefride did not look enthusiastic.

One day when Winefride was out, there was a conference in the office.

"The question is," said Evelyn Garrett, "What should we do about Winefride? *Should Winefride go?*"

I was deeply shocked to hear this. The treachery of it! It was as bad as the conspirators assassinating Julius Caesar. There was the lovely Winefride, wearing fabulously glamorous outfits, charming everyone she met, breezing in and out of the office, going to fashion shows, spending a fortune on expensive lunches and first class flights to far flung and exotic destinations in the name of writing up the whole fashion scene for the Daily Telegraph Woman's page, and being in total ignorance of this infamy, this plot on the part of Evelyn Garrett to *get rid of her!* I liked Winefride Jackson, she was always very kind to me and I could not believe they might do such a thing.

"Well, everybody," said Miss Garrett. "What do we think? Should Winefride go?"

"I think she should," said Beryl Thomson.

"Oh, I don't know about that," said Wendy. "She does write very good copy and she knows all the designers, so she gets in first with the latest trends."

In the event, after much discussion, it was decided she should stay. After a long, lingering lunch at the Savoy she breezed back in, with no idea of what had gone on behind her back.

I thought it was disappointing that the *Daily Telegraph* was so departmentalised. There we were, stuck in our little department, a million miles away from the rest of the newspaper. But then lovely Alice Hope, who wrote a lot of the news features, started sending me down to the News Room. After the first time she sent me, she said that they all wanted an introduction. I am sure this was an exaggeration, but she was something of a matchmaker. She told me someone called Michael Goode was enquiring about me, which was an exciting thought. He was a very good journalist, highly thought of. Alice also encouraged me to write, and would send me to cover a story she should have been doing herself. Much to my delight she sent me to a Sherry Party at the Indian Club in South Audley Street to represent the *Telegraph* at the Centenary of the Indian Postage Stamp. It was great fun and I felt very important, mixing with the much older representatives of the *Times* and the *Observer* and other erudite publications. They were all male, and all very knowledgeable about stamps. I knew very little, just what I had gleaned from collecting stamps when I was a little girl, and they must have soon realised this, but they gathered round me and I managed at least to make them laugh. It was my first job. Afterwards I wrote about it, but the article had to go before Beryl Thomson and of course I knew that was that – she would never publish anything I had written.

"I tell you what," said Alice. "In future, you write the story and we'll put it in under my name. Then at least you'll have the satisfaction of knowing you've been published." So that's what happened, and I wrote quite a few pieces which went before Beryl under Alice's name.

Besides being the main Features Editor, Beryl Thomson ran the Junior Page, which appeared every Saturday. Beryl could not care less about Juniors. Every week there was a competition for Juniors, quite an easy quiz and all they had to do was send in their answers neatly written on a postcard. They had to enter their name and address and their age. The winner of the competition received a printed certificate saying they were the winner of the Daily Telegraph Junior Competition, together with a postal order for seven shillings and sixpence. The following week the name of the winner was published in the paper. Every week sackfuls of postcards arrived, hundreds of them, all with the correct answers. Beryl Thomson never looked at the postcards, finding it all a colossal bore. She would just put her hand into one of the sacks and pull out a postcard, any postcard would do as long as it was reasonably neat, and that child would be the winner for the week.

One day a letter arrived from a father saying his little handicapped son had entered the competition and was sure he had got the right answers. He had carefully and painstakingly entered his answers on a postcard, and had then waited every day for the postman to arrive to say he had won – but alas, this had not happened. Why not? The little boy was heart-broken to see another child had won instead of him. He could not understand why he had not won.

I then took it upon myself to write a letter to the little boy, saying how very nearly he had won, but how his postcard had not been quite as neatly written as that of the winner. However, I said, in view of the fact he had so nearly won, I was sending him a certificate and a postal order for five shillings. I signed the letter Beryl Thomson, Junior Editor. I knew she would have been furious had she known, but she never did find out, so it didn't matter.

I did try very hard to be helpful, and you had to be quite ingenious in helping people with their problems. There was of course no such thing as the Internet and Google so I had to phone up all around London. It took me ages to research my answers and meantime the unanswered letters mounted up in the in-tray.

One day a young Russian student phoned to say he felt homesick, very, very homesick. If only he could get some dishes like his mother used to make him, he wouldn't feel so homesick. One recipe was called Kascha and another was Caucasian Shashlik. I promised I would try and find recipes for these and suggested he phone back in a few days. I asked Claire Butler, our cookery expert, but she had never heard of either of the dishes. "Just say you can't help him," she said. But I had told him to phone back in a few days - so I phoned the Russian Embassy. They hadn't heard of them either. They preferred the English Feesh and Cheeps, they said. However, if I phoned back in a few days they would ask someone in the Embassy who was on leave and might have the answer.

Sure enough in a few days when I phoned they were able to tell me that

Kascha was a sweet tart with layers of semolina, walnuts, almonds and apricot jam. Shashlik was leg of lamb cooked on skewers with green bacon. I had never heard of green bacon. Did that mean it was mouldy? Anyway, they gave me the recipes and when the young Russian student rang back I dictated them to him. He was delighted. He would ask the woman where he had digs to make these dishes for him. He was everlastingly grateful, he said. But all this had taken up a lot of time and Evelyn Garrett was not pleased. "You have spent hours and hours on just one letter," she said.

"Phone call," I interjected.

"Yes, phone call, whatever. And there are two hundred letters to answer, and tomorrow there will be four hundred and the day after that…"

Yes, I got the point.

The letters did mount up and my in-tray was swamped with them. It overflowed all over my desk and the post boy had to bring two more wire in-trays and even they weren't enough. Sometimes Rosemary helped me with the post, but I became aware that she was annoyed with me and Evelyn Garrett more so. I was meant to leave the office at 5.30 but none of the journalists left till seven and it became more and more difficult for me to get away on time, especially with the constant requests to make tea or run down to the kiosk for cigarettes just as I was trying to get through the post. Many a night I didn't get home till half past seven or eight o'clock.

Eventually it was decided I should have someone in to help me and also that I should be paid overtime. A very nice young woman joined me, called Margaret. It made a big difference having her and together we managed to get through a lot of work. She gave me lifts home in her funny little Morris car, and told me she lived with her boyfriend but he wouldn't marry her. Margaret had black hair which was just starting to go grey at the temples and the boyfriend had woken up one day and seen a couple of grey hairs on the pillow and thought he didn't want to be tied up with a grey-haired woman. More fool him, I thought for not only was Margaret a gem, she was also a very good cook.

Once a man rang the office and asked me what sort of cups we drank our tea and coffee out of. I told him they were assorted cups and mugs, some were chipped, and some were cracked.

"My firm has invented a new sort of plastic," he said. "It's called Melamine. It comes in many attractive patterns, it's durable and never gets chipped. How would you like a set of nice new beakers for your office?"

I said I'd like it very much. He said he'd bring a set and meet me in the foyer in half an hour. Sure enough I got a phone message to say he had arrived and was waiting for me down in Reception. I hurried down in the lift and was presented with a large cardboard box, which I carried back to the office and unpacked. As promised they were in a very attractive turquoise geometric pattern. I took them into Miss Garrett's office and proudly showed them to her. To my surprise she was not at all pleased, in fact she was furious.

"Phone him up at once and tell him to come and collect them," she said.

"But why?"

"He needn't think we can be bought like that!"

"Bought? I don't understand –"

"He only wants us to write up his new invention in the paper."

"But he didn't say…"

"That's what he wants. There's no such thing as a free lunch, you know."

But there was, I thought, as I sadly packed the nice bright beakers back into their box. Felicity and Rosemary often boasted of the free lunches they had had, vying with one another at not having to break into their wages for a week.

My honeymoon period with Evelyn Garrett was well and truly over.

CHAPTER FOUR

My friendship with Glen Coats had continued from the time we had met. It was only ever a friendship. I would have liked it to be more, but he said if it became physical it would end our friendship and he wanted that to continue for ever. He said we were soulmates and what we had between us was rare, something to be cherished.

He was now in the Fleet Air Arm division of the Royal Navy and was away a great deal but he wrote regularly, long and amusing letters, which I treasured. He came down to stay for long weekends when he had leave, and we went for walks in the Sussex countryside. We walked for miles over the South Downs and in the woods and meadows and along by the river, going back home on the bus in the evening for the boring last part of the journey.

His knowledge of wildlife amazed me. He could always spot the slightest movement of a bird or animal which most people would never notice. We saw a weasel, a badger, a fox, partridges, a skylark. He said it was amazing that we liked the same things, we both loved nature and the countryside.

My parents liked him enormously and could not believe we were only friends. My father was convinced there must be more to it than that, and I think there was in a way. He certainly wanted us to be together every time he was on leave, and we went out in the evenings after I was home from the office, sometimes with his family, his father who was a Naval Commander and who took us to drinks at the Berkeley and on to dinner at his club, sometimes with his beautiful elder sister Coila, or his endearing younger sister Camilla. However, usually we were on our own. We went out for coffee or to meals at the Mocambo and then on to the Corkscrew Club, that funny dark and smoky little venue nearby. We went back to our rooms in Beaufort Gardens and I'd help him with the revision for his exams or his packing. We talked endlessly, often argued but never really fell out.

In the years that followed we still told each other everything, how we felt about other people, but never how we felt about each other. We both fell in love with other people and he had a long and unhappy affair with a woman in Canada and wrote asking my advice. I was married by that time and I tried to help him, but he seemed destined to be unhappy. He was tragically killed in a helicopter accident in 1966. In his last letter, dated March of that year, he told me he suspected I had had a crush on him. He had been attracted to me too and had wondered why I had never shown him that I loved him - he believed it was because I was too shy to make the first move. I regretted not answering that last letter. And I suppose that's what it was – a crush. But I'm sure he was right and that if it had been a physical love, it would have ended.

Back at the *Daily Telegraph*, Rosemary told me she was going to leave. She had found herself another job, something very glamorous in the film world. She was very excited but would not tell Miss Garrett just yet. That was something she did not look forward to, but eventually she gave in her notice. I thought she was very brave, I wouldn't want to give notice to Miss Garrett. On the 27th April she told Miss G she would be leaving in a fortnight. There was a panic to find a replacement, but it was quickly accomplished: a job in the *Daily Telegraph* editorial would not be vacant for long.

A new, very pretty girl came into the office on the following Monday, 3rd May. Her name was Judy. She seemed to pick up the job right away but on the 10th May, Rosemary told me Miss Garrett did not like her and thought she was the wrong person. I was sorry to hear this as I liked her and thought she was efficient. There seemed to be no pleasing Miss Garrett. Nevertheless Judy was allowed to stay.

On the 20th May I had the feeling that all was not well at the office. There was a strange atmosphere and I noticed people did not always meet my eye when they spoke to me. It seemed I was out of favour with Miss Garrett because the figures were not good or something. Margaret and I did not know what to do about this, for we were both working as hard as we could. The atmosphere was awful and we felt uneasy.

One day I was asked to phone up the home of Lady Catherine Maxwell-Scott to ask about her wedding dress. Miss Garrett liked to know about the design of society wedding gowns so that they could be sketched for the Telegraph Woman's Page. I found out the telephone number of Lady Catherine but a man answered who said he was Lady Catherine's father. He said Lady

Catherine and her mother were both out, so he couldn't help me. I thanked him and went to report this to Evelyn Garrett. "That must be the Earl," she said, "Get on the phone and ask him what his daughter's dress is like."

So very reluctantly I redialled the number. Once again the phone was answered by the Earl.

"I'm so sorry to bother you," I said timidly, "I was just wondering about your daughter's wedding dress? Could you – "

"Look, I've told you," he interrupted impatiently. "They're both OUT. I can't help you."

Once again I reported back to Miss Garrett.

"For goodness sake, you're useless!" she said. "Now we need an answer, so stir your stumps and get back on that phone!"

"I can't ring again!" I said, horrified.

"Of course you can! You can, and you must!"

My fingers trembled as I redialled the number. "Hello," I said, speaking very quickly as soon as he answered, "It's me again from the *Daily Telegraph* and I'm about to get the sack so please, please I beg you, tell me *something* about your daughter's wedding dress?"

There was a long pause. "*Please…*" I said piteously.

"So you're about to get the sack, are you?"

"Yes. I can't seem to do anything right."

"All right," he said. "Hang on, I'll see if I can get hold of the housekeeper."

After a while a woman came on the phone and told me that Lady Catherine's dress was of ivory brocade in the Tudor style and it had a deep square neck edged with pearls, and wide sleeves. I reported this back to Evelyn Garrett, who ordered Hyacinth Halliwell to sketch the dress as it had been described to me. The sketch appeared in the paper two days later and for the time being I had a stay of execution.

It did not last long. On the 18th June I had a horrible shock. Judy grabbed hold of me as soon as I got back from lunch. The office was empty, everyone else had gone out.

"Delia, something awful happened when you were at lunch today," she said. Evelyn Garrett called everyone into our office and said, "SHOULD DELIA GO?"

"Oh my God!" I said.

"Yes, it was dreadful. She thinks you're too slow. She's already sacked Margaret, and maybe you as well."

I burst into tears.

"Everyone else stuck up for you," said Judy. "Alice Hope said you might be slow but you take so much trouble with your research and we've never had so many complimentary letters of thanks since you came."

It was a stormy afternoon, but everyone else was very nice to me. Alice Hope told me not to worry and said *she* might be the next. Judy also intervened on my behalf and by the end of the day she persuaded Miss Garrett to let me stay after all. I thought Alice Hope and Judy were the nicest people I had ever met. However it left a very sour taste in my mouth. I wondered how long I would stay in the job, for Fleet Street was just as Uncle Tommy had warned me. The motto seemed to be "Here Today and Go Tomorrow." Judy told me she herself had decided to leave, and so had Wendy.

Around this time the *Daily Telegraph* "discovered" 'Bon Viveur' – this was the cook Fanny Cradock. Our office arranged Cookery Brains Trusts all around Britain and these were a huge success. From my point of view it was great, because not only Miss Garrett but others of the staff had to be away from the office and be part of the back-up team. Female audiences loved Fanny, but they didn't realise what she was like. She was a monster. Wendy said one hour with her was like three days with anyone else. She had black hair and bright red lipstick and scarlet nail varnish. She liked to look glamorous and would always dress up in an evening gown with lots of jewellery. She said, "Only a slut gets in a mess in the kitchen."

Her 'husband' Johnnie (it later emerged that they had never been married) always accompanied her. He seemed to be a total dogsbody, but she said she needed him to do the wine. She would bawl "Cradock!" at him and he would rush to do her bidding. Everyone rushed to do her bidding. She demanded that everything should be just as she wanted, and her demands were more and more outrageous.

My father had been in the same house at Harrow with Johnnie Cradock and they met at a dinner one year. My father said very tactlessly, "I say, Johnnie, is it true that you and your wife are getting divorced?"

"Certainly not!" said Johnnie Cradock indignantly. We all thought him a complete wimp, but he knew which side his bread was buttered. And they could hardly have got divorced if they weren't married.

My work at the office had mounted up again and I knew Miss Garrett was not pleased with me, but somehow I didn't care. If I lost the job there was nothing I could do about it, I had worked as hard as I could. Besides, I was starting to feel ill with a sore throat and over several days it got worse. Finally I was sent home in a taxi and Mrs Harland made me go straight to bed. I had a high temperature and, it appeared, acute tonsillitis. At first I was very disappointed, as I had been invited to the Henley Regatta and it seemed I would be unable to go. Instead I stayed in bed and wrote a ghost story, to the amusement of my friends in Beaufort Gardens. But as the days passed I got worse. Badger must have told my father, because he came to visit me with a lot of nice things I couldn't eat. They then called in the doctor, who was appalled at the condition of my throat and said it was the worst case of quinsy he had ever seen. He gave me a penicillin injection, but the pain of the ulcers in my throat was so bad I could not sleep.

Next day I was in very low spirits and could not help crying. The doctor came again and said the reaction was not at all as he had hoped and my mouth and throat were full of toxin. My arm was bruised from the injection, so he gave me another in my bottom. My father and Badger both came to visit with strawberries, which I could smell but not eat. Next day I was a little better but everyone was horrified by the colour of my tongue. The doctor came again and said the ulcers were struggling now and one more injection plus M&B should wipe them out.

Badger brought me some carnations and my father some books to read, *Catalina* by Somerset Maugham and an Agatha Christie, but I no longer felt like finishing my ghost story. I also had visits from Marigold and Glen's sister Coila. The next day Doctor Gunn came back for the last time and gave me a certificate saying I was not to return to work until I was really better and certainly not for the whole of the next week. He said I had been severely run down.

Much to my surprise the *Telegraph* sent me some roses, and I was touched to see the card was signed by Evelyn Garrett and Wendy. And on the Friday Claire Butler phoned up and in the afternoon came to see me, bringing strawberries and cream which was very kind.

I did not return to work for nineteen days, and was immediately plunged into a horrible week, for Judy was ill and Miss Garrett wanted me to do her job. Margaret was called in to do mine. I hated working for Miss G and felt very depressed. Then too, she suggested I might not be strong enough to do my work and she, Wendy and Alice Hope began to discuss what sort of job would suit me better. Mrs Hope thought it should be something which brought me into contact with people. Wendy searched for some information for me from a Mr Jones of P&O and a Mr Banyard of BOAC. I wrote to them both, and waited eagerly for their replies, but both were disappointing. Mr Jones said there were no vacancies with P&O at present, and Mr Banyard rang up and said that I was too young. You had to be twenty-one to work for BOAC – but he suggested I should re-apply next year and send a photograph. Meanwhile Margaret said I should meet her brother who was a BEA pilot. I was now dead keen to become an air hostess.

Wendy left the *Telegraph* at the end of July and we had a leaving party for her with a Fuller's walnut cake. After the speeches and presentation we adjourned to the pub next door to drink her health. The pub was like a Fleet Street club, more a part of Fleet Street than anything I had yet experienced.

Judy was the next to leave, as she had found an exciting job in television. She took some time off before she went, being photographed in a TV studio, but this did not go down well in the office. Margaret and I had bought her an owl from the pottery shop round the corner, and we wondered if we would be the only ones to give her a leaving present. In the end she slipped away, her departure unheralded, unlike that of Wendy.

Miss Garrett was away for the last week of August and we made the most of her absence. It was so nice and relaxed without her. However, she was back all too soon and it was just as we had expected: as soon as she arrived, nothing was right, everything and everyone was picked to pieces. Audrey had had it completely, Sheila must buck up, everything Alice did was wrong and there was to be a showdown with Winefride when she came back. In the following days we were exhausted by this onslaught. Margaret was unsure what to do, whether to give in her notice, and as for me, I dared not think if I should even have a choice.

CHAPTER FIVE

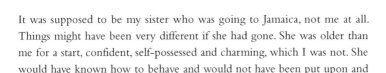

It was supposed to be my sister who was going to Jamaica, not me at all. Things might have been very different if she had gone. She was older than me for a start, confident, self-possessed and charming, which I was not. She would have known how to behave and would not have been put upon and treated as I was.

I think it was Auntie Ailsa who first told us about the job. It was the 10th of August 1954 and I was twenty – a very young and naïve twenty. Auntie Ailsa was my mother's dearest friend and she was the grandmother of little Holly, the youngest daughter of her son Peter and his first wife Lois. Ailsa was also a sort of distant cousin, as were they all. It seemed her ex-daughter-in-law was going out to Jamaica with her new husband and they wanted someone to go out and look after her small daughter Holly. Peter and Lois had had three daughters, Miranda and Merle, aged thirteen and eleven, who were at boarding school and Holly, who was six years old. Then Lois ran off with Chester Lynn, a shipping millionaire she met in the south of France. This trip to Jamaica was to be a sort of honeymoon. The only trouble was they would have Holly with them, which would be a bit of a nuisance. They needed someone to take her off their hands. Lois had always wanted someone to take Holly off her hands; she couldn't be bothered with her (because she was Difficult) so there had been a whole series of nannies and au pairs, much to Ailsa's anxiety.

"What sort of a life can it be for her?" she said worriedly to my mother, "She's had no stability in her life, she's been shipped back and forth from pillar to post all her life. She needs some stability."

Ailsa told my mother about the proposed Jamaica trip and suggested Badger might go, so it should have been Badger. It was all settled, then suddenly, somewhat at the last moment, Badger and Peter got engaged. There was a panic – what should they do?

"Perhaps Delia could go?" said Ailsa.

This was something we had not thought of, but my mother knew I was not happy in my job, so it was arranged I should meet Chester and Lois and see how we got on. I telephoned and someone with a very deep voice answered. I assumed it was Chester.

"Is that Mr Lynn?" I asked.

"No," said the voice. "This is Mrs Lynn."

Oh dear – not a good start. Nevertheless, it was arranged that I should have an interview with them and I should meet them where they were staying, at Brown's Hotel.

Lois was thin and elegant. She had red hair and looked rather like a racehorse. Chester was dark and quite good looking, though his face was a bit podgy. I had never been to Brown's Hotel before. It was grand in an understated sort of way.

I was invited to have lunch with them and the three of us sat at a table while four or five waiters circled round bearing exotic dishes of lobster and salmon and a pig's head in jelly with a ring through its nose. I was handed an enormous menu and had no idea what to choose, there were so many wonderful things on it. Chester was not feeling very well and opted for Eggs Florentine and I said I'd have the same. I was waiting for them to say, "Are you sure that's *really* what you want?" as my family always said if we went out and I chose the cheapest thing on the menu. But they never did. They were so rich – millionaires don't think of choosing the cheapest thing on the menu, they choose what they want and assume everyone else does too.

The interview went quite well. Chester didn't say much, in fact he said nothing. Lois told me that at present there was an older woman looking after Holly, called Sister. She was very efficient but she had outgrown her usefulness because she would not be able to teach Holly lessons. (In fact, she wanted to leave. She was desperate to leave, though I didn't know that then, and Lois certainly wasn't going to tell me.) She asked me if I'd ever done any teaching and I said I hadn't, and she said that was a pity because I was going to have to give little Holly lessons. Did I think I'd be able to cope with that? I said I thought I would. If I had said I wouldn't, that would have been the end of that. Anyway, Lois seemed to like me and there was no one else around and there were only three weeks before they were due to sail - so she said the job was mine. She didn't say if I wanted it, that went without saying. Of course I would want it. To go to sea on a luxury liner and stay in a beautiful house in Jamaica – what girl wouldn't jump at it?

"You will be paid five pounds a week, plus your keep," said Lois. "You'll have to have lots of new clothes. You must go to my dressmaker, Madame Morelle in Curzon Street. And you'd better go to Foyle's and get some books for Holly." I agreed enthusiastically to everything she said.

I went home very excited and told my parents all about it. They were not as excited as I was and my mother said she thought I might be very lonely, but I didn't listen. I didn't want to hear. I went to visit Madame Morelle and chose two evening dresses, a ballet length green and white check chiffon, trimmed with jade green velvet, and a rose red cotton with a black motif, a tight bodice and a halter neck. I thought the latter was rather sexy. I was delighted with them both, but Madame Morelle's dresses were all lovely even though they were terribly expensive. I had to cash all my savings to pay for them but I was sure it would be worth it.

Then I went to Foyle's to buy the books. I had been given carte blanche and had the time of my life choosing all my favourite childhood books. For once I didn't think about cost, for I knew they were rich and I wanted Holly to be the most well-read child in England (well – Jamaica). I spent upwards of a hundred pounds, which in today's money would be more than a thousand. When I gave the bill to Chester, as they had asked me to do, they were absolutely horrified.

"You spent all this money on books!" they exclaimed.

"Yes," I said lamely. I realised there was a limit even for rich people, but it was too late then. Besides they were such wonderful books, it would have been a shame to send any of them back and how would you choose which to keep and which to return? I was eventually forgiven, they even treated it as a joke that I should have spent all this money on mere books.

The next couple of weeks were busy – first of all, I had to give notice in my job with the *Telegraph*. If truth be told, I was a little uneasy at the thought of doing this; suppose they were furious and thought I was letting them down? But I suspect it was a relief to them that I was going and they were not going to have to sack me for being too slow.

On my last day there was a walnut cake in my honour, and Miss Garrett was very charming and said they were fond of me and would miss me. She said they should start an Old Girls' Club, and they *must* have some of my writings about Jamaica. Everyone was very interested and pleased for me, and they presented me with two books, *The Traveller's Year* by Elizabeth Nicholas in which Miss Garrett wrote on the fly leaf: "With love and as a reminder of your Daily Telegraph friends of the Women's Department" signed by them all (though not incidentally, by Beryl Thomson, but she had never liked me anyway and was certainly not a friend). The other book was a history of Jamaica, which was very stuffy and dull and I am ashamed to say I never read it.

I bought lots of clothes. I had told all my friends I was going to Jamaica and they envied me and told me it would be wonderful. I felt sure it would be too – little did I know...

As a sort of leaving treat, Badger and Peter invited me to choose a theatre I wanted to go to, and I chose the Duenna. There was a group of us and afterwards we went on to the Colony Night Club. One of the others in the group was a friend of Peter's called Martin Lennox. We had a delicious dinner, and Martin kept asking me to dance, even in the middle of the meal. It was the first time I had met him but we got on very well from the start and I felt he liked me as much as I liked him. I really enjoyed the evening and felt quite sorry I had met him just as I was going to Jamaica.

There wasn't much time left now. On the 12th October I was invited to London to have drinks with the Lynns and Sister and Holly. I was struck once more by how very rich they were and felt somewhat over-awed. Little Holly seemed quite sweet but Sister, whom I was to take over from, hinted how difficult she was. "And she still wets her bed, you know," she said, "that's not right for a child of six, is it?"

Sister was certainly efficient but rather colourless, also she seemed quite old. She wore a navy blue uniform and I hoped I would not be expected to wear one as I thought I wouldn't be seen dead in it. It was agreed that I should take over from her the week before we sailed, and that we should spend that week in Woking with Holly's grandparents, Auntie Ailsa and Uncle Dick. My mother thought it would be a difficult week for me and it was. Auntie Ailsa and Uncle Dick were sweet to me but now I had other responsibilities. I had never looked after a little girl before and it was quite different from what I had imagined. She was not just difficult, she was impossible, wild and uncontrolled. She flew into tantrums and refused to do anything I asked her to.

We kept going backwards and forwards to the swings in the park and into Woking, which was a dead and alive, dreary sort of place. I had no idea what to do to pass the time. The hours dragged by and I longed desperately for seven o'clock when she would be in bed. Each day seemed worse than the one before and I wondered what I had let myself in for.

On 21st October we got up early and went into London and had a dreadful morning in the park. She was sullen and disagreeable and I wondered what techniques I could use to placate her. Then we met Sister, and I went off by myself to have the yellow fever inoculation and my first TAB injection, both of which were pleasurable compared with looking after little Holly. Later I met her and Sister at the dentist and Sister left us and we went to Monsieur Rene, the Mayfair hairdresser, where Holly was to have her hair cut. He was exorbitantly expensive. He said I must be mad to be going to Jamaica with That Woman. He seemed to know her quite well. He said she was notorious. Was this an ill omen, I asked myself?

On the 22nd October Ailsa asked me if I wanted to back out, because it would not be too late if I did. But I said No, and so that was that, the die was cast. A week later my parents drove me up to London with all my luggage and we went to Claridges to meet Chester and Lois. There seemed to be a lot of muddle and confusion and they were still having their lunch at four o'clock. We left them to it, and took little Holly to Waterloo and my parents saw us onto the train for Southampton. Long after we got on the boat.

CHAPTER SIX

There was a party in Lois and Chester's sumptuous suite up on the promenade deck before we sailed. The cabin and state room were awash with flowers, and there was not an inch of room where there were not elaborate arrangements and bouquets. Also there were lots of people hugging and kissing Lois and saying "*Darling!*" They purported to be Lois's dearest friends, but even I could see they were just hangers-on and indeed, I never saw or heard of any of them ever again.

"Isn't she the most glorious ship?" said Lois, and everyone agreed that it – I mean she – was. She was called SS *Antilles*, a brand new French luxury cruise liner and this was her maiden voyage. Lois and Chester had Suite Number One, which was the best. It was called "Mexique." Also in their suite was Buffy, Lois's black Pekinese, who would be going to Jamaica with us. This little dog was Lois's pride and joy, and detailed instructions were given to the steward about his meals and his biscuits and his water bowl and the shampoo with which he was to be washed and the brush and comb with which he was to be groomed. The steward may have had other duties, but these were to be overlooked as long as was required for Buffy's daily routine.

There were four or five decks on the Antilles and Holly and I had a little cabin with bunk beds down on the third deck which felt like the bowels of the ship. The advantage of this cabin was that it was so far away from Lois and Chester. It took about half an hour to get up to their suite and I was therefore not at her beck and call – which She quickly realised was not to her liking.

A steward knocked on the door of our cabin while I was unpacking and told me I was to report to Suite One, where I was given a lot of instructions. Holly was to have supper in the Children's Dining Room at six o'clock and she was to have a full cooked meal consisting of three courses, whether she wanted them or not. I was to make sure she ate everything and we were to stay there until she had. She was then to be dressed in one of her three new nighties and negligees which were hand-made in fine Swiss cotton with broderie anglaise through which pink and blue ribbons were threaded. These were to be worn only once and were to be washed every day. This was *very* important. I was then to bring her up to Suite One to say goodnight before she went to bed, and they went down to dinner. I could have my dinner in the Children's Dining Room after Holly was in bed. They did not want me to be with them at dinner because they were on their honeymoon and they wanted to be alone. I quite understood this and felt relieved but I was sad to be having my dinner in the Children's Dining Room all by myself.

After dinner I went to the lounge to read and though I told myself how lucky I was, somehow I felt very lonely. My feelings were mixed: I loved the feel of the ship at night and it was exciting to be on board such a beautiful liner. But I woke up feeling sick and the day was long and difficult. Holly was bored. The ship lurched up and down and it was almost impossible to unpack without everything sliding backwards and forwards. Later that night Holly wet her bed. She was on the top bunk and when she called out, "Delia, I'm wet!" I leapt out of my bunk at great speed as I thought I would be showered with pee. I washed her and put her into another of the new nighties. I thought these were not going to last very long if she was going to need two every night. I decided it would be safer if I slept in the top bunk from now on.

The next day we arrived at Vigo and soon after Holly and I went ashore, which was fun. It was a quaint old place and I took a lot of photos with my old brownie box camera. At lunch time the Purser told me I should not be eating meals in the Children's Dining Room, and he put me at a special table for young people: there was Marion who was going to Trinidad and Frank, a Scot going there too, and Alan and Sheila, both going to Caracas, and Peggy going to Trinidad. It was lovely to meet them and I didn't feel sick either. I particularly liked Marion. Holly had made friends with Peggy's little girl Mary with whom she had supper in the Children's Dining Room, but meals took ages because she really didn't want to eat three courses and I had to coax her to eat every mouthful. Lucky little Mary only had to have cornflakes and milk and was finished in no time.

The next day, the 1st of November, the sea was very rough again and everything in the dining room got broken. There was a great drama on the ship when Maureen, a young girl from Manchester in Third Class, tried to jump overboard in an attempt to get away from her boyfriend with whom she was going to Jamaica. A young Swiss called Paul managed to stop her and somehow or other, the Lynns became involved. Maureen was locked up in the Ship's Hospital in case she tried to do it again.

In the evening I went to the cinema and Paul came and sat next to me; later we played ping pong and later still we danced. Lois Lynn, who I soon learnt was a creature of impulse, then took it upon herself to assure the Ship's Captain that we would look after Maureen and that she need not be locked up any longer. From then on she and Paul seemed to be attached to our party.

I think it was about the third day when the first big row occurred. Holly in her water wings and I were in the swimming pool when I was suddenly aware that Lois was standing on the edge of the pool, looking extremely annoyed.

"Delia, get out of the pool," she shouted at me in her deep voice. "Get out AT ONCE!"

I got out and stood before her dripping. There was no question of picking up a towel or anything like that. I just stood and dripped while she tore into me. It seemed that Holly had come to say goodnight in her negligee and that the ribbon threaded through the broderie anglaise was missing. "Where is it? Where is the ribbon?"

"I - I don't know," I said.

"You don't know?"

"No."

"Did I or did I not tell you she had to have a clean nightie and negligee every day?"

"Yes, and she has, but they've gone to the laundry…."

"But they should have come back by now. Didn't you notice the ribbon was missing?"

"I'm afraid not…."

"Well, this is absolutely disgraceful. It is unbelievable. I want you to find the steward and go with him to the laundry and get that ribbon back. Go now!"

I was shocked. I had never seen anyone as angry as she was.

"But – but what about Holly?"

"Get her out of the pool and get her dressed. She can go to the children's playroom while you find that ribbon."

When I found our steward, who was French as were all the ship's company, I explained to him in my faltering French what had happened. He would not allow me to accompany him to the Laundry and insisted that he would find the ribbon and bring it back to me. I waited miserably in my cabin, wondering what I would do if it was irretrievably lost. Luckily he found it for me and brought a bodkin, as I had omitted to pack one, so that I could thread the ribbon back through the holes in the broderie anglaise.

What should I do now? I thought. Should I go to her suite and tell her the ribbon was found? I did, but that was wrong too as she was now resting in her suite and did not want to be disturbed by her child's inefficient governess.

The next day there was another crisis and another row.

"Delia, why isn't Holly wearing her pink cardigan? The pink cardigan with the roses embroidered on it?"

"I – I don't know."

"She had it on this morning, so where is it now?"

"I think she must have taken it off and left it somewhere."

"You think? Don't you know?"

I didn't answer.

"This is disgraceful. So where, *where* did she leave it?"

"I'm sorry, I don't know where."

"Why don't you know?"

"I don't know."

"You don't know *why* you don't know?"

"No – I mean, Yes – I mean, No."

"This really isn't good enough, Delia. You're meant to be looking after her."

"I'm sorry."

"Well you're not going anywhere until it's found. No lunch, no tea. You are going to comb every inch of this ship until it's found."

And that is what I did – but luckily I found it quite quickly and did not have to comb every inch.

There were a few days of calm. We settled into a routine. We had our breakfast in the children's dining room at 8.30 am. Then there'd be lessons, her first ones with me. At 11 o'clock we went up to Mexique, that is Suite One, to say good morning to Holly's mother, after which Holly would go to the Children's Playroom. After lunch we'd both go back to Mexique for a rest. At 4.30 there would be a film, after which she would go up to say goodnight.

"Now Delia," said her mother. "Has Holly been wetting her bed since you joined us?"

I hesitated.

"I want you to tell me the truth – I *need* to know. Has she been wetting her bed?"

"Well – a couple of times," I mumbled.

"You must tell me every time it happens, do you understand?"

After saying goodnight there was a mad rush with Holly having to eat an enormous three-course dinner and always a tussle over every mouthful. Rene, the young male steward in the Children's Dining Room, was always on hand to help try and persuade her to finish her meal, while little Mary, who only had cornflakes, had finished hers long before. Then came bath and bed, my having to change at the same time to be ready in time for grown-ups' dinner at 8.30. I really enjoyed the evenings, I liked my table companions very much, especially Marion and Frank. After dinner I sat with them, or played ping pong with Paul. The French officers were charming and complimented me on my French which was actually not very good. They were taken in by my French accent and did not realise at first how sparse was my vocabulary, but Rene, the young steward in the Children's Dining Room was very kind and helped me a lot, so I did improve.

Lois - Mrs Lynn, as I was supposed to call her - blew hot and cold in her opinion of me. For a short while she was pleased, as she felt Holly had improved under my care, and so for a while all was well. Holly continued to wet her bed and when she told me she usually woke up beforehand but it was so nice and cosy in bed and she could not be bothered to get up and go to the loo, I remonstrated with her. "You know how much worse it is if you don't," I said, "because in no time at all, it'll be all horrible and wet and cold." But it made no difference. Then I resorted to blackmail, for it was the only thing that worked. "Next time it happens," I said, "I shall just have to tell your mother."

"Oh, Delia please don't tell Mummy!"

"Not this time – but next time I shall have to tell her."

I felt mean, but it worked a treat and she stopped wetting the bed.

After a week at sea we started arriving at the ports. The first was Pointe à Pitre in Guadeloupe, which I thought an ugly place, dirty, smelly and primitive. Mrs Lynn, Holly and I visited a little church and the priest came up to us and ordered us out of the church because Mrs Lynn was wearing a strapless dress and he said it wasn't fitting to wear that in a church. Lois was furious and said it was absolutely disgraceful and she was going to write to the Pope and report him. I am not sure if she did or not.

Disgraceful was one of her favourite words. Unbelievable was another. She was not pleased with some of the clothes that had been made for her in London by a dressmaker, possibly Madame Morell, and dictated a telegram which was to be sent from the ship, saying they were 'absolutely disgraceful'. Other telegrams were sent to other people, saying the same thing, and always that she had given instructions that had been ignored or not carried out to her satisfaction and that it was 'absolutely disgraceful'. She began to acquire a reputation on the ship, both with the crew and the other passengers, for being difficult, for being someone to avoid and yet at the same time to be fascinated by and curious about.

She had brought a crate of books with her – new books that had just come out, Booker prize winners and best sellers. These she had generously lent to other passengers and at first they were very pleased and grateful. But now she suddenly decided she wanted them back. "Delia, go into the lounge and get back all those books I lent."

So I went into the lounge and asked around saying, "Excuse me, but have you borrowed any of Mrs Lynn's books? She wants them back, so would you mind very much…"

I didn't need to go any further. "Take them, take them!" said various passengers, thrusting the books at me. Some they had started and half finished but now they all knew what Mrs Lynn was like and wanted to be shot of them as soon as possible.

The next port we came to was Fort de France in Guadeloupe. Paul had lunch with me in First Class and then Mr and Mrs Lynn went off together while Paul, Maureen, Holly and I went to the big hotel to swim in their pool. Maureen was a strange girl and I wondered if she was really as innocent as she said she was. She also became jealous of me, but for no reason. Although Paul and I spent time together, there was nothing between us.

He was strange too. He had taken umbrage with the Lynns, as he thought they had given him the brush off. Then Mrs Lynn suddenly invited him to come on to Jamaica and spend Christmas with us, instead of getting off the ship at Cartagena. I don't know if he really expected to stay until Christmas but certainly it should be for quite a long time to make it worthwhile for him to change his ticket and the expense this would entail. Perhaps he should have thought it over a bit more before accepting: my father always said guests were like fish, after three days they stank.

On the Monday we reached Trinidad. I was sad about this as Marion, Frank and others were getting off here. There was an outbreak of yellow fever, so the rest of the passengers were not allowed ashore.

The following day we got to La Guayra, Venezuela. Paul, Holly, Maureen and I set off together, but Maureen turned back, having a sulk, so we three caught a bus to Caracas. I was tremendously impressed with that rich and exotic city, at least I thought it was rich with its many fine shops, grand mansions and marble walkways. The road signs were very advanced, much more so than English ones of that time. You could practically learn to drive by looking at the road signs alone, ordering you to 'Change Down' or 'Accelerate round bend'. We did not see the poor quarters of the city, but we did see beggars, and I was shocked that Paul would walk right up to a beggar and take a photograph of him without permission or any feeling other than ruthlessly doing what he wanted. I thought it was callous but he said it was necessary for his future career as a reporter and photographer. Nevertheless, it was an interesting and enjoyable day.

It came to an abrupt end on returning to the ship: there was an almighty row, the worst yet. Mrs Lynn was furious because we had gone off without asking her permission. It was a mistake my being there, she said. I was behaving disgracefully. She would send a telegram to my parents, and I would have to be sent back to England, because she could not trust me to look after her little girl.

I lay in bed worrying for hours. I was letting down Auntie Ailsa, who would be upset, and my parents, who would be ashamed. But by the next morning Lois had forgotten it, and we came to Curaçao.

It was a clean and orderly place, like a little piece of Holland. We went shopping, and I was amazed at the amount of money she spent, buying quantities of clothes, hats, shoes, handbags and knick-knacks. It took three people to carry the parcels to the taxi that was to take us back to the ship afterwards. Chester Lynn pulled a face when he saw them all, but he didn't say anything. Maureen began to follow me around and did not leave me all evening. I thought I would be glad when we got to Kingston.

But there was still Cartagena, which we reached on Thursday 11th November, and where Paul should have disembarked. We went ashore, Maureen, Paul and I, plus two nurses, the Children's Nurse and La Fermière, the nurse from the ship's hospital. We went to a large and very beautiful hotel where we swam, but I was dejected because Paul started flirting with La Fermière. It was not as if I was in love with him, but my pride was hurt.

Later we met a Frenchman with whom I made friends, and who then attached himself to our party when we went on to a club to dance. There was a fete on in Cartagena and everyone was very happy except for me, but at least I had the Frenchman to dance with. We went back to the ship at 4 am and the next day I had a hangover. To make matters worse it was very rough and I had to do our packing. Trying to pack when you are feeling sick and the ship is rolling is no joke and I thought I would die – I would pack for five minutes, throwing things into our cases between the rolls and before the cases slid away out of reach, then lying down on my bunk for ten minutes more. At last it was finished, I felt better and was able to enjoy the ceremony of our last dinner.

And so on the 13th November, we reached Kingston. To our surprise there was an army of press people there to meet us, also the police and Robert Lake, the Lynn's solicitor, all because of Maureen trying to jump overboard to escape Kenzie McCool, her boyfriend. This was a big story both in Jamaica and back home, and I think Lois enjoyed being interviewed by the police and the press and telling them how she and Chester had become involved. Then Paul was interviewed, as he was the one who had pulled Maureen back from the ship rails. The whole McCool family were there on Kingston Docks to meet her and in the end she went off with them quite willingly and Robert Lake told us it was over and we could forget it. We had lunch on board and then Chester and Lois and Buffy went off in the first car and Paul, Holly and I followed. I was glad Paul would be coming with us as I felt he would be an ally. We reached the house in the twilight, to be met by a bevy of smiling servants.

The next day there was time to look around. Cape Clear was a beautiful white house built in the colonial style, with an enormous porch enclosed by pillars. The gardens surrounding it and the countryside beyond were splendid, there were hills above and valleys below where cattle grazed. From the road the house could be seen for miles, first on one side and then the other. It belonged to Sir Jock Jardine, and he had let it to the Lynns for six months, together with his staff of servants. All of these were Jamaican except for Harold, the head butler, who was Indian. Besides Harold, there was Ethline, an old tartar of a house-keeper who ruled her staff with a rod of iron. When I first met Ethline I was afraid of her, she looked so grim and reminded me of Mrs Danvers in Rebecca, and I felt she was criticizing everything I did. There was also William the steward and Stella who would be looking after Holly and me, and Hilda the cook, and Mildred, the laundress, Jean, a housemaid, and several other house and kitchen maids. The outside servants were Beris the chauffeur and Morgan the head groom and cattleman, and Roy the assistant groom. There were also several gardeners. Captain Lindsay Ellis was Sir Jock Jardine's agent, who lived on the adjoining estate. He came to lunch with us on the first day and gave Chester Lynn a long document listing all the things in the house, which I thought was called the Infantry.

Holly and I had a large room in one wing with a playroom underneath it. On our second day I got into trouble for typing in the sitting room after Holly had gone to bed so I went into the playroom and that was where I was to spend much of my time while I was at Cape Clear.

On the Monday, the Lynns went into Kingston and took Paul with them. While they were away, Harold the Indian butler showed me his house of which he was very proud, with its beautiful flowers on the drive. He introduced me to his wife and children.

In the evening Paul, Holly and I drove to swim at Robin's Bay. Paul kept pinching me and made bruises on my arms and shoulders, which were very embarrassing as Chester commented on them and asked me how I had come to get them and I had to say I didn't know. In any case, Lois was now bored with Paul and regretted her impulsive invitation to him to stay. It was for an unknown length of time – how long was he proposing to stay, she asked? Again I didn't know. She said he and Chester were like chalk and cheese and would I keep Paul away from them as much as possible, because she and Chester wanted to be alone. So when little Holly went to bed we went into the playroom and played endless games of Scrabble or chess, double demon, battleships, solitaire and patience. But although she had wanted me to go to the playroom and keep Paul away, she was not really pleased that I did. She was just angry that he was there.

The days passed and her dislike for Paul grew and grew. He could do nothing right, nor I, nor the servants. Sometimes I felt there was murder in their hearts. It would be the perfect situation for a murder, I thought, of the Agatha Christie sort – everyone with a motive and an opportunity.

Paul hated Mrs Lynn in a quiet but very strong way. For her part, she kept asking me what his plans were and when was he going, but I didn't dare ask him as I knew it had cost him a lot of money to change his ticket from Cartagena to Kingston and it would not have been worth his while not to stay. I also knew she had, on the spur of the moment, initially invited him to stay for Christmas and when Chester had objected, she had to deny having done so.

One day we went to a beach where we stayed quite a long time in the sun. It was a sweet little beach, full of shells, but perhaps we stayed too long, for in the evening Holly seemed to have a cough. Her mother was worried and a bit annoyed with me. Paul told her he had medical experience and he made suggestions as to what medicine should be given her. The next day she was worse and I made her have breakfast in bed. Paul took her temperature and it was 100. I told the Lynns and they asked Paul and me to look after her while they went to Kingston, which we did and either Stella or I stayed with her all the time. However Paul was worried she would get worse, and sure enough, she did. When Mrs Lynn came back she was really very angry, both with Paul and with me. She was furious, and in front of Stella. She said she and Chester did not agree that Paul knew anything whatever about medicine. He was then angry in turn, and felt very insulted. His pride was hurt and he said he was going to write to a doctor in Switzerland who would prove that he had medical knowledge - though of course he was not a doctor.

The next day Holly seemed better, but was still to stay in bed under the care of Stella, and Paul and I were allowed to go to Ocho Rios. We thought it was heaven to get away and that Cape Clear, the house, should be re-named Keep Clear. We discussed many things: Paul said no one had ever spoken to him like that and he would leave if it happened again; why had Chester ever married her, and how long would he stand it? We went to Jamaica Inn and had a picnic lunch and bathed and then had to dash back, wondering what would be the next explosion.

Luckily Holly was better, but Lois thought her illness was all my fault, mine and Paul's. She told me that all the staff disliked Paul and it was quite obvious he must go. He did not fit in. His manners were boorish (but what, I wondered, did she think of mine?) She would really like him to go now at once, just go, get out of their hair. She had thought he might take his driving licence and go round the island and take me with him, but the police station was locked so that could not happen. Instead we were sent to Ocho Rios for the day, where we started off by having lunch, which was very expensive. This was awkward as I had not been paid any salary and had no money, so Paul had to pay for me. He was already fed up, as this trip to Jamaica was costing him hundreds of pounds which he could not afford.

In the afternoon we drove up to Shaw Park Hotel where we explored the garden. It was extensive. There were exotic butterflies and fruit trees and brilliantly-coloured flowers, hibiscus and oleander, bougainvillea and jasmine and flame of the forest. There were little streams and bridges and wildernesses. It was beautiful, and I idly imagined we were Adam and Eve wandering in the Garden of Eden - except that we were not naked.

Later we had a swim at Silver Seas and Paul grabbed me and I lost the strap of my swimsuit in the sea. He kept pinching me and saying I was his slave and I thought he was very strange, but then sometimes he was silent for a long time and I wondered what he was thinking. We had no supper and sat and watched the sun set over the sea. It could have been romantic if we had been other people and not ourselves, but I was not sure Paul would ever be romantic with anyone. He was not a romantic sort of person. Did he look upon me as a friend, I wondered? No, we were not even friends.

When we got back to Cape Clear there was another terrible row. I was not sure what I was supposed to have done but I was told a telegram would be sent to my parents. This was the second time I had been told that. She said I was a very young twenty-year old and it was like looking after two children instead of one.

They had met some people and they asked them to stay for the weekend, Dennis Smith-Bingham and his friend June. June was very petite and rather pretty, like a beautifully dressed little doll. Mrs Lynn said June was his mistress but I was not to say anything about that, I was not to tell anyone they slept in the same bed. I was not sure who I was supposed to have told anyway.

Major Vaughan and his wife also drove over for the evening. They had three young children, all around the same age as Holly. I didn't like Major Vaughan. He said Holly must come over to their house and meet their children. Mary the governess would be there and would look after them, and I should help her. He was surprised I seemed to be treated as a member of the family. That was not a good idea, he said. Governesses were only one notch above servants and they should know their place, or they got above themselves. Mary, their governess, knew her place. She never ate her meals with them, she had a tray brought to her room. He suggested to Lois that I should have a tray brought to my room, so that I did not get above myself. Major Vaughan had a very loud voice and although he said this to Mrs Lynn I could hear the whole conversation. I was relieved to see she made no comment.

There was a calypso band that evening and after dinner we all danced on the terrace. Dennis asked Paul what his plans were and how long he intended to stay in Jamaica and he said till around Christmas. This made Mrs Lynn furious. Both she and Chester Lynn were fed up with Paul and wanted him gone. "Why on earth did you invite him?" said Mr Lynn. "It was an impulse," she said. "You must control these impulses," he said mildly.

Finally, on the 26th November the crunch came and Paul was told he would have to go. Mr Lynn told him they had other people coming to stay and he would have to be gone by the 5th December. That meant his time in Jamaica would have been three weeks. He was angry and said he would never have come had he known he was only to stay for three weeks, it was not worth it. I thought of my father's belief that guests were like fish and after three days they stank. Paul was certainly stinking as far as the Lynns were concerned. *I* was glad he was staying but was surprised he could not see this for himself.

The next day the Lynns went to Ocho Rios for the day and the whole house relaxed. On the 28th November they were invited to stay with the Vaughans. They took Holly with them so that she could meet the Vaughan children, and a car was lent to Paul so that he and I could drive to Port Antonio. It took us two hours to get there and we had a rafting expedition on the Rio Grande. It was beautiful on the river with the Blue Mountains rising up around us, and Paul became sentimental and said it was like our honeymoon.

We had a picnic lunch and then he drove on past Port Antonio to a spot with a steep bank on one side and a country path on the other. Here he stopped the car and tried to seduce me. I was horrified and tried to get away but we were very close to the bank on my side and Paul said if I didn't get back into the car he would shut the door on my legs and break them. I could see he meant it, he was quite ruthless. He really *would* break my legs. I saw some Jamaicans coming up the path and shouted out to them in panic and Paul said if I didn't shut up he would call them over and they could have a go first. I was shocked and afraid, for he was quite determined to have his way. So I slapped him hard across the face and this did the trick. He was furious with me, his pride was hurt and he drove off like a madman at a tremendous and terrifying speed. Not a word was spoken between us, and his face looked hard and set.

We drove down the steep hill to the famous Blue Lagoon, where the water is said to be the bluest in the world. It had rather a sinister connection, because apparently no one had swum there since a Canadian had drowned himself some three months before, but Paul and I didn't know that and we bathed at sunset with neither of us saying a word. Paul was still angry and I was struck dumb, but in other circumstances it could have been a beautiful experience.

The water was so clear you could see all the little fishes swimming about and different coloured seaweed and shells.

The sunset was lovely that evening, the whole sky was red like blood and the water reflected its glow. The palm trees stood out against the sky. You had to be there to see it, for a painting would be the sort you wouldn't want in your house, like paintings of bluebells in woods.

When we came out of the water it was twilight. We dried ourselves quickly and got dressed and then he drove dangerously fast on the way back. At one time the car skidded and got stuck and a group of Jamaicans came over and helped push the car and afterwards we drank beer and Coca Cola with them, and all this time never a word was spoken between us. Eventually we got back to Cape Clear.

Next day it transpired the clutch had been completely burnt out and the Lynns were not pleased. As for me, all I could think about was the astonishing events of the day and how very nearly I had lost my virginity.

CHAPTER SEVEN

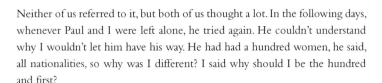

Neither of us referred to it, but both of us thought a lot. In the following days, whenever Paul and I were left alone, he tried again. He couldn't understand why I wouldn't let him have his way. He had had a hundred women, he said, all nationalities, so why was I different? I said why should I be the hundred and first?

It wouldn't have been so bad if he had loved me but I knew he didn't, he just wanted sex. I said I was saving myself for my future husband, and he said I was a romantic fool. He thought I was a prudish prig and I said it was the way I was brought up – nice girls didn't. And I thought about Fuzz, whose mother had said if she ever had a baby without being married she would be cast out, never to darken their doorstep again.

On the 1st of December Paul went into Kingston and booked his ticket from Kingston to Cartagena and early in the morning of the 5th he departed. On the night before he had tried for the last time and we had quarrelled and I had slapped his face and he had again been furious. Later we made it up and he kissed me but asked me not to see him off so I stayed in bed and listened as the car drove away. I felt sad, for apart from those times when we had so violently disagreed, he had been an ally, someone who understood what it was like living with the Lynns. He was strange but I had enjoyed his company and the innocent games we had played of chess and racing demon and croquet. So yes, I did miss him.

The day after he went, the Lynns went off for a couple of days to Montego Bay. "You are in charge," said Mrs Lynn, "Remember, if anything happens to Holly or to Buffy, it will be *your fault.*"

These words were to be said every time they went away and they haunted me: I began to have nightmares that I had found little Holly hanging by her

208

dressing gown cord from the banisters, and Buffy – that dear little dog – drowned, floating on the top of the swimming pool.

The staff relaxed when they went away and life, though uneventful, was pleasant. They told me how much they had liked Paul and how sorry they felt for me, and how sure they were of how nice Montego Bay would have been, but I was not upset at being left behind. Holly and I had begun our lessons in earnest. I had great ambitions for her to learn to read but I soon realised this would not be easy: she had a mind like quicksilver and her concentration span was zilch.

When the crate of books I had ordered from Foyles arrived I delved excitedly into them and brought out lots I thought Holly would like. There were story books and history and geography books and one on the flora and fauna of Jamaica with pictures. I started to read these to Holly but one day when she went to her mother's room to say good morning, she said she wanted to go back to the playroom to hear more of the book we had started. It was one of Rudyard Kipling's stories of Mowgli with the coloured pictures of Mowgli with Bagheera and Baloo. Another book she liked was a child's geography book, *The Children of the Ice and Snow*. Mrs Lynn was displeased that her daughter should want to leave *her* room and return to me. What could I be teaching her that could be more interesting than remaining with her mother? From then on, she told me, I was only to teach reading and tables, and we were to do this every day for three hours. In no time at all the lessons were horrible for both of us. As for learning tables, this was the deadliest thing and she refused point blank to even listen. I couldn't blame her.

There was one highlight in our daily routine, and that was riding. We went out most evenings. There were plenty of different places to ride and it was a great way to see the estate. Holly rode a small bay horse called Trigger and I rode Tina, another bay, who was lethargic and slow. The young groom Roy always came with us and led Holly on a leading rein. Most of the time I rode Tina but sometimes I was allowed to ride a chestnut called Calypso, who was a lovely horse and very fast. Roy and Holly would go on down the road and I would turn off and gallop over the hills, some of which were very steep, and explore the countryside.

After one of our rides Roy handed me a letter. It said he wished to be my lover, and not to let Mrs Lynn catch up with it. I wrote back saying this would not be possible as I had a boyfriend in England to whom I was engaged to be married. He said if the boyfriend was in England, he wouldn't know. I said, that wouldn't be very honourable, would it? He wrote another letter saying he was in love with me and he would be a very good lover. I would not regret it and my boyfriend would never know if I didn't tell him. I said, Please read my letter again for the situation hasn't changed, and this time, thankfully, he seemed to have taken it in.

One day when we came in at 5.30 after our ride, tea was brought out to me on a tray. *She* was furious and said they had had theirs at 4.30 when we had set off on our ride. She said that on the days I chose to ride I must just miss tea, and I agreed, because it did seem unfair that the cook should have to make it twice, and anyway I hadn't expected it. But Ethline came up to me and said she would bring it up to me on a tray in my room. I protested but it made no difference. She started to say that any of the servants would do anything for me, until I began to feel quite emotional. I'm sure they would have done anything for Paul too, for they had liked him despite what Mrs Lynn had said.

I wrote letters to my mother, which she kept. She later returned the Jamaica letters to me, and this is an extract from one dated 17th December 1954:

I would like to write to you more often but really these is not much time, although this may seem unbelievable. But I am not supposed to be free until after H is in bed which is about 7.30, and very often I am not. There are things to be done in the house, lists to be checked, things to be discussed and not a lot of time for writing letters... I gather you told Auntie Ailsa that I was not going down well here, and the other day Mrs Lynn said that this wasn't true and that I was not to worry in spite of the rows... I feel I am being fairly efficient in that I do everything I am told as well as I can, and I don't get any more rows for the things I do than anyone else does here. Everyone comes in for their share of blame, if they are connected in any way with the household – whether they be servants or overseers or managers of shops or customs officials – or governesses. Half of it is unfair. She is the sort of woman who, a few hundred years ago, would have been the Queen who cut off the head of the messenger who brought her bad news. The other day I was sent to Ocho Rios to collect two dresses from Mrs Lynch, her dressmaker – and told I must be back by 1.30 for lunch. Alas, I discovered the dressmaker had gone to Kingston for the day – 40 miles away and the dresses were not there. If we had had a telephone at Cape Clear we could have phoned before setting out to make sure of collecting them. I returned feeling slightly trembly and was given hell. "How dare you!" she said, "I'm not interested in where the dressmaker had gone, I told you not to come back without the dresses, and you have disobeyed me."

A couple of days later I went shopping for her in Kingston. This is the third time I have been and I have always enjoyed going, but the shopping list has always been long enough for several days, and it has often been difficult. You know how shopping for other people is hard – well here as you can imagine, it is impossible. I have to buy their Christmas presents for other people, or material for cushions and curtain covers and there is very little choice. I ask myself, is it too expensive? Is it the right size? Is this too dull, on the other hand is it too bright? And of course there's so little time to do things and whatever I get is bound to be wrong.

This is a shopping list I had given to me recently:

3 dozen tins Heinz Oxtail soup	5 packets dog biscuits
28 Heinz vegetable soup	1 packet flour
18 Campbell tomato soup	22 tins peanuts
11 chicken soup	12 tins golden syrup
1 celery soup	12 tins peaches
6 dozen tins Consomme	4 tins pears
6 Heinz beef noodles	10 tins pineapple
1 doz C&B beef soup	10 tins fruit cocktail
10 tins Oxo	5 bottles cocktail cherries
4 bottles C&B mayonnaise	5 tins baking powder
11 bottles Heinz chilli sauce	3 packets Bisto
5 bottles Lea & Perrin sauce	4 packets gelatine
6 bottles chutney	7 pots paste
5 bottles Horseradish sauce	2 bottles green colouring
2 bottles mint sauce	2 bottles pink colouring
11 bottles olives	11 tins white pepper
12 bottles pickled onions	12 tins black pepper
6 tins apple sauce	10 tins ground nutmeg
30 tins cocktail sausages	3 tins mixed spice
32 tins palethorpe sausages	3 tins curry powder
19 tins asparagus	1 tin mixed biscuits
9 tins champignons	1 box onions
9 tins baked beans	35 tins Red Stripe beer
18 tins golden corn	22 tins dry ginger ale
4 doz tins sardines	38 tins coco cola
9 tins Pate de Foie	46 Canada Dry soda water

13 packets spaghetti

5 packets macaroni

4 tins mustard

6 tins Nestles cream

6 tins coffee

5 tins tea

3 jars strawberry jam

2 jars marmalade

12 jars guava jelly

2 packets mixed peel

2 cases Cider

20 bottles tonic water

23 bottles lime juice

18 bottles Cognac brandy

10 bottles Dry Martini

2 bottles Sweet Vermouth

7 bottles Rum

6 bottles Whisky

2 bottles Kirsch

1 bottle Cointreau

9 cases Gin

7 cases white wine

And that's just the grocery list.'

(Looking at this list now, you notice strange numbers of the items – such curious decisions had been made. For instance, why 11 chicken soup and not 12, why 11 bottles of chilli sauce, why 9 pots of paste, 12 tins of black pepper but 11 of white? It must have been a nightmare for the staff in the store to count out these extraordinary numbers, and indeed, it took me two hours to check everything, sort them out and put them all away.)

The letter continues:

Anyhow, on this occasion I was sent for and told that I had bought frozen kippers instead of frozen Dover soles. I was rather surprised because I had picked them out in the shop myself, but I said nothing. The remarks were pretty cutting – phrases like "Of course there's no use in trusting you to do anything right. I should have known you'd make a mess of it. What were you thinking of?" were thrown at me. Half an hour later it was discovered that the Dover soles had been put at the back of the fridge, and the bill for them with my signature was on her desk. But of course apology is a little word we don't know here. Sometimes I think it's hard enough to do things right without being blamed for things which aren't my fault as well. But we all come in for this sort of thing and it's all right if you keep expecting it at any time. One good thing, there's never a dull moment! But I do feel worried about the servants who don't understand it at all. Strangely enough I think they hate her more when she is angry with me than when she is angry with them. They are inclined to come to me and sympathise which, as you can imagine, is very awkward. I have to smile but get up and walk away – it would be dreadful if Mr and Mrs Lynn thought I encouraged them. If they are not being sorry for me, they are worrying about themselves. Once Ethline, the housekeeper came to me and said she couldn't go on, and I had to tell her to keep on doing her best and not to worry because Mrs L was really quite satisfied with her. This, I fear, was not altogether true – because Mrs L thinks the servants are an idle bunch who laugh at us up their sleeves when they think they have got out of doing a job of work. I don't agree with her. Most of them are good old loyal servants and are most willing to do what they can to please. But with her it is like whipping and whipping a horse and if it puts on a spurt, whipping it all the more until at last its spirit is broken and it doesn't care any more. They still do their work but they are listless and all the happy enthusiasm which greeted us when we arrived has disappeared...'

The first to break was Harold. He seemed to me the perfect butler, highly trained, anticipating our every wish, courteous and gentle, but he didn't have much sense of humour and for some reason Mrs Lynn took against him. He irritated her profoundly and she decided he was useless. The poor man could do nothing right, and William the steward and under butler was promoted over his head. William was brash and cheeky but Mrs L thought he was wonderful. It must have been very hard for Harold to take his orders from the younger man. After a while he began to lose his confidence, he stuttered and made more mistakes. Finally his nerves broke down and he had to go off sick.

Ethline too was out of favour. No longer the grim-faced housekeeper who had reminded me of Mrs Danvers and whom I had thought frightening when we had first arrived, she was now a scared shadow of herself. She too was demoted from her job and reduced to just an ordinary servant. Ethline now had to take her orders from Stella, whom I did not trust. She still looked after Holly and me and was quite liable to tell tales about me to Mrs Lynn. Sometimes Stella would come into our room and say, "Missee Lynn want to see you, Miss Despair," and I suspected she had revealed the bad things I had done, or omitted to do. Whatever went wrong someone always had to be blamed, and more often than not it was me.

Sometimes it was Holly who would tell me. After saying goodnight to her mother, Holly would come into our room in a state of fear and say, "Oh Delia – Mummy wants to see you and she's *very, very angry!*" We would then both burst into tears and I would have to dry my eyes and go to Mrs Lynn's room and face the music. There were so many things I had seemingly done wrong. Holly could be very sweet and she would say, "Are you sad because Mummy was cross with you? I feel very sad about it. Mummy never seems to be satisfied, does she?"

Oh, how I wanted to agree — but I could not. Instead I had to say, somewhat priggishly, "But you see I was wrong, and I deserved it."

Sometimes there were periods when I was in favour. Mrs Lynn would be surprisingly generous and nice to me. There was row after row after row and then, suddenly, a lull. I was all right, Holly was getting on well, I was a success, they were, after all, glad they had employed me.

And there was someone else to blame.

CHAPTER EIGHT

On the 12th December the first of the Christmas guests arrived: it was Mrs Kavanagh, Lois's mother. She was a stately-looking old lady with white upswept hair and a soft Southern Irish accent. Great preparations had been made to ensure her bedroom and bathroom had every comfort. An armchair was brought in from another room, and a writing desk on which writing paper and pens were placed, together with a selection of books and magazines. There were flowers in a pretty jug on a side table, and a trolley with tea and coffee making facilities, a tin of biscuits and chocolates in a silver bon-bon dish. There was a radio on the bedside table, and in the bathroom a selection of toiletries including Roget and Gallet carnation soap with matching talcum powder and body lotion. A soft white towelling bathrobe was laid out on the bed. These preparations were an eye opener for me. Why did my mother never prepare the spare room for our guests in the same way? Other than putting in a vase of flowers she would not have dreamt of providing all these luxuries.

I was not sure I liked Mrs Kavanagh at first. She seemed an interfering old busybody who was always turning up and asking me questions, and was shrewd enough to know if she was answered evasively and suspicious enough to find fault with everything. Oh Lord, I thought, not you as well. I had thought it would be nice having her there and that she would be my ally, instead of which she was constantly criticising me and adding to my trials. I thought she was an irritating old woman and now there were two people I must be wary of.

Her first day was dreadful, with rows all the time and no riding because Holly had taken a long time over lunch and I was blamed. We enjoyed riding so much and it seemed to me this was stopped for any excuse at all. In the evening the Cargills came to dinner. Maurice Cargill was the editor of Jamaica's main newspaper, the *Daily Gleaner,* and the meal started off well, but then Mrs L suddenly turned on me and said Holly was not learning anything in the way of lessons and the books I had bought were too expensive and too old for her. I was astonished. Barely a week ago she had thought the opposite and was pleased with me. I could not understand what had happened to make her change her mind and felt angry – but of course I could not say anything. The next day Holly and I had terrible struggles over her tables but she would not concentrate and could not get them into her head.

On the Wednesday the Lynns took Mrs Kavanagh into Ocho Rios for the day and Holly went with them. It was a relief to be alone. Then Captain Ellis came for lunch and it was interesting to talk to him. He promised he would take me riding one morning, if I was allowed to go. After lunch he took me for a lovely drive all around the estate. It extended for miles, much further than I had imagined. He said his technique was to treat people as they treated him – be charming or tough, just as they were to him. A good idea if you had the courage, I thought. I certainly didn't have it, not that sort of courage.

A few days later the Vaughan children came over with Mary, the governess. The children all got on very well together and I was delighted to meet Mary. She was only thirty years old and very pretty. We had a long talk and she told me her history. To some extent we were both in the same boat but her situation was much worse than mine and I felt very sorry for her: she had had a tragic life, for her husband had run off and left her penniless in Jamaica. She was then employed by Major Vaughan as his secretary and governess to his children, and had been working for him for two years. She told me she was deeply unhappy living with the Vaughans but there was nowhere else for her to go. It was lonely, for she never met anyone, not even allowed to meet the guests who were invited to dinner, and was restricted to her room most of the time. She planned to leave in July 1955 if she could save enough money by then. We exchanged addresses and hoped we might meet some time in the future when we were both free. A few days later Holly and I paid a return visit to Brimmer Hall where the Vaughans lived, however I found Mrs Vaughan difficult to talk to and was disappointed that Mary had to stay in the office, so I didn't see her.

A week later Mrs and Mrs Lynn went off to Montego Bay to meet Miranda and Merle, the two older girls who were flying out for Christmas. Little Holly was spending the day with the Vaughan children, and I was supposed to be free, but had to spend most of the time putting up Christmas decorations. In the evening Beris and I went to Brimmer Hall to fetch Holly, who had had a lovely time, and when she had gone to bed Mrs Kavanagh and I had a polite evening on our own. Then suddenly she changed. It was as if she had been putting me through some sort of examination for her own benefit, and had now satisfied herself that I was all right. Next day it rained so much that Holly and I were not allowed to ride the ponies – there had been quite a row about that already. So Mrs Kavanagh and I went into Annotto Bay together to do some Christmas shopping. That evening I found myself quite liking her. I found she had a good sense of humour.

The two girls, Miranda and Merle, had a very tiring journey over, and as the plane was delayed 24 hours, their mother was in a great panic. They finally arrived on the 23rd December, in the evening. I was in Kingston at the time, doing all the shopping for Christmas in the way of Christmas tree, turkey etc and I found they had arrived when I got back. I soon got to know and like Miranda and Merle very much indeed, and Arthur Prothero, the friend who had brought them, was an old dear. He was a Falstaff-like character, a great big jolly man with a beard and a moustache. He could dance the calypso beautifully, had a gift for mimicry and was very funny. He should have been discovered by Hollywood for he was almost as good as Danny Kaye.

For Mrs Kavanagh, the honeymoon period was now over. She was quite well aware her daughter thought her interfering so she never made suggestions, knowing they would be turned down on principle. If she had any good ideas she would tell them to me – I being not out of favour just then – or get someone else to tell them. Sometimes poor old Mrs Kavanagh was snubbed whenever she opened her mouth. Much of the furniture that had been so lovingly put in her room before her arrival was now moved out; some was put into Arthur Prothero's room and some into the Smith-Binghams', for they too had been invited to stay for Christmas.

While they had been away at Montego Bay, Captain Ellis was kind enough to invite me out on Christmas Eve. He said he could get me an invitation to Sir Harold Mitchell's cocktail party and would take me on somewhere for dinner if I could have permission. I was surprised and delighted to be allowed to go, as it was the first time I had been invited out since our arrival. I enjoyed the cocktail party very much, as Lindsay took me around and introduced me to lots of people. They all knew each other, as most had lived in Jamaica for years and it was very interesting to meet them, if a little embarrassing on many occasions; I realised Mrs L did not go down well and many a rude comment was passed before someone let on that I was of the same household.

After the party I was taken on to dinner at the Shaw Park Hotel, and after that we went on to Jamaica Inn and met Donald Pringle, whose father built

Cape Clear and some twenty-five other great houses in Jamaica. The Pringles were an enormous family and one of the oldest living there. After Jamaica Inn we went to the Tower Isle Hotel where I had gone with Paul, with its beautiful 'Garden of Eden'. All of this was the spice of life and there was only one drawback: Lindsay was much older than me and although he was very polite and kind, he made me feel rather uncomfortable.

We didn't get back till 2.45 am, one hour of which was spent driving back from Tower Isle. To my dismay I found myself locked out completely – not a window left unlatched on the ground floor. Lindsay managed to waken Hilda the cook in the servants' quarters and she let me in. I crept upstairs feeling a little apprehensive, and more so on going into our bedroom to find little Holly not in her bed. This was ominous - where could she be?

The next morning it was Christmas Day, but for me there was hell to pay for I had blotted my copybook once again. She was furious with me for getting back so late. I was not a fit person to look after a little girl and they had had to put up a bed for her in her grandmother's room. I had apparently kept them up late when on that night of all nights *she* had decided to go to bed early. I hadn't meant them to stay up of course, but had expected to be able to slip in quite easily.

Although Chester forgave me and the others were very nice, I was ignored by Lois, and sat in the playroom all morning feeling miserable. There was to be a party that night and I was supposed to help, but perhaps I was to be banished, I didn't know what would happen. After I had done up my Christmas presents I tried to read but could not concentrate. At 12 o'clock I put my presents round the tree and I apologised to Mrs Lynn. Luckily she accepted, and I was forgiven.

The present-giving took place after lunch. The children had some lovely presents and were very excited. I gave Holly a book and a Japanese tea service with a blue willow pattern design on it which I found in an old Japanese bazaar shop in Kingston. It was difficult to think of something she had not got, and the same applied to Mrs Lynn, to whom I finally gave a leather writing case. Surprisingly she hadn't got one, and she even used it subsequently. My present from the Lynns was to be a dress in a material of my choice to be made up by Mrs Lynch, the dressmaker. I was also given a very attractive black basket-work evening bag with a bird perched on top, and a stick of Bond Street frozen cologne. All afternoon I did the decorations in the dining room and then the Cargills arrived. Maurice Cargill dressed up as Father Christmas and all the children around the compound came up and each received a gift. I wrote to my parents about it:

The delight on their faces when they saw the large lighted up Christmas tree and all the decorations, then received presents from Father Christmas was indescribable and well worth all the trouble we had gone to in the preceding days. It had certainly been a lot of work with long intervals of waiting around for orders, or re-doing things until everything was just so. But when she decides to give happiness to people she puts everything into it. Her generous gestures could not be more whole-hearted and I like her for that. All is well as long as people are happy through her doing and not through their own, but at any rate a lot of people would never have been able to anticipate the pleasure they could give to the handful of kids around here by giving them a share in the festivities too.

After dinner Charlie Pringle and his wife Marjorie came over from their house Grays Inn, and brought with them their niece Patricia and two young army officers who were staying there. We had a calypso band and danced on the terrace. They were the first people I had seen of my own age since Paul, and we had a most enjoyable evening. I can't for the life of me remember the name of the one I was dancing with most (it was Roy) but he was quite pleasant. Patricia, or Patsy, as she is called, is a ground hostess with British West Indian Airways and lives in Kingston. She is 23 and very pretty. She has given me her phone number so if I am in Kingston again on my own I can look her up. At the end when they were going, she asked Mrs L if I could come to a party at Grays Inn the next day, starting at 10.30 and lasting till around 2.30 after lunch. I was allowed to go. It turned out that Ian Something- Brown, one of the army officers, was married but that his wife had been unwell, and so had not come the night before. I gathered that his marriage was not going too well and imagine Patsy could be the cause of this. Ian had a very fine singing voice and also played the guitar and piano beautifully. He gave a performance which went down very well with everyone but his wife, who sat away from everyone looking irritated beyond words – she is apparently very jealous of his musical abilities. I had talked to her earlier and liked her. They also live near Kingston. She asked me to contact her if I was free, as did Patsy and the two army officers who said I should ring up next time I go to Kingston. It was a funny time for a party but fun. The Charlie Pringles have a beautiful house and garden, and we swam in the pool and had a delicious rum punch on the lawn.....

Two days after this, an American family came to call – Mr and Mrs Brindsley and their son John, and asked us all to a party they were giving two nights before New Year's Eve for John, who was going to be 21. I thought John was quite nice but Mrs Lynn does not like Americans and although I was allowed to go, they sent a telegram excusing themselves. They were out that day and were late getting back so I could not start until 9.30 and did not arrive until 10.15 but that did not matter as it was to be a late party and the buffet supper did not start until 11 o'clock – but unfortunately I had to be back by 11.30 so that I would not keep Beris the chauffeur up late as he had an early start to make the following morning. Beris is a nice old chap and a very loyal servant, and he was very upset that I could not stay longer. He said he often had to stay up late, and 7.30 in the morning was not early for him, and he said he would wait till 3 a.m. if I wanted, but I dared not disobey and repeat the Christmas Eve episode. It might have been hardly worth going but for the fact that I thoroughly enjoyed my hour, and the Brindsleys were not so hurt as at least one member from Cape Clear had shown up. There was dancing and at 11 o'clock the buffet supper started, followed by toasts to John and speeches. I was seated in the place of honour next to him and spent all the time with him, which I did not mind as I found he had a great sense of humour. He had just finished three and a half years in the US Navy doing national service. To my horror I suddenly discovered it was 25 minutes past 11, and had to dash off feeling I am sure, just what Cinderella must have felt when she had to rush away from the ball at midnight. I was late – but luckily nothing was said.

There was to be a party on New Year's Eve at Cape Clear, and I had to go into Kingston to buy all the things we needed for it. Arthur Prothero came with me as he wanted to see Kingston. The road to Kingston was very twisty and rough and Arthur felt rather car-sick. We did the shopping, but I was terrified I had not got everything as the shops were shutting early. We met a charming man, Mr Macrae, known as Mac, for drinks and had lunch afterwards at the Balcony Inn. In the afternoon we visited the Hope Botanical Gardens, which were famous for all the beautiful and exotic flowers and shrubs there. Arthur asked me how I was getting on and if I was happy, and I found myself confiding in him and telling him the true state of affairs. He was very kind. He said he was on both sides of the fence as it were, and he warned me I should never look as if I were enjoying myself.

All week there was a great deal of preparation to do for the New Year's Eve party. Holly was to stay with the Vaughan children so that she would not be kept awake. Major Vaughan suggested I go over to Brimmer Hall and help look after the children, as he and his wife and his sister and her three children who were staying for Christmas, were coming to Cape Clear; but luckily for me, Mrs Lynn said no, she did not see why I should miss their one party. I was very relieved and thought how I disliked Major Vaughan and poor *poor* Mary having to work for him. Holly and I moved out of our room as an American middle-aged couple were staying for the weekend, also Dennis and June, and we had a full house. She went to the Vaughans and I moved in with Miranda and Merle, which was fun, like being in the school dorm.

I spent the afternoon of the party decorating the house and making lots and lots of fruit salad. Then I changed into the new dress Mrs Lynch had made for me. It had a bell skirt and a halter neck, and the material was ivory shantung with a lustrous sheen. John Brindsley and his parents came to the party, also Noel Coward and John Gielgud. John Brindsley knew Noel Coward and introduced me to him. I liked him very much – he was in a good mood and very amusing, although he was wearing rather odd clothes. He stayed and talked to us for ages and we discussed the kind of people who were always coming up to him and gushing over him, as several did at this party, and when they did he winked at us. One woman drank a glass of champagne and threw it, glass and all, over the side of the veranda.

I did not like John Gielgud much as he seemed bored stiff – though perhaps one could not blame him – and his fishy eyes kept shifting about the room. He seemed a cold fish, disinterested in anyone but himself, unlike Noel Coward, who was warm and kind and genuinely interested in people.

Much later I read Noel Coward's account of that party. He did not mention any names but I knew who he was talking about. He wrote:

January 1st 1955
The first day of the New Year. We drank it in last night at a curious party consisting of most of the locals, ghastly and fun at the same time. Our hostess was not only pissed but raving mad, but there was something about her that I liked. Our host, younger than she, was podgy, good-looking and, I thought, a pig but I may be misjudging him. (I thought he *was*.)

Years later still when I was working at Ringway Airport, I saw that Noel Coward was flying from Manchester to Paris. I was checking in the flight and I determined to speak to him. He came up to the Paris flight desk and typically he was alone without an entourage. There was a long queue but it was a chance in a million – I asked him if he remembered a party at Cape Clear in Jamaica on New Year's Eve. He was tremendously interested and said he remembered it well. We then had a long chat, despite all the passengers queueing out of the door.

Back to that night – the night of 31st December 1954 - the party was deemed a great success. The decorations looked wonderful and the food was excellent, though I was much teased about the fruit salad that never seemed to get finished up. The calypso band was in good form, and the members got rather drunk. I spent all the evening with John and we danced cheek to cheek and later had a bit of a smooch outside in a hidden part of the garden. He was very gallant and complimentary to me. He said I was cute and a nice kid and I must remember that, when things were getting me down.

Mrs Lynn had one of her impulsive moments: she thought John Brindsley and I seemed to be getting on quite well and just as his parents and he were leaving, she asked him to stay the night – so he did, and slept on the balcony outside Arthur's room. The next day was very pleasant. Mrs Lynn was charming to me and as Holly had gone away I was considered free.

In the evening Arthur drove John and me over to his parents' house. John was leaving the next day for New York, and as it had been his first Christmas home in four years, I think his mother was a little upset that he had spent his second last night away from home. Even so, she asked me if I would stay the night with them and drive with them to Kingston the next evening when they saw John off, saying they would then drive me back to Cape Clear. As the Vaughans had decided to keep Holly with them until the following Wednesday I was rather tempted to accept the invitation, but did not as I was sure it would have gone down badly if I had. So we said goodbye and he asked me to write to him. He also invited me to come and stay with him in America if ever I could, though I didn't quite gather whereabouts as his home was in Jamaica. Did he mean his student digs?

Altogether Holly stayed six days with the Vaughans, which was a wonderful holiday for her with the three children there, and also for me. I had grown fond of her but it was quite a good time for a break from both points of view. During this time Miranda and Merle asked me to go on sleeping with them in their room, and it was like having two younger sisters. Merle, aged eleven, was clearly her mother's favourite and this was apparent to Miranda, the elder girl, who was thirteen, and at an awkward age. She was apt to get into moods and would have tantrums over nothing, but I felt under this bossy and domineering front she was sensitive and shy, and I felt sorry for her. I liked both girls very much, we had fun together and laughed a lot.

I had received two letters from John, one by return of post, and the girls teased me endlessly about him. We got up late and when it was raining we lay on our beds and read or talked; we spent quite a lot of time swimming and went for several rides through the Jamaican bush, sometimes down over rocks, crossing streams and over the hills. One day we all went off to Jamaica Inn and bathed at the beach there, and then on to Tower Hill. We played croquet and a sort of squash and went on Merle's pogo stick. Merle asked me if I would stay on with them when I went back to England which was a little awkward. I said I liked being with them but that I would want to go home at weekends, and that little Holly would soon be too old for me to be able to take the responsibility of teaching her. Merle understood perfectly. After all, in this job there was no place for any other life.

Unreasonable demands were made, even for them. At night when we were asleep in bed, their mother was apt to come in suddenly and switch on the main lights and demand they should wake up and talk to her. They would be almost drugged, in a deep sleep and having the very bright light switched on and shone into their eyes made them blink and want to bury their faces in the pillow, but if she wanted to talk to them she would force them to wake up. That was almost cruel, I thought.

CHAPTER NINE

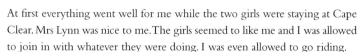

At first everything went well for me while the two girls were staying at Cape Clear. Mrs Lynn was nice to me. The girls seemed to like me and I was allowed to join in with whatever they were doing. I was even allowed to go riding.

On the 6th January Holly returned from Brimmer Hall, and the two younger Vaughans, Victoria and David, came with her to stay for a couple of days. She had so enjoyed her time with them and they all played very well together. On the 9th everyone went off to Port Antonio to stay with Denis and June, everyone but Holly and me. I was not sorry – I loved the peace of living by ourselves at Cape Clear, just for that short time. We did lessons every day, sitting in the hammock. Then we swam in the pool and had lunch at the back of the house overlooking the pigeon loft, and I told Holly an on-going story about Mr and Mrs Pigeon, refusing to continue until she ate another mouthful. In this way she soon ate up all her lunch.

She had her afternoon rest, then we went riding, Roy leading Holly so that I could have a glorious gallop over the rocks. One day Lindsay Ellis came to lunch, bringing his sister, who had recently arrived from England, and Geoffrey the piano player also came. Another day Harold's child Beverley came to tea with Holly. Every evening I wrote short stories, and it was wonderful to be as free as the air. The nights were warm and clear with a slight breeze. I would sit on the veranda and smell the sweet, almost sickly smell of the jasmine that grew all around us, and listen to the croaking of frogs and the sound of a million crickets.

I was reading *My Brother's Keeper* by Marcia Davenport, which had a great effect on me, for it concerns two old men who hoard everything and never throw anything away ever until finally they are living between tunnels of old newspapers that are stacked from floor to ceiling. And then one has a stroke and the other one, who is blind, dies of starvation and their bodies are discovered long after, buried in the tunnels. It doesn't sound very cheerful but it made me think with horror how easily this could happen, especially to our family who were great hoarders. I thought, I *must* warn Badger. I remember it vividly to this day.

On the 13th January everyone came back from Port Antonio, and the next day I went crayfish fishing in the river with Arthur Prothero and three of the servants, Harold, Ricky and Roy. It was one of the most exciting things I had ever done. We went at 9.30 in the evening, and they carried great torches made of bamboo sticks filled with paraffin and stuck up one end with earth. Then we had to wade through the river which in places came up to our waists, and there were great rocks to climb up. At first Harold said he could not take me: it was dangerous for I would not be able to climb the rocks, so I said that I was used to climbing mountains in Switzerland. This was quite untrue but anyway I got on all right and it was tremendously exciting every time we caught a crayfish. You had to watch the water and when you saw one, pierce it with a spear, grab it so that it would not bite (as they could bite a man's hand off) and shove it into a closed bag. I was not a bit good at spotting them but Harold, being Indian, was very quick. He looked like a cat, creeping over the rocks. I felt rather as if I was in one of those Hollywood jungle films, but luckily no snakes or spiders pounced on us. Nor did Clark Gable turn up... We got back at 12.30 a.m. with about a dozen crayfish of different sizes.

On the 18th January Chester's mother, Mrs Lynn senior, arrived. Once more a lot of time was spent in preparing her room, and more things were removed from Mrs Kavanagh's room including most of the toiletries. Mrs Lynn senior was charming. However, at dinner there was another terrible row: Miranda and I had gone into Kingston and it appeared I had omitted to get the right things – I had tried my best but had found the list impossible. Lois was very angry with me and I burst into tears, and cried as if my heart would break. Arthur Prothero was very supportive, as were the servants, especially Mildred, but I was inconsolable and next day my eyes were still puffed up and sore. Then Lois made it up and was amazingly nice to me. For a little while I was off the hook, but the servants were not and were having a rough time. They had to endure prolonged rows that were awful and very upsetting. They were accused of being lazy, good-for-nothing and useless. Harold in particular suffered and his nerves broke down. Once again he had to return to hospital, and I visited him there a few days later. I said I hoped he would soon be back with us at Cape Clear, but he said he didn't know if he would ever be well enough.

My mother wrote and asked me why I never mentioned Chester Lynn. I told her that he was, as everyone thought (everyone but Noel Coward, that is) very nice, kind and understanding. He was also shy and reserved and there were many things in him that I found difficult to understand. Every now and then he called me to his study to give me my wages and I noticed his hands shaking uncontrollably, and assumed this was because of all the alcohol both he and Lois were drinking. I tried not to come into contact with him too much for that would not be wise, but Aunt Ailsa had said I could rely on him to help me if anything went wrong. Yet how could I? Things were going wrong all the time but I could not let Aunt Ailsa down, nor my parents.

On the 21st we went to dinner on the adjoining estate of Fort George with Lindsay and his sister. The house was sweet, and full of beautiful things. Lois said it was the sort of house where one should spend one's honeymoon. There was a party at Cape Clear the next night but I did not enjoy it, for I found Lindsay's attentions embarrassing.

Later Mr and Mrs Lynn collared me and told me Lindsay was in love with me and his sister was going blind and I *had* to be nice to him. It was practically an order. Did they realise how uncomfortable I felt with him? I had the feeling they did. How I wished it could be different, for he was a really kind and decent man. He told me he was worried about my position with the Lynns and I was to send him a telegram if there should be trouble at any time.

Three days later I was invited to spend the day at Fort George, this time by myself. I went off early in the morning, and he and I rode all over the estate. It was a beautiful day and we rode for miles. At one time we had to cross and re-cross a winding river which kept coming across our path, and there was no more delicious feeling than the cold water splashing against our hot feet as we rode over. I was given quite an intensive geography lesson about the fruit, trees, crops and animals of Jamaica which was very interesting. There were superb views from the hills. I did enjoy the ride, and even more so if I had been with someone else, Glen for instance, and I hated myself for being so ungrateful. We got back and had lunch with his sister, who had come to stay for a few months. She was nice, and it was tragic that she was going blind. I was not sure if she knew or not. After lunch we had a rest, as everyone did in Jamaica, and then a drive to see over the Great House. I enjoyed the day, in spite of my stupidity, and I don't believe he realised it.

The following days passed uneventfully. Lessons with Holly continued, she was in a good-tempered and easy mood, and I felt she was making progress at last. We swam in the pool, and went riding most days, provided it was not raining and Morgan was able to take us. Sometimes we went up to a field where there were bulls. Once I went with Holly to see a new-born calf and the mother cow ran at us and Morgan was quick to come into the field and drive it away. He said we should never go near a cow that had a newly-born calf, it was extremely dangerous as they were likely to gore us with their great horns. Another day Holly and I went to a Jamaican market, and at dusk it was all lit up with candles.

The rest of the household went out to dinner and parties with various people we had met, including the Ronald Grahames, whom I had liked so much when I had met them at Cape Clear, and I felt a little sad at staying behind. Later the Grahames asked me why I hadn't come too, but I hadn't been told the invitation was for me as well. Arthur told me that invitations to me caused little jealousies in the house. He warned me again never to look as if I were happy.

As for Arthur himself, he was becoming increasingly irritated. He and Chester went on a three-day fishing expedition to Port Antonio but it was cut short – they were hauled back after two days. Lois did not like Chester doing things without her. She and the two girls went to fetch them and they all got back tired and dispirited. One night at dinner there was such tension between Lois and Arthur that I thought there would be an explosion. There was murder in the air.

On Saturday, 5th February Arthur and I went into Kingston to do some shopping. We set off very early at half-past seven, before the household was awake, and had a glorious day away from everything. He was very good company and it was fun being with him. For a change there wasn't a huge shopping list, so we were relatively free. We went to the Jamaica Inn and had a delicious rum punch with lime and chipped ice. On the way back we stopped at a dairy where there was a café service. We sat in the car and a tray was pegged onto the window, and we ordered chicken sandwiches and enormous cherry milk shakes with cream and ice cream and cherry syrup which were brought out to us. Arthur chuckled and said how shocked *certain people* would be if only they could see us, they would think it *very* vulgar - only the Ritz or Claridges for them, he said, and what a lot they would miss. It was such a very good day and I felt sad that he and the two girls would soon be leaving us.

Before they went there was a party at Cape Clear, to which the Ronald Grahames came, also Maurice Cargill, Mr Macrae, the Pringles and the Stuarts.

All Monday I helped with the packing. On Tuesday everything was piled into the car, and we all said goodbye. Then, with Chester driving and Lois beside him, Arthur and the two girls set off for Montego Bay, where they would spend the night before flying back to London.

Holly and I were left behind with the two Mums. We played Canasta, but we felt curiously flat.

Granny Cooper when young

Grandpa Cooper

My parents

Granny Cooper

My mother

DD

Parents, Badger and DD

Badger and Bretton

Badger and Bretton in the sea   Badger and DD in the sea

DD, Pop and Badger on beach

Bretton and Badger   Susan Bayly, Bretton and Badger

DD and Susie Roberts (1st best friend)

James and Richard Van den Berg with DD

Bretton, Winks, DD and Badger

Richard Van den Berg and DD

Bretton, DD, Auntie Joan P
and Badger

Auntie Joan Priestley

Badger and DD

Nice gardener at Fownhope

Westwood School (DD 2nd left, 2nd row)

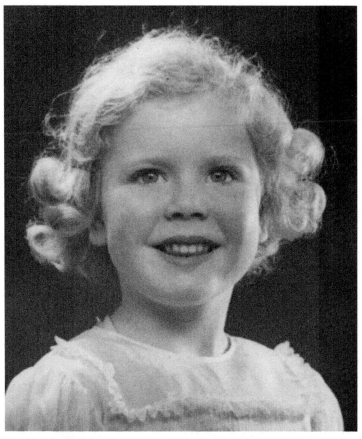

DD

Susan Bayly, Granny and Winks

Winks and Sue Bayly

Robin, DD, Badger and Sue Bayly

Yorkshire - DD with sheep

Margot (my second best friend)
in Yorkshire

DD, Wendy and Jasper in Whitby

Jonathan and Badger in Whitby

Mum, DD and
Mary Ann Cat in Yorkshire

DD and Jasper in Whitby

Wendy, Badger, Jasper, Jonathan and DD

Badger and DD at the
farm, Kirbymoorside

Ditchling, Sussex. DD, Chips, Pops, Damps and Ali

Badger, Elizabeth,
DD and Clive

My cousins
Clive and Elizabeth

Josephine (best friend in Ditchling)

Polyfoto pictures of DD with Twinkle

Twinkle (always known as The Cat)   Cousin Jean

51 Shirley Drive, Hove

Junior House (Millfield, Keswick): Fuzz back row 2nd left, DD 3rd left, Jane Bowman in front of DD, Wally, most hated matron, 3rd row 7th LHS

Tilda - housemistress, Jane Bowman 2nd left, Fuzz & DD

Roedean, Brighton, Junior House

Junior House girls

Miss Shipley (Games)

On the beach: Veda, Margaret A, Cocky, Phillida & Fuzz

Miss Mortimer
(favourite Irish
English mistress)

Roedean School No. 3 House

Hal and Fuzz

DD, Chips and Fuzz on the Downs

Colleen

Robert Donat (my pin-up)

Fuzz, DD and Felix

Nigeria: Elizabeth Wall,
DD and Naomi

Parents in Nigeria

DD and Naomi (in tennis gear)

Onitsha and DD with Daisy and Feet

Dennis Gibbs' house in Awgu

Dennis Gibbs (big crush)

DD, Dennis and Pop

Uncle Tommy (right) with colleague

The Despair family in gardens at Hove

Cuckfield Park

Cuckfield Park Gatehouse

Principals Miss Black and
Miss France with Benjy

Girls at Cuckfield: Sally, DD, Liz A, Ann H, Molly, Lily, Bridget

Elspeth

Pam, Pat, Christine
and Phil

Ann H, Elspeth, Molly, Jill, Judy R, Flick and Lily

A MERRY
CHRISTMAS
AND A
HAPPY
NEW
YEAR.

10 Chemin du Grand Praz, Chailly, Lausanne

10 Chemin du Grand Praz, Chailly, Lausanne

Antilles on her maiden voyage, bound for Jamaica

Little Holly

Cape Clear, Jamaica

Lois and Chester Lynn at Cape Clear

Little Holly at Cape Clear

Badger with Pym

Kenah Hill, Ireland -
Mrs Kavanagh's house

DD in the garden of 51 Shirley Drive

Glen and DD

DD in blue skirt

Bill and DD in Zermatt

Martin

Kyrenia Harbour

Kyrenia (view from our balcony)

Kyrenia
(our house LHS)

Nicosia, road block

Nicosia, Ledra Street, near Paphos Gate

St Hilarion Castle

Alec

Teddy, Ray, Alec and DD   DD

Teddy, Margaret M and Selma

Platres, Gillie, Pop and Mum

DD and Gillie

Gillie and Pop

Platres

DD

Alec camping at Troodos

Bellapaix

Ringway Airport, excursion to
Liverpool - Len, Stan, Val S, Jeanne,
Ralph, Val Dwek and DD

Jeanne, DD, Ralph, Hodders, Stan,
Val Dwek, Alf, Val Shaw, Mr Briggs,
Len Sefton

Val Dwek, Len, D,
Ralph, Val S, Stan,
Alf & Mr Briggs

Ringway - Mary Hanman, aka Pusscat

Ringway - Raye Jones of Sabena

Pauline Leigh

Wedding - DD & Pop
(he could not bring himself to smile)

Hotel Milano (our honeymoon hotel)

DD in Pallanza

Milan, Alec at the Duomo

Milan, DD at Grand Hotel Duomo

Milan, DD at the Duomo

DD on publication
of "How To Get On
With The Boss"

CHAPTER TEN

It was the 16th February, and the household was reduced to six: Lois and Chester, Mrs Kavanagh, Mrs Lynn senior, Holly and myself. Some guests came for dinner but I was asked not to appear. Mildred brought a tray to the playroom and I remained there all evening by myself. Mrs L said it was for reasons of business, but I wondered if it had something to do with Major Vaughan's advice that governesses should be kept in their place or they would get above themselves.

When it happened again the next night and the night after that, I felt sure this was the case. Was I really above myself? I did not think so. I felt abandoned and miserable, and the servants were sad for me. During the day Holly and I did lessons as usual for three hours and then I had work to do for Mrs Lynn, letters to write, stores to sort out, flowers to collect and arrange. There were umpteen duties to perform.

At the same time there was great excitement, for Princess Margaret was touring the Caribbean and was soon to visit Jamaica. There was to be a ceremony when she arrived on the morning of the 19th and Robert Lake, the solicitor said that as he and his wife were not going, Holly and I could go in their seats. However, there had been such chaos caused by the crowds getting out of hand when she went to Barbados, it was decided that it might not be a good idea for Holly to go. Then she was invited to stay with the Vaughan children for the weekend and I was told I could make any arrangements I could to see the Princess.

Everyone wanted an invitation to Government House where there would be a reception for her, and anyone of any importance on the island had received an invitation from Sir Hugh Foot to go to the evening reception at King's House. I didn't think I would be able to go but I was lucky: Maurice

Cargill, the editor of the *Daily Gleaner*, offered to try and arrange things for me. He subsequently sent a wire to say he had managed to get me an invitation, and would call for me and take me in his car.

That Saturday was a sort of holiday for me. We set off early and stopped at Kingston at the house of some friends of his called Phoebe and Herbert Hart, where we had tea and changed. Their house was very attractively decorated. The floors were tiled and in the sunny little sitting room there was a handsome and unusual desk. The walls were covered from floor to ceiling with books, and there were two mirrors opposite each other in which you could see yourself endlessly reflected.

All the very important ladies of the island were in a dither wondering what they would wear, whether they would be the only one in a strapless dress and if there would be anyone else without a hat. I wondered if I should wear the green organza dress I had worn for the garden party at Buckingham Palace when my father had been awarded his OBE, but I thought I could not, for Princess Margaret would have seen it already - as if she would have noticed! - so just to be on the safe side I wore a gold corded silk dress with a vee neckline.

The garden of King's House looked beautiful with all kinds of exotic flowers and shrubs. Princess Margaret appeared on the balcony at the beginning of the reception and at the end she walked round the lawn on a red carpet. At one time she stopped quite close to me and was presented to two large Jamaican ladies who trembled all over while she spoke to them for several minutes. I thought she looked very pretty and had the most amazing cornflower blue eyes. As Noel Coward was to record later, her visit was a great success.

We wandered over the gardens and drank Pimms or whisky and soda and I was introduced to a succession of very old retired Brigadiers and Colonels, each one looking more wizened and decrepit than the last. Then I ran across the two young Army officers who came to Cape Clear on Christmas Eve, Ian Something-Brown and Roy – who were most charming and asked me to go to the Yacht Club dance that night and to the Ball on Monday, neither of which I could. They had also rung me up the previous week via Maurice Cargill, but not being free or independent I was unable to accept any invitations. "Well anyway," said Ian, "if you are *ever* in Kingston, please give us a ring as we'd both love to see you again."

Maurice took me to dinner at Courtleigh Manor. He told me if I liked to give him some of my stories, he would read them and give me his opinion, and I said I would like that very much. He had to stay in Kingston that night so I was taken home by Ian Miller and his wife. Holly was brought back from the Vaughans, looking brown and wishing she was still there.

The next day I went into Kingston and met the correspondent from the *Daily Telegraph* who was covering the Princess Margaret story. He was very interested to hear I had worked at the *Telegraph*, and gave me all the latest news. Then a whole lot of other gentlemen of the press came up, photographers and all, and I was introduced to each one as Delia Despair, once of the *Daily Telegraph*, which made me feel rather proud but a bit of a fraud. He had to go out then, but he asked me to go to the Myrtle Bank Hotel at 5.30 when he got back and have drinks and stay to dinner. I could not have dinner but met him for drinks and sent a wire to Cape Clear to say I would be back at 7.30.

He showed me the stories he had written covering Princess Margaret's activities for the day, and the cables he was sending off to London. It seemed that when HRH was trying to land at Nassau, the only boat which was allowed ahead of her was the press boat. Three times the press boat tried to come in and each time the tide swept it past. Then, as Princess Margaret's boat was coming the police told the Press to keep back, which they did. Then Jean Pierre someone of *Paris Match* and David Johnson of the *Sketch* jumped into a rowing boat and came behind and tried to take photographs. The police were angry and told them to push off and when they wouldn't the police started a scuffle and beat them with their truncheons. David Johnson was injured and Jean Pierre's trousers were torn off. All this was watched by HRH and the Governor, and the Princess was very upset because she had made friends with some of the press during the tour – and Jean Pierre was quite an Adonis, tall, thin and very good-looking.

The Governor was furious with the police for being so heavy handed, and sent someone to break it up and tell them to lay off. Later on the two photographers were called to Government House and given an apology, and promised that Jean Pierre's trousers should be replaced. Douglas Williams told me that the photographers for royal tours were specially picked for the job because they were very experienced and knew exactly what they should and should not do and when they were or were not allowed to take photographs. So when the bossy police came, making trouble and telling them to go away, they were rightly very angry.

I had rum punch with Douglas Williams at the Myrtle Bank Hotel, and he was very charming. He said if I liked, he'd help me with my career when I got back to England, and he gave me his address. He asked if he might come over to Cape Clear and Mrs Lynn agreed and suggested he should come to dinner and stay the following night. The next evening he arrived. At dinner he kept winking at me and when no one noticed, said when could we have a private chat? He only wanted to speak to me about my future and how he could help me, but there seemed no opportunity, so he suggested I should leave my door open that night. I thought this would be much too dangerous. If discovered it would be taken entirely the wrong way. So instead we got up early next morning and before Holly was awake we met downstairs and went out to see the bulls and there we were able to have our talk. In the end it did not amount to much. He just asked me to come and see him when I was in London, that was all. It seemed ridiculous that we had had to go to such lengths just for a private chat but we both knew it would have been frowned upon.

That day the staff at Cape Clear were given a truck and told they could all have the day off to try and see the Princess when she passed by at Port Antonio. We in the household also went off for the day, to the big hotel there called the Tichfield which used to belong to Errol Flynn. We swam in the pool and Holly and I went down a chute from one pool into another. The place was packed and I saw all the press crowd again, with Jean Pierre giving a splendid display of crawl. I talked to another journalist who had apparently travelled out on the Antilles whom I had not noticed, and he gave me news of some of the people he had seen me with on board, including Marion, the girl at my table. I could not speak to Douglas Williams however: there was much antipathy on the part of Mrs Lynn and he and I were continually kept apart.

After lunch Holly and I were sent off like a couple of kids, and we made our way down to the big square to see if we could see HRH again as she passed by in her car. The square was filled with Jamaicans seven and eight deep, and just after we had waited about half an hour there was a sudden heavy downpour of rain and everyone had to dash for shelter. As we were rushing, we were hailed, and an English policeman who was in charge let us sit in his car, and later got one of his men to clear a space for us, so that we did watch the car come round the corner after all. It was a bit difficult to see and Holly said she didn't see the Princess and was terribly disappointed. But later we passed by a paleish woman in a full skirted dress standing in the doorway of a pub and little Holly thought that was the princess and I agreed that it was, so she went away quite happy after all. And the policeman gave us a lift back to the Tichfield, and much later on we all went home.

I was sorry I had not been able to say goodbye to Mr Williams, but the next day Chester Lynn asked me to ring him, which I did. He was very charming once more and said he'd be seeing me later on in the year.

On the 28th February I went into Kingston as usual for the shopping. Kingston was packed, as there were two tourist ships in and an American naval ship with 1100 men and most of them seemed to be in the Myrtle Bank Hotel. Mrs Pringle's niece, Patsy Robinson, had asked me to contact her if ever I could, and had arranged to have that Monday off so I was able to meet her for lunch. It was so nice. Patsy worked at British West Indian Airways as a ground hostess. This meant she had to meet the planes, pass the passengers through the various ground formalities, book hotel accommodation for them if required and generally be helpful to them. She had irregular hours and that morning had to be up at 4 am and be collected at five past four and taken to the airport. It sounded exciting to me. She loved her job, she told me, and an extra bonus was getting reduced rates for travel.

She treated me to lunch, which was so kind. She told me a little bit about Ian and Daphne Something-Brown. I was sure she and Ian liked one another. Ian had said I was to ring him if I came into Kingston. They were all very kind but the trouble was I never knew in advance if I was going or not, so it was impossible to make any arrangements.

Another driver was employed by the Lynns on a temporary basis. His name was Cox and he drove terrifyingly fast. After being at Cape Clear he needed another job and was offered one at Brimmer Hall but having heard about Major Vaughan, he declined it. I wrote a letter of application for him and he was fixed up elsewhere.

On the 2nd March Harold was given the sack. He had come out of hospital and seemed to have made a full recovery. He had returned to work, but once more had failed to please. Within a couple of days his nerves broke down again and he was a gibbering wreck. I felt sorry for him – he was a good man and he had always done his best.

Also that day the Ian Millers gave a drinks party, but I was not asked. I felt very hurt as I had liked Ian and he had always been so kind and understanding. Then later he asked me why I had not come to the party, and it seemed I had been asked after all.

One day I was sent into Kingston as usual to do the shopping. There were people coming to dinner that night and I was told to go to the Myrtle Bank Hotel and get some lobsters. Once a week they went fishing and lobsters would be available the next day. But when I asked about them, there weren't any.

"Are you *sure* there aren't any?" I asked.

"Not today. The boat did not go out, but there will be lobsters tomorrow."

"But I *have* to have them for tonight!"

"I am sorry. No lobsters today. Tomorrow there will be lobsters. Not today."

Mrs Lynn was very angry. At dinner she said to the assembled guests:

"You should have been having lobster tonight, but I'm afraid Delia could not be bothered to get them."

Everyone looked at me and I blushed scarlet, but said nothing. It was useless to argue, it only made it worse.

There were two constant visitors to Cape Clear, one was an American Roman Catholic priest called Father Gary, who came often to talk to Mrs Lynn and give religious instruction to little Holly. The other visitor was Mr Wint, an elderly Jamaican who came to give Mr Lynn massage and exercises. He would come on a Thursday, have dinner and stay the night and return to Kingston the next morning. Once he said to me that he had always known there were black slaves, but had not realised there were white slaves too, until he met me.

Then something happened which was a piece of luck for me: I received a letter from the Governor of Jamaica, Sir Hugh Foot. It seemed that a Colonel Veasey who had spent many years in Nigeria and whom I had met on the day of the Princess's reception, had told Sir Hugh Foot about my father. Sir Hugh said he remembered him well, and had thought him one of the best in the Nigeria Service. I felt very proud, and everyone else was too. He said he would like to have news of my father from his offspring, and I was to be invited to lunch at Government House. His secretary would arrange it, they would send me a cable. My standing in the house was greatly improved by this letter: I was not just the governess and no longer to have my meals alone in my room, but a young girl staying with them at Cape Clear. I was sometimes even taken for Mrs Lynn's daughter. She was not sure she liked that but decided it was rather amusing.

We all went over to San-San, the house of Denis Smith-Bingham and June. It was very contemporary, with a tiled floor, bright colours, modern pictures and ornaments and all most attractive. The views from the terrace were splendid. We went down to the famous Frenchman's Cove where HRH had her moonlight picnic. It was a lovely beach with a fresh water river on one side and palm trees. Holly loved it and was splashing about all day. Her swimming was good and I was credited for this – wrongly as it happened but I made the most of any praise that came my way.

In the morning I washed Holly's hair and packed for her as she had been invited to stay with the Vaughans. In the evening we went to Lindsay's supper party and I was delighted to see Patsy there. I also talked to Colonel Veasey and Maurice Cargill, and took great delight in cutting Major Vaughan. Colonel Veasey was a funny old boy – rather nice – tall with a military moustache and bearing. The next night Mac came to dinner with some Scottish friends of his.

There were always people coming for drinks or dinner or the night. Mrs Lynn loved to be the hostess and to give parties, but she didn't enjoy being a guest at other people's. Once she went to a party at someone's house and Mr Lynn was enjoying himself when suddenly she made a terrible scene and said in her deep voice, "CHESTER! WE ARE LEAVING!" Patsy told me that. And for some time I had been noticing Mrs Lynn's astonishing ulterior motives when talking to people: for instance, she would say to Celia of her best friend, "I cannot understand why Joyce should say you were a hypocrite – I don't think you're a hypocrite at all!" And to Joyce she would say, "I can't understand why Celia should say you were two-faced..."

And Joyce would look very upset and say, "Did Celia really say that?"

"Well – yes, I'm afraid she did. I shouldn't really have mentioned it,"

To me this was premeditated and awful. It was almost as if she planned these little barbed remarks weeks in advance. At the same time she was being very nice to me and I was happy enough.

CHAPTER ELEVEN

I had liked Chester's mother, Mrs Lynn senior, and she and Mrs Kavanagh and I had enjoyed playing Canasta together when Lois and Chester were away. She was a nice, sensible, dignified woman. But now it was time for her to leave Cape Clear. Chester and Lois, together with Mrs Kavanagh, were to drive her to Montego Bay, where she would catch the plane back to England. They would then spend a few days at Montego Bay, and I would be free. My only worry was the usual warning: "Now Delia, you are in charge, and if anything happens to Holly or Buff, it will be YOUR FAULT!" – and the recurring nightmares of finding Holly hanging from the banisters by her dressing gown cord, and Buffie drowned, floating on the surface of the pool.

Thankfully this did not happen. Holly behaved beautifully and our lessons, sitting in the hammock by the pool, went well. We were reading the Knights of the Round Table, and other stories. We swam and went riding every day. Buffie slept on my bed at night and seemed as fond of me as I was of him. He was a dear little dog. Lindsay Ellis and his sister Sheila came to lunch, and one day Lindsay came by himself, and another man, Duncan, very amusing, came for tea.

In the evening I wrote letters and short stories. One I read to Holly. It was sad but she loved it and wanted it read again and again – it was a fairy story, called *The Lonely Rose*. The servants were relaxed and although they looked after us as well as ever, I more or less let them do as they pleased. They needed the rest as much as I did, but they never took advantage.

One day Holly and I were invited to spend the day with Mrs Johnson, a dear old Jamaican lady who was Marjorie Pringle's mother and Patsy Robinson's grandmother. We had a pleasant day but I was shocked by the behaviour of the servants there: they were the rudest and most insolent bunch

I had ever seen. They were taking advantage of a helpless and frail person who had no means to instil discipline. When she called to one and asked her to bring tea, the woman said, "Get it yourself!" I looked at Mrs Johnson to see what she would say. She said nothing, so she and I went into the kitchen and made the tea. When we went into the garden to sit in the hammock, there were four of them lounging in it already, playing very loud music. Mrs Johnson said we wanted to sit there, so they got up reluctantly. Then they decided to have a jaunt and drove off in her car. They were just running wild and she was letting them. It was horrible the way they bullied the poor old woman and I decided I must tell Patsy about it.

Three days later Mrs Kavanagh got back at ten o'clock in the evening. She was alone, the others would be back in three days. We went to Jamaica Inn at Ocho Rios, and swam, and another day to Kingston. Ian Miller came with his wife and two little boys. Mrs Kavanagh had to ring Mrs Lynn one day and it came out that I had left Buffie while we went riding and Mrs Lynn was furious. I expected a huge row when they got back, and it was a relief to find out I was wrong. All was well. Holly had been invited to go to Montego Bay for four days, and I was to be allowed to go there for the day on the Thursday when she was coming back. I asked if I could possibly go on the Wednesday when they were going and stay for the night and then come back, and it was agreed. I was overjoyed.

There were some people in Hove we knew slightly, a Lady Leicester and her two daughters, Meriel and Margaret. I had met Meriel before leaving UK as she was going to be in Jamaica at the same time as me. I had liked her and we had arranged to meet if ever I was free. She had a job at the Casablanca Hotel in Montego Bay, so when I heard I was able to go there, I telephoned her and asked if she could possibly find me somewhere really cheap to stay, for I had by then scarcely any money at all. She said she could get me a room in annexe of the hotel for £3.10s.

On Monday the 14th March Holly went off to Montego Bay, I having got everything ready and packed for her. I was to go into Kingston taking Hilda and Mildred with me, but they took ages getting ready and we didn't have long. I rang Ian Something-Brown but there was no time to see him and he asked me to ring next time I came in. I had a sandwich and met Lindsay at the Jamaica Arms before we went back, Cox driving very fast. When I got back there was another letter from John. Apparently he seldom wrote home, yet I got one by return of post each time. His letters were a bit disappointing

– not nearly as amusing as Glen's - but he said he enjoyed mine and I was to keep on writing.

On Wednesday I packed for Montego Bay, but we had to go into Annotto Bay first thing and I knew we would be very late in leaving. Mrs Lynn was always late leaving to go anywhere as she didn't get up before eleven. Finally we set off, with me champing at the bit, and after stopping at Jamaica Inn for lunch, we were on the way. The drive was wonderful. We arrived at six o'clock and I was let out of the car at the Casa Blanca Hotel, and I rushed in to find Meriel. Unfortunately she was on duty from four till midnight as she had been expecting me that morning when she was off. I was shown my room down the road from the hotel, and I had a lovely swim and then a bath and changed and came over to the hotel for dinner. Sadly there was no one to have it with and I felt a little bit lonely. But I spent a pleasant night in a dear little room with bathroom attached, and in the morning I got up and had my breakfast on the wooden balcony. It reminded me very much of Switzerland as the blue sea looked just like the lake and the hills in the background were like the mountains and the house was like a Swiss chalet.

I met a young American who also came out on the balcony for his breakfast. He had travelled a lot and was very interesting. Then Meriel arrived and we went down to Doctor's Cave and spent the morning on the beach. We swam and sunbathed and chatted for ages. She was very sweet and kind to me, and it was lovely to see her and to exchange all our news. She was very happy indeed and having a wonderful time. She was as brown as a berry. She worked at the hotel alternately from 8 am till 4 pm, or 4 pm till midnight, which meant that she either had most of the day or a long evening free. Every day she played tennis, went riding, yachting, and swimming in the day time and dancing at night. She knew lots of people and they all had fun together – beach and tennis parties galore. She once flew to Kingston just for a dance. The other receptionists at the Casa Blanca were very nice and she shared a room with one. They had two wirelesses and a very nice balcony where they gave bottle parties.

We spent all morning talking and swimming every now and then, and we came up to the large veranda for a picnic lunch. I was delighted with Montego Bay and loved seeing everything and all the liveliness of the place, although it was apparently much quieter then as it was nearing the end of the season. When it did end Meriel said she would automatically get the sack, but she had managed to find herself a wonderful job at the Airport as a Traffic Controller, normally a man's job so I thought she was very clever to have got it. She would take a year to learn how to signal planes in and so on. The pay was good, £8, soon going up to £11 a week, so she was naturally very excited about it.

I loved being with Meriel and was so pleased to have seen her, but eventually at half past three my visit ended: Beris arrived to collect me and take me back to Cape Clear. On the 18th March Lois and Chester got back, having picked up Penny Kavanagh from the Airport. Penny was Lois's sister-in-law, for she was married to Lois's brother Monty. She was blonde and glamorous and lost no time in lying by the pool and getting herself a suntan. I liked her. But Lois was annoyed when someone referred to her as a girl. "A girl?" said Lois. "How can a woman of thirty-six be described as a girl?" Lois herself was thirty-six and looked much older than her sister-in-law.

The next day I received a nasty shock, which I described to my mother:

How quickly minds change! Last time I wrote, she thought that Holly was doing wonderfully well with her lessons and had given her a prize. Well now, all that is changed. From being in advance, she is now behind-hand. Mrs L met the Jamaican woman who taught Holly last year in Montego Bay and she says Holly is no further on than she was last year – and that she could then read as well as she can now. I don't quite understand how she makes that out but still. After all do you remember in Woking little H used to get bored after reading Ba Ba Black and never even got to Sheep? Now she can read the Beacon Readers quite fluently and all she needs is lots and lots of practice. Still, what is my opinion worth? I only teach her....

It is so very nice being here on our own at Cape Clear. Little H and I have such fun. We don't have to be so quiet all the time and can borrow Auntie Penny's wireless and turn it on in the early morning and the evening, and we dance around the room to the music. Very juvenile. The servants are inclined to be a bit slack. 'When the cat's away the mice will play' can certainly be applied to them.

Here is a list of sacked staff so far:

Ethline, one of the laundresses (she was the housekeeper but was demoted some time ago)

Harold, the head butler

Jean, a kitchen maid

About to be sacked: 3 more – but not, I hope, yrs truly..

We now had only another month before the lease of Cape Clear came to an end and there was much discussion on what they should do next, and where.

Chester Lynn wanted to do so many things: he had the necessary cash but couldn't make up his mind. Sometimes I wondered if he would end up doing nothing at all. He was drinking a lot – they both were – and I hoped they would not decide to stay on in Jamaica where tropical rot could set in so quickly. Maybe Switzerland, they thought – would I go to Switzerland with them? Or perhaps the south of France?

I didn't know what to say. The thought of it horrified me. Well, I would be letting them down if I didn't go with them, said Mrs Lynn. I should be thinking about little Holly and not about myself. But then they were not sure what they wanted to do or where they should go in any case. Maybe they would get a French governess. Wherever it was, *she* would need plenty of servants. Maybe they could rent a house in the south of France with a staff of servants, and make that their base. Meanwhile it was agreed I should stay at least one month after getting back, and this would probably mean two weeks with each of the two grandmothers, Auntie Ailsa and Mrs Kavanagh, for they had booked a suite at Claridges, and I couldn't see us going *there*. But nothing was decided, and their plans could change at any time.

On Sunday the 20th March there was to be a party for Auntie Penny, who had just arrived, and for Mrs Kavanagh who would shortly be leaving and going back to England. Holly went to stay with the Vaughans for the night. I made three mousses - one banana, one strawberry and one pineapple. Mrs Kavanagh helped me. She said she was glad I was looking after Holly and she hoped I would come and stay with her in Ireland when we returned. I was pleased to see Patsy at the party and also Ian Miller, but am ashamed to say I spent most of the time dodging Lindsay. The next day I said goodbye to Mrs Kavanagh senior, and the Lynns took her to Montego Bay to catch her plane. They were then going to stay on and show Penny around, so we would be alone.

That Monday I was to have gone into Kingston with Beris to do the shopping. Ian Something-Brown had asked me to lunch, so I was most disappointed when at the very last minute it was decided Beris could cope on his own. However, it was so lucky I didn't go, a blessing in disguise, for Holly came back from the Vaughans complaining of a tummy ache and feeling sick. I took her temperature and it was 103. I called the doctor and he said she had malaria. The poor thing felt awful and he gave her an injection. That night William the steward got it too and his temperature soared to 104.

I was very worried about Holly and stayed nursing her for three days and two nights while she was being sick and having violent diarrhoea. The second day her temperature was down but I never left her for longer than half an hour. We got no sleep at all, day or night, as she had to keep rushing to the bathroom, and alas, was rarely in time. She couldn't help it, poor little girl, but it became difficult to find clean sheets and nighties. There seemed to be a number of monstrously large spiders of which I was terrified. They were in the bathroom and around the bed in our room and it was all I could do to stay there.

I was so tired, so depressed and so unhappy I kept weeping for no reason, except tiredness. Holly played up a lot over taking the medicine the doctor had ordered and would *not* – flew into a horrible rage and was more unpleasant than I'd ever seen her. All the servants came up to help me give it to her and in the end they forced it down her like we had to with Buffie. I went out of the room – it was too awful to watch and I couldn't bear it any longer. And then when for the third time the doctor came, he said he'd like to have a talk to me too, and took me into another room and asked what the matter was. I said I was very unhappy and to my shame I wept. He was so *very* kind and understanding and said he thought it would be a very good thing when I got back to England.

The Lynns and Penny Kavanagh had gone to Port Antonio for a long weekend, and on Saturday 26th March Mac came and fetched Holly and me, and he took us to his house where we spent the day. He was very sweet to us, and he thought Holly was delightful. We had a wonderful lunch and saw round his house and met his rather stout Dachsie called Doctor Fritz. After lunch little H had a rest and I saw a lot of Mac's photographs. We then went for a long drive up to the sea – a perfect evening – and sat up on the cliffs above Robin's Bay, and looked at the blue, blue sea and the spray on the rocks. There were some old ruins up there with quite a lot of legends woven around them. The White Witch of Rosehall was a famous story. You could see the gutted house of Rose Hall near Montego Bay.

The days passed slowly. Many people came to Cape Clear and the Lynns were invited back. Sometimes I was invited as well, but was not allowed to go. It seemed to me that Mrs Lynn's behaviour was becoming increasingly bizarre. One night she got me up at four o'clock in the morning, saying she wanted me to go through her glove drawer. Half drugged with sleep, I was messing around putting the gloves in little piles for over an hour while she was reluctant to let me go back to bed. She had lots of pairs of gloves that she never wore in Jamaica but she said she would need them when she got back to England so they *must* be sorted out *now*, at four o'clock in the morning.

Another day I was sent to Port Maria on a flower begging quest. I had to go and ask various people the Lynns scarcely knew if they had any flowers in their gardens they would give so that Mrs Lynn had some with which to decorate her house when her guests came. This was deeply embarrassing and made me lose my nerve, for nobody had lots of flowers so why should they give away the few that they had, for an occasion to which they would not be invited? I was mortified.

Then there was the riding. Half the time I found Tina would not go for me and when she did, she was very slow, so I would be offered Calypso who was a beautiful horse and we would have wonderful gallops. Now Aunt Penny was given Calypso and I was offered October. She was fresh so I could not gallop but still enjoyed riding her – but when we got back somehow Mrs Lynn had found out and was furious. She said from then on I was to ride no horse but Tina. I could not believe it – she *knew* what Tina was like and that no one enjoyed riding her. It was just pure spite. "No," I thought, "I will *not* go to Switzerland or to France with you." But of course I did not say it to her face.

I did not think she and Chester were getting on very well. There was no fun, no jokes, no laughter. They were both drinking and Chester's hands shook more and more every time he gave me my wages.

On the 5th April I was sent into Kingston to get some Chinese soup cups and saucers and spoons from China Town. This was an exciting quarter of Kingston and I hoped for an adventure but Robert Lake the solicitor said I should not have been sent there as it was very dangerous. What were they thinking of, he said, to send me? I didn't know what he meant – perhaps I could have been abducted or murdered. Anyway, nothing happened. I thought the soup cups were very attractive and got some extra ones for Badger's wedding present. Her wedding day was to be on 16th April, just a few weeks before our return. Sadly I would miss it.

On Easter Sunday they went to Mass and I arranged the breakfast table with flowers and presents and eggs I had painted. Maurice Cargill and Barbara, his wife, came to lunch and I gave Maurice four of my short stories, as he had promised to read and criticize them. In the evening there was another dinner party to which the Howells came and Mac and his friend Mr Jarrett and two RC Fathers. On Easter Monday I made a fruit salad and there was a children's party and a treasure hunt for which I did the clues. Then there were races which the children enjoyed, and afterwards we swam in the pool. Supt Howell tried to duck me and Ian Miller came to my rescue and pushed him away and it was all very jolly till Mrs Lynn appeared looking annoyed and ordered me out of the pool. I remembered what Arthur had said, warning me never to look as if I was enjoying myself.

I had received a telegram from Sir Hugh Foot's secretary inviting me to lunch with the Governor on Tuesday the 12th April. I went into Kingston and at Kings' House mistook the housekeeper for Lady Foot. I said, "How do you do, Lady Foot," and she said, "I'm not Lady Foot, I'm Nancy." On the sofa before lunch I was seated between Lady Foot and Mrs Sharpe and felt like the dormouse between the March Hare and the Mad Hatter. But I did enjoy the lunch and meeting them all – although Sir Hugh Foot was really more interested in the test match between Australia and the West Indies. All through lunch he had a little radio beside him so he could listen to the commentary. Afterwards I returned to Cape Clear and received a rather cool reception.

And then on the 13th April there was a bombshell: Chester had received a letter from Major Vaughan, which he showed me. It was a stinker, and most unpleasant. It said, amongst other things, the sooner he and Lois went back to England the better. Mrs Lynn had caused more trouble between old friends than he would have believed possible, her spiteful and insidious remarks had stirred up trouble and caused great distress. Friendships were broken and could never be mended… and so on and so on. It had been arranged for Holly to stay with the Vaughans for the next week. Of course now this could not happen.

The 'friends' alternated as they were flavour of the month to begin with and then lost favour, to be replaced by others. To begin with there were the Vaughans, but after this vitriolic letter they were definitely out. At the end there was Father Gary, a colourless priest to whom little Holly had been rude. I recorded that Chester had beaten her for it. Could that really have happened? In retrospect I can't imagine nice quiet Chester beating anyone. There was also Mac, whom I had always liked and respected, Maurice Cargill to some extent, and the new favourites on the block were Supt Charles Howell and his wife Maureen. I liked both of them and they were stalwart to the end.

There was not much time left at Cape Clear. Life continued much as before, the servants getting into trouble; Harold could never return, Stella had lost favour at last, and for me, rows for the many sins I had committed: I had not changed Holly's nighties every day as she had decreed, I had not noticed the ribbons threaded through the broderie anglaise were missing. I had been riding when I should have been doing something else. The lessons were a failure. They were not producing results – and after all the money I had wasted on books, too. It was disgraceful and unbelievable, and once again I was to have dinner on a tray in my room.

Sitting upstairs alone I wept many bitter tears and wished I was out of it. Never again, I thought, would I work for one person where I was a prisoner with no freedom to choose anything for myself, but forced to do their bidding at all times. Afterwards she made it up with me. She thought it was all right again and it was for her, but not for me. It would never be all right for me.

CHAPTER TWELVE

It was the 21st April, two days before we were to leave, and Maurice Cargill came to dinner. There were other people there as well but I don't remember who they were. Afterwards he said he had brought my short stories back and wanted to discuss them with me. We sat on a sofa in a corner of the sitting room while he went through them. He said he thought the stories were 'bloody good' and used such adjectives as 'splendid' and 'excellent'. His favourite was 'The Lonely Rose' and it had nearly brought tears to his eyes. He also liked 'Agnes Mallory' which was based on an incident in a bush station in Nigeria where we had stayed with friends of my parents. Maurice thought it could be turned into a Somerset Maugham type story. "I was expecting to tell you to take up knitting," he said, "but no, you *must* go on writing. You can certainly write, there's no doubt about that."

Then Mrs Lynn appeared and said, "For heaven's sake, Maurice - you've been closeted with Delia for over an hour! What can you have been talking about?" And he said: "Something *far* more important than anything you could say to me or I could say to you". She was very annoyed at this, but I didn't care. I had given him the stories to read on the 10th April and had decided I would carry on writing or give up, depending on what he said, and I was much too excited at having had his verdict. It meant everything to me. He was my first-ever critic and I was proud, pleased and so grateful.

There were two more days and they were spent in packing. It was hard and exhausting. All the trunks and crates were brought out and we had to sit on the trunks to make them shut. Goods that were to be returned to Kingston had to be sorted. The 'Infantry' was supposed to be taken but of course, was not, there was no time for that. I had to pack for Mrs Lynn, Holly and myself and was terrified it would not be finished in time. It was all such a rush. Charles and Maureen Howell went ahead to Kingston taking the Hold luggage. All the servants kept saying how much they were going to miss me. How I wished it could have been different for them – they had been so unhappy, so defeated. If only I had been able to do more to help – Harold who had been so dignified, so correct – it was pitiful to see him reduced to this shambling wreck. And then after his stay in hospital he was fine again, seemingly recovered. And barely after two days at Cape Clear his nerves gave way and he was right back to what he had been before, a shambling wreck.

I did not know what had become of Ethline, of whom I had been so nervous at the beginning, likening her to Mrs Danvers. She wasn't a bit like that, she was sweet. But after she was sacked I never saw her again.

The day of our departure was very hectic and I was in despair because I had so much to do and so little time to do it in, but at last there we were with all our luggage. Mac came to see us off, and Charles and Maureen Howell and Father Gary – they now seemed to be the only friends left. And so we said goodbye and went on board the Swedish ship SS Patricia where we would be for two weeks. It was Saturday, 23rd April.

CHAPTER THIRTEEN

Unlike the voyage out, when Holly and I had been on the 3rd deck and well away from the Lynns, we now had a magnificent suite on the top deck, but there was a snag: it was adjoining theirs, so I was right under her eye and could not get away.

On the first day at sea we did not do any lessons but unpacked, and I had to stay close at hand in case Mrs Lynn wanted me to do something for her. If there was nothing, she still wanted me to stay around in case she should think of something. I was to stay within earshot all the time, except at meal times and in the evening. Then I would be free.

After two days at sea we reached Trinidad. Holly and I waited around all morning until she was ready and then we all went ashore. We went shopping – window shopping in my case – and afterwards to swim at the Country Club. Trinidad was rather beautiful with many new and amazing buildings. Having been unable to visit on the way out because of the yellow fever outbreak I was pleased to have the opportunity of seeing it. The next day we landed at Barbados but no one went ashore. While at sea Holly and I settled into a daily routine of lessons all morning, then lunch, then a rest, then a play – sometimes a swim in the pool, or a film in the little theatre, or we'd read a story. There were a couple of children's parties which Holly enjoyed.

The crew, who were mainly Swedish, were very good-looking. Especially so was the Chief Deck Steward, who showed me his slides on our first night at sea. At meal times I was seated at the Purser's table with a half-Chinese woman called Mrs Ching. Also at the table were the Chief Engineer, an elderly man known as Uncle Andy and, whenever he was not on duty, the First Officer. I liked them all and we had a very jolly evening.

The second day Mrs Ching did not appear at dinner, I didn't know why.

I liked her, and wasn't sure if she was seasick or very unsure of herself so I went down to her cabin and tried to persuade her to join us, but she wouldn't. She said she might come tomorrow, so the Purser and I were alone. He was rather a strange man with dark good looks, quite charismatic: at times charming but often moody. That night we got on very well and I made him laugh. At lunch next day when there were four of us, it was the same, and the days after that. I christened him Big Bully and he was delighted.

We were clearly having a jolly and raucous time and Mrs Lynn did not like it. On the voyage out she had told me she did not want me to sit at her table as she and Chester wanted to be alone, but now they did not seem to enjoy each other's company as much, and seeing us all laughing and having fun, she wanted to be part of it. She asked us to join them for dinner on deck, and we did, but the atmosphere was quite different. None of us spoke much and nobody laughed.

There were entertainments in the evenings, horse racing and bingo and the wheel of fortune. I made friends with a nice English woman called Mrs Bishop, and Margie Ching and I often stayed close to her in the evenings and played darts and ping pong. One night there was a display of Swedish gymnastics and the First Officer came up and asked me to dance. He told me someone on the ship liked me but he wouldn't tell me who it was. Afterwards I wondered if it were him.

As the voyage proceeded, Mrs Lynn's behaviour became increasingly erratic. Chester and she were not spending as much time together. One evening Chester invited me for a drink. We were in the bar and another passenger came up and said, "Is that wise?" I had no idea where Mrs Lynn was – in her cabin, I supposed. She did not like it when people, especially men, paid me any attention. But not even female friends like Susan Bishop or Margie Ching were acceptable. She did not want me to be around her and Chester, nor with anyone else. She really only wanted me to be in the cabin adjoining hers all the time, so that she could call on me at any time of the day or night. Everything I did seemed to be wrong and there were constant calls over the loud speaker for Miss Despair to report to Suite One immediately.

On the 1st of May there was a party in the Chief Engineer's cabin. There were about six of us there, the orchestra leader and his wife, the Chief Deck Steward, Uncle Andy, Bully and me. It was a good party, but as it was in the bowels of the ship you could not hear the loudspeaker, which I had not realised. Had I known I would never have stayed so late.

At about eleven o'clock a steward came in looking very agitated. "Miss Despair, I'm sorry to tell you but Mrs Lynn has been calling you on the loudspeaker all evening. She is *very very* angry. You are to report to Suite One immediately." Everyone looked shocked, and I was so terrified I flung myself into dear Uncle Andy's arms and sobbed against the lapel of his uniform jacket. He was very kind, they all were. Eventually I disengaged myself and went up in the lift to Suite One. I knew there would be a terrible row and I had no way of avoiding it.

"Delia, where on earth have you been? I've been calling you all evening."

"I'm sorry. I was at a party. I didn't hear the loudspeaker."

"Well, it's not good enough. You have behaved disgracefully!"

So it went on.

Next day we reached the Azores. I went ashore with Holly and Margie Ching, and we took a taxi and went all around the town. It was an incredibly attractive place, very Spanish-looking and with happy people. We got back to the ship and little boats came alongside, selling brightly-coloured knitting bags with bamboo handles. Margie kindly bought me one for a present. She was a nice woman but Mrs Lynn seemed to disapprove of both her and Bully. That night the Lynns were in a bad mood, and the ship started to roll a lot. I was hauled out of dinner and given a rocket. I sat with the Bishops and went early to bed.

Next day tempers boiled steadily all day long. I was hauled out of lunch and dinner. The scenes she made were witnessed by everyone on the ship. I received a lot of sympathy, they were all very nice, but it did me no good. Is she a bitch or a witch, I wondered? I thought a witch. I was in the power of a witch and there was nothing I could do about it.

In the evening Bully and the Chief Engineer asked me to join a Bingo game. We won and went down to Uncle Andy's cabin to celebrate. The next moment the steward arrived to tell me I was to leave and go immediately to Suite One. I wept bitterly for I was now frightened that she really had the powers of witchcraft.

When I got to her cabin she was incandescent with rage and I didn't really know why. She told me I was not to mix with either Margie or Bully for the remainder of the voyage.

"In fact," she said, "you are no longer fit to be looking after Holly. I simply can't trust you. From now on you are to stay in your cabin and she can sleep on a day bed in our suite."

I was then locked in my cabin, and my meals were brought to me by the nice deck steward. But this time she had gone too far. After three days I slipped him a note to be handed to the Purser. If I was not let out by the end of the day, I asked him to send a cable to my parents asking them to pick me up when we docked at Southampton.

I was released just two days before we docked. Everyone on the ship seemed to know what had happened and were shocked and angry. Susan Bishop said, "I am not getting off this ship until you promise me you will not go to Switzerland with that woman."

On the 5th May it was the Captain's Dinner, and I spent the evening with the First Officer. On the last night Mrs Lynn decided to host a party in the Captain's private dining room, but she hadn't asked his permission and he was furious. He stormed in and shouted: "Get out woman! Get out!"

I spent our last day on the ship packing. That night the weather was very rough and stormy and a lot of people were afraid, but I was exhilarated. The First Officer told me one more roll and we'd have been over – another ship was broken in two the same night. I watched the pilot boat come and in the distance I could see the Seven Sisters. Not long now. It was sad saying goodbye to everyone and I wished I could give some tips but I had received no wages and had no money.

And so we reached Southampton.

CHAPTER FOURTEEN

I had promised to stay on for one month, of which the first weekend would be in London with Peter, Holly's father, and his wife Elaine. After that we were to go to Auntie Ailsa and Uncle Dick in Woking, and for the last two weeks to Ireland to stay with Mrs Kavanagh, the other grandmother. During this time the Lynns would be in their suite at Claridges.

On Tuesday the 10th May Holly and I took a bus to Claridges, where we had tea, and then Auntie Ailsa arrived to take us to Waterloo and thence by train to Woking. Lois Lynn was jealous of Ailsa and did not really want us to go there. She gave me strict instructions: Holly was to continue with her lessons every day and I was to see that she had a cooked supper and went to bed at half past six each night. Did I understand? Yes, I understood.

It was so nice being with Dick and Ailsa, they were sweet and charming and it was wonderful to be free and happy. But within two days it was all spoilt. Lois kept ringing to check up on us. Dick's job as a film director meant that he didn't get home till seven or after, and of course he wanted to see his little granddaughter, on whom both he and Ailsa doted. So at half-past seven on Thursday evening, Holly was still up and having her supper when the Witch phoned. She spoke to Dick and asked how we were getting on and how Holly was.

"Oh, she's fine," he said.

"Is she in bed?"

"No, I've only just got home, so she stayed up to see me, but she's bathed and ready for bed. She's just having her supper in front of the fire."

"And what is she having for supper?"

"Cornflakes and a banana, I think – is that right, Ail? Yes – cornflakes and a banana and some milk."

They chatted amiably enough for a few minutes, then she said she wanted to speak to me. As soon as I was on the phone the storm broke. She was beside herself with rage. I had deliberately disobeyed her wishes. It was half-past seven and Holly was *not* in bed, and she had *not* had a cooked supper, as she, Lois had instructed. She had had *cereal, cereal* and a *banana*, Dick had just told her so. And she had *known* Ailsa would not give her a cooked supper because this had happened before, and she was not a fit person to look after Holly and neither was I. Tomorrow morning I was to pack our cases and return to London.

I relayed this conversation to Dick and Ailsa. Ailsa was very hurt and upset. "I would never give a cooked supper to a child of six years old," she wept. "I don't think it's good to have a heavy meal before bed, not for a little child. I have looked after lots of young children and I have never given them a cooked supper."

Uncle Dick was very angry, he said he had never been angrier in his life. "She is like a snake!" he said, "a poison ivy, an evil menace!"

We talked of her till after midnight. Ailsa continued to cry. "I greatly fear she is going to ruin the lives of everyone who comes into contact with her," she said.

"She is like a vampire or a flame, she consumes everything in her path," said Dick. So – *were* we really to pack up and leave and return to London next day? Of course that was not what she wanted, for she would not really want the bother of looking after her little daughter in the suite at Claridges. As so often, the threats were empty, the row subsided. And so we stayed in Woking.

All continued peacefully enough until Friday May 20th. Ailsa suggested I should go home for the weekend as it would be my 21st birthday on the 23rd. I collected my trunk from Claridges and caught the train to Brighton, where my father met me. That night we went to see *The Reluctant Debutante* at the Theatre Royal with Wilfred Hyde Whyte and Celia Johnson. It was brilliant. My birthday was on the Monday: we went to the Sussex Grill for lunch, then I went up to London and to Badger and Peter's flat. Peter's friend Martin Lennox was there, whom I had first met and liked on 15th October 1954. We all had champagne and some of the top layer of Badger's wedding cake. Then we went to a comedy, *My Three Angels* with Ronald Shiner, and afterwards to the Coconut Grove, where we had dinner and danced to the music of Edmundo Ros. Once again Martin and I got on very well. We could have danced all night but at 4 am the others wanted to leave, so we did, but it was a wonderful evening, the culmination of a lovely birthday.

The next day I went down to Woking and spent the day washing, ironing, mending and packing for little Holly. On the 25th we went up to London and had lunch at Claridges. To my great surprise and delight I was given a beautiful grey fur stole, my 21st birthday present from the Lynns. Lois was such a contrary creature, and she could be exceedingly kind when she wanted to be. Then we took a taxi to the BEA terminus and went on the coach to London Airport for our flight in a Viscount aircraft to Dublin. Mrs Kavanagh met us and took us to her house above Killiney Bay. It was called Kenah Hill, a large square house built of grey stone with a great big garden and wonderful views overlooking the sea and the mountains. The view from most of the windows was of trees, hundreds of trees of all kinds and colours, and the sea beyond. I loved the sound of the sea breaking on the shore as I went to sleep at Kenah Hill, and I woke to hear it pounding against the cliffs. It was all just as I'd imagined Ireland to be.

In the next two weeks I was shown much of her country. Lessons with Holly were fitted in if we were not going somewhere, and if we were, they were abandoned. What would Lois have said? But Lois didn't know. On the first day we motored over to Dolland, another beautiful and romantic house where her brother Mont and Penny lived and where Mrs K herself used to live and where Lois was brought up. Ireland was full of large romantic houses that reminded me of *Rebecca* and *Jane Eyre*. Mrs K was very good to me, she seemed to want me to have a good time, and not a day passed when we didn't go somewhere or meet someone.

A highlight was visiting Glendalough, where I sat by the lake and looked at magnificent views of the mountains. We walked on the seaside promenade at Bray, drove twice into Dublin, that fine city, to the cinema to see *Carmen Jones* and to a tiny theatre to see three Irish plays by O'Casey, Synge and Sheridan. I was surprised and perturbed that she did not have a babysitter for little Holly when we went out in the evening. We just put her to bed and left her. "She'll be all right, it's quite safe," said Mrs K and I didn't argue. Fortunately Holly didn't wake up and was fine, but that was something Ailsa would not have done and I think Lois would rightly have been very angry had she known.

Mrs K had a huge family and she introduced me to lots of them, her sister Cherie, her brother Robey and his wife Molly and their girls Denyse and Rosemary. One night Rosemary took me to a cinema. I met the niece Avril who, intriguingly, had behaved very strangely that year, though I wasn't told why, and Tom her husband. I met her friends Mary and Lynette and we went out to dinner at the house of Frances and Ossie. I think Frances was another sister. I thought it must be nice to have such a huge family. They were of course, all Roman Catholics. Robey and Molly came to dinner at Kenah Hill one night and her nephew Charlie and June another night, also a young man called Alex Mitchell who spoke to me at length about his cousin Lois. I liked him particularly: he was very discerning, for without my having to say anything he guessed much of what I had gone through in Jamaica. One day when it rained I walked into the town to take some shoes to be mended and the cobbler's baby had just died and his wife told me all about it and wept. There was poverty in the town, her house was very poor in contrast to the large opulent and romantic houses of Mrs Kavanagh and her family. I noticed a sharp divide in Ireland; houses tended to be very large or very small, there did not seem to be much in between.

On Saturday the 4th June, towards the end of my visit, we went to Aunt Cherie's house. We were to have gone to the races in the afternoon but the weather was bad so it was called off. I met her son Ken. He was very attractive - tall, dark and good-looking with a wonderful Irish brogue. Charlie and June had tried to arrange something, but Ken asked me to join him and three student friends instead. They planned to go to the cinema in Dublin. It was a marvellous film called *The High and the Mighty*, about the RAF. I felt very shy with them as I was not sure if any of the students was his girlfriend, but seemingly not for they sat apart from us.

Afterwards they said goodbye and left us and we drove back to Killiney and went for a walk to the top of Killiney Hill. It was still early and the views were far-reaching, you could see the sea and the mountains, the foothills of the Wicklow Mountains and Bray Head. Ken was very flattering to me but we had only met that day and I was not sure I could believe the nice things he said. He was cross that Mrs K had not introduced us before and asked me to go out with him again the next night. First we went for a drive in his uncle's car, then came back and had tea and cake with Mrs K. Then we went for a beautiful walk by the sea. We climbed over the rocks and sat for a long time listening and watching the sea as it tumbled towards us. He held me and kept telling me over and over again he had fallen in love with me and I wanted, how I wanted, to believe it.

Holly and I were supposed to be flying back to England the next day, Monday the 6th June. I *had* wanted to go, for then there would be only two more days with the Lynns and I would be free. But now having met Ken, I was glad to find our flight was postponed till the Tuesday so we had one more evening together.

I packed in the morning and his mother came to lunch. He was at college in the daytime but in the evening he came to supper and took me to the cinema. We wanted to go back to our place in the rocks but it was pouring with rain so we stayed in the car, and when we went indoors I could see that both Aunt Cherie and Mrs K seemed displeased with us. However, they left us alone and we stayed in the drawing room at Kenah Hill till late.

He was very ardent. He said he'd be on the same plane tomorrow if he only had the cash. Over and over again he made me promise to write to him. I was to write first, and I was to send photographs and I was not to forget him. He would look up to the sky and watch my plane as it flew away from Ireland and he'd wish we were still together on the top of Killiney Hill or the place on the rocks above the sea. And as soon as he could get the money he would come over to England to see me. And then we said goodbye.

Mrs K took us to the airport next day but our flight on a Wayfarer aircraft was delayed for two hours because of thick fog. She was very sweet and I was sad to leave her, and say goodbye to Ireland and to her. From Heathrow we took a taxi to 7a Melbury Road, to the flat of Peter and Elaine. There I met the new governess, who seemed very nice. Wednesday was my last day with little Holly. That too was sad for both of us. Ailsa came for lunch, for she was taking Holly back to Woking until the new governess started. I did my packing and gave Holly her supper and finally said goodbye. I thought she would be happy with the new governess. Then Ailsa and Holly and I went to Claridges so I could say goodbye to the Lynns. We ended on a good note – 'Thank God,' I wrote in my diary, 'It is finished.'

Ailsa told my mother, "It's such a strange thing, when Delia is with Lois she is like a rabbit that is hynotised by a snake." Ailsa was very discerning, for she also guessed I had met someone in Ireland. I thought about Ken a lot and I wrote to him and sent him a photo as he had asked me to – but he wrote back and asked why I hadn't written. I wrote again and he didn't reply. My mother commented that he was a half-hearted lover and I began to think she was right. That Irish charm – how deep did it go? Was it just a lot of blarney?

Then about three months later he wrote again saying he still hadn't heard from me, and why not? He wanted the photos quickly for he still felt the same way and just wished we were together again by the sea. But he never did receive my letters. I found out his mother Cherie had intercepted them and destroyed them. She had disapproved of our relationship because I was English and a Protestant. Of all things, that was not to be borne.

When I got home to my parents in Hove, there was a package for me with a letter from Lindsay Ellis. He was a very kind and decent man and I wished I had been nicer to him, it would not have hurt to be more generous spirited. His letter read as follows:

Fort George Estate, Annotto Bay, Jamaica, B.W.I. 23rd April

Dear Delia

I am glad to say that I was the one to find the enclosed very personal and intimate things of life which seem to make life worthwhile. I promise I haven't read any of the letters and forward everything just as I found them.

Seeing everybody off this morning was of course a difficult job and one which is always unnerving; as much as I disliked Mrs L I must admit even saying goodbye to her was somehow not enjoyable. The House seemed very dead as soon as you had all gone and I shot away as soon as I could, though somehow happened to see these things of yours.

I have to admire you very much for the way you stuck to your job and you really do deserve the greatest credit for having done so, though it is likely that you will never receive the full credit due. At times I really did feel sorry for you, but I must say you were a brick! I truly hope Jamaica was a joy to you and that it will always bring back happy memories; however small those memories may be they are a reflection on the past and that tiny bit of past can stick in ones mind forever; happily the human mind only stores chiefly the best of the past and what best you found in Jamaica I hope will remain as being good and if possible useful for the future.

It will always be a regret of mine that I was not able to see you more often, this a genuine thought and one which has passed through my mind often with a tinge of sadness here and there. You were unapproachable to me because of the repercussions Mrs L might have had.

Fort George has sad and happy memories for me in as much as Cape Clear has also, but for what it is worth I want you to know that though Cape Clear, through the Lynns, gave me a bit of worry it will come to me as a streak of happiness the different glimpses I will have of you.

I don't expect ever to see you again, but with this letter goes the most sincere thoughts to you for your happiness in the future and a sincere admiration for all the things you have achieved, overcoming different difficulties, in the immediate past. Yours in admiration, Lindsay.

I began a novel called "The Trapped Ones". It began, 'I have just escaped from a woman of whom I am afraid…" but I couldn't go on with it. I have never been able to write about that time in Jamaica, until now.

PART THREE

———◆———

THE CHOICE
CHAPTER ONE

"Why don't you stay at home for a bit?" said my mother when I got back from Jamaica. "You can surely take your time about looking for another job."

And so I did, but first there was a holiday in Spain with Bretton and his girlfriend Marguerite and his friend Julian with whom my sister had been in love. Luckily there was no heartbreak, for neither of us fancied the other. Then followed a lazy summer lounging about, going to parties, to the cinema or the theatre, playing tennis, swimming - in the sea, of course, for the weather was always hot and sunny in those days. I wrote a short story called *The Cherry Stone* and sent it up to *Woman's Journal*, but most of the time I was very idle. That was a favourite word of Guy and Peter's, they were always saying someone or other was idle – and now I was extremely, exceedingly idle. I don't remember doing any cooking and I don't remember doing any housework. I do remember lounging in the garden with dear little Pym on a rug, reading a book. My sister used to say her idea of Heaven was sitting in a deckchair with a book and a Mars bar and that was pretty much my idea too. My mother's cooking was delicious after the bed-sit days of boiling eggs or warming up horrible tinned stew on an electric fire turned on its side.

My mother bicycled down to Cullens and rode back uphill, only realising when she reached our house that her bicycle basket was filled with someone else's shopping. She had absent-mindedly got on the wrong bicycle. Luckily she was able to speed downhill and return the wrong bicycle before its owner had noticed its absence. She was always absent-minded. She once discovered on arriving at the theatre to see Beatrice Lillie that she had a damp tea-towel over her arm instead of her fox fur with its cross little foxy face that she usually wore.

Something terrible happened while my parents were in Nigeria: we found out that our beloved Mrs Marshall had hanged herself. I couldn't believe it - that poor little woman who had come to clean for us three times a week and had always been so cheerful, it was unbearable to think of what she must have suffered. My mother felt that if only, if only she had been in England, it wouldn't have happened. She and Mrs Marshall were such friends and each confided in the other and perhaps it would have made all the difference to be able to talk about her problems. We didn't realise, at least I didn't realise, what an awful life she led. Her son was gay and her daughter, who was bad-tempered, had decided she was a lesbian, in times when these things were unacceptable. Her first husband went missing during the Second World War and after quite a long time she found someone else. And then one day her husband walked in through the back door. He wasn't best pleased to find someone else in his house. So he was there, and his horrible spiteful mother moved in as well, and continually nagged her and made her life a misery. I only remembered how sweet she had been, how she sent me two Mars bars for my birthday at school, and all the times she came to our house, and how I confided in her – as did my mother – and how we all felt things couldn't be too bad if she was coming in. She was the sort of person who cheered you up just to see her. She was the last person you'd expect to do such a terrible thing.

Our old friend Damps had a cottage in Wales and my parents bought it from her for two thousand pounds. We three then drove to Wales to see it, stopping off at a hotel in Broadway. The cottage was in a rather dreary terrace and there were coal pits around and a dank stream, but a bit further afield the countryside was beautiful like Switzerland, with mountains and a lake. We met Mr George the caretaker and his wife and daughter, and a man with a red dog and a Polish doctor and two little old women like Mrs Tiggywinkle. It was decided we would let the cottage when we were not using it ourselves. Mr and Mrs George would continue to look after it and keep up the small garden and we would provide the furniture. We went to some antique shops in Aberystwyth and picked out some quite nice pieces including an oak gate-legged table and four Windsor chairs. Later, when my parents went back to Nigeria, it fell to Badger and me to let it, so we put an advertisement in the

Sunday Times saying, "Welsh Cottage to let, sleeps six, fishing available, £2 per week."

This turned out to be an irritation: although one nice person wrote, "Is it possible there is really a cottage to let in Wales for only £2 a week?" others were not nice at all. Someone wanted to know what sort of fishing it was. I had absolutely no idea. I went to the Library and looked in various natural history books hoping to discover what sort of fishing it could possibly be in that part of Wales. The books, besides being huge and very heavy were much too technical and no help at all, so I wrote back, guessing carp. I had no idea if that was the right answer or the one he wanted to hear.

After the first let, we got a very nasty letter from someone who complained about everything. First, the beds in the second bedroom were hard – Badger and I had slept in these beds for years and hadn't noticed this, but then we had been to boarding school and you get used to anything there. "Furthermore," said this man, "Just what is one supposed to use to get an egg out of a frying pan? My wife had to go out and buy a spatula!" We felt indignant at receiving this – after all everything else had been provided and it was only £2 a week!

We went to Wimbledon, for Aunt Chattie always had an allotment of complimentary tickets which she handed out to deserving relatives. However they were often less than deserving. Rather than watching the tennis Aunt Chattie would spend the time looking at them through her binoculars, and woe betide any relative caught chatting or eating sweets from those large bags of Pick n' Mix that people bought as they went in. That was it – no more tickets for them! My parents were given tickets and they generously passed some on to Badger and me, and we saw Tony Trabert and Ken Rosewall.

Mrs Harland, my dear friend and former landlady, gave a fork supper for her sons Roger and Geoffrey (whom we thought were drips, especially Geoffrey) and I met a lot of old chums there including Marigold. Then suddenly who should walk in but Glen, on leave from his job in the Fleet Air Arm. We were overjoyed to see each other and talked for hours, until someone else came along and attached himself – but it was extraordinary and delightful to see Glen again.

He asked if he could come and stay, and this he did for a week in the middle of July. He made me laugh all the time, for he was so ridiculous, and yet my parents and I were charmed by him. As always when staying with us, he played Chopin's *Nocturne* on our baby grand piano and went over and over it until he'd got it right. He was a perfectionist, and told us, with a complete lack of modesty: "I could have been a very good pianist, you know." Somehow it didn't seem like boasting, although I don't think he could play anything else.

We talked a lot all week, and played tennis and ate orange water ices and went swimming - we swam all the way from the beach in front of Queen Victoria's statue to the West Pier. We went to the Eaton restaurant in Hove and he and my father argued about whether they would take a job like mine in Jamaica for £100 a week. They both said they would, and I said I would not, not for a thousand pounds.

On the third day he and I went to Cowdray Park to watch the Polo. I wore my new blue skirt which he admired and I wondered what he really thought about me - but he would never say. He only said he did not intend to get married until he was forty. We went to the cinema to see *Two Thousand Leagues Under the Sea* and to lunch at September Cottage in Poynings, and to an art gallery in Brighton where he bought two paintings that he couldn't afford; but his philosophy was that if he ever became rich he would regret it if he hadn't bought them. He treated me like his best friend.

We were both sad when the time came for him to leave and he asked me to go into his room and keep him company while he packed, but that was all. He asked me to keep on writing to him and said he would come and stay with us in the Welsh cottage and in Hove next year and would see me in the interim. He was sweet and caring, but I don't think he would ever have made a good husband, for me even if he had wanted – which he didn't - or for anyone else.

There were other boyfriends that summer, but none I particularly liked. There was Leonard the Pole, who was a lodger in the house of the vicar who lived opposite. He told me he could see my outline through the bubble glass of our bathroom window, which I thought a bit suspect. Nevertheless I agreed to go out with him. I was warned by my parents and a girlfriend that Poles are always attracted to English girls and were very fast, but it rather irritated me to think they thought I couldn't look after myself.

The evening started off well. we went to Howards' restaurant and had a delicious steak, and he was sweet and kind and very flattering. Then we went to a marvellous French film called *The Bed* – I can't remember what it was about but I can imagine. Afterwards he kissed me and I felt awkward because I didn't enjoy it but didn't like to hurt his feelings by drawing away too much.

A few days later he rang and asked if I would go to the theatre to see *Guys and Dolls* with him and Mr and Mrs Gill, and I thought it would be all right as long as they were there. We mustn't lose them, I thought. When the day came I sat between Mr Gill and Leonard, but I decided that soon it must end for Leonard was becoming very amorous and made me shy and afraid. Perhaps my parents were right and I couldn't handle it – not that they knew what was going on.

A few days later he rang and asked me out again, and this time there would be no Mr and Mrs Gill. I dreaded the evening, and felt very depressed, not knowing how I would handle the situation, but at first it was all right; we had a delicious meal and went to a film but then on the way home he drove through the park and suddenly stopped and said we had run out of petrol. He got hold of me and was about to kiss me – so then I told him I already had a boyfriend. He seemed sad to hear this. He told me he loved me and asked a lot of questions about this mystical boyfriend (who was a cross between Glen, Martin Lennox and the Irishman, and of course all three of them lived nearby) and then we drove home, for it appeared there was petrol in the car after all. I was greatly relieved to have told him about the mystical boyfriend, for now I was off the hook.

Three days later the vicar and his wife and daughter came for drinks – long overdue - and the daughter, who, it appeared, was keen on the Pole, asked me a lot of questions and gave me an intensive cross-examination, which was embarrassing. She wanted to know where we had been and what he had said and what we had done. Of course I could hardly tell her, so I didn't say anything much, except to gloss over the theatre visits and what we had had to eat in the very vaguest terms.

CHAPTER TWO

I was now anxious to get a job and thought I would like to work in a hotel, on a temporary basis, before applying to BOAC. I applied to two hotels, the Lawns and the Kingsway, but the Lawns was dark and depressing and full of old ladies and the Kingsway wanted someone permanent. Later in the month my father introduced me to Mr Billington, the Manager of the Grand Hotel in Brighton where Badger's wedding reception had taken place. We asked if there were any jobs available and then and there he gave me an interview and agreed to take me on as a temporary hotel receptionist, starting in two days' time on 28th July. It would be shift work and I should come in at 9 am on Thursday and report to the Head Receptionist. I would earn £4 13s a week. Even for those days it was not much, but I was delighted. There was no special uniform, said Mr Billington, but we had to wear black. I immediately went out in search of something suitable, and managed to get two smart black dresses in a sale at Westerns, for £7.

On Thursday I got up early and my mother suggested my father could take me in the car. He agreed, though he hadn't had his breakfast and was a bit grumpy. "I shan't be doing this every day," he warned me. "You'll have to get the bus." He dropped me off at the front door of the Grand Hotel. I went up the steps and reported to the Head Receptionist, whose name was Miss Kyle. She was elegant in a rather tired way, with jet black hair streaked with grey and a face shiny with make-up like women behind beauty counters in department stores. She wore a white blouse with a frilly pussy-bow neck and a black suit with a greenish tinge to it and a spray of artificial lily-of-the-valley on her lapel. She had a very attractive smile but she was quite stern.

"Did you come in by the front entrance?" she asked.

"Yes. I didn't know there was any other entrance."

"There most certainly is, the staff entrance is round the back. Don't ever use the front entrance again. Are you good at mental arithmetic?" she asked.

"Not really," I said apologetically.

"Pity. You will have to get used to doing sums in your head here, you'll be handling money all the time. If there are any discrepancies in your float at the end of your shift, you will have to make up the amount out of your own money."

"Oh dear," I said.

"It will certainly be Oh Dear. Oh Dear won't be in it if you have to fork £20 out of your wages."

She then introduced me to Eunice, one of the other receptionists, who was also on the morning shift. Eunice was plump and pert with short blonde hair. She seemed very friendly and was full of chat. "You'll soon get the hang of it," said Eunice, reassuringly.

"I do hope so," I said but I was a bit worried at the thought of doing sums in my head. I couldn't even do them on paper, let alone in my head. Yet from that very first day I knew I was going to love my job at the Grand Hotel.

Miss Kyle then proceeded to tell me about the other work to be done in the Reception Office. "You're not here just to look pretty, you know," she said. "Your main function is to allocate rooms to the guests and with over four hundred rooms that's no mean feat. There are big charts for each floor which have to be kept up to date. I am very strict about this. If you let a room you must be sure to mark it off on the chart. I don't mind if you're dying, you must mark off on the chart first and then you can go off and die afterwards – that's how important it is."

"The biggest cardinal sin," she told me, "Is overbooking. That is, allocating the same room twice to different guests. It is easily done when the charts are not kept up to date or if you don't remember to enter your bookings immediately but as far as I am concerned it is something quite inexcusable, something I will not tolerate in any circumstances. Now would you like to go to breakfast? You have half an hour."

She told me to go down a passage leading to the back of the hotel, near the staff entrance. The staff dining room was a dark, dreary room that faced onto the well of the hotel. It smelt of grease and stale food. The only nice thing in it was a long polished oak table at the top end of which seven ladies were sitting, engrossed in conversation. I sat next to one of them. She was flat-chested with a beaky nose, and she looked round and said, "You can't sit there. That's Doreen's place."

"I'm sorry," I said, and sat further down. Unfortunately all the things to eat were at the top of the table, presided over by a plump lady called Alma. She had rollers in her hair and wore a mauve nylon dressing gown.

"....terrible griping pains in the pit of my stomach," she was saying. "Right across here." She indicated a lower portion of her mauve dressing gown.

"Very nasty," said one of the ladies.

"Do you think it could have been last night's macaroni?" asked another.

"Could be. Cheese is very indigestible," said a third, a lady with rimless glasses and a spotty face. "Personally I never like to take cheese before bed. It lies heavily on the stomach, cheese does."

"Could you pass the cornflakes, please?" I asked.

"I didn't really feel like getting up," said Alma. "Not to work, that is."

"I'm not surprised," said the one who never took cheese before bed. "You don't want to worry about what Mr Howard says. You don't want to push yourself."

"No. You get no thanks for it," said someone else.

"I thought, sod Mr Howard," said Alma, "Mr Howard can get stuffed. If that man dares to say anything more to me – " words failed her, momentarily, at the idea. "Anyway I thought I'd just nip down and have a bite of breakfast and then stagger back to bed again." She took a large mouthful of bacon and egg and patted her headful of rollers, which bristled like a porcupine under a green silk net.

"Could you pass the cornflakes, please?" I said "And the sugar?"

"I must say, I don't like the sound of those pains," said someone eagerly. "I had a cousin who –"

"The cornflakes," I murmured. "And the sugar."

"Perhaps you should have taken something, Alma?"

"Well, I thought I had some Alka Seltzer –"

"And phut! Just like that. Ever such a shock to her family....."

"Just a minute," said Alma, looking at me from her place at the top of the table. "You wanted the sugar?" she boomed, "Well, here it comes!"

Then astonishingly, she picked up the sugar basin and sent it skidding down the centre of the polished oak table. "And the milk?" Along slid the milk jug at a great rate in the wake of the sugar. Then the packet of cornflakes which toppled over and spilled flakes along the way. "And I suppose you'd like the toast, would you? And how about the butter? And the marmalade?" All of them were sent sliding along the polished surface of the table. "Salt? Here it comes. Pepper? Mustard? Tomato Ketchup? Brown sauce? Here they come. Coffee?"

"Oh no, not the coffee!" I squeaked.

"Here it comes!" It bounced along in its tall white jug, narrowly missing the ridges on the way, till it came to rest next to the tomato ketchup, which had tripped over the salt and lay on its side, rocking gently in a steadily growing pool of red.

"And now," said Alma heavily, "Perhaps we can have some peace! Where was I?"

"You were saying you thought you'd got some Alka Seltzer."

"Oh yes. Well I thought I'd got some Alka Seltzer —"

I thought, I've got to get away from here quick, and before the half hour was over I got up to go. As I was going through the door, I heard someone say, "Who was that?"

"Haven't a clue, dear," said Alma. "Never saw her before in my life."

"Eunice," I said when I got back to the Reception Office, "Who is Alma?"

"Alma?" said Eunice, pulling a face. "She's the Head of the Book-keeping department. She's got her own little empire. There are ten of them, and Alma's the kingpin. They work in the inner office, behind ours. Why do you ask?"

"She was having breakfast at the same time. She was still in her dressing gown, I think she was ill. She didn't seem very pleased that I was there."

"I should warn you to keep on the right side of Alma, she can be a very dangerous and difficult woman," said Eunice. "In any case the book-keepers don't like the receptionists at all, there's an on-going war between us."

"Why is that?"

"Oh – they're just jealous because we have all the fun in the front office, seeing people, meeting guests, getting tips and so on. All they do is make out the bills, which must be bloody boring."

I soon saw why the book-keepers didn't like the receptionists. Several times during my first morning Miss Kyle and Eunice went to the door of the inner office and ordered them about in quite a peremptory way, calling out: "The bill for Mr Evans, please," or Mrs Jones or whoever, and Miss Kyle added: "Look sharp!" Goodness, I thought – no one likes to be told to Look Sharp, it is bound to put their backs up - but neither Miss Kyle nor Eunice seemed to care about that.

"Eunice," I said, "Who is Mr Howard?"

"He's the Assistant Manager. Tall and good-looking but a funny stick. Not much humour. I call him Fancy Pants."

"Eunice," said Miss Kyle. "Will you stop gossiping and get on with your work." She then gave me a pile of letters to type, which mainly confirming reservations.

Quite a few people booked in during the day and I was asked to take them up to their rooms. I didn't know where the rooms were at first but luckily William, a young page who took their luggage, came with us in the lift, and he knew which room was which. He was very cheeky and he made me laugh: we were waiting outside a bathroom while a short fat woman in a long leopard skin coat examined a faint but unmistakeable tide-mark on the side of the bath, when the page hissed at me, "Lock her in!" This was nearly my undoing, for I got a fit of uncontrollable giggles and could not look at the woman with a straight face. The page and I giggled at the walls of the lift all the way down to the ground floor. To make matters worse, the woman in the leopard-skin coat said she did not want the room after all.

Just before four o'clock the third receptionist came in. Her name was Vera. She was a quiet girl with brown hair and brown eyes and a lovely gentle nature, and I liked her at once. She would be working the late shift, finishing at midnight. Later in the week Miss Kyle had a day off and Vera and I were on together, while Eunice did the evening shift. Two or three people phoned up while Vera was at lunch and I made several bookings. One man asked if he could have a double room for two nights for himself and his wife at the end of the month. It would be his wedding anniversary and he wanted a nice room with a bathroom and a sea view. I looked at the chart and booked him a room on the second floor. I thought I had done everything all right and was upset when Vera came back to find I'd made a bad mistake. "Fine – quite good," said Vera, checking what I had done, "Except that you let Room 201 on the 30th August and it's let already."

"Oh no, surely not? It doesn't say so on the chart."

"'Fraid so, love!" She pointed out the entry and I looked at it in dismay.

"Oh dear, I'm sorry. Overbooking, the cardinal sin."

"Never mind, Miss Kyle's not here to notice. The charts get such a lot of rubbing out when people change their minds and it's quite difficult to see what's what, that's why we always have to write in pencil. Look, we can switch your booking to Room 307 on the third floor. They won't know the difference. You're bound to make mistakes to begin with. I can't tell you the things I did wrong when I was new – this is nothing to what I did – and I still do!"

I liked being on with Vera, who was nice. She did not mind how many stupid questions I asked, and she also made mistakes and admitted them.

The next few days were fun and I did not feel I was working at all. This was partly because I wasn't given much work to begin with, for I don't suppose Miss Kyle felt she could trust me not to make a hash of things. So all I did was show people up to their rooms and type a few letters. It was interesting watching all the different people booking in and out. The hotel staff were all very friendly and there was a lot of joking and fooling about. One of the floor waiters gave me a couple of cream cakes left over from room service. Some of the people who booked in were unknowingly funny. One woman with a strong northern accent complained that she had not been "CONsulted" and I went home at the end of the day and imitated her and others to my parents who were very amused.

I soon met Mr Howard, the Assistant Manager, and he was just as Eunice had described him, tall and dark and very good-looking but cool and aloof with not much humour. He wore a dark coat and smart striped trousers and he walked past the reception office very often and watched what was going on, but without comment. "He's a spy," said Eunice. "He watches us to see if we make any mistakes and then goes and tells Mr Billington."

One of the residents came to me one day and said she had diarrhoea and would I buy her some knickers. I wasn't sure what sort to get but thought she wouldn't care much as long as I got them quickly. There were a number of permanent residents in the hotel, most of whom were elderly and rather sweet. They liked to come and chat to the reception staff to whom they often gave presents, for after years of living in the hotel and looking upon it as their home, they found themselves more fond of people like Miss Kyle and the others than they were of their own grown-up sons and daughters. These permanent residents turned to the hotel staff who were always agreeable and ready to listen and to sympathise: with Mr Hobson-Wells, who had yet again misplaced his Austin Reed umbrella, and with Mrs Finch who had had another attack of sciatica. Miss Kyle had heard about this umpteen times but could be relied upon to commiserate and offer advice and was far more sympathetic than the grown-up sons and daughters who, in any case, seldom came to visit.

But there was one resident, an elderly lady called Mrs Calvert, whom nobody liked. She was querulous and bad-tempered, she never smiled and continually found fault. The first time I came into contact with her was when she came to pay her monthly bill. She made out her cheque for more than the amount on the bill and she asked for the difference in cash. On being given this she handed me a ten shilling note and asked for some small change. I put the note into my drawer and gave her some silver, whereupon she asked me for the other ten shillings.

"What other ten shillings?" I asked, aghast.

"Why you stupid girl, the other ten shillings to make up my pound!" said Mrs Calvert.

"But you only gave me ten shillings in the first place!"

"Nonsense, I gave you a pound. Are you trying to tell me you didn't just put it away in that drawer? Why I watched you do it with my own eyes. I will not be done out of my ten shillings."

"Wait a moment," said Miss Kyle very quietly. "Now what's the trouble?"

When it was explained to her she simply requested Mrs Calvert to place on the counter all the money she had just been given. Then she looked at the cheque, and what lay on the counter agreed with the amount over and above the monthly bill. "Well now, Mrs Calvert," said Miss Kyle, "If you had given my colleague a pound as you say, you would now have ten shillings less than you wrote the cheque for; but you have the right amount here, so I'm afraid I must agree with my colleague in this."

Mrs Calvert grunted and stuffed the money into her handbag. When she had gone away Miss Kyle said: "You're going to have to be much more careful when you're dealing with money over the counter. You were lucky not to lose your ten shillings then. I wouldn't have argued with everyone, but I happen to know Mrs Calvert of old. She's apt to try this sort of thing on, especially with new girls. She wouldn't have tried it with me! Another time when someone asks you for change, don't put their note away in the drawer: hold it on the counter with one hand while you collect the change with the other. That way there can be no arguments about what they gave you in the first place."

From that day on I was very wary in my dealings with Mrs Calvert, whom I thought of as a mean, odious old woman. One day as I was passing the restaurant I collided with her as she was coming out, carrying a straw bag.

"You clumsy girl!" cried Mrs Calvert justifiably as the bag with all its contents including a table napkin filled with cakes, was scattered over the carpet. I helped her to pick them up, then went into the restaurant to have a word with one of the waiters. "Did you see that?" I cried indignantly, "That mean old Mrs Calvert has been pinching cakes to eat upstairs in her room!"

But the waiter was not shocked, on the contrary he laughed. "She's been doing it for years," he said. "They are her own cakes, but she doesn't eat them herself so she takes them upstairs and gives them to her chambermaid. You wouldn't believe it, would you, not of Mrs Calvert? But she's got quite a kind heart underneath."

I thought that because I had found out this benign streak in Mrs Calvert's nature, the old woman would be nicer to me in future – but she was not, she was as bad-tempered as ever and continued to find fault with everything. Who would have thought that she had this one redeeming feature? "You can't judge a book by its cover," said Miss Kyle sagely.

After a while I was allowed to do the cash and given my first bills, and Miss Kyle was pleased. She said she would like me to stay on and she would train me up, but I had set my heart on joining BOAC and had, in fact, sent up my application form. I had also bought a set of Spanish Linguaphone records, as I had decided to teach myself Spanish as an added inducement (I hoped) to BOAC. Every day at home I did my Spanish exercises and got top marks each time I sent them off – yet despite these wonderful marks I never did learn enough Spanish to carry on any sort of conversation, because no one in real life ever talks as slowly as the people on the records.

Meanwhile I loved working at the hotel and thought it the most entertaining job I had had. Every day one of the receptionists would go on a tour of inspection during which she would see the head chambermaid on each floor and receive any unusual reports. There were many of these. The chambermaids were a good bunch and presumably when they were taken on they were asked to report anything suspicious they happened to notice. This they did with huge enjoyment. Old Daisy, who had a broad West Country accent, came up to Vera and me one day and said in a shocked voice, "I think you ought to know dear as 'ow her in No. 281's had a man in with she. I know 'cause I goes in this morning and I sees they both in the little narrow bed." Now Daisy did not in the least mind the moral side of this, if she wanted he in she's bed good luck to they, all that concerned Daisy was that the hotel was being done out of the price of a double bedroom. This was of equal concern to the reception staff, who would dash up and down having excited conferences with each other. It was a tricky situation. If the receptionist could walk into the room and find the guilty couple, well and good, if not it was the chambermaid's word against she's. Sometimes when suspicions were very strong Miss Kyle or Mr Billington would confront the woman as she was checking out and say, "I have reason to believe there were two people sleeping in your room last night. We're therefore having to charge you for a double room."

Oh, how brave, I thought, but what if it were not true? I would never have dared to say such a thing. It was, however, surprising how often the guests paid up without a word and then slunk off. It seemed a little bit unfair in a way, because if you paid for a single room and were prepared to put up with the discomfort of squeezing two people in one person's bed, surely you should not have to pay the same as if you had had a bed each; but the Management did not see it this way. Miss Kyle said they were revolting old women who were using the hotel for their activities. They were picking up men, she said, gigolos they met on the Palace Pier. That was a good hunting ground. It was a disgrace. Anyway, quite often the women didn't pay at all, and we discovered afterwards they had done a moonlit flit down the fire escape. That was even more disgraceful.

I was now doing shift work, just like the others. The evening shift in particular was fun. We started at 4 pm and finished at midnight, and it was more like being at a party than being at work. Often the guests felt like chatting to the receptionists and sometimes they would offer us a drink. We always thanked them and asked for a gin and tonic because we had an arrangement with Jock, the Scottish barman. We were not allowed to drink on duty so Jock would bring us a glass of plain water with a slice of lemon in it and slip us three shillings and sixpence afterwards. This could be quite profitable. Male guests gave us drinks or sometimes perfume, and we also received gifts of chocolates, handkerchiefs and nylon stockings from female guests, particularly the older ones. These were perks which the bookkeepers in their dingy back office never got, so no wonder they did not like us and felt sour.

On Saturday nights there were dinner dances at the hotel and we reception girls would watch the guests arrive and see the blind dates meet in front of our desk. "Rather you than me," we would think as an eager girl who had probably spent hours in the bath and after, making herself pretty, was confronted by a well-boiled, well-oiled young man with protruding teeth and no chin. Or we would see the face of a handsome young man fall as he espied his partner, thick ankles and fat arms and grubby bra showing at the back. Oh, the disappointments – but for the receptionists it was an entertainment, for we were uninvolved. It was like watching a play, except that we never saw the last act. Quite often young men would come up and ask me to dance and I always refused for we were not allowed to mix socially with the guests.

"I think it's a shame," said Miss Kyle who had a romantic streak in her. "I thought that last one looked very nice." He was the President of the Conservative Association and Miss Kyle, being a bit of a match-maker, thought him very suitable for me. It was a quiet night so she told me to go off duty and go to the dance, so I did, and the young man made a great fuss of me and danced with me for the rest of the evening. Waiters kept coming up to me and winking and giving me drinks and the next day I heard one of the bookkeepers say, "I can't understand how Reception can go and join in with the dances, can you? I would hate to have drinks served to me by my friends!"

"Lots of unlikely friendships start up here," said Eunice, "but you must be careful. There's no one you can trust, not a soul."

But I liked them all, well most of them, and I was very happy. I loved working at the Grand Hotel, it was a lot of fun and not like being at work at all. The night porters were very matey and we discussed cremations at breakfast. They, the waiters and the barmen paid me lots of attention and there was much teasing but it was all light-hearted. The flattery I received from them never ceased and though I knew it was not to be taken seriously, it did a lot for my low self-esteem.

One friend I made was a girl called Dizzy. She was about twenty. I think she worked in the kitchens but I can't really remember. She was funny with a sharp wit and she made me laugh. One day she told me in a very matter of fact way that she had a daughter of two by a window cleaner to whom she had once been engaged. I was amazed and could not imagine what her life must have been like. It must have been difficult. I suppose the child was looked after by the grandmother but it didn't stop Dizzy going out a lot and having a very good time.

Life at the Grand was constantly amusing. The page tried on some woman's outlandish hat and everyone sang, "Close the doors, they're coming in the windows" and "We're going to rock around the clock tonight" with which even the elderly residents joined in while sitting at their separate tables in the dining room. I liked the pages as much as anyone. There were four of them and they were all very cheeky and looked much smaller than their years. William, the cheekiest of them, was my favourite, and he always made me laugh. Someone came in and asked if we were full and he said, "No, I'm empty." And when Eunice asked who some old woman was he answered, as Mr Ward the head waiter had said of Mrs Scott-Findlay, "Oh – some ruddy old cow." This seemed a favourite term of abuse. "Don't be cheeky, Page!" said Eunice but he would take no notice.

The others in reception thought him too forward. Miss Kyle was always snubbing him in the most cutting way, the others cried "Be quiet, Page!" as soon as he opened his mouth, but I could not help laughing at his facetious remarks. He and I discussed guests in whom we often saw something hilarious and we would giggle away in a very undignified manner. He was very rude to me too, but I did not mind. I was delighted to see him strutting up and down in someone's fur coat that had been given him to take upstairs, or trying on someone else's hat, or pulling faces behind someone's obnoxious back. "Page!" Miss Kyle would call out sharply and he would skip gaily into the lift, the doors closing smoothly to hide his impish grin.

Mr Ward, the head waiter, was tall and thin and hardly ever smiled but he had a very dry sense of humour and was amusing. One day a party of four people came in, a man and three women, one of whom was his mother. The man ordered wine, which was a rarity in those days, for wine was very expensive and not many people could afford to drink it. When the bottle was opened the man said it was corked and he sent for Ward and told him to take it away and bring another bottle. "Certainly sir," said Ward with his usual dead-pan expression. He then took the bottle down to the cellar and smeared a bit of dust over it, shoved the cork back in and brought the same bottle back to the table. He opened it with a flourish and poured out a little which the man tasted, sloshing it around in his mouth as he knew you were supposed to do. "Ah, that's better!" said the man, "I can always tell when a wine's corked."

"There's nothing our Ernest doesn't know about wine," said his mother proudly. Ward came past the reception desk and shared this little gem with us, adding scornfully, "Bloody idiot!"

Apart from dinner dances there were conferences for various things. The people who came for these were often dreary: self-important little men with glasses and bald heads. Another time there was a conference of midwives. They too were a dull lot and the waiters made plenty of rude remarks about them.

When I had a quick turn-round, that is a late shift followed by an early one next day, I was allowed to stay in one of the two tower rooms on the 7th floor. These were lovely rooms facing the sea, which at that time could be occupied by members of staff but later were prime rooms which were charged at £300 per person per night. I loved staying in my little tower room. It had a stone balcony outside the window, but not the sort you would go onto – unless you were thinking of jumping – because you had to climb out of the window to get onto it and it was so narrow when you got there. But there was a wonderful view. I would open the window and look at the moon shining on the sea and listen to the waves pounding on the shingle. There was a telephone on the bedside table and one of the porters would ring with my alarm call at 7.30. One day I rang down to the hall porters and asked for my breakfast to be sent up, but to my surprise they did not think this was funny. I assured them it was meant to be a joke but they never quite believed me and thought I was putting on airs.

Sometimes when I was in reception on my own, there would be a sudden rush of people and it could become quite frightening. Once when I had been interrupted by two drunken women and it was difficult to deal with them, I got flustered and made two bad mistakes: first I let a man have £27 without giving a receipt and then I let the same room to two lots of people. "Oh woe is me," I wrote in my diary. I should have got a rocket from Miss Kyle but she was very decent about it and covered up for me. Miss Kyle was a fair-minded person and if she felt her girls were pulling their weight she would support them in every possible way, taking their side in disagreements with other departments, and giving them the off-duty time that suited them best. But Miss Kyle had her knife into Eunice and when they were on duty together, the poor girl could do nothing right. She was ordered to do the most wretched jobs like clearing out the filing cabinets, and spoken to in the most cutting way as if she were a bit of dirt. Luckily Eunice did not seem to care. She answered back with cool insolence and argued persistently when she did not agree, often proving Miss Kyle to be in the wrong.

I liked Eunice, she was bossy but fun. She told me she thought I should go to Mara, her hairdresser who would cut my hair in a much more interesting way. So I went and she was certainly good. I looked quite different. Everyone at the Grand said it was stunning, even Mr Howard seemed interested.

"There, you see?" said Eunice. "I knew it would make all the difference, much more flattering." She obviously didn't think much of the way I'd had it before.

In the summer vacation an art student was taken on as a chamber-maid. Her father was a big wig in the City and he had had a word with Mr Billington and got him to take her on. Her name was Carol, she was blonde, lively and full of fun. I often encountered her on my morning rounds of the floors. ""Hi," she said one day, "Give me a hand with this bed, there's a love. It's so much quicker with two."

Another time she said, "Am I sick and tired of cleaning basins! My hands are awful. I've taken to helping myself to their Elizabeth Arden hand cream." Then she offered me a chocolate from a huge box on someone's dressing table. "I can recommend these," she said, "They come from Fortnum and Masons."

"But what if they notice?" I said fearfully.

"Oh go on, take one!" cried Carol. "The way I look at it, if they eat all these themselves they'll put on pounds and pounds – so really we're doing them a favour." This seemed logical, so we each had several. Another time we found a bowl of lustrous black grapes and Carol noticed that one or two large ones at the back of the bunch were just beginning to go off, so we thought we had better eat them in case they infected the rest of the bunch. In spite of being off they had the most superb flavour.

One day when Carol was making someone's bed more thoroughly than usual, she found some pornographic literature under the mattress. She and I were just sitting on the bed engrossed in it when the owner of the room came in and caught us. He looked a most ordinary little man, slim with spectacles and a moustache and reddish hair parted in the middle.

"What are you doing? Where did you get that?" he demanded angrily, hastening towards us. I leapt to my feet but Carol continued to sit on the edge of the bed with her legs dangling.

"I found it," she said, "under your mattress."

"Give it to me," he said, "it was very wrong of you to take it, I shall report you both to the Manager. Going around interfering with people's property – it ought not to be allowed!"

"It is your property, then?" said Carol.

At this the little man's whole attitude changed. He went grey and shook.

"What do you mean by that?" he asked.

"Nothing," said Carol.

"You'd better go, both of you," he said grabbing my arm and urging me towards the door, "I won't tell the Manager if you promise not to say anything. You won't, will you? We'll forget the whole thing, shall we?"

When we were outside Carol said, "You realise we could blackmail that fellow for the rest of his life."

We thought about this and it seemed quite a good idea, but in the end we decided we were not quite nasty enough.

Every day the rooms were cleaned out by the chambermaids and if something was found belonging to a guest who had checked out, the article was given in at the reception desk. The custom was to send it to the address of the previous occupant on the understanding that if the article had belonged to anyone else it would have been found before. One day however, the system broke down. It so happened that one day Carol, who was not the most thorough of chambermaids, brought down to the desk a very frilly lilac nightdress and gave it to Vera. "Found this in No. 138," she said and sauntered off. When Vera went to check the book she found the last occupant was a Mr E. H. Harper with an address in St John's Wood. He had stayed for one night. Without considering the implications of a male guest having a female's nightgown in his bedroom, Vera made it into a parcel, put a compliments slip with it and posted it off to the address in St John's Wood. The parcel was opened by Mr Harper in the presence of his wife, both of whom were horrified on seeing its contents. No amount of reasoning on his part could persuade her that he had not been having an affair with some woman at the Grand Hotel, "Because," she said, "Hotels are like banks. They just don't make mistakes."

The Manager then received a letter from Mr Harper in which he said he proposed to sue the hotel for the mistake they had made, as a result of which his wife threatened to divorce him. Mr Billington made enquiries and it was discovered that the nightdress belonged to a Miss Murray who had occupied Room 138 on the night previous to Mr Harper. Mr Billington called Carol and Vera to his room and rebuked them very severely, Carol for not doing her job properly and Vera for showing so little common sense. Fortunately Mr Billington was able to convince Mr Harper's wife that a genuine mistake had been made, and the matter was dropped. The staff at the hotel however, particularly the reception staff, were very shaken by the whole thing and resolved to be very careful in future.

Yet in spite of our extra care another mistake was made, this time by me. A Mr A. White had been staying in the hotel for three weeks. He came several times a year and was well-known to the older members of staff. It so happened that a week after he checked out, a second Mr A. White, this time with wife, came for a single night. A week later a letter arrived addressed to Mr A. White and I, who was dealing with the correspondence that day went through the book, spotted the entry for the second Mr A. White and without giving it another thought, forwarded it on to him at that address.

It turned out to be a most unfortunate mistake. Mrs White, who found the letter with the Grand Hotel label on it, had never been with her husband on the night in question. As far as she knew he had never been to Brighton in his life. She wanted to know how there happened to be a letter for him re-addressed from the Grand Hotel, Brighton when he had told her he was going to Hull. He was much too taken aback to think of a satisfactory answer, and another marriage hit the rocks. Or so we heard. It had come about due to my error which, admittedly had been made through lack of experience rather than through carelessness, as Miss Kyle pointed out to Mr Billington. It showed what grave consequences could come of an innocent mistake. Such a mistake would not have been made by Miss Kyle and from then on she was given the sole responsibility of re-addressing letters and belongings to guests.

One morning when Daisy went to clean Suite No. 5 she found the occupant lying cold and dead on the bathroom floor. He had apparently had a heart attack and slipped as he was getting out of the bath. It gave her ever such a turn, she said, because it wasn't what you expected to see when you went into a bathroom with your tin of Vim and your floor-cloth. At first she wasn't quite sure that he was dead, although he looked a funny colour and his mouth was all twisted to one side. She touched him gingerly on the shoulder and it was cold as marble. It gave her ever such a funny feeling. "Him were naked o' course," she added with relish, "and all slippery like a fish with soap an' lather." She gained a lot of attention with this story, which she told over and over again.

After finding him she ran out of the suite and informed the housekeeper, who rushed downstairs to the Manager's office. He took the matter in hand at once. There were all sorts of arrangements to be made to dispose of the body, which was laid on the bed in the meantime. Later on when I came on duty I saw that Suite No. 5 was scheduled to be free from that night, and I took rather a jolly family up to see it. They were very impressed with the sitting room. Then I walked across to the bedroom and flung open the door and there was the body still lying on the bed covered by a sheet. You could see exactly what it was because of the way the feet stuck up, pointing to the ceiling.

"I'm sorry, I made a mistake, the suite is let," I said, shutting the door hastily, but not before the family had seen the figure on the bed. They were strangely silent as we went down in the lift. I suggested they might like to see another suite, No. 6 on the sixth floor, but somehow they seemed to have lost their enthusiasm for staying at the Grand.

Sometimes guests would skip out without paying their bills. The sort of people who did this generally came for one night and were inclined to be shabbily dressed and shifty-eyed, couples often, wearing grubby mackintoshes and down-at-heel shoes. They would just have bed and breakfast and you wouldn't see them again until night time, if then. If it was suspected that they might do a flit their luggage was held in reception and handed back only when the bill was paid. If they had no luggage when they checked in the staff were justified in asking for a deposit in advance. Sometimes it was discovered that they had gone before breakfast, before anyone but the night-porters were on duty.

It was not difficult to do a flit, either via the fire escape or the staff exit on the ground floor, which came out in the car park. When this happened Mr Billington was annoyed with the girls in reception. I was on with Eunice and Vera and he came in and said he was fed up with the Bloody Reception Office and he'd like to change the lot of us. Vera was very upset but Eunice answered him back and said coolly, "How were we to know that couple would do a moonlight flit?" He said that we should be able to foresee such a thing if we used our common-sense. It did not happen to the people checked in by Miss Kyle, for if she had any doubts whatever she did not hesitate to ask for a deposit. I dreaded to ask people for a deposit and it seemed wrong to suspect someone of being dishonest just because their skirt was hanging down below their coat and they had shifty eyes.

The hotel could not refuse to let a person have a room if there was accommodation available, unless of course they were drunk and likely to cause annoyance to other guests, but Miss Kyle kept a list of people who were liable to cause trouble. People who got drunk or were offensive or had disgusting habits or were generally difficult were marked down on the Black List, and a careful watch was kept on them by all departments.

On the other hand, Miss Kyle was not impressed with name-droppers, people who thumped the desk and said they were on the Board of Directors or they were Alderman Thingummy or Councillor So and So. Then there was the old chestnut: "I'm a personal friend of the Chairman," which was like a red rag to a bull. Nothing infuriated Miss Kyle more. "Name-droppers, little tin gods," she commented tersely, "Give them a room on the back."

One day a man came up to the desk and asked me for a room. "The nicest room you've got," he said. "I don't know how long I'll be staying, at least a week, maybe longer."

"Would you like a suite?" I asked.

"A suite? You mean several rooms? Marvellous! Then I shall be able to have parties and entertain all my friends. What a brilliant idea of yours!"

His name was Doctor Ryder. He was about thirty-five years old, tall with black hair. He wore horn-rimmed spectacles and walked with a bad limp. He was charming – everyone thought so. He never passed the reception desk without stopping to talk to us. He was very generous, always buying us drinks (water with a slice of lemon and 3/6d on the side.) "Well," he'd say to me, "And how's my favourite receptionist?" I didn't take this seriously as he probably said the same to Eunice and Vera, but he was so charming and had such a marvellous sense of humour that it was fun to have him around. He livened things up a bit.

When I was on in the evenings and it was quiet, he would come up and talk by the hour, leaning on the counter and hooking his stick over the top. He would tell me about his practice in Harley Street and about the cottage he had bought in Southern Ireland, how it was right on the edge of the cliff and you could lie in bed at night and see the waves pounding on the beach without even raising your head from the pillow. There was a goat in the field behind the cottage, it was very tame and when he was there it would come right inside the kitchen and lie down in front of the fire, like a dog. He called it Alfie. Once he found a seagull perched on the edge of the cliff with its wing broken. He had brought it inside and made a splint for the wing and gradually it got better. One day it flew away and he thought he had seen the last of it but a month later it was back again. After that it often came back and perched on top of the larder door. He christened it Douglas.

"Why Douglas?" I asked.

"Because it looked like a Douglas."

He soon made friends amongst the other guests and would invite them up to his sitting room for champagne cocktails. Everyone spoke of him in glowing terms. He was the most charming, generous guest to have stayed at the hotel in years.

It would be difficult to say when anyone first noticed anything odd about him, but one day when I was on duty with Eunice and we were chatting to one of the waiters, he said, "Have you noticed he never actually pays for anything?"

"What do you mean?" I asked.

"Well, we know he's very generous and all that, but he puts everything down on his bill. Everything, even a packet of fags. And my word, his bill must be something! He orders whatever he fancies you know, all the out of season stuff, no skimping. It wouldn't surprise me at all if he was to do a flit one of these days."

"Oh Harry don't be daft," cried Eunice, "He's a nice respectable gentleman. I don't know how you can think such things. It's that nasty suspicious mind of yours."

"Well I'm not the only one," said Harry, "there's one or two has said it besides me."

Soon after this the staff started laying bets as to whether or not he was genuine. Even the Manager, briefed by Miss Kyle, started to watch him. I, who firmly believed in him, thought they were being quite absurd.

After he had stayed at the hotel for two weeks he announced that he would be leaving the following day. He wanted to have a farewell luncheon in his suite first, he said, for twelve people – smoked salmon, champagne, the lot. He would leave after lunch and would like his bill to be ready.

"There you see?" I said triumphantly, "if he were going to do a flit he would never tell us when he was leaving and ask for his bill to be ready. He would just go quietly one day."

"There's still time," said Miss Kyle, who did not trust him.

After breakfast on the morning of his departure, Dr Ryder announced that he was going up to the golf links for a round of golf.

"I don't anticipate being late back," he said, "I've asked my guests to come at 1 o'clock for 1.30 and if anyone should arrive early I'd be glad if you would show them up to my suite."

"Oh I will, certainly," I said earnestly.

"Thanks honey. You're a good girl," he said, giving me a pat on the cheek.

"Right," said Mr Billington when he had gone out, "we'll hold his luggage in reception."

A very handsome pigskin suitcase was brought downstairs and left behind the reception counter. I was embarrassed. Whatever would he think of us, to suspect for a single moment that he wasn't going to pay his bill? I hoped I would not be around when the suitcase was handed back to him.

There was an atmosphere of excitement in the hotel. As 1 o'clock approached the luncheon was laid on. Tables and chairs were carried up to his suite, flowers were taken in, drinks and champagne on ice.

"Where's he gone?" said Mr Billington.

"He's having a round of golf. He'll be here in a minute," I said.

But he wasn't. He never came back at all. Mr Howard opened up his suitcase and found it full of second-hand books marked 3d and 6d each. It was a beautiful suitcase made of pigskin with silk-covered compartments: it had been hired from a firm in Bayswater. When Mr Billington and Mr Howard went upstairs to his suite they found everything had gone, every stitch of clothing. They checked his name and address and discovered he was not on the medical register, and the number he had given in Harley Street was a false one. The police were notified and they said he was probably a man who had been staying at hotels up and down the country for weeks at a time, using different disguises at each place. The glasses and the limp were part of the disguise, they said, and probably the hair colour. He was quite brazen, they said, though charming. Everyone agreed he had charm. But the audacity of the devil. Goodness knows where he might be by now.

The hotel buzzed with it. No one spoke of anything else for weeks. I was stunned. "I shall never trust anyone ever again," I said. "I can't believe it. What about the cottage in Ireland and the goat called Alfie and Douglas the seagull with the broken wing?"

"All a pack of lies," said Miss Kyle. She could not help being a little complacent.

CHAPTER THREE

Meanwhile things had been happening at home: *Woman's Journal*, to whom I had sent my short story "The Cherry Stone" had forwarded it on to another magazine called *Good Taste* and they wrote on the 23rd September to say they thought my writing style was young and gay and easily readable. I had to make a few alterations, but to my great joy they accepted it and were going to pay me 15 guineas. This seemed like a great deal of money.

Then, on 7th October while I was working at the Grand, my parents and I moved house. I was sad to leave 51 Shirley Drive but they said there was no point living by the sea if you were not by the sea (we only had what my mother called a landlady's view from an upstairs window) and they had found a maisonette on the top two floors of 23b Adelaide Crescent, which of course was much nearer. On the day of the move we said our goodbyes to the neighbours, the Websters and the Herberts and the Kirkleys and Leonard the Pole (who nearly wept), and had dinner in a Chinese restaurant. Of course we had Mr Chips and Pym with us and I was a bit worried that Pym would not settle down, as he would no longer have our garden to run about in. Admittedly, the maisonette was nice. It was spacious with a mushroom-coloured fitted carpet throughout, over which we put the Persian rugs.

My parents had a large bedroom on the ground floor and there was a sitting room, dining room and kitchen on the same floor with four bedrooms and two bathrooms above. All the rooms that faced the sea were bright but the ones that faced the back, including the kitchen and the two bathrooms, were dismal, dark and old-fashioned. The bathrooms were painted green and the walls papered with glossy green paper, having a predictable pattern of seaweed and fish that was popular in the 50s.

I liked my bedroom. It faced the sea and got a lot of sun. My furniture was painted yellow, and the curtains had a bright honeysuckle pattern with a matching dressing table and stool. So much yellow added to the sunshine effect. I spent a lot of time kneeling on the floor with Pym beside me. I'd be writing short stories, listening to classical music on my gramophone or doing my Spanish Linguaphone records (even though my Spanish never got much better). My mother complained that I wasn't very sociable and I wasn't, for I despised the sort of television they watched and thought it was a waste of time.

Now that we lived near the sea we were able to swim every day. My parents liked to go in the evening, wearing long towelling dressing gowns over their bathing things. My mother could now walk to the shops instead of going on her bicycle, and she could walk to the large department store Hills of Hove and meet her friend Eve Fyffe for coffee. Every day my father went to his local pub the Wick, where he drank a pint or two of bitter. They could take our dog for walks along the front or in the gardens. There were no such things as dogs' lavatories in those days so there was dog mess all over the place and if you sat in the gardens with your book you had to watch where you were sitting.

On the 8th October I received a letter from BOAC asking me to go for an interview on the 20th. When the day arrived I was on tenterhooks. I dressed very carefully in my black polo-necked dress with emerald green coat, black pillbox hat, black suede Louis-heeled shoes, black gloves and bag and glass earrings. I thought I looked very smart, but I didn't really, I was deluding myself. I went up to London on the train and a very nice taxi driver took me to the glass office where the interviews were being held. It was pouring with rain, I was the first to go in and trembled with fear. Alas, it went off very badly. I didn't like the Chairman at all and came out feeling rather sad.

To my surprise I got a letter five days later saying I'd been accepted for the final selection board, date not known. "Oh thank you God, you are a brick!" I wrote in my diary. (I wonder how many other people called God a brick).

Meanwhile my father, having retired in 1953 from his job as Senior Resident in the Colonial Service in Nigeria, had been looking for something else to do to occupy his time. (At one time he had considered buying the Duke of York cinema but did not in the end. I also had played a joke on him and sent him a spoof letter inviting him to 'travel in ladies' underwear' which my mother thought very amusing - I'm not sure he thought so.) In 1955 there was a State of Emergency in Cyprus where the Greek Cypriots wanted Enosis (Union with Greece) and the Turkish Cypriots were bitterly opposed to it.

British personnel were required by the Colonial Office to go out there and my father was offered an administrative post as Commissioner of Kyrenia.

For what seemed an age he debated whether he should go or not. He was alternately keen, then unenthusiastic. Finally he decided he would definitely go. My mother had misgivings but I was all for it. The only problem was, what would I do about BOAC? I wrote to them and said my parents were going out to Cyprus and wanted me to go with them, and would it be possible to be based in Nicosia? But they wrote back, a very nice letter, saying they did not employ girls unless they were based at London Airport, however they would hold my application over for 18 months. Having set my heart on joining BOAC I was a little disappointed, but I had promised my parents I would go to Cyprus with them, and my mother said my father would never have taken the job if he had thought I would not keep my word.

Now I too had to have a job there. Things happened quite quickly. On the 15th November my father managed to get me an introduction to Mr Teriyapoulos of the Cyprus office and helped me fill in an extensive application form. On the 18th I went for the first interview. My father would be leaving for Cyprus in two days and we had a farewell family lunch at the Sussex Grill and a last drive in his old Jowett Javelin. The next day we all got up early and saw him off from Victoria.

I had my second interview a week later. I thought it went fairly well, but I don't know why, for it seems to have been a disaster: they wanted people to go out right away, which I could not do, they wanted girls with very good shorthand which I did not have and they said I was too young, which I could do nothing about. Nevertheless, I was sent for a medical and X-rays in Harley Street. In due course I received a rather discouraging letter from the Colonial Office, but they didn't close the door altogether, and I decided to go to a local secretarial bureau and brush up my speeds.

On the 5th November Badger and Peter came down from London with their friend Martin Lennox and we all went to Bonfire Night at Lewes. It was an amazing night with fireworks and numerous processions of local people in fancy dress and masks marching down Lewes High Street, some with brass and drums, some with flaming torches. They burned an effigy of the Pope as a protest against the burning of 17 Protestant martyrs in 1755 under Bloody Mary. Today people exclaim in horror at this political incorrectness, but in those days the Catholics were very laid back and didn't mind a bit. After watching the various processions, we went to one of the five big bonfires which are held in Lewes every year.

I had not seen or heard anything from Martin since the previous year, just before I went to Jamaica, when we had gone to see *The Duenna* and afterwards to dance at the Colony. I had liked him then and thought he liked me too but having heard nothing, came to the conclusion that men were fickle – for otherwise why had he not been in touch with me?

Yet this November 5th it was just as before: I was close to him all evening and he held me by the shoulders while we watched the fireworks and the bonfire. The next day we walked along the front by the sea and fed the gulls and got soaked by the spray. He asked if I would go to Zermatt on a skiing holiday with him in January and I was delighted. Later I was working late and he drove me to the Grand Hotel. The following week a group of us were in London to see *The Pyjama Game* and afterwards we went on to dance at Hatchetts until 3 am. I wore a black chiffon evening dress which I'd had copied from a picture in a magazine. I thought it was very sophisticated. It had a narrow skirt and a sheath of black velvet draped around the hip and a fresh rose pinned to the bodice. I wanted to look like a femme fatale, for I knew I would be seeing Guy again – the first time for nearly two years - and was afraid of him seeing me as a wallflower. Luckily that did not happen, for once again Martin stayed close to me all evening. It was all right with Guy too, although I think we were both aware of how close we had once been. Felix, who had met him since, said he treasured the memory of our relationship and I was comforted by this thought – but anyway it was now in the past. And meanwhile Martin and I danced till 3 am and afterwards he took me in his arms and kissed me and I was very happy.

Two weeks later Martin rang up and invited me to go to Reigate the following day and meet his family. I was pleased but worried at the same time, half dreading to meet his parents – suppose they didn't like me? He met me at the station and drove me to the lovely detached house in which they lived. I thought they were one of the nicest families I had ever met. His mother in particular was kind and charming to me, his father too, and I adored his younger sister Pam, who had a job at the Army and Navy Stores and was contemplating going round the world. I would have gone with her like a shot if I had not been going to Cyprus. We had a very good supper and then played Scrabble in front of a blazing fire. Afterwards Martin bought my ticket for me and saw me off at the station. I hoped his parents did like me - at first I thought perhaps yes, but later I wondered if I was assuming too much. I really liked Martin and everything about him.

The next day in London I had another interview at the Commissioner of Cyprus office, but the funny thing was I didn't realise the interview had started. I was sitting in an office chatting casually to a couple of people there, not knowing who they were and being quite frank and probably coming out with all sorts of unseemly remarks as I was apt to do, and suddenly they laughed and said that had been the interview. It must have gone reasonably well I suppose. Afterwards I met Pat Pears and as usual we had stacks to talk about. She was funny, we could let our hair down and I always loved meeting her.

At home life was difficult, for my mother was very depressed at being separated from my father; she blamed herself and me for his having gone out to Cyprus. It was difficult and embarrassing and I wished she wouldn't. She was a person of mercurial moods, and her depressed state was worst of all. Nothing I could say would cheer her up. I decided to buy her a hyacinth blue twin-set for Christmas but there wasn't one in her size and they cost £6, which I didn't have. I thought in some ways the sooner we went out to join my father, the better.

I was also a bit despondent as I had heard nothing from Martin, and when I eventually got a Christmas card simply signed 'From Martin', with a capital F, I felt that was It. It was over. How fickle men were, I thought. First there was Guy, then Ken and now Martin. They were all fickle. The only faithful one was John, the American boyfriend I'd met in Jamaica, who had continued to write regularly. He said he was glad I'd got away from the Lynns, it was not right the way they treated 'a sweet girl like you.' I thought, not so sweet, if you only knew it.

I walked along by the sea. It was just getting dark and the sea looked very beautiful. It was strange but however unhappy and troubled I was, I could always be comforted by the sea. I watched the waves as they rolled, almost singing, onto the shore; and then the next one would come and the one after that, it was inevitable as time itself that the waves would keep rolling onto the beach; and presently my troubles rolled away with them.

It was a relief to get away from home and go to the Grand Hotel. Christmas was coming up and there were lots of parties and dinners. At the Staff Luncheon I was toasted at the top table. I sat next to Dizzy and wore my new tangerine dress which seemed to be quite a hit, even with Mr Howard. On Christmas Day I received lots of chocolates and £1 6s in tips. I helped with the Children's Christmas party and passed round endless plates of sandwiches, sausage rolls, cream cakes and biscuits to fat little children who stuffed everything into their mouths as fast as they could. "They'll probably be sick now," said Dizzy, and they were – one in front of the reception desk, and we had to jump to avoid stepping in it.

Badger and Peter had come down and after my shift I went home and we had a lovely evening, opening all the presents. After getting my wages I had had enough money to buy mine and got a rust twin-set for my mother which she liked very much. (Or said she did – for I remembered how, as a small child, I had bought her little bottles of poppy scent from Woolworths and she had said she liked those too.)

On Boxing Day Graham Wimbolt asked me out for a drink and Mr Brown asked Vera. Graham Wimbolt had been to a dinner dance at the hotel and kept coming to Reception to talk to me. Mr Brown had been staying in the hotel and kept talking to Vera. He was a widower, quite rich with a very nice house in Haywards Heath. He asked Vera to marry him and she did, but the trouble was he continually compared her to his first wife and would not let her make any changes in the house. She had to use all the first wife's china and sheets and everything and Bill kept telling her what a wonderful cook and housekeeper the first wife had been, which was a bit much, I thought. A second wife doesn't want to hear endless stories about this tedious paragon of virtue. However, all that was to come later.

On the 4th January 1956, Mr Billington told me I would have to leave before I went on my skiing holiday, which meant I only had another two weeks at the Grand Hotel. This was sad, I had so loved working there. Also on the 4th I received a letter from Douglas Williams of the *Daily Telegraph,* whom I had met in Jamaica. He asked me to meet him for a drink at the Park Lane Hotel, which I did. He said he would like me to meet a friend of his from Cyprus, a Commander John Proud who worked for the Cyprus BBC, and who might be a useful contact if the job with the Colonial Office fell through. The three of us met on the 6th January. They were both very kind, but I didn't know why they should have bothered, and wished I had been brilliant and witty in my conversation.

My last days at the Grand passed quickly. Everyone was very sorry to hear I was leaving, even Mr Howard, who was surprisingly pleasant and who talked to me at length when we were both on the evening shift. The waiters teased me endlessly, calling me the Queen of Cyprus. Two of the waiters were Greek Cypriot and they said they thought the troubles would soon be over, but this seemed unlikely, for every day in the news there were reports of more bombs and more murders.

I slept for my last night in the little room in the tower and the next day said my goodbyes. It was sad. Everyone was charming, especially Jock the barman who had given me all those glasses of water with a slice of lemon and sneaked me 3s 6d on the side. Eunice gave me some ski clothes, including a super black and white sweater. Miss Kyle said how she would have liked me to stay on. Vera of course, I would stay in touch with for she had become a good friend.

CHAPTER FOUR

My mother had very decently given me some money towards my skiing holiday and I bought lots of clothes, including a lovely tangerine velvet skirt and a black evening sweater. I went to Lillywhites and got black ski pants and a coral and white jacket. Our holiday started on 19th January 1956, under the auspices of the RAF Ski Association. We met at London Airport and flew to Berne. There were initially five in our group, Martin, his friend Colin, Virginia, Valerie and myself. I thought they were all very nice, but at the airport two other girls joined us, Sue and Sally, and I was uneasy to note how pretty they were, especially Sally. I didn't think I stood a chance with them in our group.

From Berne we took a little mountain train up to Zermatt. At our hotel Martin and Colin shared a room with a Pole and a very fair young man called Bill, while I shared with Virginia and Valerie. Of the two I liked Valerie the best.

On the first day we got our bearings, sorted out our skis and sticks and explored the pretty little village of Zermatt. The next day we had tests to check our level of proficiency: we had to ski down a steep slope. I went very fast, which impressed everyone. They were expecting me to do a stunning stem-christie but I didn't know how, so I just crashed at the bottom. I had only ever skied once before when I was in Lausanne and I'd been pretty hopeless then. Anyway my crash landing caused a sensation and after they'd stopped laughing I was put in the lowest class, the next one up from the beginners, with Hans as instructor. Virginia and Valerie were in the same one, but the three young men were much more advanced and were higher.

I did not get on well at first, I kept falling over and by the second day it was worse. I felt exhausted and dizzy and had to go back to the hotel. Afterwards the others came back and said Hans thought it best if I did not go to Riffelburg with them the next day in case of accidents. This was very depressing – to come on a skiing holiday and not be able to ski made me feel very unhappy and I wept. Martin's friend Colin was incredibly kind and understanding. He was different from the others in a way I cannot explain.

The next day was no better. I went into Toni's class but could not keep up and dropped out. I was obviously rubbish at skiing. I had just gone off on my own when Erik, a tall bearded Swiss-German instructor saw my plight and asked me to join his class of two – a German and a Belgian, who were very polite and kept clicking their heels. Erik made a great fuss of me, but we had to communicate in French as he could not speak any English.

The next day I was put in Ambrose's class which was a bit better, though I was still dispirited by my lack of skill, and greatly preferred the après ski. There were lunches with plenty of Glühwein at little mountain inns and hot chocolate at the Jug or the Alpina, where we danced in our ski boots. The RAF Ski Club had a cocktail party and I chatted to Bill and lots of others. There was a moonlit excursion by horse-drawn carriage up a mountain, and a Gala night at Mont Cervin where I danced with King Farouk's son but can't remember if he was as grossly fat as his father.

Martin took me out to places where we could dance at night. We went to Bernadetti's on the Schweizerhof and to the Chez Nous Bar. The hit song at that time was Frank Sinatra singing "Love and marriage go together like a horse and carriage", which Martin said was very true.

Colin and I travelled up in the train to Gornergrat together and had a good chat. He said he had guessed I was a writer – potentially, I said quickly. (It was flattering but I didn't think I could claim to be a real writer on the strength of just one short story in *Good Taste* and a letter published in a cat magazine when I was ten.) One night when the others had all gone to bed, Bill begged me to go out with him and in the end I agreed to go just for one hour. Martin would not have been pleased and I felt a bit guilty, but I enjoyed it, for Bill was good company. We talked of many things – fate and the colour bar – and the complexity of my nature. I didn't think I had a complex nature, anything but. More a bit simple really. Coming up in the lift he suddenly kissed me, much to my surprise. He said he never thought he would come all the way from his home in Eastbourne to Zermatt to meet a girl from Hove.

After a while my skiing, under the tuition of Ambrose, got better. Five of his class went up in the chair lift and skied down, and Martin joined us. Another day we skied six times from Rotenboden to Riffelburg, and again the next day seven times, the last time very fast with just Ambrose, Tom, David and me. We then had tea in the Jug and David danced with me, and Erik the Swiss ski instructor joined us and flirted outrageously. On the last day we took the train up to Gornergrat, and coming down the Wall of Death I hurt my knee and could not ski down to Zermatt with the rest of the class in the afternoon. But Ambrose said never mind, he was very pleased with my progress.

That holiday was extraordinary. It sounds conceited to say so and no one was more surprised than me, but both Martin and Bill told me they had fallen in love with me. I wasn't sure Martin really meant it but he told me again on subsequent nights. And while I danced cheek to cheek with each of them in turn, Eric the handsome Swiss ski instructor followed us everywhere and watched, winking at me over their shoulder.

On our last day Martin told me, to my surprise, that dear Colin had enjoyed this holiday more than all the others, and when I asked why, he said "Because you were there."

On our return I carried on with my shorthand and typing lessons at Clarke's College. I worked very hard but the stipulated 100 words per minute in shorthand eluded me. I kept taking the tests, but my speeds fell far short of the requirements. I went back to see the Crown Agents. I had not been offered a job in Cyprus, yet we must have been confident I would get one, for my mother and I booked our passage from Venice to Limassol in a month's time. My old friend Ion Collas, whom I had met in Switzerland and whose father had been the Greek ambassador there, wrote to say he would see me when we went through Greece en route to Cyprus.

It would be sad to leave our pets behind. Winks was going to have Mr Chips and Pym was to be boarded with a woman known to Auntie Joan P, at a cost of five shillings a week. I wasn't sure I liked this idea, as the house was in a very depressing street and there were dirty white lace curtains at the windows. However, the woman's daughter, a nurse, had fallen in love with Pym and I felt she would be kind to him. Besides, there was no alternative.

Martin asked me to go to a hockey dance and stay for the first weekend after we got back from Zermatt. His family were out when we arrived, the house was all in darkness and we had to change by candlelight. Next morning his mother was very kind and brought me breakfast in bed and put my fire on. Then Martin and I went shopping in Reigate and had coffee at the Old Wheel, and in the afternoon I watched him play hockey and met his cousins and various friends.

On the Sunday we went for a walk on Reigate Hill and talked of many things and he told me he loved me more and more each day. He took me to tea with his sister Peggy and introduced me to her two sweet little children. Also on Sunday I was nearly late for breakfast – there was a bit of discipline about that, I noticed – and then Martin, his father and I went to church. Charming as they all were, there was quite a strict routine in their household. It was precise, everyone had to conform. Breakfast was always at the same time and you shouldn't be late; they always went to church and had a glass of sherry afterwards and the men always cleaned the shoes while the women cooked the lunch.

It was all very different from my own home, where things were chaotic and the most nostalgic smell was of burnt toast. At home there had once been a burglary and the police came and reported there were signs of disorder and confusion in my parents' bedroom, drawers left half open, clothes and papers scattered about, whereupon my mother had to confess the disorder and confusion was of her own making. I could not imagine such disorder in the Lennox household, but I was undaunted, for I liked the family as much as before.

Later Martin drove me home and Badger and Peter were there and we all had supper together. Then we went out on the sea front to get some air, but really to be alone so that we could say goodbye. He kept telling me he loved me and I was sure I loved him too. He wrote and said he had to make a decision but I didn't know what he meant.

I had had a letter from Colin asking me to have lunch before I went to Cyprus, so I did, with him and Virginia. He was such an unusual and nice person and I felt honoured that he should want to stay friends. I wondered if perhaps Virginia was in love with him, but feared he wasn't the marrying kind. Bill also wrote, saying he wanted to see me and asking me to go out with him the following Saturday. He then telephoned. This was a bit of a quandary as I thought Martin might be angry, but I went nevertheless. I took him home for lunch and all the family liked him enormously.

In the afternoon we went up to Devil's Dyke and had a walk, then we found a delightful farmhouse where we had brown bread and strawberry jam and cream for tea. In the evening – and I'm surprised I wasn't as big as a house eating all the time - we went out for dinner at the Sussex Grill and had Chicken Maryland, and then on to dance at the Metropole. Bill was good company and a superb dancer so it was a very pleasant evening, but he kept saying he was in love with me and I didn't want to lead him up the garden path. I told him I was very involved with Martin and it might be better for us not to meet again. He came round to our house two days later in spite of my telling him not to - but only stayed an hour.

Martin came to stay with us the next weekend. We went to see a film called *Love is a Many Splendoured Thing*. In the night it snowed and the next day when we tried to go to Poynings Church we got stuck in a snow drift and had to get out and walk. We got as far as the Shepherd and Dog about three miles away, where we had a drink, then walked the three miles back and did not get home till half past two. In the evening we had high tea by the fire with chestnuts and Cointreau, and he told my mother he was going to miss me very much when I went to Cyprus, because he was very fond of me. I was sorry he said that because after he had gone she questioned me for ages. She was dying to know if we had an understanding, and I really didn't want to tell her anything.

I took several more shorthand tests and when I got 90 words per minute Miss Haddow, my teacher very kindly wrote and told the Crown Agents, so that they would not give up on me. Then on the 22nd February I took the 100 wpm and managed to get it. So at last I had my Certificate. I was delighted and much relieved, and gave Miss Haddow a huge bouquet of flowers.

I went up to London two days later and stayed the night with Felix and the next morning we had hot buttered toast and lots of girly chat. Someone had asked her to marry him and she didn't know whether to or not – she didn't, and decided to join BOAC instead. My other girlfriends were having similar traumas; Pat Pears was deeply unhappy because her father had put a stop to a passionate love affair and had the young man sent out to Africa. His last letter was so sad. Jill M was in love with a Jewish guy whose mother interfered and put a stop to it. Ann C had married an old bald man, which appalled me, though she seemed happy enough. The vicar's daughter was besotted with Leonard the Pole and her mother rang and talked for half an hour, saying how unsuitable it was. And Ann H was in love with a Catholic priest.

I saw the Crown Agents and they told me I had got the job, and gave me an agreement to sign. My job title would be Confidential Assistant and I would join a team of British girls who were being recruited in preference to the Cypriots because we would be handling Secret and Top Secret files and were expected to be more trustworthy.

That evening I went to Peter and Badger's flat and a group of us went to see *La Plume de Ma Tante* and then on to the Sloane Court Club for dinner and dancing. Martin drove me back to Badger and Peter's flat and on the way we stopped and he asked me to marry him. Of course I said yes, so there it was, we were engaged. It was about three o'clock in the morning.

After that life was a whirl. We went down to Hove and he asked permission from my mother, who was so overcome with gratitude at the thought of getting her wayward younger daughter off her hands that she cried "Oh thank you, thank you very much!" We told Badger and Peter and then Martin's parents in Reigate, and they very correctly drove us down to Hove to meet my mother, and everyone seemed to like everyone else and to be delighted.

Martin knew I was going to Cyprus for at least a year – though the contract was for two - but he hoped I might perhaps come back earlier so that we could get married. He arranged for us to have our photographs taken professionally and we had them done by someone called Fayer who draped a lot of black velvet stuff around my shoulders so it looked as if I was wearing a strapless evening gown.

To my amazement there was a letter from Ken, my Irish boyfriend, the next day. He said he would come to England if I still wanted him to. All that year I had longed for him to write to me again and he never had. Even if his mother had stopped my letters to him, he could have written to me. Well – it's a bit bloody late now, I thought. So I ignored it. But I had to write two very difficult letters, one to Glen. I did so hope he would understand and that we could continue to be friends. He wrote back at once, a very sweet letter saying it made no difference to our friendship, for we had never had any kind of affair, he had taken good care to see to that, and we would be friends for the rest of our lives. (And we were too, continuing to write for many years until he was tragically killed in a helicopter accident in 1966.)

The other difficult letter was to Bill. Unfortunately my letter crossed in the post with an ardent love letter he wrote to me. Later Martin found out about this and was upset because I hadn't told him about it before. So I showed him the letter and it was so innocent and sweet, he understood and was all right about it.

I was now worried about my mother as she was very ill. Her smallpox vaccination had taken badly and her temperature was 101.2, so I persuaded her to go to bed, and she gradually got better. Then came the goodbyes – to Granny Hove and Auntie Joan P and everyone at the Grand Hotel. They were all delighted to hear my news.

There wasn't much time left now. The packing for Cyprus was difficult, for my mother was in an awful state of nerves. I went up to London, taking some of the luggage, on which there was quite a lot to pay, then on to 33 Beaufort Gardens to say goodbye to Mrs Harland and Alan, and later still to Badger and Peter.

I met Martin and we went to Mappin & Webb to choose the ring. He had been there earlier and made a selection from which I was to choose, the prices having been removed first. He was so correct in everything he did. The rings were laid before me on a black velvet-lined tray and I chose one with my birthstone, a beautiful emerald with a diamond on either side. It was too large for me but they promised they could make it smaller in time for our departure. I gave Martin a record token and he chose the music from *Love is a Many Splendoured Thing*, because he felt it was our theme tune.

Then it was Sunday 4th March, the last day. I did my last-minute packing, then Martin arrived and we drove to Rottingdean and walked along the undercliffs. It was a perfect, beautiful day and the sea and the sky were very blue. We sat on the beach and Martin gave me my ring and I was very happy, and at the same time, sad at the thought of parting. But we told ourselves that lots of people had been through this before and it would be worse if it were wartime.

We went to the Sussex Grill for lunch and he asked my mother if she and Daddy would come home for two weeks' holiday so we could be married next spring, but she was not keen. We drove to Surbiton, where we met Auntie Joan and Jean, then on to London, where we had booked three rooms at the Grosvenor Hotel, for Martin, my mother and me. Badger and Peter joined us for drinks, then he and I decided to go to the Savoy Grill. There were a lot of very rich people there and we felt we were doing everything wrong, but we laughed and managed to be cheerful.

Back at the Grosvenor my mother had gone to bed and Martin came to my room. He longed for us to make love but knew I wanted to keep myself 'pure and virginal' for my wedding and was much too honourable to insist. I was such a prude, but it was the way I had been brought up. Besides, my mother would have been shocked, and it was altogether unthinkable. He stayed a long time and it was very difficult for us both, but eventually he went to his room, and after a last phone call we said goodbye. I cried myself to sleep.

The next morning he rang to wake me up. We got up and dressed and had breakfast, finding the notice of our engagement was in the paper. Then there was a frantic rush to get everything done in time, and at last there we were in the train with all our luggage. We had to say goodbye once and for all. I wept again, and he looked unbelievably sad. Then the train moved slowly out of the station and we were off on a journey that was to change the entire course of my life.

CHAPTER FIVE

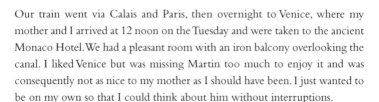

Our train went via Calais and Paris, then overnight to Venice, where my mother and I arrived at 12 noon on the Tuesday and were taken to the ancient Monaco Hotel. We had a pleasant room with an iron balcony overlooking the canal. I liked Venice but was missing Martin too much to enjoy it and was consequently not as nice to my mother as I should have been. I just wanted to be on my own so that I could think about him without interruptions.

A telegram was delivered to the hotel saying "Thanks for everything darling writing Cyprus love M". It was a new experience to be called darling, no one had ever called me darling before, until Martin (and also, Bill in his letters – where it was every other word).

We went on a tour of Venice with some Americans, and the next day we looked round the shops and saw beautiful glass. My mother was very worried because I went off on my own to sit by the canal and finish my letter to Martin. I think she thought I might jump in and be drowned. We took a gondola to the customs house and waited there for what seemed hours, and I wrote in my diary that it was like a slaughterhouse – not that I had ever been in a slaughterhouse – and eventually we boarded the ship SS *Grimani*. It was a nice little Italian ship with not many passengers, certainly not in first class. We went to our cabin and unpacked, and I was touched and delighted to receive a delivery of a dozen red roses done up in cellophane and tied with red ribbon. We then went early to bed for we were very tired. It was bitterly cold.

On Thursday it was rough and we both felt ill and lay on our beds all day, having no breakfast, lunch or tea. I felt not ill so much as tired, and slept solidly, not getting up till seven o'clock, when I had some roast beef. On the Thursday we reached Brindisi and an American whom my mother had been talking to, showed me the Appian Way, the staircase leading from Rome where Pompey and Caesar once came to their ships. I was very impressed by it and drank in the atmosphere of everything that had happened all those centuries ago.

On the Friday I spent many hours looking out to sea, and as we began to pass the Greek islands I thought of Odysseus coming home to Ithaca. There was a good-looking Sicilian officer called Salvo who fetched me a deck chair. He had seen my roses being delivered and he teased me about Martin while I was trying to write a letter. In fact I found it impossible to be alone on deck without various irritating characters who came by and started talking. The only way to put them off was to close my eyes and pretend to be asleep, which was a waste of time. Then when I opened my eyes I'd see them still standing at the ship's rails waiting to pounce. I got sick of the way so many men stared, but the Captain paid me a great compliment and said I looked like Grace Kelly. I didn't of course, but my mother was pleased about it.

In the evening there was dancing to the music of the ship's orchestra and I was asked to dance by Salvo and various other officers. They also asked my mother who was sitting beside me. She was embarrassed as she felt they saw it as their duty and were just being polite.

"I suppose they think I'm expecting them to dance with me," she said, "but it's the last thing I want. I only wanted to sit here and watch – now I suppose I'll have to go back to our cabin."

On Saturday we reached Piraeus, the port for Athens. My mother was going on an excursion with a group of other passengers, but I had decided not to go, for I hoped to see Ion Collas as we had arranged. However, there was a lot of trouble; Archbishop Makarios had been deported from Cyprus and Ion, who was serving in the Greek Army, had his leave cancelled and had to report for duty. The American who had shown me the Appian Way told me he could arrange for me to go with some Greek colleagues in his company. He introduced me to the Greek director of his firm, who was unbelievably kind and hospitable. He lent me his car, with Allen his driver and his secretary Maria. They treated me royally. We drove to Athens, where I was shown the Acropolis and lots of temples. Maria bought me presents of pottery souvenirs and took me out to lunch. We continued on our tour in the afternoon, but Athens was seething with fury about the deportation of Makarios and suddenly we were in the middle of a riot. Shop windows of English travel firms were broken, also one belonging to an American airline. The next moment our car was surrounded by a howling mob of students shouting and screaming and pointing at me.

"I'm not going any further," said Allen, our driver. He started to reverse, but the students thumped the windows and started to rock the car backwards and forwards.

"It's because you're so blonde," said Maria, "they suspect you're English. Quickly - can you speak any other language?"

"A little French," I said doubtfully. "Je suis Française!" I shouted through the open window, "Je ne suis pas Anglaise!"

It seemed to do the trick, for they backed off and allowed us to drive away, and we were able to get through to the port of Piraeus without further incident, but it had been a most astonishing day, for which I thanked Maria for her kindness and both of them for putting themselves at risk on my account. I saw my mother and it appeared the ship's excursion had been cancelled due to the riots.

On Monday 12th March we got up and packed, and presently we arrived at Limassol. Salvo said goodbye to me with great sadness. He told me he had been in love with me since the first night we arrived and thought Martin was very lucky. I said he would soon fall for someone else but he said no. I promised to send him a postcard.

We went ashore by launch. My father was not there to meet us, which was the first disappointment for my mother. We spent a long time at Customs with half the British Army running around, then took a taxi to a very dreary hotel, where we were to stay the night. At last at five o'clock my father arrived, and they had an uneasy reunion: he seemed on nerves and she was disappointed and depressed.

"I've got such a lot to do at the office," he said, as if he resented the time he had taken off to come and meet us. "There's so much going on."

I told him about my day in Athens and the riots and asked him what had happened to cause such anger to the Greeks – why had Archbishop Makarios been deported?

"He was a troublemaker," said my father. "He refused to denounce the violence, in fact he was inciting it. The Governor, Sir John Harding, felt there could be no settlement as long as he was here, stirring up trouble. So it was decided he should be deported."

"Well it seems to have made it worse," I said.

"You don't understand," said my father.

CHAPTER SIX

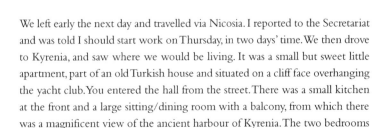

We left early the next day and travelled via Nicosia. I reported to the Secretariat and was told I should start work on Thursday, in two days' time. We then drove to Kyrenia, and saw where we would be living. It was a small but sweet little apartment, part of an old Turkish house and situated on a cliff face overhanging the yacht club. You entered the hall from the street. There was a small kitchen at the front and a large sitting/dining room with a balcony, from which there was a magnificent view of the ancient harbour of Kyrenia. The two bedrooms and bathroom below were reached via a spiral staircase, which also continued up to the flat roof. Next door to us on one side was a similar apartment used by officers of the Blues, and on the other side was the castle, once held by Richard Coeur de Lion, and now taken over by the Wiltshire Regiment.

We had not been there for long and were just having a drink when suddenly there was a knock at the door. My father went to open it.

"Ah, Joy!" he said, "Come and join us."

She came. He introduced her as Joy, his secretary. She was forty-something, red-haired, heavily made up with a coarse sallow skin in which you could see the open pores.

"Were the flowers all right?" she said.

That was a big mistake. My mother had been so pleased to see vases of flowers in the sitting room, thinking my father had bought them for her. It wasn't the same thing at all to know he had asked his secretary to get them. Nor did my mother want her to join us on our very first day when she had not seen my father for three months, but it seemed Joy was determined to do just that. She also asked him about the supply of cutlery and linen in the house, about which he must have consulted her. She stayed for ages and I thought she was very tactless, barging in like that, and also rather common.

That evening we went to the Harbour Club, which was just across the way from our house. It was quite dark inside and full of people. "I'll get some drinks," said my father, disappearing to the bar. We sat down and waited for ages, but no drinks appeared. Eventually I went to the bar to see what was happening, and there was my father standing chatting to Joy, who stood looking up at him and fluttering her mascara- laden eyelashes.

"So what about our drinks?" I said.

"Yes, I'm just bringing them," he said.

"About time," I said.

"Oh dear," laughed Joy, "Are you in trouble?"

He laughed too. "Probably," he said.

The next night he took us to dinner at the Octopus. "You'll like it," he told us, "It's one of my favourite places."

It was a little restaurant further round the harbour, and it was run by a woman called Lottie.

"Hello Kenneth," she said when we went in, kissing him on both cheeks. She seemed to know him quite well. I thought the restaurant was aptly named, for Lottie was like an octopus herself, wrapping her tentacles around every man who came in. This included my father. She even came and sat down at our table while we were having our meal, talking animatedly about people we didn't know, and I was sorry for my mother, who felt miserable and neglected.

Later my mother came into my bedroom and talked for a long time. She said she did not feel she was going to settle down here. My father had been here for three months as a single man and got to know everyone and they obviously liked him - all these women who kept milling around.

"It's all right for him" she said. "He knows everyone here, and he's got his job, and it's all right for you, you've got a job too, but what am I supposed to do, stuck in this little house all day?"

I tried my best to cheer her up and thought I had succeeded. But indeed, I did not know what she would do stuck in the little house.

Meantime the news in Cyprus was bad: there were riots in Nicosia over Archbishop Makarios. On 14th March Sergeant Paddy Rooney from the Kent constabulary, the first policeman from the UK Unit, was shot and killed in Ledra Street. A school was burned down.

"So where's he gone - the Archbishop?" I asked.

"I can't tell you, it's classified."

"Oh go on - I won't tell."

"All right then – to the Seychelles. Also Bishop Kyprianos of Kyrenia and some others. I have to be on duty, there could be riots in Kyrenia too."

He showed us the gun with which he had been issued, it was in a holster and he said it would be quite difficult to get it out. We couldn't help laughing for he said, if someone came up and tried to shoot him he would have to say, "Hang on, hang on a moment…." while he tried to get the gun out of the holster.

"Can I have a go?" I asked.

"No."

"Why – is it loaded?"

"Of course."

He told us that when he first arrived he used to go every night to the Coeur de Lion Hotel to drink with the locals, and then someone came and told him he should not be going there. He was annoyed. "Why not? I like to drink with the locals" he had said. "I make my own friends, I don't need to be told who not to meet."

"But don't you realise, your so-called friends are all hardcore EOKA people, that's where they go. You're the Commissioner of Kyrenia and you're meeting with EOKA every night."

This had not occurred to him.

I thought it was exciting. I wanted to explore Kyrenia and went for a walk by myself. Kyrenia was a pretty little place. I walked around the harbour and then back into the town, but when I came face to face with a group of Cypriot boys they looked at me with such hatred, I instinctively bent down and picked up a stone in case they attacked me. I'm not sure if I would have thrown it, but I kept it hidden in my hand.

On Thursday I went to the Secretariat in Nicosia and worked in an office there. It was unbelievably boring work, and I was not even very good at it either. The morning seemed endless, and I thought it would go on for ever and ever. I had lunch in the canteen with a Cypriot boy in the office and it was the most extraordinary lunch, just a small pile of rice with a bit of oil on it, in the shape of a mud pie, one of those sand pies you make on the beach with a bucket and spade. It might just as well have been sand for all the flavour it had. The next day the work was just as boring but at least I had an excellent lunch at a place called Le Bon Gourmet. Two older rather distinguished Cypriots insisted on taking me in a car round Nicosia. They told me I would have only one more day in that office and next week be transferred to Police Headquarters at Paphos Gate.

On Saturday night bombs were thrown and one soldier was killed at Lapithos village near Kyrenia, which was very sad. My father immediately went out to see what was going on. I felt sure I could help in some way and was keen to go with him, but he refused to let me, much to my disappointment. There was a lot of extra work for him and he spent all Sunday at his office. My mother and I went to the Kyrenia Country Club where you could swim on a beach known as The Slab, and sit in rather a pleasant lounge and see all the newspapers and the latest magazines. We sat and read all morning, much to the irritation of the owner, Colonel Anstis, a grim-looking man with a military moustache who ran the club and constantly checked up to see if people were there who had not paid their subscription. My mother said she would join but if I wanted to I would have to pay the subscription myself.

I never did pay it and went to the club occasionally, spending all the time dodging the colonel. He had a beautiful and languid wife who lay on a chaise longue all day with two Great Danes mounting guard like lions at the feet of Cleopatra, fawned upon by a stream of doting young subalterns. Her daughter Sally was also very beautiful. She had had an unhappy marriage and it was said, her appalling husband had decapitated her beloved pet dogs, so she had left him then and there in the middle of the night and arrived at her father's house in Cyprus. She had then run off with the handsome Turkish harbourmaster. They lived in a little house in Kyrenia and had terrible rows and people passing by said they did not know if the Turk was killing Sally or Sally was killing the Turk.

On Monday it was the first day in my new job. I was given a lift into Nicosia by a Wing Commander Furzeman and some other RAF people. Our journey along a beautiful mountainous route took about forty-five minutes. I was dropped off at Paphos Gate, where Police Headquarters was situated, and there taken upstairs and introduced to the seven English girls who were on contracts similar to mine.

It was delightful to meet some normal people at last. In one office was Margaret from Lancashire who had come out to marry Joe Mounsey, a UK police officer in the CID. She was a tall, wholesome girl with a lovely fresh complexion and curly hair. In my office there was Enid, who seemed to be the senior one, for she was older and more experienced than the rest of us. She was a big girl with a quick sense of humour and a very sharp tongue. There was also brown-haired Gillian, a friendly girl of my age who took me home with her for lunch, and Edwina who worked next door. Edwina was the youngest of us, sweet and child-like, vivacious and warm-hearted. She had great blue eyes and oozed sex appeal. She worked in the Secret Registry under Maclouzarides, or Uncle Mac as we called him. We three girls in the adjoining office were in a pool, working for anyone who asked us, but Mr Robbins the Commissioner of Police had his own office at the end of our passage, and Philippa, his secretary, worked only for him. Mr Robbins was in the Colonial Police and his senior officers were mainly British from former colonies, while the rank and file were recruited locally from both Greek and Turkish communities.

The UK Police had been brought in by Field Marshall Sir John Harding, who was Governor and Commander in Chief. He had said that the citizens of Cyprus must provide themselves with a strong, highly-disciplined, well-trained and properly-equipped police force. He said that the Cyprus police force had not yet developed up to the standard required to provide the degree of security needed in a modern civilised country such as Cyprus. It was also common knowledge that EOKA had infiltrated the Cyprus Police and could no longer be trusted to perform impartially. London therefore decided to send out a contingent of British officers to form a special unit. The purpose of the UK Unit was not to act as a replacement but to supplement the existing Cyprus police. Thus in late December 1955, 150 British Officers were flown to Cyprus together with several police dogs and their handlers. The dogs were immediately set to sniff out arms dumps in the Troodos mountains. The UK Unit was in the charge of Chief Superintendent Tom Lockley. They were fully armed at all times and their accommodation was guarded 24 hours a day by armed units of the British Army and Turkish Cypriot policemen.

Gillie worked mostly for Mr Biles, the Colonial Deputy Commissioner. He was a handsome man with black hair, sarcastic and brilliant. He was also dynamic, highly efficient at his job, and he expected us to be equally efficient. He gave me lots of Situation Reports to type on my first day and shorthand dictation, which was scary. I'm sure he dictated faster than 100 words a minute. I tried to take it down, shaking like a leaf, and was a bit depressed to note that I did not seem to be as quick as Enid and Gill, and could not get through as much work.

That evening I went to the Ledra Palace Hotel to pick up my lift home as arranged, and found I had missed it. So I hitched a lift back to Kyrenia and arrived very late, to the alarm of all. My mother had rung the police and when I arrived at police HQ next day I found there was a great flap on about my 'disappearance' and I had been posted as missing. That evening I got a lift back with a taxi firm called Theoharis. This was a brilliant idea: you went to the taxi office and waited and when there were three or four people who all wanted to go to the same place, you shared the taxi with them. I did not have long to wait and my fare was only three shillings, which was very satisfactory.

I settled into the work quite easily and became much quicker, though never as fast or efficient as Gillie. It was fun in our office, there were periods when we had nothing much to do except chat and have laughs. One rather tedious man we worked for was nicknamed Precious and was quite unaware we were laughing at him. But the others, mostly Colonial police who had been in Cyprus before the Emergency, were very nice. There were also the men of the UK Police Unit for whom we worked occasionally.

During the day we ate oranges on sticks brought to us by one of the Greeks in the canteen. The canteen manager was always chewing garlic cloves, so the oranges had a slight flavour of garlic, but they were so delicious we did not mind. The other girls went home at lunch time but it wasn't feasible for me so I brought sandwiches. When I unwrapped them they were always covered with little ants, but I found if I put them out on the windowsill in the sunshine, the ants soon crawled off. I suppose if I had eaten the ants it would not have mattered, seeing you could buy chocolate-covered ones in the delicatessen. Uncle Mac - as we called Mr Maclouzarides, the head of the Secret Registry - also stayed in at lunchtime and he would come into my office and chat. He was a dear, sweet man, kind and funny. We all loved him.

On Thursday night, back in Kyrenia, there was a party at the head of the Turkish community's house, and lots of dubious-looking little things were handed round, including sheep's eyes. "This is a Turkish delicacy," someone said. So I took one but it was slimy and chewy and horrible and I spat it out into a vase of roses – luckily no one noticed. I also met some senior Greek Cypriots, when my father took my mother and me to meet the Greek-Cypriot Mayor of Lapithos and his wife. They gave us tea and very sweet cakes. They were charming and seemed very pleased to see us, but as we drove away I turned to look back and saw their twelve-year-old daughter standing on the balcony of their house making the sign of the Greek curse, so we knew the charm went only skin deep, and really they hated us. We were told you could not trust Greeks – they would smile at your face and stab you in the back. Sunday was Greek Independence Day and trouble was expected, so there was a curfew all day.

At home I was missing Martin very much. He wrote me many letters which I read and re-read over and over again. But one he wrote upset me for it seemed he had not been receiving my letters to him. He had heard nothing since 18th March and was understandably hurt. He wrote sarcastically, "Are you still living in Cyprus?" This was upsetting, for I had spent hours writing to him, choosing a beautiful place to sit on the cliffs by the castle, overlooking the sea, as if I could transmit the beauty of the location with the letter. I resolved to write shorter air letters twice a week, instead of very long ones only once.

Life at home in our little apartment in Kyrenia was very difficult at this time, for my mother was deeply unhappy. She had always had misgivings about our going to Cyprus and now, at the age of fifty-nine, she was going through the 'change of life' and this added to her feelings of hopeless inadequacy. Knowing nobody and being alone in the day time, she had nothing to look forward to but the weekend when my father and I were at home and we could go out somewhere. We would go to the Mad Hatter for tea, or a drive to the beautiful monastery of Bellapais. But often enough on the Saturday my father was working in his office, and if there had been an incident resulting in a curfew, we would be stuck at home all day. And besides, there was Joy, my father's red-haired secretary, a divorcee and very, very available. He had always been attracted to red-haired women and had once had a passion for Rita Hayworth.

In the evenings my father liked to take us to the Harbour Club. It was run by a very nice couple called Judy and Roy Findlay. Judy had been on the stage, she was glamorous and Roy her husband had been in the Navy. There was a friend of theirs called Bill who played the piano. Every time we went, my father would tell us he was going to get the drinks and then he would spend ages chatting to people at the bar, leaving my mother and me sitting on the periphery. I liked the Harbour Club and thought it had a great atmosphere. People came up and talked to me but they ignored my mother, so it was no wonder she did not want to go. "Why do we *always* have to go to the *bloody* Harbour Club?" She said one day, so we remained in our sitting room after dinner; but my father could hear the music coming from the club and started to pace up and down like a caged tiger. At last he could bear it no longer and said, "I'll just go and see what's going on at the Harbour Club," and off he went.

I tried to cheer her up, but then I went to the office the next day leaving her alone and when I got home she was depressed again. Every day it was the same. She thought she was a failure and that everyone liked my father and not her; she thought he was bored with her and would have a wonderful life on his own.

One night she began to talk of suicide, how people soon forgot, and I knew she was talking about herself. I was shocked and miserable and cried all night long. The next day she came into my room before I went to work. She was weeping, and I felt very sad and depressed about her. I could think of nothing else all day but how awful that it should have come to this. And what should we do if either their marriage broke up or else if my father walked out? I wrote to Badger and Peter, and told them all about it and asked them to write back quickly and tell me what I must do. But that didn't work, for what could they say after all?

On Easter Saturday he had promised to take us out for a picnic, but first, he said, there was something he had to do at the office. He would come back as soon as it was finished, he promised. The picnic lunch was all prepared - by half past ten I think - and standing in readiness waiting by the front door in a basket covered with a white cloth. All morning we waited, but he didn't come. At one o'clock I phoned the office, and there was no reply. "He must be on his way back," I said. Again we waited and again he did not come. My mother looking white-faced then urged me to go out with her, and I followed, having no idea where we were going. We went to parts of Kyrenia I had never seen before.

Suddenly we found my father's car parked below an apartment block. My mother went mad and looked up at the windows and started shouting, "Kenneth! Kenneth!" Of course there was no reply. "Come away," I said, and we went home. My mother went into the bathroom and was sick and I called my father's office. He answered.

"Where have you been?" I demanded.

"Here, of course, in the office."

"No, you haven't. We saw your car. It was parked – outside Joy's apartment. What was it doing there?"

"Yes, I gave her a lift home."

"Well, I think you'd better come back straight away. Mummy is very upset."

He came. We sat opposite each other at the dining room table, and I interrogated him.

"So what's going on?" I said bossily.

"Nothing."

"We phoned up and you weren't there."

"I told you, I had to take Joy home."

"But your car was parked there – why didn't you just drop her off and come home?"

"She asked me in for a coffee."

"But it was after one o'clock. And then you went back to your office. You *knew* we were going out for a picnic. You *promised.*"

"There was something I'd forgotten."

He looked at me stony-faced and refused to admit anything was wrong. And all the time my mother was in the bathroom.

The next day was Easter Sunday. My mother and I went to church and I wrote that it was very disappointing. I don't know why this was – surely one shouldn't describe church as disappointing? That is hardly the right reaction. We were asked to a cocktail party and I didn't want to go and was tearful and bolshie because I was longing to get away from what I thought of as the evil little house, out into the fresh air where I could think about Martin and write to him. But I did enjoy the party in the end. It was given by some charming people called Spinney with a very nice daughter of my age called Elizabeth, known as Buffy. My mother too felt a bit better, having now met several very pleasant and friendly people who invited her to coffee. Thank God, I thought. Perhaps she will be happier now.

But then came the next chapter of the wretched saga, when she found The Letter. One day sitting in the house all day, she happened upon a book my father had brought with him when he first arrived in Cyprus. She opened it and out fluttered a letter. The handwriting was spidery and unfamiliar and of course she read it.

"My own darling Kenneth," it began. "It was so terrible that day when you went off from Victoria and I couldn't come and say goodbye because She was there –" The letter continued with all sorts of banalities. She wrote that she had washed her smalls and hung them on the radiator. It was signed, "All my love darling, Lydia"

My mother was horrified and angry. When my father came home she taxed him with it: "And if you *had* to have an affair, couldn't you have chosen someone who could write more interestingly than about *washing her smalls* and hanging them on the radiator?"

But my father denied having any kind of affair. He told us all about Lydia.

He had been having dinner at his club in London and saw this woman sitting alone at the next table.

"Oh yes," interrupted my mother, "You had had lunch at the club with Mervyn and when I asked who you had dinner with you said, Mervyn. I thought it was strange that you had lunch with him and then dinner as well. Anyway, go on."

This woman was about forty, said my father, not pretty, quite plain in fact, but he felt sorry for her and invited her to join him for coffee.

"As you would," interrupted my mother sarcastically.

The woman was overjoyed. She said it was the best night of her entire life. She dreaded the evening coming to an end. She said she had lived alone with her mother for many years and no one had ever asked her out before. She had never even been kissed. She had no friends because of the demands her mother had made upon her. The mother had recently gone into a home and the house had been sold to pay for it so Lydia would soon have nowhere to live. My father said he might be able to help her out, as his sister had a friend with a house in Beaufort Gardens and there were sometimes rooms to let there. Would she like him to find out? Oh yes, indeed she would. They arranged to meet the following week and he took her to 33 Beaufort Gardens and introduced her to Madge Harland. There was a room, just a small one (maybe the same one I had occupied before I went to Jamaica) and she agreed to take it.

But oh dear, how would she manage if she didn't see my father again? She couldn't bear that thought. It had been the only thing that made her life worth living. So he weakly agreed to meet her again the following week, and the one after that. He had foolishly become involved in something he had no wish to continue and longed to be away, far away, and out of it. And then the job in Cyprus came up. Thank God, he thought, now he would be off the hook.

My father finished telling us, and this time, though we thought he had been very stupid, we believed him. With Joy it was a different matter. She was, after all, quite attractive in a brazen sort of way. I never knew if there was anything going on with her or not, but people sometimes hinted that there was. The Colonel of the Wiltshire Regiment, who could be charming when he wanted but was sometimes malicious, came to drinks with us and always asked me how my father was getting on with 'that red-haired secretary of his'. Was he insinuating something? Or was he just being spiteful, because he and my father rubbed one another up the wrong way? I felt very sorry about all this, knowing the background of their marriage. Badger and I had once been rooting through a desk at 51 Shirley Drive and had found his diary and a bundle of letters. We had a quick look and had been shocked. We thought them disgusting and embarrassing but it was obvious they had been terribly in love when they were young.

There was nothing I could do to help, but gradually - gradually - things got better for my mother. She was invited out by a number of people whom she liked, and they liked her too, so they asked her again, and soon they became friends. It was a great relief. We gave dinner parties and I helped with the food. Once my mother was making chocolate mousse and asked me to decorate the top with blanched almonds. I thought some of the almonds were blanched already and arranged them on top of the chocolate mousse and that evening when we came to the pudding one of the guests spat it out. "What the hell?" he shouted angrily. "That's garlic!" It was indeed, for what I had thought were almonds were actually garlic cloves. The guest, whom we didn't much like anyway, was not amused and never came again.

I continued to enjoy working in the office at Paphos Gate with the other girls, but to my annoyance my father interfered and asked the Commissioner of Police if I could be transferred to Kyrenia, and the Commissioner agreed. I desperately did not want to do this, for I could not imagine it would be half as entertaining there. I so enjoyed being with the girls in my office, Gillie and Edwina were very sweet and Enid was most amusing – sarcastic and quick-tongued but great fun. I accepted it was a bit difficult sometimes to get transport but was sure I could manage, especially as Edwina would soon be living in Kyrenia too, so that we could share taxis. So I went to see Monty Rich, head of Administration in the Colonial Police, and my immediate boss, and asked him if I could possibly stay where I was, and he said he didn't see why not, for the time being anyhow.

There were many incidents of terrorism in Cyprus at this time: bombs and murders happened every day. People rang Police HQ to pass on information about EOKA suspects, and quite often these same people were later found murdered. It seemed there might be a traitor in HQ but we didn't know who it could be. There were Greek Cypriots working there but they had been vetted and were thought to be loyal. It could have been anyone, though obviously none of us Brits. All day long Army Jeeps drove past Paphos Gate with soldiers on their way to investigate terrorist incidents.

One day in the lunch hour, when as usual I was alone on our floor, I popped next door to the Secret Registry to have a chat with our beloved

Uncle Mac. Usually he came into our office to chat but this day he did not come so I decided to go to his office instead. I was shocked to see he was standing in semi darkness, photographing Top Secret files. So it was he – could it be? Yes. He was the traitor who had been passing on the information to EOKA. All these thoughts rushed through my mind with lightning speed. I backed out of the Secret Registry, unsure if he had seen me or not. I was horrified. I didn't know what to do. If I exposed him, told someone like Mr Biles or Monty Rich, he might be arrested, he might even be hanged. On the other hand if I confronted him myself and asked what he was doing, he might feel – and this was a gruesome thought – he might feel that *I* should be silenced. Wasn't there a saying that you should beware of Greeks bearing gifts? He didn't exactly bear gifts but he did give me the occasional sweetie, and people said you couldn't trust Greeks, they would smile at your face and stab you in the back. He might do it with regret, but he *might* do it.

I thought of telling my father what I had seen but immediately rejected the idea, for I knew he would not hesitate to expose Maclouzarides, whom he did not know and would have no sympathy for. I couldn't tell Edwina or anyone. I looked upon Uncle Mac as a dear friend and I didn't want him to be hanged – so in the end I did nothing. But I never felt the same about him after that. I don't know if he saw any difference in my attitude and often wondered if he had seen me that day, standing in the doorway of the Secret Registry while he photographed the Top Secret files.

Edwina was in love with someone called Ian who was in the South Staffordshire regiment and she rushed to the windows every time a Jeep with the South Staffordshire regimental flag went by. She talked all the time about Ian and the South Staffs, which made me wonder what she talked about when she was *with* Ian. Gillie was in love with a man in the dog handler unit of the UK Police unit. He was called Joe, but he was married, and his wife would soon be joining him, a matter of great angst for Gillie. She also had a short fat admirer she didn't like at all.

I had the same problem and was invited to go out to dinner by various tiresome people I wanted to avoid. There was one I described as 'the wretched Oscar' who was apt to turn up uninvited and another with a moon face called Batchie Brown who phoned up late at night and asked me to dinner and I could think of no excuses not to go. In the office we all laughed very much and devised ways of putting off these dreary admirers, which was not unkind because they were pushy and deserved it. I thought the best way was to take them to the Octopus where hopefully, Lottie would ensnare them with her tentacles.

It was difficult being engaged. I met a very beautiful girl called Eve whom I liked enormously. She was also engaged and had been apart from her fiancé for eight months, but would soon be returning to the UK. She and I discussed the difficulties at length.

"Do you go out with other people?" I asked.

"Well – yes," she said. "But not if I can help it, alone. After all you can't live like a nun. You have to have some sort of social life."

Yes, I thought that was true. You did have to. I couldn't help enjoying life with the girls in the office, and yet life at home was not good and Martin was so far away. In my diary I wrote, *"Sometimes I wonder what I do think, and whether I am a worthy person. And then I think, No – I am very unworthy. And then I am depressed."*

Some RAF people had invited me to go on an expedition at the weekend, to Buffavento Castle. I set off before 8 am with Beatrice and the Furzemans and joined up with the others at Bellapais Monastery, from where our walk would commence. There were twenty-one of us altogether, and we walked a distance of fourteen miles, seven there and seven back. We were accompanied by several Cypriot boys including a fat boy with red hair on a donkey bearing our picnic lunch. The last and steepest lap of the climb was to the actual castle of Buffavento itself, situated high up on a rocky crag in the Kyrenia mountain range. I felt very happy and excited, for the views were stunning and I was carried away by the enchantment of it all. We got back tired and footsore.

"What was it like?" My father asked.

"Just magical - but very hard going," I said, adding tactlessly "You two couldn't have done it."

My mother was indignant. "What rubbish – why we used to trek for miles when we were in Nigeria."

But that had been some years before and I didn't think, inwardly, they could have managed it.

CHAPTER SEVEN

The hostilities on the island increased. I loved going to Bellapais Abbey and would sit for ages by a window in a tiny alcove, looking out over Kyrenia. But one day when I went there a group of Greek Cypriots spat at me. It was unpleasant being hated for what I did not consider to be my fault.

We met an author, Sir Harry Luke, an elderly and learned man in his seventies. He was a very interesting and unassuming person who knew Cyprus well. He had written a lot of books about it, both about Cyprus under the Turks from the 16th century, and in more modern times, and he explained a lot to me about the background of the present troubles.

One night Superintendent Philip Atfield of the Colonial Police was murdered by EOKA. It was a great shock to all of us who knew him and we grieved for him and for his wife. The funeral took place without delay, and he was buried in the British Cemetery in Nicosia. It was so sad, and the atmosphere at Police HQ was awful.

I went to Eve's house and was struck by the happy environment there, very different from ours. It was a pretty house, quaintly furnished and with beautiful views all around. A few days later she invited me to come and swim on their little private beach, and we took books and magazines down there, but mostly we talked. We had so much to discuss and I wished very much she was going to stay on in Cyprus.

At the weekend I went up onto our flat roof and sunbathed. Buffy Spinney and some of the Blues from next door came and chatted. I did not think much of them and thought them a rum lot. Later on a bomb was thrown in Kyrenia and my father was out for most of the evening. The next day a Greek Cypriot policeman was shot. He died immediately and a curfew was imposed and no one was allowed in or out of Nicosia. When I was in the office the day after, the trumpet siren was sounded, which only happened in cases of extreme emergency. It was exciting. I shouldn't have felt excited but I did. A lot of Greek properties were set on fire by the Turks and we wondered what would happen next.

Amongst the people who came in and asked for typing to be done were two men called Tom and Alec. Tom was an Inspector and Alec a Sergeant from the Lancashire Constabulary of the UK Unit. I had never met anyone from the North before and I found them unusual and quite different. They were free and easy, open and very straight talking. They talked a lot about money, and discussed their terms of employment in a way quite different from the Colonial Police.

On Wednesday Edwina and I were in trouble as we found we were unable to get transport home: we could not get a taxi with Theoharis because of the curfew and did not know what to do. So I went into Alec Kay's office and asked him if he could help us, as he was in charge of the Transport Section. Tom Watkinson was there too, sitting on a desk swinging his legs. Alec said he could probably drive us home, provided we could leave the office at half-past three. This we did, though I did not think Monty Rich seemed too pleased. Edwina was dropped off first and then when we got to my house I invited him in for a drink. My mother liked him very much and our conversation flowed easily. He talked easily with a strong Lancashire accent which we thought quite funny. Instead of saying cooks and books, he called them cukes and bukes. He asked me about the Blues next door and I told him, "But I don't like the Blues very much."

"Do you like policemen?" he asked, a warmth in his voice. He said that some of the police crowd sometimes went swimming on Wednesday or Saturday afternoons and perhaps I would like to go with them? Next day Edwina said she thought that Alec rather liked me - I had thought so too.

Gillie and I were planning to go to Beirut for a weekend, but it was quite difficult to arrange. We went down to the office to ask about tickets, and Gillie wrote to the St George's Club in Beirut to see if we could get accommodation.

Sir Harry Luke came to dinner with Fred Maxie, an extraordinary friend with whom he was staying. We stood on our balcony and looked out at the harbour, and Sir Harry Luke said it was the finest view in the whole of Europe. That evening my father had brought me a letter from Martin delivered to his office which he had forgotten and Sir Harry Luke could see I was desperate to read it.

"Go along," he said kindly, "and read your letter. You'll want to be on your own." He was so understanding and so wise.

I was excited about Beirut and mentioned my plans to go there for a weekend and asked Sir Harry if he had been there. He said he had, but Fred Maxie was very disdainful. "Beirut? That cesspool!" He said. "Beirut is a hellhole. A den of iniquity."

We could not help laughing. I got the message but it didn't deter me from wanting to go there, and Gillie and I went ahead with our arrangements. We managed to get our air tickets and accommodation sorted out, and off we went on 4th May. We were immediately impressed with Beirut and thought it a most exciting and glamorous place – certainly not a cesspool. We had booked a double room at the St George's Club, and we went there first of all and had lunch. In the afternoon we went to look at the shops, which were wonderful, very different from the small and scruffy shops in Nicosia. In one shop I fell in love with a most beautiful scarlet nightdress, hand sewn by the nuns at the convent. It had yards of very soft material trimmed with broderie anglaise, but it cost 10 guineas, which was a lot of money.

The following day we went to the ruins of Byblos, the most ancient city in the world. There we saw the tombs and skeletons of babies in clay pots, which was a gruesome sight. We had lunch in a café in the rain, and went into a hut with goats, cats, kittens, hens, chicks – and Arabs of course. The next day we went to Baalbek. I had never before been as impressed by a place as I was by Baalbek. The mighty columns looked as if they had just fallen, as if a terrible catastrophe had just occurred, moments before. I could have wept, so moving was the sight, and the feeling I had about it. We went for a walk over a hill and there saw another sight, totally different, which shocked and appalled us: we saw a shepherd performing with a sheep. One look was enough – we rushed away. Afterwards I would always remember Baalbek for those two very different things.

While we were in Beirut we went to a night club, where I danced with a Frenchman. I wrote that it resembled Madame Tussaud's, but I am not sure why I thought so. We went to a glass-sided restaurant, and twice to a very luxurious cinema, and saw two films starring Grace Kelly, 'The Swan' and 'Dial M for Murder'. On the last day we went back to the shops and I bought the beautiful scarlet nightdress, which I thought I would wear on the first night of my honeymoon. I also bought a crocodile-skin cigarette case for my parents and a brocade smoking jacket for Martin. My parents liked their cigarette case, but admired the nightdress more, and my father was so fascinated that he insisted on showing it to everyone who came to the house, which was embarrassing. People said to me, "So you're the girl who bought a fabulous red nightdress in Beirut!" and a young officer in the Wiltshire Regiment told me it was so famous that the whole of the British army had heard about it.

Martin wrote some very ardent letters, saying how much he missed and needed me and couldn't see why we had to wait. In another he wrote "I love you, I want you and hope you can read between the lines…" I could, of course I could, and felt the same. I had told Glen I was planning to break my contract and go home the following April so that we could get married, instead of continuing for the two years for which I had signed. He had been shocked, for he thought I was wrong to sign a contract knowing I was going to break it, and my parents would probably have thought the same - though even next April seemed far off. But then around this time the mail from England was very erratic and there were unbearable periods of time when I received no letters from Martin. It was probably no more his fault than it had been mine when he had not received anything from me. Days would pass and I would rush home to see if there was a letter and there would be nothing and I could not understand it. I had, surprisingly, received a letter from Lindsay in Jamaica, and also an embarrassing love letter from Salvo, the Sicilian officer on the SS *Grimani*. I heard from John in America and Glen from RNAS Lossiemouth and Bill from Eastbourne, but nothing from Martin for what was to me an eternity. It seemed endless, though it was probably no more than ten days, but the thought of having to wait another hour, another day, was intolerable, how could I possibly bear it? I felt sad and bitter; and then two or three letters would come at the same time, saying he loved me more and more every day.

But that period of waiting had taken a toll. I wrote in my diary *"Would it be hurtful to him if I sometimes go out with others, like Police people, once in a blue moon? I think not. I can't bear to be surrounded always by sugar daddies."* The next day I wrote *"A is a nice person, he is straight, very easy and is going occasionally to take me out. A platonic friendship can do no harm I think. One gets very narrow if always with married couples…"* I went to the little cove at Eve's house and bathed, which was delicious. I wanted to ask her about platonic friendships – but really I knew that only I could be the judge of that.

On the 3rd May we had learnt that Michael Caraolis was going to be executed for the murder of a Greek Cypriot police constable, and on the 10th May he and another Cypriot were hanged. Caraolis was in the civil service and had been caught with a letter in his pocket from an EOKA leader recommending him as a good patriot to the point of self-sacrifice. He would be the first Cypriot to be executed by hanging and we all knew there would be trouble. There was a curfew on but Edwina and I managed to get through with our police passes and went home via Theoharis taxi.

In Kyrenia a medical officer was badly wounded by a bomb in the harbour and Tex, a man in my father's office, was suspected of being behind it. I was told off for walking about by myself. After two RAF wives were ambushed between Nicosia and Kyrenia, on the road taken daily by Edwina and myself, it was decided that in future British personnel should be escorted home by British police, starting on 15th May. Alec took this duty mainly on himself and Eddie and I were taken home in different cars, usually the official dark blue police Vauxhalls. Often for various reasons Edwina was not with us, and many times I remember being taken on my own in a Land Rover with a loaded gun in the front and the doors taken off so that we could jump out if ambushed. I thought it was exciting and the journey home across the Kyrenia mountain range was beautiful.

One Saturday afternoon Alec came to fetch me and took me up to St Hilarion Castle. St Hilarion was one of three Crusader castles which had formed a defence of the island against pirates invading the coast. It was like an entrancing fairy tale castle, very eerie and romantic. We stood at the ruined top of it and looked down on distant Kyrenia and the sea, and to begin with there was no one there but ourselves. Then suddenly there was a lot of activity, vehicles and motor bike outriders arrived and Sir John Harding, the Governor and Commander in Chief stepped out of an army vehicle. It was astonishing and unbelievable that he should be there. We watched him from the battlements and then he was there quite close by, having come to inspect the site. He gave us a shrewd look and said "Good afternoon". He and his escorts stayed a short while then drove off, leaving us alone again.

That day at St Hilarion was the beginning of something I did not believe was happening. Alec and I got on so well and it seemed so natural and so innocent. How happy we both were! I found I could talk to him about anything in the world. I would not admit it even to myself, but I liked and was attracted to him even then.

CHAPTER EIGHT

Summer hours meant that we worked from 7 am till 1 pm, had the afternoon off and returned from 4.30 till 6.30, making a total of 8½ hours a day. It was considered too hot to work in the afternoons during the summer and most people went home to have a siesta, returning to work in the evening. We also worked Saturday mornings but to compensate, we were generally off altogether on Wednesday afternoons. It was not feasible for me to go home in the afternoons, so I would have to stay in Nicosia.

"It's quite ridiculous," said my father. "I told you so, but you think you know it all. You should be transferred to Kyrenia, then there would be no problem."

But I didn't want to work in Kyrenia. I much preferred being in Police HQ at Paphos Gate. Someone suggested I should join the Nicosia Club, where I could go in the afternoons and play tennis or swim and relax by the pool. Also we had met some people called Edmondson who, by an extraordinary coincidence, turned out to be second cousins of my mother's. There were four of them, Evelyn and her husband Don Tarbet, known as Fish, and her two brothers, Trevor and Edward. They were charming and became good friends at once. They lived in a house in Nicosia and they suggested I could go there during the afternoon and have a sleep in their spare bedroom. These arrangements worked very well, and I spent a lot of time both at the Nicosia Club and at the Edmondsons. Gillie was probably my best friend and she often came to the Club with me to play tennis and swim.

There were also two army pilots called Tony and John who were based in Nicosia, and they would grab me to play tennis with them and a girl called Mimi. They also had a number of parties and once played a joke on me, telling me their next party was a black tie event. I arrived to find myself the only one there in a long evening dress. But I had the last laugh: I told them I was going on somewhere, ordered a taxi and swept out, half way through their party. They were quite impressed.

Meanwhile one Saturday afternoon, Alec asked me to go with him and his friends Teddy and Ray to a beach to swim. Teddy worked at Paphos Gate but not in the same office as me. We went to a cove past Sandy Beach on the north coast, and changed into our bathing things. I hung my clothes on a bush and was shocked on returning after our swim, to find that my knickers were not there: someone must have been watching and stolen them. I had to go back to Kyrenia holding onto my skirt and hoping it did not blow over my head. When I got home I told my mother that someone had stolen my knickers. She was quite amused.

"Oh dear," she laughed, "I do hope they were clean!" It was the sort of humour she had that I loved about her, but it did not happen enough.

That day with Alec and Teddy and Ray was the first of many such occasions: we went to all the beaches on the North Coast, and all the little coves, but our favourite place was Snake Island. After swimming there we would drive to Newman's Farm, where we would have tea and delicious milk shakes. Often Alec and I were alone, and we'd go back to St Hilarion, mysterious and romantic, surrounded by clouds. Each day that passed we got to know one another better and I found I was depressed and unhappy on the days that I did not see him.

One day I told my parents I would be late home – they thought I was working - and Alec drove me down to a small cove on the Lapithos road where the moon was very bright. I ran over the rocks in my bare feet and in and out of the sea, feeling the sand between my toes. We talked of many things and it was peaceful and lovely in the little cove and I was very happy. "*Surely,*" I wrote in my diary, "*It can't be wrong to be so happy…*"

One day at Paphos Gate we were with a Turkish lady called Selma. She was a clerk working at Police HQ, a very large lady, and Alec said to her, looking at me, "Is she a nice girl, Selma?" She said, "Yes, she is, very." "I think so," said Alec. Selma said, "Everyone does, everyone likes – or loves her."

I was touched and pleased, particularly as I was starting to hate myself and had very low self-esteem. I was also beginning to feel guilty about Martin. He had written, "I hope you realise how much I love you, darling" and "I love you better than anything else in the world." I really wanted things to work out between us and wrote in my diary "*I dread that the year will never pass. I want us to be safe and together again.*"

Safe, because I knew we were not safe at all. I was falling in love with Alec and lived for the day, trying not to think about the future. He felt the same and our feelings alternated between being ecstatically happy and utterly miserable. He knew I was engaged to Martin and that I would be going back to England to marry him. So we decided it would be best if we saw less of each other, and I made arrangements with a lady called Janet Gooch to take me and bring me back twice a week from Kyrenia and Nicosia. It didn't make any difference. We counted the time till we saw each other again.

I saw other people as well. My parents saw to that. At weekends there were people they wanted me to see, mainly middle-aged couples, friends of theirs. Colonel Prince, a neighbour from Hove took me sailing several times. I wrote that he was 'quite a nice old stick,' which was praise indeed, and he deserved better for I was an ungrateful little bitch. I was also taken sailing by Tim Burberry, one of the nicer Blues. There were a lot of cocktail parties that I did not enjoy and thought as dull as ditchwater, but I did like some of the Wiltshire Regiment who were stationed at Kyrenia Castle and who were my own age.

We were invited to lunch with officers of B Company at Morphou. Then there was John Holroyd at the castle, and Mike and Judy his wife, and Vivian, a Lieutenant at Aghirda Camp, who in particular became a good friend. Edwina and I would go to the Harbour Club with a group of Wiltshire officers and have dinner and dance. At other times Vivian came over to fetch me to play tennis. I really enjoyed his company for he was very amusing, and with him our conversation seemed to go back and forth, fast, like balls on a tennis court. He said I made a good sparring partner. He also invited me to supper at Aghirda Camp and we played Liar Dice, which was fun. I enjoyed evenings going to the Harbour Club with him, Edwina and the other young Wilts, but apart from these people, found I was longing for the weekends to be over.

Sir John Harding and his wife invited me to a party at Government House. They were very kind and my parents were delighted with such a prestigious invitation, but I did not enjoy it. Lady Harding had very bright eyes, like a little bird.

When I arrived she introduced me to a young couple. "This is Delia, the daughter of the Commissioner of Kyrenia," she said. They said hello, and when she had gone away, the young woman turned to her companion and said, "Isn't it a bore having to meet new people?"

I wish I could have thought of some cutting remark but I just stood there stunned for a moment before leaving them. I remember nothing more about that evening, except that at the end I was driven home by a young man in an open sports car who drove very fast and kept trying to run over cats which he obviously regarded as fair game and the scum of the earth, saying, "Nearly got it!" Fortunately all the cats managed to get away unscathed.

Later on I was invited to another party at Government House, and this time it started with a film showing of *Sabrina* with Audrey Hepburn and Humphrey Bogart, which I loved – though not my companions. Again Lady Harding was very kind and I must have been a disappointing guest. She organised games of the sort I hated, including having to pass an orange from one person to another without using hands. Some people thought this hilarious but I disliked people rolling their orange up and down my body and was heartily relieved when it was over. I stayed the night with the Edmondsons and my parents were disappointed to hear I had not enjoyed the party.

On the 20th June I started to feel ill at work and Monty Rich arranged for me to be sent home in a police car. I felt very sick and tired and continued to feel ill next day, and the following days. I had to get a message through to Alec to tell him I couldn't see him that evening as arranged. He was very sorry and worried for me. I was off work for a week altogether. Vivian sent me some carnations and a note saying he hoped I would soon be better. I knew Vivian had feelings for me, there was a softness in his eyes when he looked at me and one night when he came to supper he made me learn a song about "two lonely people too much in love to say goodnight." I liked Vivian very much but only as a friend, no more than that.

When I eventually went back to work it was to find Gillie very unhappy about Joe, and Edwina in a state about Ian. Enid came in and we had a discussion about the awfulness of men. I was really worried about Gillie, her affair with Joe was going nowhere and I wished she could find a nice boyfriend.

The next day I saw Alec, who had been away in Famagusta. He took me out and later we went back to the Kutchukian flats where the police were billeted. He had a nice little flat next door to Joe and Margaret Mounsey, and I taught him to play Battleships. We talked for ages and he told me a lot about himself: he had joined the Royal Navy at the age of seventeen and a quarter – I thought 'the quarter' was a funny detail – and had served in the Far East and Malta in the Second World War. Then he had joined the police.

He told me how he had come to be in Cyprus. It seemed he had had to drive his Chief Constable somewhere, and the Chief had told him that there was a State of Emergency in Cyprus and fifteen men were to be chosen from the Lancashire Constabulary to go out there. He thought Alec might be suitable to be one of them and said he would recommend him. There were hundreds who applied from Lancashire but Alec was selected, and went out to Cyprus with the rank of Sergeant. I then told him how I came to be there, how my father had got the job of Commissioner of Kyrenia and, even though I then got engaged to Martin, I had promised I would go out there too and could not break my promise. Eventually Alec drove me back to Kyrenia, but we did not get there till midnight and my parents were worried and cross.

As the days passed Gillie grew increasingly unhappy, saying she had 'had' Cyprus and would like to collect her pay and take the next ship home. I felt really worried about her and wished I could introduce her to someone. I invited her to come and stay for a weekend in Kyrenia and resolved to give a party for her. I was worried about the party as I didn't know how many men would come and how many girls and if there would be too many of one group and not enough of the other. However, it was fine, in the end there were eight men and seven girls. It was a success and everyone enjoyed it. Later Tony, Bill Turner, Vivian, Gillie and I went to the Harbour Club. As I'd hoped, Bill got off with Gillie. I kept hoping he'd ring her afterwards, but he never did.

Vivian had a friend called Richard, a brother officer in the Wiltshire Regiment who fell in love with Edwina, and she couldn't decide who she liked best, Ian or Richard. She had decided to leave Police HQ and get a job as an air hostess with Cyprus Airways and her last day was the 30th June.

After this date Alec and I were always alone on the days he took me home after work, and I also saw him on Saturday or Wednesday afternoons as well. He made me laugh a lot and I thought he had a lovely sense of humour. He told me I made him very happy, but my mother was not pleased. At the beginning of July she said, "Aren't you seeing too much of Alec?" I wrote in my diary, *"Well yes, maybe I am but surely it cannot be wrong to be so happy. It is such an innocent happiness that exists between Alec and me, and I dread to give it up."*

I told Alec what my mother had said and he was upset and rather sarcastic. Often he was in a bad mood when he thought I was seeing other people. If I told him I could not see him for a while he was furious, disappointed and hurt. I would tell him I couldn't help it, for my mother had intervened and was stopping me, but he didn't like it and was jealous and moody and our time together was spoilt. I thought he took offence very easily. I told him it made no difference to the way I felt about him, but he thought that it did, and we quarrelled. For a few days he sent me home with Andreas, his number two assistant. I was then upset and angry and told him I was engaged to someone else who I was going to marry and he had no right to criticise what I did and who with. He was deeply hurt, and I instantly regretted saying it. Every time we quarrelled we would decide to call it a day, and were then miserable - but the sweetness of making up afterwards more than made up for the misery – and we were closer than ever.

It was very hot in Kyrenia in July and I often slept outside on our flat roof, under the stars. Time passed and there were cocktail and dinner parties. In Kyrenia I dined at a nice little Greek restaurant called the Hesperides where the food was good and not expensive. Sometimes I went there with Alec, sometimes with Vivian and sometimes with my parents. They also had a busy social life. They saw a lot of the Edmondsons and went to several parties on HMS Manxman, a naval ship that patrolled the Mediterranean and was anchored off Kyrenia. They became friends with the Colonel of the Blues who used the flat next to ours as a holiday base. The Colonel was worried about a Captain in the regiment who was friendly with a handsome young American. I liked the Captain, who was gay, but the Colonel said the two of them were corrupting half his young subalterns.

I was invited to a party there and took Gillie. It was held on their flat roof and was very well organised by the young Captain, but I thought most of the Blues an odd crowd, very drippy. Some of them got drunk and would not let us go home, though it was twenty to four. The next day we discussed it with amusement and said what an extraordinary party it had been. Gillie got off with Tim Burberry, who was about the best of them. I hoped something might have come of it, but she was still stuck on Joe. *"What it is to get tied up with a married man,"* I wrote, *"yet as Somerset Maugham said, 'Better to sin and to regret than to regret for not having sinned.'* Gillie loved that saying, she thought it very true, and she would carry on sinning.

My parents gave a cocktail party, which I thought was boring. Most of the cocktail parties were, the chat was superficial and I felt I was as boring as everyone else. I passed round plates of hors d'oeuvres and noticed there were tiny ants crawling over them, and didn't know whether to ignore them and hope they didn't see, or to draw attention to them by saying, "Oh – watch out for the ants…" It was quite dark so I said nothing.

Colonel Hunter said, "How's that red-haired secretary of your father's?" He always said the same thing, could be malicious and I thought him dangerous. But there was a very amusing Major Robbins in the Wiltshires, known as DIM Robbins, not because he was dim but because those were his initials. He and his wife Mary became great friends of my parents. He liked to play practical jokes and often got into trouble over them. He wrote on the blotter of Kasmiris, my father's Greek Cypriot assistant, "EOKA WILL GET YOU!" Kasmiris was terrified. Another time Dim went to a restaurant and put silver cutlery into the pocket of one of the diners whom he did not know, then called the Manager and suggested he look in the man's pocket. The cutlery was discovered and the poor man was embarrassed having to admit he had no idea how it had got there.

Dim went to a cocktail party and told a woman that he was the King of Egypt. He was very dark and quite short, so she believed it and said to another woman, "I've just met the most extraordinary little man, he says he's the King of Egypt!"

"Oh yes," said the other woman, "I'm afraid that's my husband." This was Mary, Dim's delightful and long-suffering wife.

Dim went to see someone in another regiment, and did not like it when he was told to wait in an outer office, so he wrote a note saying, "Never keep a General waiting!" This caused great alarm and he was shown into the office at once. Another time he was in his own office and called a young officer in to see him. The officer knocked on the door and went in and thought there was nobody there – Dim was hiding behind his desk. Vivian and the other young Wiltshires said it was sometimes very difficult for them to know when he was joking and when he was not. He would order them to go down a hill and they would laugh and then Dim would roar, "Bloody well get down that hill!"

There continued to be terrorist attacks and Sergeant Reginald Tipple of the UK police unit was shot and killed in Larnaca. There were incidents in Nicosia, and Ledra Street was known as Murder Mile. News was out about Operation Pepperpot, it had been a great success and everyone was very excited. A thousand troops of all the services were involved in this massive operation, including the Army, Navy, RAF helicopters, Police and tracker dogs. Three EOKA gangs were wiped out altogether and another almost eradicated. Two men were captured for rewards of £5000 each. We wondered how many EOKA there were in the police. I wondered what Uncle Mac was up to these days and hoped he was not responsible for any more murders.

On the 8th July Mr and Mrs Kaberry were shot dead in their car on their way to the coast for a picnic. Their car was halted by a road block, then the terrorists opened up with automatic weapons and shot guns. Mrs Kaberry was killed instantly and her husband died on the way to hospital. She was the first British woman to be killed since the terrorist campaign began.

When Alec heard about the Kaberry murder, he first thought it might be my parents. He was shocked and said it made him think he wanted to marry me. Marriage? I was startled. That was not on the cards. I was engaged to Martin. I was going to marry Martin. I loved Martin – *didn't I?* So - what was he thinking?

In August there was a battle at Nicosia General Hospital. A hardcore EOKA terrorist called Yorgadjis, who was in custody, was taken there for an X-ray and a gang of four members tried to rescue him. There was a shoot-out in the hospital corridor and Sergeant Eden and Sergeant Demmon of the Metropolitan police were shot. Tony Eden, though wounded, fought off the attackers, but Demmon was killed and so were two hospital employees and two members of EOKA. We had to live with such incidents all the time and so we lived day to day, never quite knowing what might happen next. We knew we could be ambushed at any time. When I went shopping in Ledra Street's Murder Mile, Alec, unknown to me, followed by car. I don't know what he thought he could do, but I know he would have died for me.

CHAPTER NINE

A new regime of senior UK police officers now arrived to take over some of the duties from the senior Colonial Police. Both Mr Robbins and Mr Biles, the Commissioner of Police and his Deputy, were replaced by Colonel White from Kent constabulary and Mr Webster from Leicestershire. There was also Mr Saunders who was very tall, 6' 6½". I was shocked and disapproving, because the very first letters Mr Webster and Mr Saunders dictated were about their terms of employment and about the bonuses and material perks they could claim, not about the Emergency at all. This was very different from the attitude of Mr Biles of the Colonial Police who had been dedicated in his resolve to defeat EOKA, and the thought of claiming benefits for himself would have been the last thing on his mind.

I had mainly been working for Monty Rich, but now I also had a lot of work from Mr Webster, who treated me as his personal secretary. He was a handsome man and Enid was very smitten, but I did not much like him, nor Colonel White whom I thought was ruthless. He seemed to be popular with the UK police but not with the Colonials, and I took their side and was loyal to the old regime.

On the 25th July there was a crisis in Egypt when President Nasser closed the Suez Canal. I wrote "they say it is the most serious thing that has happened since the war. Will it cause another? Who can say. I talked to Janet (Gooch) about it and we were very worried."

We continued to be worried and on the 1st August I wrote that we were still wondering what would happen. Later that day I went round to see Edwina and found Ian there. Richard, Vivian's friend in the Wiltshire Regiment who was in love with Edwina, also came and we all stayed for supper. "It was very awkward as Eddie now cannot decide who she likes best, Ian or Richard" I wrote. Afterwards she and I had a chat. She said Richard had told her Vivian was absolutely mad about me but could not understand why I was there. I wondered too – why was I here? I still loved Martin, or thought I did.

On the 4th August Colonel Prince invited me for a picnic at St Hilarion, but Alec had offered to take me to Famagusta and Lefkonico and I managed to get out of the picnic. I was very excited. We saw Famagusta and went on to Salamis, the site of an amazing town, half hidden in the sand dunes, dating back to the 5th century BC. There was nobody there but us and we wandered all over the Roman and Byzantine ruins of basilicas, colonnades with classical statues and royal tombs. I was entranced by it all. We went back via Lefkonico but after a sinister warning by a Turk that we should not go there, did not dare attempt the Pass. On the way back to Nicosia we stopped at a roadside restaurant for supper and *"saw a fire on the mountain side and looked at ships. That was all, but I was happy."*

On the 6th August all the lights in Kyrenia went out and the Manxman assisted with searchlight and signals. The next day the Government announced there would be three hangings and lots of precautions were taken, for instance only security forces and government vehicles were allowed to go anywhere.

I was still getting a lot of work to do from Mr Webster and Monty Rich and felt exhausted by the end of the day. Alec took me back to Kyrenia on a forest and river road. We found a little glade by the river. It seemed very peaceful and far away from the violence of those days, but we were deluding ourselves; the hangings of the three men took place on the 9th and two bombs exploded in the evening. Alec was going to take me to a film after work but there were curfews on and we could not go.

After that life returned to normal – as normal as it ever could be. On the 16th August the magazine *Good Taste* came out and my story, 'The Cherry Stone' was published. It was exciting to see my name in print. My parents seemed quite pleased about it but Alec was the most pleased and very proud of me. I sent my story 'The Lonely Rose' to the Cyprus Broadcasting Service and they rang to say they would like to use it but did not say when.

On the 20th August I was taken to the Dolphin by Bill A, an officer in D company of the Wiltshire Regiment. He said he wanted to transfer to the Guards and I thought that would suit him better. He wanted us to go to a beach and swim afterwards. I said I had no bathing costume and he said that didn't matter. He said he had been brought up on the west coast of Ireland and he and his cousins always swam in the nude, and he expected me to join him. I was probably very prudish but I was shocked. I thought he was very fast and I had no intention of swimming in the nude, so he stripped off his clothes and went into the sea alone. The next day I told Gillie and we were amazed and thought whatever had the world come to? He telephoned me continually for the next two days. I pretended I was out, but Alec was furious.

My mother was uneasy that I was seeing so much of Alec. We had a sort of row and she said, "I think it would be best if you went home and got married earlier than next April." I rather agreed that it would. But I felt all mixed up. I had a lot of time to think and I didn't want to think. My parents suggested we might have a long weekend up in the Troodos mountains and that we could take Gillie, so she and I asked Mr Webster and Monty Rich if we could have two days off the following week. It was a struggle but in the end they gave permission, saying we would have to work overtime to make up.

We started our little holiday on Saturday, 1st September. We picked up Gillie in Nicosia and drove up to Troodos and then down to a hotel in Prodromos where we were going to stay, and where we had lunch. All afternoon we slept, and then had drinks in the bar with some friends of my parents'. Our first night was very depressing and we all retired early with books. Next day we played tennis in the morning and had two excellent young Greek ball boys. We offered them Coca Cola but they wouldn't accept it – maybe they sympathised with EOKA.

We arranged to go riding on Troodos in the afternoon. I loved the scenery, the mountains and the pine trees. Gillie rode a bay called Stella and I a dark stallion called Othello. Neither would go very well and we were a little disappointed. We had a serious talk and found ourselves rather unsettled somehow. I wondered if Alec was thinking about me and missing me as I was missing him.

In the evening I went alone to a place where I watched the sun set far away in the mountains. It was so beautiful and peaceful and I felt nothing mattered in a hundred years. The next day we went to Platres, an entirely army-occupied village. Gillie and I went for a last ride, and it was the most beautiful I could ever hope to do: a winding mountain path, the tremendous precipice, the thick blue sky, the pine trees and the mountains rising up all around. I was overawed. Sometimes we seemed to go off the edge of space, it was like being on top of the world. We left Prodromos and Berengaria and journeyed home feeling refreshed and optimistic.

Alec and I were very glad to see one another again after my holiday and

I arranged to spend the night with the Edmondsons so that we could go out in the evening. As so often we went on the Hilarion Road and had supper in a dear little Turkish restaurant, and I marvelled that all the time we seemed to come closer. But I knew uneasily we were heading for a clash. I had refused to think about the future, but we both knew it was becoming more serious. It was as if I had covered my head with a blanket and wouldn't face what was happening.

The next night when I went home there was a horrible row with my mother. As usual it was about Alec and I knew she was right, but I didn't want to listen to the vitriol she poured over me. It was bad enough that I was hating myself more and more with every day that passed. I felt miserable all day and all evening because of her bitter accusations and the acrimonious things she said. I told Alec about it and he was sweet, very gentle and understanding. In my diary I wrote, *"if a bus should run me over, if the sea should drown me, if a fire should burn over my head, I should be content to let it."* I was being melodramatic but I really believed it, so guilty did I feel and so much was I hating myself. It was an unhappy morning at work. Alec comforted me and said many nice things. He told me I had changed his entire outlook on life, that I had great character and great virtue. I was touched and proud, but we wondered if we should end our relationship because of the rows I kept getting. At home the next night it was all right, but I was fearful of being questioned further by my mother. She made barbed little remarks about him.

"Brigadier Pickthorn says he saw Alec working outside and he was wearing a *vest*," she said.

"Just a vest? No trousers?"

"Oh, trousers too – but a vest – beyond the pale. *And* it had holes in it."

"A holy vest? That *is* beyond the pale."

"You may scoff, but it isn't what a gent would wear."

"Brigadier Pickthorn is a silly, puny little man."

My father entered the conversation.

"You don't get to be a Brigadier by being silly, Delia. You shouldn't make such stupid sweeping statements."

"I must have learnt it from you, then." Which was rude – but I didn't care. And he *was* a silly, puny little man.

"But he's a *gent*," said my mother, as if that made up for everything.

On Saturday, Enid and Gillie took me to Shilling Beach in a hired car and we had an ant-ridden picnic. Gillie told me she had arranged to go to Rome with her parents for two weeks from the 3rd October and asked if I would stay at her flat and look after her cats. They were sweet cats, only young, hardly more than kittens, and they were called Harriet and Henrietta. I gladly agreed, for I was not happy living at home and dreaded being alone with my parents. It wasn't just that I would see more of Alec, but that I would be free – free as air, to read and write, to lie in bed and do whatever I wanted. That sounds selfish and I was.

On Sunday Paul asked me out for the day – he was Gillie's sister's fiancé who was in Cyprus for a while – Gillie had introduced him to me and the three of us went out in his Morris Minor for a picnic. This time he asked me on my own. I thought him rather arrogant but I agreed to go and we went in his open Morris Minor to Cape Kormakiti, right to the very point. We had to travel twelve miles down a very rough road through two not very nice villages, Greek Cypriot and unfriendly to the British. The Paras were at the Cape. We swam and had a picnic, then drove back at a startling pace. Alec was rather jealous about Paul but there was no need. I thought of no one but him. We continued seeing each other constantly, going to swim at the beautiful Snake Island, or our favourite romantic little coves where the sea tumbled over the rocks, or to the lonely and mysterious Saint Hilarion Castle.

On the 17th September my father said there were going to be hangings and this would cause more trouble. The next day Alec and I were very depressed to hear that winter hours were to begin the following week. This would mean we would not be able to see each other in the afternoons. It was getting serious and I knew I was on dangerous ground, dancing with the devil. Sometimes I didn't know what I thought any more.

In the next days there were many curfews and I was warned to be on my guard at all times. On the 20th September three men were hanged. Alec was out on a job all morning, taking prisoners to Larnaca. It was dangerous and I was very relieved to hear he had got back safely. There was an operation in Kyrenia and the Dome Hotel was searched. Nothing was found.

Winter hours began on 24th September. It was not easy at home. On the 27th there was to be a police dinner at the Acropole Hotel, and I asked if I could stay the night with the Edmondsons so that I could go. The idea was not welcomed but I selfishly thought I would go anyway. It was a very good evening and Alec told me he felt very proud of me, but before I left home that morning things were not good and I felt unhappy that it should be like that. I didn't want to cause them pain but it seemed inevitable that I should do so.

I tried hard to find a present for my mother for I felt it would cheer her up, but two police sergeants were tragically killed and there were curfews on and I could not get out. These murders were so awful – how many more? On the 28th September there was an ambush on the Kyrenia road and a soldier and a woman were killed. We had to be on guard all the time. I felt uneasy because I had told my mother I was going to stay at Gillie's flat to look after her cats while she was on holiday and she had seemed to accept it, but I was afraid she had not taken it in. Gillie's flat was in a bad EOKA district of Nicosia and Alec was worried about the security there and probably my father would be as well, but they had said nothing, so I left well alone.

I was reading a book at this time, called *Against the Law* by Peter Wildebloode. He had been imprisoned in 1954 for homosexual offences together with Lord Montagu and Michael Pitt-Rivers. My second cousin, Peter Rawlinson, had been his defence counsel and Arthur Prothero was the solicitor. When I wrote and told Martin about this, he said he was surprised I should be reading such a book and strongly disapproved. He said it was a subject one saw in a paper like the *News of the World* and quickly turned the page. I was very disappointed with this response. In fact it made me wonder how well I really knew him.

On the 2nd October Gillie gave me last-minute instructions, as she would be going the next day. I got home and did my packing and nothing was said. Then there was a terrible crisis when my father suddenly said at supper:

"What is this about you going to Nicosia?"

My heart beat very fast. "You know I'm going, it's all arranged,"

"What do you mean? I know nothing of the sort."

"Yes, I told you. I *told* you! I'm going to look after her cats."

"You most certainly will not. I won't hear of your going."

"I told you about it weeks ago and you never said anything. I've got to go, I've got to. It's all arranged. The cats can't feed themselves, can they?"

"Don't be ridiculous."

"Well I'm going anyway, whatever you say."

"We'll see about that," said my father looking very grim.

I rushed downstairs to my room. I was very nervous and keyed up and could not sleep. I decided that if he stopped me, I would leave home altogether. The next morning I got up, feeling very scared, finished packing and was all set to go. It was early in the morning and no one was up. I looked for a long time from my window at the sea and the coastline of Turkey. I thought quite calmly that if he tried to stop me I would leave – for ever. My father was furious and said he was going to stop all this and he was going to ring Geoff White, the Commissioner of Police.

Janet Gooch arrived to pick me up and I was in floods of tears as I got into the car. When I got to work I was still in tears, and Alec drove me away and I cried on his shoulder. I said I was going to America and he said if I did he was going with me. I wondered what my father would do but he did not ring Geoff White in the end, and later he rang me to apologise. I also spoke to my mother and it seemed that all was well – at least for the time being.

That night I went to Gillie's flat. There was a friend of hers, Lillian, staying there with Roy, her fiancé. She had some lovely classical music and that evening when they went out we lay on the sofa with the cats and listened to the *New World Symphony* and were happy. Alec said that in these two weeks we would get to know one another better and must take the opportunity to think very seriously about a future together. Yes, it had really come to this: that I should think of breaking off my engagement to Martin and marry him instead. But we had to be sure, and neither of us were. Sometimes he became very passionate and I had to push him away. He knew I had very high principles and would never dream of letting him sleep with me. I said, "Is it only sex with us?" and felt very hurt when he said he did not know. I kept thinking of that remark. I thought, if that is true, what am I doing with him? What am I doing to think of giving up my future with dear Martin whom I truly love? I felt very confused. But the next day Alec said that he was a clot and a mug and of course it was not just sex, and that he loved me better than anything in the world.

One night there was a mysterious telephone call, and there was a Greek voice on the line. He said, "Who is that?" and refused to say who he was. Lillian and Roy had only stayed a few nights and I was now on my own and Alec was very frightened and hated leaving me in case it was EOKA. He locked up all the doors and windows very thoroughly. Then he gave me his gun and said I should put it under my pillow and if I heard anyone come I should not hesitate to shoot. I too was a bit nervous and kept thinking about Uncle Mac and wondering if I was on the EOKA hit list.

After Alec had gone I lay in bed and suddenly I heard footsteps on the gravel outside my bedroom window. I picked up the gun and went to the window and was about to shoot when I realised it was Alec, who had returned just to see if I would hear if someone came. And he certainly was a clot, for I had nearly shot him.

On the last night Alec brought Teddy and Ray and I cooked supper for us all and he said he was very proud of me. Afterwards they insisted on not leaving me alone in this EOKA district, so they took me back with them and I slept in an empty flat at the Kutchukian building. The next day Gillie came back, full of beans, and we all went to the Acropole in the evening.

On the 18th October I wrote, *"I am very happy. Oh dear, what a beast I am. Yet perhaps human. I didn't ask for this to happen to me. What an utter mess it all is. Sometimes I think it would solve things if I should get killed by EOKA. It would end everything then. Little did I guess what would happen to me in my life. A good thing none of us know our fates."*

27th October: *"Went back to Kyrenia in the afternoon. He said he wished I would make my mind up to marry him. He is very serious, we must decide soon, but what choice can I make? It is either my happiness or my parents', and if I am to choose theirs and I am unhappy, will they not be unhappy also?"*

My mother talked for a long time about my father's affair with the girl at his club, at least it was not really an affair but she had built it up into one. I told her she *must* try to forget about it, but I felt very worried about her. She seemed so unhappy at present and had lost weight.

On the 30th October Evelyn Edmondson rang up and asked me to meet her at John Odger's for a chat about my mother. I thought at first she was going to talk about me, in which case I had decided to tell her all, but it was not about that after all, but my mother's unhappiness because of my father and the girl at his club. We could not think what to do about it, but then my mother got a little job as a Censor and that seemed to make a difference.

31st October: *"The news is very bad, there could be war with Egypt. The Russians are squashing the Hungarian anti-communist rebellion and killing thousands of Hungarians. I dreaded to go home but A said we must concentrate not on us but on my mother's health. We were both very sad and unsure – at least he is sure but I am not."*

On the 1st November Mr Webster told me he would take me to Kyrenia, as he was going to a party. Saunders was also going and taking Enid, and they were all staying at a hotel. Alec said he thought W would make a pass at me but I did not think he would. Then sure enough, Webster drove the car up a side road saying he was going to teach me to drive. He put his arms round me and I shoved him away with all my might, thinking how extraordinary it was that Alec was right. Next day we laughed about it. Afterwards Enid told me Webster had come to the hotel and grumbled that 'the little Despair girl wouldn't play ball.' They had obviously arranged the whole thing. Both

Saunders and Webster were married men, but that didn't stop them - or Enid – and it never did, she would jump into bed with anyone. Why was I so different? It was the way I had been brought up.

From then on Webster treated me like dirt and I was quite surprised. I always thought men would respect you more if you didn't behave like a tart than if you did. It had been the same with Paul in Jamaica, he had not respected me or appreciated my point of view. But at least I knew Alec did.

CHAPTER TEN

2nd Nov: *The news is terrible. The Para's have landed in Egypt. Perhaps there*
              will be a world war. I should like to join the WRNS – oh but I do not
              know. I think I should like to die.

5th Nov: *"What a stupid muddled girl I am. I don't know where I am at all.*
              One thing is clear, I must be a horrible person. The 5th November has
              been an eventful day in my life but today finds me, a horrible girl, utterly
              utterly confused."

              Enid said I should go ahead and marry him but suppose Tom was right?
              Tom Watkinson had said it would never work with Alec and me, I
              would never settle down to be a Sergeant's wife and live in Lancashire.

8th Nov: *"Mum asked me if I had gone off Martin. I said, Of course not – but*
              I felt awful and wished she had not. I am not ready to tell anything.
              When I am I think I shall tell Daddy first. I met Edwina. Richard
              says Vivian is madly in love with me.

10th Nov: *Horrible talk with Mum. She asked me if I were happy, I said Yes but*
              please don't keep asking me, I hate these talks.

13th Nov: *I kept wondering what to do and wishing I were dead. I wish it could*
              be done for me so that I do not have to go through with this. I can't
              bear to think of marrying anyone but Alec yet it is going to cause such
              tremendous complications and unhappiness for Martin. What am I to
              do? I fear M and D will never understand or forgive me. I am at the
              cross roads of my life, one way says The way you Want to go and the
              other says The way you Should go. Which to take?

14th Nov: *A beautiful sunny day. Alec drove me back to Kyrenia and we discussed*
              the future. First we thought we would part and on thinking this we

both wept and I was moved at seeing Alec cry. We sat on top of a hill and thought if we were to end it, it would be a good place in a beautiful spot like this. But we could not. We tried and we could not bring ourselves to say goodbye. I walked home – having decided to tell M and D. I walked miles, feeling glad and sorry at once. As soon as M came in I told her and Daddy came, and it was terrible, worse than I had imagined. We wept and Daddy was alright at first, quite calm, but not Mum. What a terrible night.

15th Nov: This morning early it was simply awful. They were both shouting at me and I was in floods of tears. They were horrible, oh so horrible.

"I wish I was dead," I sobbed.

"Were dead," said my father. He was such a stickler for good English.

"I wish I were dead. I wish EOKA would kill me. They kill other people. Why not me?"

"You're so melodramatic, Delia. You always have been. And now you want to marry a working-class police sergeant from Lancashire. It's unthinkable."

"But why? Why do you think our family is so superior to everyone else?"

"Don't be ridiculous. I've never said that."

"But it's what you believe. When Badger was in Nigeria you refused to let her go out with young men because you thought they were common. Someone told me afterwards, no one was allowed near the daughters of the Resident."

"That's nonsense. You don't know what you're talking about. You're behaving very badly and you've got to stop all this at once. You think of no one but yourself. You're making your mother ill."

When I came to Nicosia I thought we must end things. I talked to Alec and cried in the car and he could not have been sweeter to me. In the evening I could not feel like eating but had to repeat everything to him over again. This time last year I said Men were fickle – but what is it to me? I am far, far worse. I was deeply unhappy yet A was marvellous to me.

16th Nov: *We decided that A should go and see Daddy tonight – although he had said he would not see Alec. Still it would help, I'm sure. In the evening A and I got ready, cleaned his shoes, pressed his trousers and with the good wishes of Gillie, Enid, Margaret, Ray and Jimmy we set off. We were both terribly nervous. M and D were very nice and asked us in but A does not think he made a good impression.*

17th Nov: *No – we were right. We did not make a good impression. Daddy was horrified and furious. I feel much more sure now. We know where we stand. We stopped on the Hilarion road and talked very seriously. He is happy to think I am so sure. I went home and M was awful at first. They went out, and I found a little beach all by myself and thought for a long time. They went to a film but after the film she was sick.*

18th Nov: *Today I kept myself to myself for I felt I was not wanted. Daddy was very cold towards me. Mum has lost weight. Both accuse me of doing this and I feel guilty as the night. But it is Martin that really makes me sad – having to tell him. How I dread it.*

19th Nov: *Monty Rich gave me a long talking to and I felt very depressed. He said marriages can break up over lots of small things: religion or background or his parents staying with us, or something. After I told A and he was incredibly sweet. I was sad for a long while. Then suddenly I felt quite different and tremendously happy.*

20th Nov: *I asked Monty to talk to A and he said he would, tomorrow afternoon. In the meantime he helped me with the letter to the Establishment Secretary asking for my penalties, passage and month's pay to be waived, and Saunders kindly recommended this.*

21st Nov: *In the afternoon A went to see Monty and after he felt much better, so did I. Monty said he would like to have a talk with my parents and he would ring them. When I got home I wondered if it would be alright. I had a feeling they might be awful. I was right. We had three whole hours of terrible wrangling. It was a great strain and I felt like a wet rag. How little they understand. Then we made a pact: they to stop and me to wait. I am to go home at once.*

22nd Nov: *Daddy grumbled that now he would not be able to go to the MCC, of which Martin is a member and he thinks that he, being able to go to Lords, is one of the advantages of my engagement. I thought it a little ironic that he should put this forward as a reason for not breaking it off.*

He was horrible before I left and said I was thinking of no one's happiness but my own. It made me sad. I wonder if they will ever come round. I met Evelyn for coffee and she was incredibly kind and sweet. I talked everything over with her and felt much better afterwards. I was delighted she had understood and given me such good advice.

23rd Nov: The nicest time is when Alec comes to collect me in the mornings. How intensely happy I feel then and so does he. I am only happy when I am with him and unhappy at home. In some ways it will be good to get away and leave them — but how I dread to leave him. He fears often that I shall not come back. Sometimes I wonder too. Last night we had a tiff and loved one another more than ever afterwards.

24th Nov: M and D had seen the Riches. They criticised Gillie. They criticised all the girls out here. But they don't know Alec — don't begin to.

I wrote a long letter to my dear Badger, trying to explain. I told her how I had done the unforgiveable thing and fallen in love with someone of whom our parents totally disapproved — a police sergeant from Lancashire. I so wanted her to forgive me and understand.

24th Nov   Mum was very cold towards me. I went out to dinner with the Cobbolds. Vivian took me home and stayed hours. He is a good friend. I hope I shan't hurt him. I'm sure he has no idea. Yet I have tried not to lead him up the garden path. Another weekend over. Parents are very cold with me these days. But what can I do?

26th Nov: Another week. I still cannot bring myself to write to Martin — I must do it. But first I booked my ticket for England.

27th Nov: A letter from Badger, such a sweet letter. She says if only I will wait six months she thinks M & D will come round and be on our side, whatever they may say now.

28th Nov: I showed Badger's letter to A and he was very pleased. Daddy wanted to know about Alec's financial situation, and he wrote it all out very carefully. An uncle had given him quite a large legacy on his 21st birthday which he has in a savings account so he is not without money, in fact he has a lot more than I have. We had the afternoon off and went on the road past Hilarion where it was very beautiful. We saw a small church right up on top of the mountain, deserted but very lovely.

29th Nov: *We took Margaret to a film about a German girl called "Frieda". It was sad and I felt depressed afterwards. A noticed at once. It is uncanny the way he can read me. He thought I was beginning to have doubts, but it was not that.*

30th Nov: *I heard that my penalties have been waived and if I eventually return to Cyprus I can go back to my job on the same salary. I was delighted and thanked Saunders and Webbie and everyone else. What luck, for now I am financially secure.*

2nd Dec: *Daddy blamed me for Mum's health and I wept. I missed A very badly and had a foretaste of the loneliness of the next months.*

3rd Dec: *A and I were very happy to be together. We love one another very much. I wonder if anyone realises how much. We must find presents for one another before I go away. He feels I'll not come back.*

4th Dec: *I dreaded telling M & D that I did not want them to see me off. Mum took it very badly but I did not mean it to be hurtful, just that it would be easier for all of us. Still she was very hurt indeed. I feel awful about it. A & I went shopping in Ledra Street and I looked everywhere for a little present for her so that she won't be hurt and realise that I don't want her to be unhappy about not coming to see me off.*

6th Dec: *When I rang FBS to ask for my story back they said they wanted to use it and asked me to come up and make the recording on Monday.*

7th Dec: *We were glad I was coming up tomorrow and we didn't have to say goodbye.*

8th Dec: *A and I went to the bank and got the money I shall need. We got £50 in travellers' cheques and £10 sterling.*

9th Dec: *The Riches came in the morning when I was in the middle of packing. Mum was upset and got very intense. I packed my trunk. The atmosphere in the evening was awful. A felt angry and said he wished we could get married straight away. I wished that too. He said he thought none of my family were being fair and writing out what money he had made him feel he was trying to sell something. Why couldn't they accept him for what he was? I felt sad at these words. Why indeed? Yet they cannot.*

10th Dec: *Had to go to the FBS to make the recording of my story. I was nervous but to my surprise the recording sounded fine with just the right expression at all the different places. I spent the night in Margaret's flat with Joe away and we gossiped endlessly.*

11th Dec:	*I showed my m/s to Enid, she seemed very impressed and I was glad to have her as a critic for she is a stern one. M&D were difficult making digs all evening and I was relieved to get away from them to my room and its privacy.*
12th Dec:	*A bought me a beautiful present. I bought presents for Mum and others. In the evening a cocktail party and Vivian and the Cobbolds there. I told them I was going soon and V was fearfully upset about it. They were impressed to hear about my story. After we went to the Harbour Club.*
13th Dec:	*My story was broadcast. Alec, Margaret and I listened in her flat. It came over well and they liked it and A was v. proud. I've only a short time left and I was overcome with sadness.*
14th Dec:	*Enid and the others full of praise for the broadcast, saying I had missed my vocation and should go on the BBC. I had hidden talents and it was beautiful. Mr Rich asked to see me, he was awfully kind and nice, unbelievably so, very sweet of him to take such an interest. I found to my sorrow, a lovely present from Martin, a marcosite brooch of a sailing boat.*
15th Dec:	*I longed to see A again after yesterday. He was a little bit depressed especially at things Tom said. Tom is horrible I think.*
16th Dec:	*Dinner at the Harbour Club. All the Wilts were there and Mike, Judy, Bill T and Vivian congratulated me on "The Lonely Rose" very much and I was glad. We danced. I did my packing. V did not come up after all and we said goodbye on the phone.*
17th Dec:	*In the evening I changed into my rust and gold dress and A liked it a lot and we had dinner at the Acropole and discussed a rosy future. It was a truly wonderful evening and we were incredibly happy.*
18th Dec:	*There's so little time left now. I was sad because everyone was being so nice. A and I were very close on the way home and my heart seemed to be bursting partly with happiness and partly with sorrow as the time grows less. M & D were rather sweet and M cooked a special supper for me.*
19th Dec:	*I came up with my case for it is my last night with A. I went shopping after lunch and bought a book for Pop and a lovely card for A. Saw the Edmondsons and said goodbye and they were very nice. The key would not fit at Enid's so I had to sleep in Alec's bed and he with Harry.*

20th Dec: *A lovely day. A was so sweet to me. How could we ever have quarrelled? Yet it made no difference to us. How sad we both of us are that I am leaving. I gave him the card, then we went to Ledra Street and I bought a watch for him and he was delighted with it. In the evening I went home and said goodbye, first to the Riches. Then we had our last evening together. How I dread to leave him! When I went home I had a lot to do, doing presents up and packing cases. Talked to M & D till 10 p.m. and still they are dropping hints about working class people etc.*

21th Dec: *At last the day has arrived. Got up, had a tearful breakfast, finished packing and said goodbye. Mum v upset and I was too, that things should be this way. Found Alec and he helped me label and reload luggage. Then said goodbye to Nick at bank and all Headquarters, and I was upset and cried, so was Enid, and Saunders so sweet, also Teddy, Margaret, Gillie, Jimmy etc so nice. Alec then took me away and we were both terribly sad. We drove to Larnaca and had lunch at the 4 Lanterns. On the way to Larnaca he said, "I do hope that soon I shall be coming down to Limassol to meet you and you'll be back again." We were both very sad at the thought of parting – he because he was afraid I might not come back and that he would never see me again. But he said he thought of it this way, if I really loved him I would come back and if I did not it was better that we should find out in time. Oh God I do hope that I do love him enough. I feel certain now that I do – make me go on feeling sure. Then we said goodbye. They would not allow him aboard and I wept bitterly and was miserable. I stood for hours watching the shore where he said he would wait. The sunset was very beautiful. At last the 2nd Lieutenant came and the man from Special Branch before they went ashore, and they made me drink lots of brandy. They wished me all the luck in the world. Our great separation had begun.*

CHAPTER ELEVEN

———◆———

The SS *Messapia* of the Italian Adriatica Line sailed from Larnaca on the 21ˢᵗ December, bound for Venice, but on the next day for some reason we dropped anchor outside Limassol, and did not leave till 9 pm. At first I was very excited, thinking we were still in Cyprus and I could see Alec again, but much to my disappointment no one was allowed ashore.

For the next six days I was at sea, and in some ways relieved to be on my own and in others, sad and lonely. I missed Alec and spent a lot of time crying in my cabin, or out on deck staring at the sea. I studied the other passengers and they studied me. There was a strange English couple, I thought he was with his mother but it turned out she was his wife. There was a vegetarian and an African and a Turk and someone I called "Angel" but can't remember why. I had a very kindly steward who brought me breakfast in bed each day.

We reached Athens on Christmas Eve in the pouring rain. We climbed up the Acropolis looking like a lot of miserable, drowned rats. In the afternoon we passed through the Corinth Canal. I thought Christmas Day was the strangest I had ever spent. I sat on my bed and opened my presents and was deeply touched on opening my mother's to find it was a beautiful cockerel, made of sapphire blue and gold Venetian glass. I knew she had treasured it very much and it was so sweet of her to give it to me.

I thought back on the past days in Cyprus. It was awful that I had fallen out with my parents. We had always been such a close family and I had never before done anything really bad, had never incurred such disapproval and wrath.

We reached Venice after lunch on Boxing Day, and I ate well for I did not expect supper that night. The vegetarian took me across Venice for very little money. It was so extraordinary to be in Venice again and I thought of everything that had happened since I had been there last when I was on the way to Cyprus with my mother all those months ago. Looking back, it was crazy to have got engaged before going away on a two-year contract. But there were no excuses for how I had behaved, and for what I would now have to do to Martin.

I boarded a Cypriot train, which was dirty, uncomfortable and alternately hot and cold. I kept all my luggage with me. In my carriage was a police inspector Demetriou, also the Turk. I read a lot of the time and wished I had something to eat, for there was no food. We none of us got much sleep and after twenty-four hours felt as if we had been on the train for ever, but at least we did not have to change at Paris.

At Calais I got on a ferry boat and talked to an aristocrat who had shipped oranges from Port Said to Famagusta. At Dover I passed safely through customs and boarded a train with thousands of Cypriots and refugees. Finally we arrived at Victoria where Badger and Peter met me. It was good to see them again. They were on their way to a party and took me, looking scruffy and dirty, with them. After we got back I was happy to find a letter waiting for me from Alec. Badger and I talked till six o'clock in the morning. She was not encouraging about Alec, but did not rant and rave at me as my parents had done. That would never be her style.

I received two more very sweet letters from Alec. He had received the letters I had written him from the ship and was pleased; he said he thought I wrote good and interesting letters. I thought his were good too and I loved the way he put things. Getting his letters was a great consolation.

It was decided I should see Martin earlier than we had planned, for he knew I had returned to England. I don't know what he thought, but as I had decided to tell him face to face rather than in a letter, I had not told him why I was coming. Badger and Peter went out to dinner in the evening and he came round to their flat. There I told him I could not marry him.

It was awful – awful. He could not believe it. He said he loved me more than ever now – and for him I felt nothing, except overwhelming regret. I had decided not to tell him about Alec because I thought it would be too cruel and would hurt him so much, but in retrospect I think it was the wrong decision and I should have told him the truth. However, rightly or wrongly, I had told him there was no one else and then it was too late to go back on it. I was trying so hard not to hurt him but this probably hurt more and anyway he could not understand why I had changed my mind. In fact he just refused to believe it.

He stayed for two hours and it was the worst two hours of my life. I felt so sorry for him and oh, so sad. The next day I went out and bought some real gold cuff links for him. He was pleased, but so upset afterwards that he could not eat and seemed about to break down. I felt desperately sad and grieved that I should have to hurt anyone like that. We agreed we would meet again in a week's time, and then he left.

On the 31st December there was a letter from him, a very sad and pathetic letter saying his world had broken up completely. I felt wretched and wept bitterly. The trouble was, I no longer had feelings for him, so even if there was no Alec, I would not have wanted to marry him. When it's over, it's over.

On the 4th January I was typing out short stories I intended taking to Curtis Brown, when the phone rang and I went to pick it up. To my horror it was Martin: he had had lunch with Badger and seemed not to believe I didn't love him. He wanted to meet me, but I said I couldn't. Then I burst into tears again. How long could I go on hurting someone like that? But if I *had* given up Alec and married Martin, I could never make him happy, not feeling the way I did.

I saw him three more times: the first time on the 15th January when we had lunch at the Charing Cross Hotel. It was a dreadful two hours – he would not understand or allow me to feel differently. I should have told him then about Alec, and afterwards I wished very much that I had, but I still thought it would hurt him more, and anyway it was too late, so I persisted in saying that I had simply changed my mind. He could not accept this and I found myself almost disliking him. In addition, I had started my period and was feeling very ill.

The second time we met was on the 18th January. We went to Lyons Corner House where we had a drink and then supper in the Salad Bowl. I could hardly swallow my salad. Then we went to see *HMS Pinafore*, or 'The Lass Who Loved a Sailor'. Rather ironic that, I thought bitterly. Unlike Martin, I was not a devotee of Gilbert and Sullivan.

The third and last meeting was the following afternoon when we went to *The Messiah* at the Royal Festival Hall. It was beautiful music, but once again I could not relax and felt very unhappy. Afterwards we walked along the embankment by the river and he asked if anything was worrying me. I told him I still felt the same, so we agreed to break off the engagement. He was very upset and broke down and I felt terribly sad. I struggled to pull off my glove so that I could give him his ring back, but he refused to take it. He saw me into a taxi, and the last I saw of him was walking towards Victoria. It was exactly a year since we had started our skiing holiday in Zermatt. How I hated myself.

I wrote to him and also to his mother, whom I had liked so much and who had been so kind to me. I said how very sorry I was to have made Martin so unhappy and how sad I was to have caused this trouble to him and his family. It probably would not make any difference, for they must all think so badly of me, but at least they would know I was sorry.

There was a huge amount of opposition to my relationship with Alec. First there was a barrage of letters from my parents, repeating over and over their anger and disappointment in me. There were bitter recriminations from my father at what it was doing to my mother's health: I was thinking of no one but myself. There was such a lot of stuff about Class, not only from my parents but from everyone else. It does not happen nowadays but then it seemed the most dreadful crime to get mixed up with someone who was "working class." If I married Alec, they said, I would end up wearing clogs and a shawl.

My beloved Auntie Winks wrote that I should stop all this at once, it was causing my mother's health to break down. Auntie Margaret had met someone who told her I was the talk of Cyprus, the daughter of the Commissioner of Kyrenia who had fallen in love with a police sergeant from the North of England. Philippa Knox, Geoffrey White's secretary, wrote and said I must not take any notice of what Enid said, for it suited Enid and her ilk that someone in my position should marry someone of working class, because that was what *she* was. I should not think of marrying Alec, wrote Philippa, for it would never work out and we would both be unhappy. Even the young gay Captain in the Blues who had lived next door, was planning to come to England and tell me not go ahead with Alec, it would be a terrible mistake - he did not come in the end.

Auntie Joan Priestley wrote and said my mother seemed very unhappy in Cyprus. Why? Why was she so unhappy? My mother wrote to Peter that I was gossiped about in Nicosia and they said I behaved badly. What rot, I thought, and how dared they? They didn't know me, they didn't know how I had behaved, and anyway, what had I done to make them say these horrible things? There was a letter from Mr Symons, denying the possibility of a job if I was to return to Cyprus. Symons was one of my father's chums and a big noise in the Administration department and I felt sure it was a trick, but I felt very dejected. The whole world seemed to be against us. I seemed to be causing unhappiness to so many people. I was in despair.

I went down to Hove to stay with Auntie Joan Priestley and Granny Hove at Airlie House. It was a shock to see Granny, for she had aged. She was now bedridden, and didn't seem to understand much of what was going on. I was sorry to think that my mother would no longer be able to confide in her in the same way she used to, and thought what a terrible thing old age was.

I now had a job to do at our flat in Adelaide Crescent, so I got the keys from the agent and went round. It was bitterly cold and depressing. It had been my home but I was unsure if I would ever be welcome to go there again, so I packed up all my things into a trunk and three crates, including one of books, and arranged for them to be picked up and stored at Harrods. I don't think Auntie Joan noticed anything.

Before going back to London I went round to see Pym. He looked well and happy, was as playful as ever and burst the blue balloon I had brought him, which I supposed was a good sign.

Back at Badger and Peter's there were letters, two from Alec, in one of which he was very depressed having received my despondent letter of 4th January. There were also letters from my mother, Auntie Margaret, Winks, Enid and Vivian. The one from Winks made me cry. She asked me again to give up Alec and I just could not do it. If only they would understand. If only they knew how I hated myself.

What was I going to do now and where should I go? One thing, I had decided to leave London. I wanted to get away from everyone I knew, even including my dear sister, for I was afraid they would try and introduce me to eligible young men. I thought of Switzerland and went to the Swiss Legation, but they said you could only get work there if you had had a year's experience. (I always think that's stupid, it doesn't make sense: how can you get experience if they won't let you go *without* experience? Why don't they think of that?) So anyway, Switzerland was out. I thought maybe I would go to Edinburgh.

I got my stories back from Curtis Brown, which was a blow. They said they were well written but not marketable because of the choice of material, and the characters were too childlike. However they asked me to go in and have a chat, so I went to their offices and saw Miss Dorothy Daly. She said she had been very impressed and thought I had a lot of talent. She suggested I should write a novel. They would always be pleased to see it if I did, and if I really worked hard I could make a lot of money. I left, feeling pleased and hopeful.

I went down to stay with Fuzz at Spitzbrook. It was so good to see her again. We went to see *The King and I* and she was bitterly disappointed that the King of Siam did not end up marrying the English governess. Fuzz was a romantic and always liked a happy ending. We talked in bed the first night till 1.30 am. She was dubious about Alec and me, although she did like his photograph. But she said her mother would have a fit if she wanted to marry a man who worked in the fish market and lived in East Ham.

"But it's not like that with Alec," I said.

"Isn't it? But he's working class," she said.

Back to Class again. Why did everyone, even Fuzz, go on about Class?

The next day we had a lazy time and in the evening we put on our dressing gowns and had supper by the fire and soon I had heard all her love affairs and she had heard all mine. I wished she had been more enthusiastic about Alec and me, but I showed her two of his letters and she liked those. We got pleasantly tipsy on four stiff whiskeys, and felt wonderful and drank a toast to Philip, her latest love, and to Alec.

I rang up Pat Pears and she asked me to spend the night at her flat in Dolphin Square. It was lovely to see her and have a good chat. She asked me all about Alec and at first seemed quite favourably disposed to the idea of my marrying him. However, when I saw her again a few days later, she was rather against it and said whatever happened I *must* see him in England first.

In Alec's next letter he said that Monty Rich had asked to see him. It appeared that my mother had written to Monty, asking him to find out what was going on and what I was planning to do. Her letter was somewhat wild and hysterical. Monty showed Alec the letter and when they had deciphered it, asked what he thought of it. Alec said he thought my mother was rather highly strung and Monty agreed. Monty was very nice indeed and they had a good chat. He seemed genuinely interested in our problems. He said he thought the police force was a good occupation, but later Mrs Rich came in and she said she thought if I married him I would miss having servants. *Servants?* She seemed to think this was an essential part of my life.

Alec said very few people in the North of England managed to employ servants except perhaps the daily cleaning woman and was this not so in the south? I wrote back, saying it was laughable and assuring him that it was exactly the same in the south. I could not help wondering what planet Mrs Rich was on.

I had a letter from Vera, my friend from the Grand Hotel, inviting me to stay with her and her husband Bill, so I went. They lived in a pretty, detached house in Haywards Heath. Vera and Bill were by no means encouraging. They thought Alec and I would have to face very many problems and that my parents might be right. They also felt that people from the North were not easy and might not accept me.

However, they thought it was a good idea for me to go to Edinburgh. Bill said he had a friend who lived there, a Mr Gibson-Kerr. He was very rich and influential and would be able to help me get a job. Bill wrote to him and it was arranged for us to meet at the Regent Palace Hotel when he came down to London. He seemed to take a fancy to me and I was a bit alarmed, for he was much older than I had expected. He was convinced that he would easily be able to get me a job and I began to wonder if I wanted one in Edinburgh after all. However I didn't want to let Bill down after he had arranged the meeting for me.

When I told Badger I wanted to go to Edinburgh at the end of the week, she was very upset and cried. She said she thought she would never see me again for years, and I felt dreadfully sad that I had hurt her. It seemed I was destined to hurt everyone I loved. I tried to make it up to her, buying her bunches of daffodils and anemones and a bag of peaches. She asked me not to go for another week, and that I *must* see Lancashire before making any more decisions. Alec too, had thought this a good idea, and had devised an itinerary for me. Badger said she would come with me for the first couple of days, so on the 9th February we left Euston on a train bound for Manchester. Peter came to see us off.

The journey was enjoyable for we passed through some lovely country, but depression set in when we reached Manchester. Everything looked black and gloomy. Badger thought the buildings were of black stone but it transpired they were just very dirty. We left the luggage and set off by bus for Edenfield, Alec's home village in the Pennines, and Ramsbottom, the village nearby. Edenfield was where he had grown up. Sometimes he had helped his grandfather on his farm way up in the hills and had to plunge through thick snow for miles. He had left school at the age of fourteen and became a butcher's boy, cycling miles to Ramsbottom every day. I wished I could find it romantic, but I hated it. It was not my idea of a pretty village, just rows of grey terraced houses, no picturesque little cottages. Badger and I thought it unbelievably depressing. Away from the village, everywhere you looked there were tall chimneys from which black smoke spewed forth, blackening the atmosphere. Even the sheep were a dirty grey colour. The more despondent I was, the more cheerful Badger became. We spent the night in a hotel in Bolton, but I could not sleep for depression.

The next day we went back to Edenfield, then on to Accrington. I thought it was horrible. Then we continued to Clitheroe, where the countryside was really lovely, and I began to feel more cheerful. Badger was to leave me at Clitheroe and return to London, but first she told me something terrible: that our mother had tried to commit suicide by taking an overdose of sleeping tablets. I was shocked and horrified. I could not believe my ears. How was I going to tell Alec, and what now? How could we go on after this? She then made me promise that I would not marry Alec until I had first seen him in England. I gave her my word. Then we parted and I was very sad.

Altogether I spent a week in Lancashire, following the route Alec had suggested. I walked round Pendleton in the sunshine and Downham in the rain, and thought them lovely villages, quite different from Edenfield and Ramsbottom. I went to Preston, where I stayed at the Bull and Royal Hotel, then to Garstang, Lancaster, Morecambe and Blackpool. I visited the Barretts, Margaret Mounsey's family, who lived in a nice semi-detached house near St Anne's. I thought Margaret's sister was very pretty and her husband reminded me of Glen. I don't know what Margaret had told them about me and they probably thought it odd that I was on a tour of inspection of their county before I could make up my mind to get married. What a strange girl - probably. But they made me welcome and were all very nice and made me stay for supper, before seeing me onto a bus back to Preston. The next day I went to Southport, then Blackpool via Lytham St Anne's and Preston, then Ormskirk and Liverpool, finally back to Manchester where I stayed the night.

There was a letter from Alec waiting for me in the hotel, and I wrote to him and told him about my journey. We had promised one another we would always be honest and tell one another everything we were thinking, and I was able to give him quite a favourable report, though I did say I had not liked Edenfield. I then asked if he could possibly get some leave and come back to the UK, but not telling him I had promised my sister not to marry him until I had seen him in England. I only hoped he would think this a good idea, but I was a bit worried as I did not know how he would react. It was so difficult being separated and not being able to discuss things face to face.

On Friday 15th February I collected my luggage and caught the 1.30 train for Edinburgh. I had no money left, just one and three pence halfpenny and a cheese roll I had bought in Manchester, for supper.

CHAPTER TWELVE

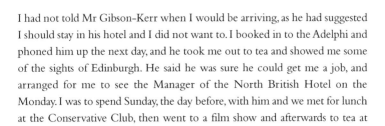

I had not told Mr Gibson-Kerr when I would be arriving, as he had suggested I should stay in his hotel and I did not want to. I booked in to the Adelphi and phoned him up the next day, and he took me out to tea and showed me some of the sights of Edinburgh. He said he was sure he could get me a job, and arranged for me to see the Manager of the North British Hotel on the Monday. I was to spend Sunday, the day before, with him and we met for lunch at the Conservative Club, then went to a film show and afterwards to tea at the North British Hotel.

However he was beginning to make me feel uncomfortable and I wished he was not Bill's friend. He paid me lots of compliments, called me his 'little squirrel' and kept telling dirty jokes which were not funny. In the evening we had coffee at the Caledonian Hotel and I did not like the way the waiters looked at me, with I thought, disgust, guessing he was a sugar daddy. The thought of this was repellent and I was thankful I was not staying in the same hotel.

The Adelphi was all right, nothing to write home about - it seemed to attract rather dreary commercial travellers, but there was a girl there called June who was staying in Edinburgh on business. She had rather a yellowish complexion, but I thought she was pretty and I liked her sense of humour. We became friends immediately, and had long chats about our lives. She was married, but I was not sure how happily. We drank endless cups of coffee and ate bananas surreptitiously in her room in the hotel. We also went to the cinema and she stopped me feeling lonely.

Monday was a bad day; I received a letter from Alec in which he sounded depressed and impatient with me. He said he would not come back to England on leave for various reasons - although he thought it a good idea to see one another in England, he could not get any leave before next January. I am not sure if he said could not or would not, but at any rate it made me unhappy and I wept.

To make matters worse I had my interview with Mr Allen of the North British Hotel, and he said there was nothing doing in reception work until April. He said there might be a job there for a stenographer but I thought I would try other hotels first. I rang Mr Gibson-Kerr and said I was going to stand on my own feet and try to get a job by myself. I then went round all the hotels, the Caledonian, the George, the Queens, the Royal British, and others. None of them had any reception work until April, so I went to the Labour Exchange to ask for temporary work and they had nothing either. I then went back to the North British to ask Mr Allen about the stenographer's job. He said they really wanted someone permanent, but they would ring me tomorrow.

I now had very little money left and was feeling pretty desperate. A fat lot of good Mr Gibson-Kerr had turned out to be. If I couldn't get the clerical job at the North British I would have to leave Edinburgh and try my luck in Manchester.

There were more depressing letters from my family: they made further demands and stipulations, not only that I should see Alec in England, but also that we should not get married for at least a year. My sister asked me to promise that I would not and I had to write and tell Alec this.

On Tuesday there was a letter from him in which he apologised for having been impatient, and on Thursday there was another in which he said he just might be able to get a cheap fare and come home in May, but I was not to count on it. I was delighted to hear this, especially when I got a call from Mr Allen offering me the job of stenographer at the North British Hotel on a temporary basis, with a salary of £5 8s a week. Now I would not have to leave after all. I was very cheered up and went out in search of digs, and was really lucky to get a room on the top floor of a house at 72 Princes Street, above a shortbread shop. The landlady was called Mrs McPhee and she seemed very nice. She said there would be hot water between 2 and 4 pm and the rent would be thirty shillings a week. For that I had a lovely big room overlooking Princes Street, the gardens, the Art Galleries and the Mound. There was a good fire and the room got a lot of sun. I checked out of the Adelphi and brought my luggage to Princes Street. I bought a lampshade, an adaptor and some fruit, and once I had unpacked, everything looked very cosy. Later on June came round to see it and spend the evening with me. She thought it was nice and for a little while at least I was contented.

The next day was Friday and I started my job at the North British Hotel. There were two other people in my office, a sharp-tongued Scottish girl called Shona who said she didn't like English people, and a very fussy elderly woman called Miss French who kept trying to tell me what to do, but as she herself seemed to be in an awful muddle, it was quite difficult. It was a very busy day and there was a lot of shorthand. It was even busier on Saturday. I spent Sunday with June, and it was to be her last for she was leaving Edinburgh to go home.

After she had gone I felt very lonely. I was now extremely short of money. I spent 6d on my supper and had only 3d left. There were no such things as credit cards in those days and there was no way of getting any money until payday at the end of the week. I was hungry. Luckily I was able to get breakfast, lunch and tea at the hotel but right now it seemed a long time till breakfast next morning.

I was upset to get a letter from Badger. She said she had been so unhappy lately that she had not dared write. To add to my woes there were no letters from Alec for six days. I counted on his letters to sustain me and keep up my spirits. They were always so loving and supportive and he said over and over again how much he wanted to make me happy, so when there was a gap with no letters I grew increasingly worried.

When I received one on 27th February, it was a horrible shock: he wrote that he had been staggered to receive my last letter. He could not agree to our waiting to be married for a whole year. He thought we had agreed to get married in Cyprus before coming home at the end of October. He felt he had given way over so many things, being separated, first till April, then June and it seemed to him that my family were making more and more demands. He felt they would never accept him and he wondered if I would ever break away and have faith in him. He wanted to make plans for us and could not. People told him I would never come back to Cyprus and he too was now wondering if I would. He said he loved me but he could not go on like this – I must make up my mind, either to go back to him or for us to part.

Now what was I to do? I felt wretchedly unhappy and kept crying in the ladies' lavatory and even in the office, not caring if anyone saw or not. I wrote, *begging* him to get a month's leave in May. But I could not expect a reply for at least a week.

The next day there was a letter from him written before yesterday's and forwarded on from London. He had heard nothing from me and was very depressed. He said that he was very much in love with me. I now made up my mind. Even if he refused both to come home and to wait to get married till next year, I would not give way on this. I would keep my promise to Badger, but I would go back to Cyprus in June, and I would persuade him. I *must* persuade him. And whatever happened we would see each other again.

I had a horrible letter from my mother enclosing one from Mrs Lennox. The latter had written to her as follows:

"Thank you for your letter. My husband and I have been very sad and worried because Martin has been so terribly upset. As you know I had very little opportunity of getting to know Delia, though of course I hoped to see more of her in the next few months, but I knew she was a dear child because Martin was so in love with her. I felt she was a very honest straightforward person and perhaps it is just this quality which has come to the surface now, and has wrecked the engagement, but probably saved an unhappy marriage. In our wildest moments neither you nor I would dare risk that for our children. Please don't be hard on Delia. She must have been having a terrific battle on her own. Maybe in time Martin will be able to sort things out for himself. I hope so. Yours sincerely, Joan M Lennox."

What a lovely woman she was, and how understanding. I had liked her immediately and was doubly sorry for causing such upset to her and her family and of course, to Martin. My mother enclosed this letter and hers to me was full of bitter reproaches: "*Why* did you have to do this to Martin of all people?" she asked. "He would probably never have looked at you if you had not run after him." I was very upset, but also hurt. I wrote to her, "It may be some very small consolation to you if I remind you of this: you know that I did *not* run after Martin. I have never run after anyone in my life and would not dream of showing my feelings unless the same feelings had been shown to me first…" But she would probably not believe me any more than she believed anything I said.

Meanwhile a letter came from Alec saying he was very unhappy and could not believe there was a difference of opinion between us. Then there were no letters for a week. I felt desperate. I didn't know what he was thinking. It was just so difficult being separated and not able to talk to each other. The situation between us kept changing and our letters were constantly behind and out of date.

Then Enid shocked me by writing that Alec was very depressed, unhappy and fed up. "He loves you," she wrote, "but if you upset him any more you will lose him." She said he was hovering between making more suggestions and calling it a day.

CHAPTER THIRTEEN

I was a little cheered up to receive a letter from Dorothy Daly of Curtis Brown to whom I had sent a short story called 'The Other Passenger'. She said it was delightful and had great charm, and they would try to place it.

Another cheering thing was that a very nice girl called Pat started work in my office. She had been in Zaria in Northern Nigeria and also in Lagos. We became friends at once. On the Sunday she and I made an excursion to the estate of Lord Roseberry, going first by bus, then crossing a small river by boat. We walked through some beautiful woods with the sea on our right and gulls crying. Later we saw the amazing Forth Bridge and crossed over in a ferry to the county of Fife but we did not like that. We then took a bus to her digs and had supper and I told her my story. She was really nice to me.

The next day I had Alec's reply to my letter begging him to get some leave and come home in May. He said he would agree to come home before we got married, but did not see any chance of coming to England in May because the fares were so expensive. However, he suggested that we should have a holiday in Italy together on my way back to Cyprus. I was delighted and wildly excited, and although I knew there would be further opposition from the family, I was past caring.

There was another letter the following day, a sweet and tender letter, and two days later another, not annoyed but only sorry to hear how upset I had been because of my mother's letters. He was sorry to think he had been the cause of such unhappiness and it made him realise how much I had done for him. He promised he would always look after me and do everything in his power to make me happy.

On the 16th March there were more horrible letters, one from my mother and one from Winks, who said it was obvious I must give Alec up. How could she say such a thing? Yet I *did* understand it. What a position I was in and how I hated it. There was also a letter from Mrs Fuller, a friend of my mother's, full of malicious accusations about Alec, which were upsetting but which I did not believe. There was another letter from Philippa Knox who had apparently been talking to my mother. It was a very nice letter but depressing. It was kindly meant but I did not want or welcome it. She said she too had had an attachment with someone of working class. She had broken it off and was now perfectly happy with her husband David. It never worked to marry below one's social station, she said, and though I might not think so now, I too would find someone of my own class. Look at her and David, she said. I looked, and thought *she* might be happy but David was not, for at one time he had given me regular lifts from Kyrenia into Nicosia. He was a strange, introspective man whom I knew was deeply unhappy, and this was destined to cause an extraordinary and insurmountable rift in years to come.

Edwina wrote a sweet and rather breathless letter, begging me to come back to Cyprus. She said Vivian was pining for me and they all missed me very much and she was sure I was miserable all alone in Edinburgh, especially when Vivian was so fond of me… I did not know how to answer her for I did not dare tell her I was intending to come back, with Alec. The heavens would open if that leaked out.

There was then a period with no letters from Alec but yet another from Winks, telling me *not* to marry Alec. All these letters made me sorrowful and bitter. It was all very well, I thought, but my parents and family would not be living with me all my life – and really, *why* was I so disgracing them? Winks said Princess Margaret had given up Peter Townsend, but for goodness sake I was *not* Princess Margaret.

I had decided to see something of Scotland while I was there, and on Sunday I went for a walk in the Pentland Hills. I chose my route and set off quite early. It was lovely in these hills, much nicer than the Braid Hills which I thought were just a disappointing golf course. The Pentlands reminded me of the Kyrenia range, but this made me lonely and homesick for Alec. Then I got lost and joined up with a girl who told me she was an artist and an orphan. We went back through Swanston, where Kipling had a cottage, and she invited me back to her typical artist's flat for supper. She was a strange girl but I liked her.

The following Saturday I determined on a longer excursion. I caught a train at 7.30 am to Aberdeen via Montrose and I stopped at each. They were both very cold towns and not beautiful, but I went to the jagged coast by the sea where there were larks singing, and thought of that poem by Masefield, 'I must down to the seas again, to the lonely sea and the sky…' and wondered why he didn't say *go* down but perhaps it would have upset the metre. It was icy cold, a vicious clawing cold.

I took a bus to Banchory on the way to Balmoral, going north of the Dee and south of it on the way back. I ate my lunch at three o'clock by the river. Then at 6.30 I caught a train to Inverness, arriving at half past ten, and stayed the night at the Queensgate, where Shona had said they had the cheapest rooms.

The next day was sunny. After a large breakfast which would see me right for the rest of the day, I saw the castle, then took a bus to Beauly along the waters of the Moray Firth. I walked miles from Beauly (received a proposal from a good-looking but drunk farmer with a dog) to the Ness Islands and caught the 3 pm back. I had a great warmth of feeling for Inverness and its people. The countryside of sea and pine trees along the coast to Forres was lovely and this reminded me of the Troodos mountains in Cyprus. The train journey back to Edinburgh, on which we were joined by parties of skiers, mountaineers and horsemen, covered the whole of Perthshire. It was scenically beautiful with its pine trees, rivers, mountains, and bracken and heather-covered moors.

I returned to my room in Princes Street sated with the splendour of these parts of Scotland, and sat down and wrote a long letter to Alec, drawing a rough map of where I had been, including the jagged coastline round Aberdeen. I also enclosed some postcards of different places.

On the 5th April I was invited to dinner by the Hamiltons. Martha had been one of my sister's best friends at school and also the head girl of Roedean. I liked the Hamiltons very much, especially Josephine, the elder sister, who was clever and interesting and prettier than Martha. The Hamiltons lived in an enormous house, they had a maid and the gong was sounded for dinner, yet they were socialists. Those are the right sort of socialists, I thought, the ones with lots of money. I had a delicious dinner and wrote and told Alec how good it was to have a square meal, but it worried him that I was not having enough to eat, and he wrote telling me not to miss out on meals. I bought bread and cheese and ate them in my room in the evening, but quite often I had run out of money and had to wait till next payday.

The next day there was a cable from him to say he had received no mail from me and was anything wrong? I cabled back to reassure him. The mail was hopeless and both he and I were constantly worried when there were gaps and we heard nothing, but on the 9th he cabled again to say two letters had now arrived and he was so happy he had had to send an expensive cable to tell me so. He said he was finding letters inadequate and frustrating and it was far superior to receive a cable and know my thoughts just a short time after I had sent them, rather than five or seven days later when I might be feeling very different. When he had not heard anything he began to wonder all sorts of things, about my parents, whether I was having enough food, my shortage of money and all sorts of stupid things. He also wrote to say he was really delighted with the letter and postcards describing my tour of Scotland, and had found it so full of interest that he had read and re-read it five times.

Pat and I had arranged to go to London for a long weekend, and on Friday 12th April we caught the 10.20 pm train, travelling overnight to make the most of our time. I had bought a tin of shortbread and a honeycomb for Badger and Peter, and was very excited at the thought of seeing them again, though I knew there would be trouble when I told them I was planning to meet Alec in Italy in May and then go back to Cyprus with him. I felt rather awful as Badger had rung up the day before and sounded hurt that Pat and I planned to go shopping together on the first day, but we didn't know when the train would arrive, and anyway they were going out themselves.

We had quite a good night, despite snores from other passengers, and then after having breakfast in a café, we rushed around the shops. It was a beautiful sunny day and it felt good to be in London again. Then we parted company and I went to Badger and Peter's flat, and later on they came back. It was really lovely to see them again and they were very sweet. Badger was pregnant but did not show much and she had some pretty maternity clothes.

That evening we went to the theatre with their friend David Lock, to see an amusing play called *Plaintiff in a Pretty Hat*, then we came back for a delicious dinner, cooked by Badger, and apart from the one with the Hamiltons, the best meal I had had for ages. Next morning she told me that she and Peter were going for a holiday in Cyprus and I was amazed. I then crossed my fingers and told her I planned to go to Italy and she was furious at first. Then she calmed down but when I told her about Cyprus she was very upset and we both wept. It was awful.

We went to a pub for drinks, then drove out in the country with some of their friends to look for houses. In the evening we went to dinner with some other friends. Badger was very silent but it seemed to go all right. But that night was terrible. We both cried and Peter talked to me till very late.

"If you go ahead with this, you are going to have a very hard life," he said. "Maybe I will," I said, "but I don't care."

I was quite hysterical and felt ashamed afterwards to think how he must scorn me. Neither Badger nor I slept at all.

In the morning I felt guilty and awful for causing them all this trouble, yet I loved Alec more than ever. In a way I could see their point of view that I was going to have a very hard life, but I couldn't think about that. So be it. We all tried to put it out of our minds and Badger and I went shopping and had lunch at the Chocolate House in Regent Street. I bought a grey suit. In the evening Badger and I had another talk, but a reasonable one this time, and then they took me for a very nice meal at the Metropole in Knightsbridge. That night I caught my train back to Edinburgh by the skin of my teeth. It had been a nice weekend, except for the same old trouble. That was always going to happen, I thought sadly, just as long as I continued with Alec. I hated being at odds with my family, it had never happened before, and it seemed so unfair. He was such a very decent and honourable person, and despite knowing they hated the idea of my marrying him, he never held it against them. He genuinely wanted them to like him as he would have liked them. He had been so pleased at the idea I was going to see them again and stay for the weekend, and was always so nice about my family. So whatever they said I would not give up on him.

When I got back and went straight to work, there was a cable from Alec addressed to the North British Hotel, saying he was going to phone me that evening at half past five. I was very excited and could think of nothing else all day. Everyone at the hotel seemed to know about it. What could it be?

When the time came I waited breathlessly by the phone, and the call came through at ten to six. It was incredible news: he asked if I'd like him to return to England. Oh, I would, I would. He could get a flight, arriving in London on the 16th May. I was very excited, very happy. He must have seen my parents, for he told me my mother was looking much better and had more colour in her cheeks and had put on weight. He told me his plan was for us to spend some of his leave touring Scotland before taking me down to Lancashire, where I would meet his parents. We talked for nine minutes and I wanted to tell him how much I loved him, but was too shy and in any case he did most of the talking. The call cost £18 but he said it had been well worth it for us to be actually speaking again, and we would really see each other in a month's time.

I was particularly glad he was coming to England, for now we could carry out our half of the bargain to see one another in his home surroundings and I felt it would make Badger and Peter feel better. And indeed, they were very pleased. Soon after this they flew out to Cyprus for their holiday, staying in Kyrenia with my parents. They planned to meet Alec while they were there, and I did hope they would like him, it would be so wonderful if they did. I prayed it would go well.

I had a letter from Gillie. She said she had seen my parents – and that in some ways it would be mad to marry Alec and in some ways it would be mad not to. I wasn't sure what she meant but supposed my mother had voiced her opinion.

In the next weeks there was a great deal of work in our office. Miss French was usually in a funny mood and you never knew with Shona, for often she was fun to be with but sometimes she was sarcastic and spiteful, and you never knew which it would be. "Wha' a nairve!" she would say to me, and I'd say it back to her, "Wha' a nairve!"

Pat was always lovely and I went out a lot with her and with Shona. We went to the cinema and out for meals to places like the Coffee Mill and Browns' restaurant, where you could eat quite cheaply. One evening Pat and I went to the mound and joined a group of communists. They were ranting and talking a lot of rubbish so we argued with them. We were rather brave, telling them things they had not thought of, which was startling but fun.

On Easter Sunday I went to St Giles Cathedral for the mid-morning service. I wrote to tell my parents that Alec was coming home on leave and hoped they would not mind because I was so happy. In a way I felt as if I was being swept up by the tide, and eventually would be dumped somewhere on the beach like a piece of flotsam – and I wondered what would happen.

One Sunday, Frank the restaurant manager invited Pat and me to go out for the day with him and his friends. He had a car and we would drive up to the Trossachs and Loch Katrine and other beauty spots. We accepted eagerly, but it was the most extraordinary day. First we were rather dismayed when we saw the strange crowd who would be going. There were two blowsy women called Magdalene and Jean in very low cut dresses that showed too much décolleté. They looked like barmaids – maybe they were. There was Frank's friend, Willie and a pale young man called Ian and a great big red-faced man called Charlie.

We all squeezed into the car and Frank drove off. To our surprise and disappointment we had not driven very far before we stopped at a pub and that appeared to be the object of the outing: we would drive a short distance, find a pub and there would be a lot of drinks before continuing. We went to the Trossachs but hardly saw them as the others wanted to find yet another pub. "This is just a pub crawl," Pat whispered.

Before long Charlie and Ian were both very drunk. Charlie kept ordering green chartreuse for me, and after drinking half a glass I left the others, a bunch of six liqueur glasses lined up in front of me like a band of little marching soldiers. Then Charlie became angry with me. He said belligerently, "So ma drinks aren't good enough for ye, eh? Ye're a bloody snob." He was behaving like an oaf. He *was* an oaf. Then he and Ian started to argue and people were looking at us and Pat and I were ashamed to be with them. The argument with Ian became more heated and suddenly Ian produced a knife and lunged at Charlie. Frank and Willie pulled him away. It was unreal, the worst situation.

"I'm going," I said to Pat. "I'm going to hitch a lift back to Edinburgh. Someone is sure to give us a lift and no one could be any worse than this lot." She agreed and we went together.

The next day Frank apologised to us for what had happened. He said that Ian was very much in love with me and that was why he was so angry with Charlie. I said, how could he be in love, he doesn't know me?

We learned that Miss French was leaving and being transferred to the Caledonian Hotel, and on her last day we had tea and cakes with her and Mr Allen. The next day Pat and I were alone in the office, for Shona had gone on holiday and there was a lot of work, but she had been very spiteful to us both lately and it would be nice to have some peace. On Thursday Pat and I went out for dinner with Frank and Will. I was unhappy because I had not heard from Alec, and wished the dinner was over.

Then for a week there were no letters. Every day I longed for one and every day there was nothing and I grew increasingly worried. What could have happened? It was unbearable.

On the seventh day I sent a wire saying how worried I was. In the evening there was a reply, "Delia please don't worry, minor difficulties, have not written recently, All my love Alec." I burst into tears. Something must have happened. I was more worried than ever. I wrote to him asking him to write to me and beseeching him to come back, for I just knew something had happened. It was now the 4th May and I didn't know whether I should give in my notice to the hotel.

I sent a letter telegram, saying I was still worried – was he coming home on the 16th? – and at lunch time there was an answer saying I shouldn't worry, there was a minor problem with the air passage and sending all his love. For a few days I felt better – but when there were still no letters I began to feel dreadfully unhappy all over again. Surely he must have received my urgent letter asking him to write and to say when I should give in my notice to the hotel? But there was just silence. He kept saying I *shouldn't* worry, but how could I not worry? Why hadn't he written? And why wouldn't he confirm if he was coming back or not? *Something* had happened, but I didn't know what.

The days went by. Eventually I gave in my notice. Every morning I woke at half past five, waiting for the post, and every day there was nothing. I grew more and more desperate. I wrote to Enid, begging her to tell me what had happened. One evening I was crying so much Mrs McPhee came into my room and said if I didn't stop crying I would end up in the mad house. That made me feel worse than ever. I felt so sure something had gone wrong – and of course I was right. He would never not have written otherwise. I felt so unhappy that I seriously contemplated suicide. I thought I would drown myself, that way everyone would think it was an accident. They would just think I had gone swimming and got out of my depth. I suppose if you were really, really desperate you would not care what people thought, so I had not reached that final degree of despair – but it was close.

After that night I just felt numb. There were no more tears, just an awful pain that would not go away. I wanted to cable Badger to make him come, or Enid, or both – but managed to stop myself. The sands were running out. I must accept that something had happened and it was not going to work out for us.

I went to St Giles Cathedral and sat there in the semi darkness. It was very beautiful there and very quiet. It was now two long weeks without a letter. It seemed a lifetime. I thought, what shall I do now? Where shall I go?

Then on Monday 13th May there was a cable from Enid. It read, "Alec battling well still endeavouring convince parents feels exactly as you loves you million per cent - Enid"

That made me feel very much better - and it seems very stupid, yet by now I was so used to this aching misery I hardly dared to hope he really would come. But that night I had a phone call from my parents. Someone, I did not know who, must have told them how desperately unhappy I was. They told me he was having supper with Badger and Peter and that he was coming back.

And on Tuesday there was a cable from him saying he would cable full details of his passage tomorrow. He said "please stop worrying will see you soon darling all my love Alec" Finally the same day he sent another telling me he would leave Cyprus at midnight on Wednesday and arrive at 72 Princes Street early Friday morning…

Now at last I could believe it. But it's a funny thing – when you have been very *very* unhappy the pain seems to stay with you. It is a deep ache inside. There's a poem written by Byron called 'The Prisoner of Chillon' in which the prisoner is incarcerated in the Castle of Chillon. he writes: "At last men came to set me free, I ask'd not why and reck'd not where. It was at length the same to me, Fetter'd or fetterless to be, I learn'd to love despair."

I could understand how the Prisoner felt. I won't say I loved despair, but I was so used to it that for a while it would not go away. This was how it was for me - but gradually, gradually I could accept that it was over.

CHAPTER FOURTEEN

In the end I stayed in my job at the hotel till Thursday evening, for there was such a lot of work. There was now a new regime, a very efficient older lady who had to clear up all the muddles left by Miss French, and we were all having to work late. She certainly expected results, and she would get them too - there was no time to talk. However I was leaving them all to it. I saw Mr Berry the Manager, who was very charming and wished me lots of luck. I said goodbye to Pat and Shona and the others and continued working till well after nine pm.

Alec arrived at half past three on Friday morning, and it was just so good to see him and to be together. We had such a lot to talk about, I wanted to know what had happened and he said he would tell me everything. He slept in my room until breakfast time, when I introduced him to Mrs McPhee. She did not seem too pleased. That first day I took him all round Edinburgh, to the castle and the gardens and in spite of the rain it was wonderful.

The next morning when he woke up he was very upset and depressed and had lost a lot of confidence. Then he told me what had happened in Cyprus. He had met Badger and Peter at St Hilarion and they had had a picnic. Then Peter had talked to him for a long time and said that if he *really* loved me, he should give me up because he would never be able to give me the sort of life I could have with somebody else. They told him I had hated Lancashire and would never be happy there.

This had shaken Alec's confidence and for the first time made him question if he was doing the right thing for me. He wanted to give me everything but perhaps it would not be enough. Peter could be very persuasive. He had tried to persuade me and I had held out against him, so now he had turned the pressure on Alec, and the only way was to point out that he would not be able to make me happy. Once again it was back to the old Class thing. Then he had been invited to supper and given, of all things, asparagus. That was a mean trick. Poor Alec didn't know you were supposed to eat asparagus with your fingers. As if it mattered, for goodness sake, but he was meant to feel humiliated, though knowing him he would have laughed it off, laughed at himself so that their invidious little scheme would have backfired. Yet little by little they were making him see that he was different.

He had stopped writing to me because he didn't know what to say, didn't know what to do. Perhaps they were right and he should just walk away. Their strategy so very nearly worked. I hated what they had put him through, yet I could accept why – they thought they were doing their best for me, but I felt cold inside to think it really might have been the end. Now I had to restore his self-confidence and make him realise I loved him and I would be strong enough to withstand whatever they said and I would stand by him whatever happened.

Mrs McPhee told me she would like me to leave as she had let my room to someone else. We had been going to go in any case, but I was sorry I would not be able to introduce Alec to my friends Pat and Shona. We packed, then caught a train bound for Perth where we stayed for two nights at the Royal British Hotel.

Altogether we stayed a week touring Scotland. We went to Pitlochry and sat by the river and walked miles up into the hills. We went to Callender and stayed for two nights at a comfortable homely little hotel called The Eagle, which cost 17/6d per night. We met David, a Scottish commercial traveller who drove us to Tyndrum then to Loch Katrine and the Trossachs, where we walked for eight miles through majestic countryside. From Callender we took a train to Crianlarich, intending to go to Fort William, but were misinformed and went to Oban, which we liked much better. On the way we stopped somewhere on the shores of Loch Awe which was incredibly beautiful, the best place of all. Oban was a lovely little town and we stayed for two nights at a sweet little hotel there called the Argyll.

While in Oban we did a boat trip round the Sacred Isles. It was my birthday and I recorded it as the nicest and happiest birthday I could remember. We stopped at Iona and were greeted by monks, then on to Staffa and finally to the Isle of Mull, where we landed at Tobermory Bay. On our return to Oban we saw the fishermen coming in with their catch, and later had a delicious dinner at the Argyll.

We were very sorry to leave dear Oban but had to return to Edinburgh the next day. First we went back to 72 Princes Street, where we had left some stuff, but I was disappointed to find Mrs McPhee very abrupt and not a bit friendly or pleased to see us. I didn't know why but I was destined to find landladies a disappointing breed on the whole, and really more interested in your money than in you. So we collected our stuff and went to my old haunt, the Adelphi, for the night. The next day we bought some presents for Alec's parents and caught the train to Manchester, and then a bus to Edenfield where I was to meet them.

I was worried about this, first because he had told them nothing about me and I thought it would be a shock to meet this strange girl from Cyprus whom their son – their only son – wanted to marry. At the very least it would be a surprise, and perhaps not a welcome one.

CHAPTER FIFTEEN

Alec's father was a tall thin man wearing glasses. He seemed genuinely pleased to meet me and I thought he was sweet. I told myself I liked his mother as well but if I am totally honest I found her depressing. She was short and fat and had grey hair scraped back into a bun and red-rimmed eyes rheumy with tears, which overflowed as soon as she saw Alec. She had more than a hint of a moustache. She didn't know what to make of me and I am sure I was as big a disappointment to her as she was to me. She was as different in every way from Martin's mother as it is possible to be.

I remembered what Monty Rich had said, that marriages so often founder on little things like having his parents to stay with us. Oh dear, what a shallow person I must be. But I was determined not to let it come between us.

The cottage at 14 Rochdale Road, Edenfield, where they lived, was what Alec described as 'two up and two down'. Other houses he talked about as being 'back to back'. This was all a revelation to me, as I had never heard of any of them. The Kays' cottage was in a terrace and you went through the front door straight into the front room. Beyond that was a small kitchen with a stove and a sink and a tub for washing which they called the back boiler. In the corner of the front room a steep open staircase led upstairs to the two bedrooms. The Kays slept in the back bedroom, and I was to sleep in the front which led out of theirs. In the corner of the Kays' bedroom there was a lavatory, which was considered a great improvement on some of the cottages where you had to go outside to the privy. As there were only two bedrooms, Alec was going to stay with his uncle and aunt who lived round the corner, in a more superior house as it had a separate bathroom. I wished I was going to stay there instead of Alec, but I supposed they felt they must make me a welcome guest – and I have to say they did make me welcome, whatever misgivings they might have had.

At five o'clock we had tea, which was really more like supper. There was bread and butter and ham and some sort of flat cheese and onion pie and beetroot and a dish of sliced raw onions in vinegar. There was cake and tinned peaches with evaporated milk, all washed down with strong cups of tea. We ate it at a table in the front room, where there was a heaped coal fire. His mother said she liked to have 'a good table.'

After our tea his mother and I went into the kitchen and 'washed t'pots' while Alec and his father sat by the fire and talked. I looked at my watch and it was only eight o'clock and what seemed like hours later it was twenty-five past. At nine o'clock Alec said he would go to his uncle's house, as it seemed to be bedtime. He did not kiss me goodnight and I was glad, for I would have been embarrassed.

They asked me if I would like to have a bath, and I said I would, so the water was heated in the boiler in the kitchen and his father set up a tin bath in the front room. He said when I had finished I could leave the bath there and he would deal with it in the morning. They went up to their room, closing a door at the foot of the stairs, and I had my bath in front of the fire. When I went upstairs I had to go through their room into mine and I saw they were already asleep. My bed was made up but there were no sheets, so I had to sleep between blankets which were scratchy. I thought this very odd, but looked upon the whole visit as a rather extraordinary experience.

In the morning his mother said, "Percy, d'yer want ter make water?" he said he did, so he went to the lavatory in the corner of the room. She said to me, "D'yer want ter wash yer?" and I was shown where to wash myself in the kitchen sink. Her accent was very broad and she found it irritating when I did not understand what she said. For instance when she said, "Are yer goin' oop pad?" I had no idea what she meant. In fact it was up the path that led to the back yard of the cottage. I had no idea why I should want to go up the pad or the path anyway. I tried really hard to understand what she was saying to me, but sensed she was impatient and irritated that I did not. As far as she was concerned I could have landed from Mars.

It was a relief when Alec appeared, all jolly and hearty, and asking how we were getting on. We made some sort of polite noises. He said he was going to take me out to see 'the Plunge'. This was a deep pool in the countryside round the back of Edenfield where he had gone as a boy, to swim and to fish. He had loved the Plunge and had played there for hours, and I could imagine him there as a boy and understand why he loved it. He showed me the road leading

367

up to the hills (oop t'hills, his mother called them), where his grandfather had his farm. I liked the sound of his grandfather. So what had happened to his farm? They had to get rid of it when his grandfather died, during World War Two, when Alec was away in the Navy. His parents both worked in cotton mills and that was why his mother shouted so much, because of all the noise of the machinery in the mills.

We stayed in Lancashire for two weeks, during which time Alec took me to meet various friends and relations, including the uncle and aunt with whom he was staying. Most of them were nice to me and I tried to like them, but really we had nothing in common. We lived in such different worlds and I felt they were just putting up with me for his sake.

Several times we went to see his old landlady, Mrs Platten, who lived in Droylsden, a very slummy and depressing district of Manchester, where he had been stationed. She was delighted to see Alec and was quite possessive of him, which was a bit scary. It was extraordinary to see three large television sets lying in her garden, and it seemed she had recently won some money on the football pools and had bought the television sets, one after another, discarding each one and then chucking them into the garden. They quickly got ruined in the rain. In this way she had spent everything she had won and had nothing left. I thought she must be a very stupid woman, but she had been very good to Alec and he was fond of her.

We picked up my luggage from the left luggage place in Manchester and took it to her house, so we were more or less bound to keep going there, which was depressing. He seemed so at home with the Plattens and I felt he did not need me. I also met Harold Taylor, the butcher to whom he had been apprenticed before he joined the Navy. He was nice, but I disliked Mrs Taylor intensely. She asked lots of nosy questions, making many digs at me and my family. The next day I felt very unhappy and lost a lot of confidence in myself and although Alec was very sweet to me, he did not altogether understand. How could he? If only we could make a fresh start somewhere else, for I dreaded the thought of living in Lancashire. And I was ashamed of myself for being so shallow.

It was a bit better when we were on our own. After high tea at Edenfield we went for a five-mile walk, going round a farm and passing reservoirs. Another day he took me for a walk by a river and fields with cows in them. There were extensive views, but everywhere you looked there were tall factory chimneys spewing forth smoke – no wonder the sheep were a dirty grey.

We went into Manchester several times, to Cooks to fix up about my ticket to Cyprus and to arrange for my luggage to be crated up and sent out by sea, which would cost £30. In a bookshop I bought the *Complete Works of Oscar Wilde* and *The Snow Goose* by Paul Gallico. I met his friends Peter and Norah who had moved down to Berkshire and who were very nice. But they had only come back to visit their parents. We went everywhere by bus and one day went to Blackburn, hoping to see his friend Margaret, a school teacher who had lived in the same digs and who had helped him with exams. She was not in, only her father was at home. He gave us tea. Alec found Blackburn very depressing, yet there was some lovely country thereabouts and we had a long walk.

Next day I was introduced to his cousin Alice and Jim, her husband. They took us out in their car to Whalley and north of Clitheroe into Yorkshire. It seemed Alice was not a popular member of the family, they thought she was pushy and above herself, but I thought she was one of the best. She reminded me of Auntie Joan Priestley and she was fun. She made no bones about wanting to better herself and had even taken elocution lessons, which was endearing, not that they had made much difference, for her Lancashire accent was as broad as everyone else's.

One day I woke up with a sore throat and felt very rotten. I stayed in bed but had to get up in the evening as there was a family party. Ten people came, uncles and aunts, and also the Plattens, and it was quite crowded in the hot little front room. I was sorry Alice was not there but I liked his Uncle Alf very much, and his aunt. Better still was when they all went home and Alec and I could get out and go for a walk on our own. It was always better on our own. I didn't have to tell him I didn't like Lancashire, for he knew, even though I thought I had covered it up. And now he was seeing it all with my eyes and didn't much like it either. He said he felt he could go far if he could just get away, and I was sure he could too.

We went to Preston via Blackburn, where we finally met Alec's friend Margaret. I thought she was a very straightforward, friendly person who was nice to me and not possessive like Mrs Platten or nosy like Mrs Taylor. Then we went on to Preston to Police HQ, as Alec wanted to see his old Superintendent, John Wren. He wanted to ask his advice about whether to stay in Cyprus for another two years or come back at the end of his present tour. It was difficult, all the police in the UK Unit were in a quandary not knowing what to do, for they did not want to jeopardise their careers in the

UK. He was nervous about this meeting but I was in tremendously high spirits that day. While he was seeing Mr Wren I was entertained by Muriel, the Chief Constable's secretary, in her very beautiful office. For Alec it was a disappointing encounter: he was told nothing and did not know whether he should stay in Cyprus or come back.

The next day we went to Ormskirk via Wigan, which was a horrible depressing place, full of slums. Perhaps it would have looked better if it had not been raining. Then we went to his last police station at Ormskirk, and there was no doubt what the Inspector and Sergeant thought – stay out in Cyprus.

Our last day in Lancashire came and it was raining. We packed in the morning and after lunch went to his aunt's house, where I had a bath and washed my hair, and so did he. Actually I liked his parents' little cottage much better than the 'superior' houses of the others in his family, even though there was no bathroom. It was very simple but cosy and warm. Whatever they thought of me, his parents showed me nothing but kindness and for my part I really liked his father and tried my hardest to hide my innermost and unworthy thoughts about his mother. When we said goodbye to them his father got very upset and emotional. Alec was sad and I could understand that he loved them and he loved Edenfield, even though I could not.

We went to Manchester and caught a train for London just before midnight, arriving in the small hours of the morning. Badger had sent me an express delivery letter, saying we would be going to Haslemere for our last weekend with them, before we went back to Cyprus.

First we had a few hours to spend in London – it was so good to be there again. I showed Alec parts he had never seen, Piccadilly and Bond Street and St James's Park and the Palace and Harrods. It all looked wonderful and he was very impressed. Then we took a train to Haslemere, where Peter met us and took us back to his father's house where his father and stepmother lived, and where he had grown-up. It was a very busy and sociable weekend. We saw countless friends of theirs, all very sophisticated and worldly, and it was totally different from our stay in Lancashire.

The first night, after a large and delicious dinner at The Georgian restaurant, we went to see their friends Robin and Judy. Their cottage was very sweet and so were they. We played charades and everyone drank too much. The next day we went to the enormous and opulent house of their rich friends Romayne and David. I felt very uncomfortable and thought we neither of us fitted in at all. I had not fitted in with Alec's people but nor did I fit in here.

Alec, though sweet and appreciative, was withdrawn and different somehow, and I wondered if he, like me, was contrasting all this with Lancashire.

During that weekend we saw Guy, my first love, now married to Sonia and with a small son. I wondered what they all thought was happening with me, but dared not ask. I hoped Guy was happy, but although I rather liked her, Sonia was a difficult girl who had made him marry her when she became pregnant, and later she became an even more difficult and unhappy woman. In the years to come I was sad to hear that Guy had died early of a massive heart attack. It is so strange how life turns out and you never know what will happen.

On the Monday we returned to London. Peter was going to work so we said goodbye to him and then went to Knightsbridge and I showed Alec Beaufort Gardens where I used to live once long ago. At Harrods he bought some gorgeous chocolates for Badger and I bought her some beautiful flowers, and she was very touched when we gave them to her. But when we said goodbye she was upset and cried and I managed not to at first, but afterwards I cried too. Alec was very sweet to me.

Eventually we boarded the plane and had the bumpiest flight ever. Everyone was ill and I had bad earache and Alec held me and comforted me. We landed at Malta and had a meal there, and on arrival at Nicosia early in the morning we were met by Tom. It was nice to see him but I was conscious of everyone staring at me and I did not feel that people were as glad to see us as I had imagined they would be. I felt tired out and dirty and my morale was at its lowest ebb.

I dreaded meeting my parents again, but it had to be done. We drove over to Kyrenia in the evening and my mother did not appear very pleased. Alec went off so that we could be alone, but it was awful. They both started on me and I was unhappy. Why, *why* couldn't they accept things? Later he came to fetch me and on the way back he took me in his arms and comforted me. He was such a nice, such a good person – why couldn't they see it too?

CHAPTER SIXTEEN

I spent the first night back in Cyprus on the sofa at Gillie's flat and was very pleased when she said she thought I would be able to stay at the flat permanently. Her friend Jean was really in charge of the flat, and she kindly agreed that I could have a room there. On Friday I went to Police HQ at Paphos Gate to see if I could have my old job back. HMS was very sweet, but unfortunately it was impossible and I was disappointed. Everything seemed to be going wrong and both Alec and I were depressed.

We had lunch at the flats and I saw Enid. She was nice enough but I felt guilty and awful as she had been expecting me to share her flat, and I had opted to share with Gillie instead. I am sure she was annoyed about this. It seemed that she and Gillie had fallen out, but I hoped things would blow over and all would be well. However, we were never as close friends as we had been before.

The next day it was my mother's birthday and I was to spend the day with them. They came to fetch me and my mother was really pleased with the 'My Sin' perfume I had bought for her. The whole day was pleasant and not a harsh word was spoken. We had a picnic lunch at Halefka and later bathed on the slab and when we went back to the house, who should come in but Vivian. I was glad to see him again, for we got on very well and always laughed at the same things. I regarded him as a good friend but would not go out with him as he wanted. We watched the passing out of the Wiltshires' 'Retreat' and then had dinner at the Harbour Club. Dim and Mary Robbins and the Colonel and his wife seemed really pleased to see me again, which was cheering, as I had not expected they would be. I thought everyone must believe I had behaved badly, both to Martin and to my parents, but whatever they thought privately, it was not evident. My visit to Kyrenia was pleasant enough, yet I found myself missing Alec. I always wanted to be with him.

On Monday I started my new job at the Secretariat. I was PA to Bob Browning, who was Assistant Secretary, Internal Security. His boss was the Undersecretary General, Mr Ramsay. Bob Browning was a married man with a young family and he was quite sharp, that is to say he expected a lot from me and was impatient if he thought me inefficient, as I was - till I got used to the work. Mr Ramsay was an older man, a dry stick with, I thought, very little sense of humour and not likeable. His secretary was Jean Yard who worked in the same office as me. There was also Mrs Davies, a nice woman in her 40s who had been in Nigeria. She worked for Mrs Chudleigh.

The first morning went very slowly. The others in my office were nice enough but I missed the girls at Police HQ and the morning seemed very long. I also missed Alec desperately, but I saw him again later and we went back to our old haunt, St Hilarion. The next day I was picked up at 7.15 a.m. and Alec collected me at lunch time. Those were the transport arrangements to begin with, but there was a lot of work in this office and many times after we were supposed to be finished for the day, Bob Browning would come to Gill's flat and pick me up to go back and work in the afternoon and evening. Thus it was not easy-going, as it had been at Police HQ. I think we had got away with murder there, now we were expected to work overtime and received no thanks for doing so. Bob Browning was a strict boss – before he went on holiday he said the work *must* all be finished. He didn't care if I had to work late into the evening and all over the weekend, as long as it was finished. Mrs Davies helped me, and it was.

After a while we were upset to learn that our transport was to be stopped. I did not know how I would get to work, but Alec hired a bicycle for me. I enjoyed riding it and it certainly went like the wind.

In the next few months I saw a lot of my parents, though not as much as they wanted. Now that I was no longer living with them they were very much nicer to me, and I enjoyed seeing them. They stopped going on at me as they had done before, but they did want me to go to dinners and meet people who were either friends of theirs or of mine. My father got me an invitation to dinner at General Kendrew's house followed by Brigadier Balfour's Dance. I didn't want to go but my father said I must. I was so used to doing what my parents wanted.

There were other occasions too, a party at Colonel Hunter's house where I was handed a note from Vivian asking me to have lunch. I did not go but saw him, Edwina and Richard at a party given by Dim and Mary Robbins.

Vivian kept ringing up and asking me to go for picnics or out to lunch and sounded very cut up when I refused. Dim said he wished I would spend more time in Kyrenia, and other friends said the same, and although Alec wanted me to stay on good terms with my parents, he was often unhappy that it involved my seeing other people, especially Vivian. This caused arguments between us.

Those next months in Cyprus alternated between being wonderful and idyllic, and stormy and difficult; there was no in-between, and it was certainly not monotonous. Either we were ecstatically happy to be seeing one another in a beautiful and romantic island, or we were quarrelling and unhappy. A young man called McKendrick at the Secretariat asked me to go out with him and although I did not go, Alec was annoyed. We had tiffs over my clothes, particularly one very close-fitting scarlet poplin dress which he thought too sexy and did not like me to wear. He was also jealous when he thought I was enjoying being back in Kyrenia and seeing other people and this made him cold towards me, which in turn made me miserable. At times he would be in a mood and did not seem to care if we were together or not, and it made me wonder if I were doing the right thing, being with him at all. Should we break up? But then he'd tell me it was because *I* had hurt him. He kept saying how much he loved me and did not know what he would do if we had to part - so we always made up our quarrels and were closer than ever.

There were so many lovely places to go to: we went out for picnics on the beach, often with his friends Ted and Vera Morgan. Ted was the image of the film actor Sterling Haydon. He was a strong, silent man and I liked him and his wife very much, and enjoyed being with them, but sometimes there were other police people I did not care for – particularly Maxie Ball, who was a stirrer and made malicious innuendoes about me.

Sometimes Alec and I were by ourselves, and that was what I liked best, when there were just the two of us. We swam, looking at magnificent coloured fish under the sea through goggles. We brewed tea over a fire on the beach. He often came to fetch me in a Land Rover so we could go off the road, down out-of-the-way tracks.

We drove through Kythrea to Halefka over the mountains. It was very misty there and rather beautiful. We went to Cape Andreas and ate peaches from a tin and ginger biscuits, and to Cape Kormakiti, where it was rough and we both fell over and scraped our legs, which bled a little. We went to Snake Island at night time and sat under the moon. We went to Makaras Monastery, and Kantara Castle. I remember Kantara because we were tired that day and quarrelled. He was grumpy and did not want to look at the castle, so I went rebelliously by myself, and a mountain rescue squad took photos of me which did not go down well.

One whole weekend we went camping in the Troodos mountains, sleeping on seats we took out of the car and filling the billy can with water from a stream. Another day I packed a picnic and we drove to Paphos, which we loved, exploring the tombs of kings and many caves. I suggested we should hitch-hike to Japan but this was not popular. We had our picnic lunch by the sea, near the rock of Aphrodite. We bathed and it was a happy day despite a tiff, but I don't remember what it was about. Once we went to Buffavento and climbed to the very top where the view was dramatic and awe-inspiring. On the way back we turned off onto a lonely road and saw the sun set and it was beautiful with the shadows on the hills.

We went to Stavaroumi Monastery on the Limassol road, and saw another majestic view from the top. The monks asked us to go in and we had coffee with them and talked about the past Abbots. There they lived all the year round, a simple life of mostly prayer, growing their own fruit and vegetables and with hens and a goat or two to provide milk and cheese and eggs. They had few comforts but were obviously content, and I could understand how people could become religious living on the top of a mountain with such sublime views: if you believe anything, you could believe you are close to your God and your heaven in a place like that.

One day when I had not felt well, I waited for Alec all afternoon and he did not come so I went to sleep and then he arrived and woke me up and took me to dinner at the Hesperides in Kyrenia. Afterwards we went to a beautiful beach and swam naked and it seemed very pure and holy somehow. I would always remember that evening and thought how much I loved Alec and Cyprus and being with him there. And of course we often went back to our special place at St Hilarion, where we could talk, telling each other our innermost thoughts – but this was not always a good idea.

And this was one of the main causes of our disagreements: he didn't know what to do about his contract and whether to stay on in Cyprus for a second term or go back to Lancashire. I was desperate he should stay, but he was uneasy, fearing this might damage his career back home. He debated the matter with increasing doubts as to what to do. He was very worried at the thought he might lose me if he went back to Lancashire. He asked me if I was happy with him and I said I was, but I did hope he would stay in Cyprus. He said he wanted to do what was best for us both in the long run. He said it was up to him to make me happy and he felt sure he could do this. I wished I could be as sure, but I was not.

He had to make a decision by the 9th August, which was exactly two months after our return. Around this time I was ill with a temperature of 102, and was sent home from work. I stayed in bed at the flat, and he came to visit me. The doctor came and suspected it was glandular fever and ordered me to stay off work. My father came over and brought me some roast chicken and a bunch of roses, and I was very touched. Alec came to see me every day and his love and concern for me was very apparent, and I was immensely happy when he said he had elected to stay on, but my joy soon evaporated as I realised he was unhappy and felt he had made the wrong decision. It was just no good – if he was unhappy, I was too. So he went to see Jock and asked for the decision to be reversed. It was what I most dreaded: he would go back to Lancashire and if we were not to break up, I would have to go too, back to the grim and greyness of it, those dark satanic mills.

It was arranged we should see Geoffrey White, the Commissioner of Police. I don't know who instigated this meeting, but it might have been my parents as they had met him and voiced their worries. Alec took me to Mr White's office and we had a long talk. He was so very kind and understanding, but the picture he painted of our lives together was very black indeed. We asked if Alec might be transferred to a southern force, such as Kent, which was Geoff White's own force. He said he did not think this was a good idea. Afterwards, when he saw me by myself, he was kinder still. He said what a problem it was and that he thought in England our marriage would not work, though in Australia or Canada it might. Then he mentioned my parents and I could not help crying. *Why* must I hurt them so much? And was I destined always to hurt people? There was Vivian – Richard and Edwina told me he wanted to know if he had a chance with me and I had to say no, I liked him but only as a good friend. Apparently he was very upset, and could not believe it. And there was Alec himself who often imagined I was changing my mind, that I was being cold towards him and must be on the verge of giving him up. Then he was deeply hurt too. So it went on, all these people I seemed to be hurting without in any way meaning to.

Geoff White was so kind but I am not sure how right he was about us, and learnt afterwards something terrible about him: a few years later, back in

Kent, he shot himself. I was shocked and upset to hear this and did not know the reason why. He must have been very deeply troubled to do such a thing. I wrote to his widow and told her how kind he had been to Alec and me and she wrote a very nice letter back, saying what a comfort it had been to know that. She remembered us well and she and her husband had often discussed our problems. Yet they were nothing compared to his.

Our life in Cyprus was so lovely - if *only* it could continue! But now the die was cast, and I would have to break my contract for a second time, which would be seen as grossly irresponsible by everyone. It was indeed – grossly irresponsible - but if Alec and I were to stay together there was no alternative, and I was too much in love with him not to do it. We had served our period of separation and were resolved not to let it happen again.

I now had to tell my parents, and I dreaded it. They came to fetch me after work on the 27th August, and that evening I told them that Alec was going back to Lancashire in October, and I was going with him. As expected, they were fearfully shocked, angry and upset. My mother was kind to me but my father said very cruel things which made me terribly unhappy.

"You've hardly been back here and now you want to break your contract – *again!*" he shouted. "This is utterly irresponsible behaviour and I am ashamed of you."

"I'm sorry you feel that, but what else can Alec and I do but go back and give it a trial? That was what you kept saying I should do."

But of course he had never thought it would come to this. Neither of them had thought so. At least, that was what they had hoped.

"Four months – that's all you will have stayed. Four months."

"Yes."

"You should give him up, that's what you should do."

"I'm sorry, but I can't. We love each other."

"Love? You don't know anything about love. Your trouble is that you don't know your own mind. You loved Martin once."

"But this is different….."

"Rubbish. People always think that and it never is. You'll be in love with someone else soon – and then it will be too late."

"No, I won't – I won't!" I began to cry. "I'll never love anyone but him."

"Have you met his parents?"

"I have, actually. I stayed with them."

"Oh yes? And what did his father do?"

"He worked in a cotton mill."

"There you are, you see. A mill worker."

"What's wrong with that? Someone has to work in a mill."

"Not the father of the man my daughter wants to marry."

"You're just a snob."

"Doesn't his accent grate on you? It grates on me, and one day it'll get on your nerves too."

"I can't believe you're saying these things. Have you any idea how shallow you sound? It's unworthy of you. You've always said it's the people who count, not where they come from, not their beginnings."

But whatever I said, I could not make him understand.

I wrote my letter of resignation from my job, feeling very worried as I did not know how it would be taken, but fortunately Bob Browning was quite pleasant. Mr Ramsay took no notice whatever, but I had not expected that he would, ever since Dim Robbins came to our office and wrote personal comments about the various Commissioners in Cyprus on his notice board. "Not reliable" he wrote about one man, and "Wouldn't trust him as far as I could throw him" he wrote about another. Against the name of my father, he wrote "A very fine fellow." Mr Ramsay was absolutely livid about this, and because Dim was our friend, I was blamed. He could never see a joke like that. I learnt I would be granted my gratuity on 24th September which was lucky, and very decent of them.

On the 2nd October Alec and I went to Famagusta and booked our passage home on the cargo ship Northumbrian Prince, via Algiers, Tunis and Gibraltar. We would sail sometime between the 20th and the end of October. Edwina and Richard were going to get married on the 15th and Edwina asked me to be her bridesmaid. I was pleased that I could do this for her before we returned to England. She and I met and went to choose the material for my dress, which was made for me by Elise, my nice Greek Cypriot dressmaker.

I went to stay with my parents in Kyrenia on a couple of weekends before the wedding. The first of these was difficult, for my parents were very glum and appeared to be in the depths of depression. Alec's name was never mentioned, it was as if he did not exist. The second and last weekend was better. The day of Edwina's wedding dawned, sadly a dark and rainy day and there was a great storm. Edwina and Richard came round with my flowers and after lunch I put on my dress and it looked quite nice, at least my parents and various other people said so, but Edwina outshone everyone. She really looked wonderful and I felt very happy for her as it was a lovely wedding and she looked beautiful. The ceremony was held at the Country Club and then after the speeches I helped her to dress for going away. Then I changed into my close-fitting scarlet dress – the one Alec never approved of - and some of us went to the Harbour Club. Vivian was very attentive and I was pleased when he said to me, "On the contrary, Delia, you are one of the most intelligent girls I have ever met. Your brain is far ahead of mine." I didn't consider myself at all intelligent but strangely enough I was quite quick when I was with him, we got on very well and our conversation seemed to flow very fast. The next day he brought some earrings which were my present for being the bridesmaid, and said goodbye.

After that there was not much time left. On my last day at the Secretariat I was very touched to be presented with two lovely Cyprus pottery dishes. We met up with Ingrid Lushington and Rex and went to their engagement party. I liked them both very much and felt we were in the same boat, for Ingrid too had encountered opposition from her parents about her engagement. Alec and I went to St Hilarion for the last time. Everything we did was for the last time.

My mother rang up and we were going to have lunch together but the agents rang to say the ship would be leaving the next afternoon. I was disappointed to hear this and she was in tears. I arranged for some flowers to be sent to her the next day and hoped this would in some way make up.

Then there was the last-minute packing. After lunch Alec and Ted Morgan came to fetch me in a police Land Rover. They loaded up the luggage and we all sat in the front with me in the middle and Ted drove us to Famagusta. When he said goodbye he shook my hand and said very seriously, "I don't suppose I'll ever see you again," and Alec said he liked me on the quiet - I had thought so too, in the preceding months, though Ted had never said anything to me. We then went on board the MV. *Northumbrian Prince* and at 6 pm the ship sailed. It was Goodbye, Cyprus.

CHAPTER SEVENTEEN

For the next fifteen days we were on the MV *Northumbrian Prince* and although the ship started to roll almost from the start, it was a very happy voyage. We had our own large and spacious single cabins, and we ate our meals at the Captain's table. The Captain was a good-looking man with a dry but rather strange sense of humour. He gave a small cocktail party on our second evening which was fun.

We met a very nice couple called Don and Maureen Braine who had been living in Limassol and were returning to their home in Surrey. They were highly educated and intelligent and although they far outshone us intellectually this never seemed to matter, for we all got on so well. We spent a lot of time with them, sitting up on deck and reading, or playing table tennis, often with them and also with the Captain and the first mate, both of whom teased me very much – I think they thought I was cocky and I resolved to be a more humble person in future - but I'm not sure how long that lasted.

Tripoli was the first port we visited and we were there for two days while vehicles were loaded. We all went ashore and did a lot of shopping, buying gifts for people back home, and also for ourselves. We went to a smart restaurant for lunch and later on we dressed up and went to the casino. Later still we met up with Maureen and Don and went to a very smart bar and drank cocktails and watched the people. We all found it an exciting and fascinating place.

Our next port of call was Malta, where the vehicles were unloaded while we toured the harbour for about an hour in a little boat. It was not much really but we were not staying long and it was enough to give us a glimpse of Malta. I had hoped we would be calling at Algiers and Gibraltar which would have considerably lengthened the voyage. I begged the Captain to stop off at those places but my pleas fell on deaf ears, for he was intent on getting back.

ought done.

So our time aboard the Northumbrian Prince continued very happily and the days passed all too quickly. We played lots of table tennis and became quite adept. We sat up on deck in the sunshine and read our books. We had terrific and very interesting discussions with Maureen and Don, drank Drambuie and listened to my records, for they also liked Ravel. Alec kept wanting to make love to me but I would not, for I still had this old-fashioned idea of wanting to "stay pure" until my wedding night. It was not only that I was a prude, I remembered how Fuzz's mother said if she ever had a baby without being married she would be cast out, never to darken their doorstep again, and I did not want this disgrace to be added to what my parents already considered my disgraceful behaviour – ending my engagement to Martin, falling in love with Alec, breaking my contract with the Government of Cyprus not just once but twice. If I were to get pregnant on top of these things it would be the last straw – so I continually had to ward Alec off, which was frustrating for us both. Nevertheless we were both very happy together and dreaded the end of the voyage when we would be parted.

We had three beautiful sunny days at sea and saw the majestic rock of Gibraltar and the passing coastline of Spain. Then the weather worsened and the ship changed from pitching to tossing. The waves looked enormous, like mountains, and in the distance we could see Cape Finisterre. The Captain was called out of dinner because it seemed another ship was too close. We had two very rough and terrible nights and no one slept much. There was a day's respite. We spent time with Maureen and Don and took photos of one another. Then we packed and in the evening the Captain had his farewell dinner and was very congenial.

The next day we landed at Liverpool. We said goodbye to everyone and walked around Liverpool in the rain. I thought it depressing, I don't know what he thought but I think he understood how I felt and he was very sweet to me. He looked at shops advertising Canada, and I thought if only we could go there, or anywhere away from here… oh, if only…

CHAPTER EIGHTEEN

Alec saw me onto a train bound for London, where I would stay with Badger and Peter. It was good to see them again, and to meet their dear little baby Mark, who was just two months old. It was the 5th November and I was told we were going to a fireworks party. It was all right, quite a nice party, but I found myself missing Alec, both then and on the following days. I felt out of place now amongst all these people who had their own lives and interests and could not care less about Cyprus.

Alec had told me he would come down to London in six days' time. In the meantime he would stay with his parents in Edenfield and report to his Chief Inspector for news of his next posting. Badger and Peter went out quite a bit and I babysat. Mark was a very sweet and good baby but obviously squeaked when it was time for his feed and they were not back. Then I walked around the flat with him under one arm and Dr Spock open at the page where it says what to do in those circumstances. Except that it didn't say. He got quite a lot of rose hip syrup and sips of water and didn't seem any the worse for it.

I went to Hove and saw our dentist, Mr Middleborough, who looked smaller and older than I remembered. Luckily there was nothing to be done to my teeth. He was charming to me, but I felt sorry for his dental nurse with whom he was as snappy and bad-tempered as always.

There were always lots of people coming and going at Badger and Peter's flat: Bretton and Julie came and we drove to Oxford to watch Bretton play squash. He was really good. Another evening our cousins Tony and Peter Cooper came round and were very amusing. They both had such a wonderful sense of humour and I felt proud to think they were my cousins. On the night of 9th November we learnt that Granny Hove had died. I was deeply sad - dear old Granny Hove, how we should all miss her. The next day we drove down to Haslemere to see Peter's father and new step-mother, who was very kind and even asked after Alec. The Reynolds' house was cold and we all huddled round the fire. We saw the litter of black miniature poodles, including the one Badger and Peter were going to have, which was sweet.

I was very excited at the thought of seeing Alec the next day, and dressed carefully in my grey suit, the one he liked. I went to Euston and was terrified he would not be on the train, but he was and we were overjoyed to see each other. We got him a room at the Regent Palace Hotel for 35 shillings, and then had lunch at Lyons Corner House. We went to collect the car he had ordered from Fords – it was a smart little grey Ford Anglia which we christened Horace, after my teddy bear. He was funny and made me laugh, and we could say anything to each other, we always could – well, almost anything.

That evening we went to an amusing play called *Dear Delinquent* with David Tomlinson, and afterwards had supper at Fortes. I then went back to Badger and Peter's flat and Peter opened the door to me and said, "I'm afraid the hotel is closed." I think he was a bit annoyed.

The next day I met Alec at the Regent Palace and we drove down to Brighton. He wanted to know all about my past life, what I had done, where I had been, everything about me, so we went via Cuckfield Park where I had spent a year, and Ditchling where we had lived when I was a child, and my beloved South Downs with Devil's Dyke slap in the middle. I then showed him Brighton and Hove, and he saw Dyke Lodge, the imposing Tudor house where my grandparents had lived, and 51 Shirley Drive, and 23b Adelaide Crescent where I had lived with my parents. We saw the Lanes, and the Grand Hotel where I had worked as a receptionist, and the Royal Pavilion and Roedean School where I had spent six years, and he was very impressed with everything he saw.

"I can see why you love it here," he said. "I understand now."

Yes indeed, for it was *so* different from Lancashire.

We met Jean and Theo Yard and went to a musical with them, then back to Jean's mother's house in south-east London, which I didn't like. The rooms were very small and claustrophobic and had wallpaper with large brown and yellow leaves close together and three flying geese on the wall and pairs of hideous vases. Apart from the Plattens' house in Manchester I had never been in a house like that before – I suppose it was a class thing – and we were back to the old thing of class, which my parents and their friends kept going on about. To me, Jean Yard's mother's house was not in London, not the London

I knew and loved. To me, London meant the West End, and only the West End. It meant St James's Park and Bond Street and Piccadilly and the Royal Academy and Harrods and Fortnum and Masons and Sloane Square and Knightsbridge. It did not include those mean streets south of the river which you could see from the windows of the train, where there were dingy bald lights with no shade hanging from the ceiling and flying geese on the wall in the front parlour.

On the third day we went shopping. We walked up Regent Street, along Oxford Street to Bond Street, and Alec bought a very nice sports jacket at Aquascutum. In the afternoon we drove out to London Airport to watch the planes taking off and landing. There were not the hordes of people you see there today, and I thought it the most romantic, exciting and glamorous place which, laughable now, it was then. I thought longingly that I would love to work there. I had told Alec of my application to BOAC to be an air hostess. They were going to hold my application over but of course it was now out of the question. However, in Lancashire there was Ringway Airport near Manchester. Perhaps I could work there - not as an air hostess, Alec would not have agreed to that – perhaps I could be a ground receptionist? But Alec was being posted to Lancaster in the north and Ringway Airport would be too far away.

When he went back to Lancashire I felt extremely unsettled and insecure. I thought how happy we had been in London and how sure we could both be if we could only be left to ourselves. I met Susie, who had just returned from Jamaica, and loved seeing her again. She, like me, was feeling very unsettled. She said she did not want to stay in Jamaica, but didn't think she would ever be able to settle down in England. She was finding that no one could care less about her, life was hard, money tight and everyone grim. Poor Susie, I knew exactly how she felt. We said goodbye and both of us were sad, for neither of us knew when we might meet again.

I went to Harrods and sorted out my bank account – I had £31 13s 3d and with my other money about £50 in all. I would soon have to find a job. We had discussed this and decided I should go up to Lancashire on the 10th December and try to find a job in Lancaster where Alec was stationed. He would come down to London to fetch me.

Meanwhile there was a lot going on in the lives of my sister and brother-in-law, for they were leaving their small flat in St John's Wood and moving to a large and spacious flat in Elvaston Place, Kensington. First we all went down to Haslemere to fetch the puppy, which they called Smudge. She was very sweet, but there was a lot more work with her food and her little mistakes and the baby as well. We went over and over again to the new flat and worked very hard, cleaning and painting all the rooms. We came back exhausted, covered with dirt and with little spots of paint in our hair and on our faces, and often had supper at midnight. Badger and Peter asked me if I could stay on with them until the 12th December instead of the 10th as had been arranged with Alec. So I wrote to him to ask if he'd mind if I did this as Badger and Peter were moving house and would like me to help getting the flat ready.

Badger put an advertisement in the paper for the flat in Circus Road, St John's Wood, at the asking price of £300 per annum, and the next day there were lots of phone calls from all sorts of dreadful people demanding, "Vere ees dees flat? I veesh to come and see eet." There was a man from Hove who sounded charming, and I showed him the flat the next day and he turned out to be awful and not charming at all. The next day there were three more, Mr Ballina came first and was very enthusiastic. "It is exactly what I am looking for," he said. "My wife will love it. Do not, *do not* let it to anyone else until I have got back to you." So we told the other two, Messrs. Cohen and Levy it was under offer, and then a few days later we got an awful shock when Mrs Ballina rang and said that Mr B did not want the flat for her at all, but as a love nest for him and his tart. It was an amazing and involved story, but sad. She begged us not to let Mr Ballina have it, for if he did he would leave her and move into the flat with the tart. He and she had had terrible rows about it. In the end he did not get back to us and we let the flat to someone else, but I did feel sorry for poor Mrs Ballina.

I received a letter from my mother enclosing the photographs of Edwina's wedding. In my diary I wrote, *"No comment on my last letter to her, which is most unlike Mummy. I guess the reason is that I was on the voyage with Alec and now she never ever comments on him, just ignores his very existence. Oh God, what a mess it all is. My family have no idea at all what a very nice and good person Alec is. They can't see beyond the fact that he's a Lancashire copper. How I wonder what will happen, for truly I dread a life apart from him in England. Yet I have so many qualms about that sort of life - mixing with people and having to pretend I like them when really we have nothing in common, knowing they don't like me either. Alec is quite different somehow. He's not like them, he is good and sweet and kind and funny and there is absolutely no chip on his shoulder… always genuinely pleased that others – like my family – should have good fortune."*

One day we had lunch with Jimmy and Margaret Parrish and their friend Michael Mott was there. He was the editor of a small literary magazine, so we had a chat and he suggested I should send him my stories, which I did. In due course he rang up and said so far he had only read 'The Lonely Rose' but he had liked it very much and proposed to send it to an editor he knew. He also asked me to a party and to lunch at his club, neither of which I could do as Alec would be fetching me, but I thought it was an exciting contact.

I also saw Eve, my beautiful friend from Cyprus, who had now married her fiancé and was living in London. They came to dinner one night and I loved seeing her. She seemed very happy with Patrick, her husband, and I thought how lucky she was that everything had worked out for her. What if I had been transferred to Kyrenia right at the beginning, as my father had wanted? I would never have met Alec, and there would have been no trouble, no strife. It would have been peaceful and easy – but oh, I would not have had it any other way.

Alec and I spent Christmas together, having booked a special break at the Old House Hotel in Windsor. It was such a lovely time, and we went to the chapel in Windsor Castle for the service on Christmas Day. Our hotel was very historic and peaceful and there were swans on the river beneath our window. I wanted to stay there forever, but the break ended and we began to travel northwards. It was a fine day and we went through Henley and Oxford, stopping for lunch at Stratford-on-Avon. Next came Warwickshire and then Staffordshire. The further north we went, the more I felt depressed, and when we got to Manchester I began to cry – I just could not help it.

At last we reached Alec's home at Edenfield. It was very cold there and raining, that sort of spiteful, stabbing rain. His mother's red-rimmed eyes filled with tears as soon as she saw Alec. Once again he stayed in his uncle's house round the corner, and I stayed in his parents' cottage. The first time I had stayed there it had been unreal, a new experience, but now the novelty had worn off. It was strange having no sheets on the bed. As I climbed between the prickly, tickly blankets, I felt very sad, lonely and homesick. But homesick for what? I no longer had anywhere I could call home. It was a hard night and I prayed I need not stay there for another one.

The next day we drove north to Lancaster. That too was a grey, dismal town. I think it was the thought of being so far away from everything I knew that so much upset me, but it was where Alec was stationed and where I must try to find a job. We did try practically everything; there was nothing in

Lancaster so we went to Morecambe. There we found two nice little flatlets but there were no jobs going in which I could be remotely happy, and besides the money was bad. At last we went back to Edenfield and in the car I could not help crying and crying. I managed to stop before I went into their cottage and I don't think they noticed, but I must have been as perplexing to his parents as they were to me.

I was alone most of the next morning, sitting in their little front room, writing to Badger and Peter while Alec washed Horace. In the afternoon I was relieved to get out of the house and go for a drive in the car. *Ah, but how grim is the countryside up here and how homesick I feel...* We went to see his old colleague in Cyprus, Tom Watkinson, and that was fun, *an amusing break in a sea of misery*. His house and his aunt reminded me of Wuthering Heights, for it was lonely and bleak and the wind howled around. Afterwards we had tea at an old barn and later went for another walk and almost decided to part, Alec and I. Then it was back to the cottage for a third night and for me, a bath in the tin bath in front of the fire, and a lonely early night.

The next day we got up very early and went to Lancaster and Morecambe again. We found a room for me in a small hotel for only ten shillings a night, where I would stay for three nights so that I could see him between shifts. On the first day I had an interview with a journalist on *The Visitor*, Morecambe's local paper, and he told me to write to the editor. It was a scruffy place but the salary was good. I did write but I didn't get the job anyway. We went to see his old friends John and Joyce Hartley, who lived in Bury. He had been at school with John, but when they were fourteen there was a parting of the ways, for John opted to go to the grammar school. Alec could have gone too but his parents did not encourage him, so he left school, aged fourteen, and got a job as a butcher's boy.

I tried really hard to get a job in or around Lancaster where Alec was stationed, but there was nothing available. We drove to Blackpool and I tried to enthuse about the countryside but really it depressed me. I was a total wimp and I despised myself but I could not stop feeling as I did. I knew I loved Alec very much and we were very happy together, yet I *detested* being in Lancashire, and the life and the people, and the thought of being up there for the rest of my life terrified me. Nevertheless I made up my mind to enjoy those three days with him – and I did, for when he was working I was happy enough in my room in the little hotel.

And on the third day it was suddenly better – a miracle, driving south of

Lancaster we went to Garstang and then on to the Trough of Bowland and there was some truly beautiful scenery, streams, woods and high hills. We drove all around it and my spirits soared and I felt different altogether. Then he said goodbye, and I went down to Manchester, to Kendal Milne's in the pouring rain and got a job as a temporary sales girl, starting on the 6th January. I would get five guineas plus commission, and it was arranged for me to stay with Joyce Hartley in Bury. Her husband was away on a course at the Police Training School, so she was quite glad to have someone with her. It was arranged I should pay her for the time I was there, and she would cook me an evening meal. And the next day I would start my job at Kendal Milne's.

CHAPTER NINETEEN

I got up at crack of dawn and caught the train to Manchester, but I had miscalculated how long it would take to get there and I was late. There was a commissionaire with a kind face at the front entrance but in spite of his kind face he waved me away when I came running up. We had a long conversation in sign language which amounted to his saying "Round the back," and me miming "Oh please, please," to no avail, so of course I was later than ever.

The staff entrance lay at the bottom of a rather sordid flight of steps at the back of the building. All the staff who entered thereby had to clock in, which was a bit of a blow. I was given a little card which said 0911 and as I wasn't sure what to do with it and it was rather damning, I let it be flushed away down the lavatory. Inside a vast cloakroom dozens of women and girls were peeling off outer garments coyly as though they were inner – scarves and cardigans and long woolly bedsocks. I removed my coat and hung it on a hanger. No sooner had I done so than a voice said, "Hey, that's Cecil's! Haven't you got a locker then?"

"No – and I can't stop, I'm late."

"But that's Cecil's!"

Too bad on Cecil, I thought, and rushed away to a chorus of indignation, up via the staff stairs to the fourth floor and the office of the woman who had interviewed me.

She was not very pleased. "You're late!"

"Yes, I know, I'm sorry but – "

"I hope this is not an example of what we are to expect from you in the future. We expect the staff to be in their departments ready to serve at nine sharp. This means you must clock in not later than ten to nine in order to be ready when the doors open."

Cecil's going to be very late, I thought. In fact Cecil, together with the band of girls who were in the cloakroom when I arrived, were Clerical Staff and weren't due to start work until nine-thirty. Besides Cecil was never late. The very idea of being late would have shocked him profoundly.

"You have been engaged," the woman who had interviewed me was saying, "together with eighty other temporary staff to help when the spring sale starts next week. That means you have a week to learn your business. Make good use of it. Learn, learn all you can."

She sent me to Model Suits on the third floor. They were hidden away in an exclusive alcove where the carpets were so deep you fell into them almost. It was an isolated department, the sort you wouldn't dream of going into normally unless you stumbled in by accident. I went up to the most senior-looking saleswoman and was told the fitter wanted me. It was reassuring to be wanted.

I went into a cupboard to find the fitter. The cupboard was long and narrow with openings at each end and inside were hundreds of suits, hanging on rails. They were very nasty suits, mostly the same in different colours and not model in any way. Actually they were not Kendal Milne's stock anyway, but had been imported from some tatty little place at £5 each and were to sell in Kendal Milne's for £9 'Genuine Reduction.' I had to unpick the label of the tatty little place and sew in a Kendal Milne's label in its place. The fitter, whose name was Mrs Slack, and I sat close together on school-room chairs and sewed, Mrs Slack quickly and neatly, and I slowly and badly. You could tell with my suits that the labels had been sewn in because they looked funny. The stitches all showed and were uneven, and Mrs Slack kept leaning over me and clicking her teeth. She was pear-shaped and glum and suffered from bad breath. At least, I suffered, especially when Mrs Slack bent over me to see what I had done.

At the end of an hour I had sewn on four and a half labels and Mrs Slack was looking very sour, as she guessed she would have to unpick them. She decided she did not want me after all, so she left the cupboard to ask for a replacement, and the senior saleswoman came in and ordered me out, which was a relief for us all. I spent the next hour at the elbow of Mrs Harries, who was tall and wore a baggy skirt. She was rather nice and explained how to make bills out and what shopping cards were and the difference between cash, cheque and account payments.

The staff at Kendal Milne's sold on commission, which meant there was no "couldn't care less" attitude about them. They cared very greatly. There was a lot of competition in the Model Suits department about who got which customer. The senior saleswomen were supposed to have priority, and the other Junior, a girl called Pamela, and I were not allowed to say "Can I help you?" unless we had first checked that the others were busy with customers. At the same time, if we saw Mrs Mop approaching with Lady Barbara Blankety-Blank in the rear, we had to grab Mrs Mop in order to leave the seniors free for Lady Barbara. (Sometimes Mrs Mop turned out to be Lady Barbara's mother, which was a blow for the seniors. More often than not, however, the Juniors got the duds.) All this required quick judgment, subtlety and precision, qualities for which we were greatly underpaid and unappreciated. The seniors accepted it as their due and probably it was; to be fair, if you had been there since the year dot, you ought to have a few perks.

There were two other seniors besides Mrs Harries, Mrs Dent, who was short and hatchet-faced and scathing, and Miss Blackburn who was tall and thin and looked a bit wet. Mrs Dent, from a customer's point of view, was to be avoided, but Miss Blackburn had a very sweet smile. You looked at her and thought, Now *there's* someone I can trust. She was like your scripture mistress at school, honourable and pure, who called lies 'untruths' and never ever told them. Alas for those who thought this, for she was the worst of all. She had no conscience and would talk people into buying anything. She would smile that frail, sweet smile and wheedle and persuade and they would think, here's the old retainer sort who really cares – not many of them left nowadays. And they'd go off clutching a suit which made them look like the back of a bus and which they couldn't afford anyway. Mrs Dent frightened her customers into buying while Miss Blackburn beguiled hers, and both did very well.

The head of the department was the buyer, Miss Bacon. She was the one who had spoken to me that morning. She was very smart with blue rinsed hair and pearls, and could be charming when she liked. To the staff, particularly the junior staff, she was more inclined to be sarcastic. She didn't actually sell – nothing so low – but could be relied upon to say graciously, "Miss Despair, forward!" now and then. Sometimes she would step in to clinch a sale if it wasn't going too well. If it had got to the stage of the person saying, "I don't think it's quite me," Miss Bacon would appear and assure them that it was or if it wasn't, it ought to be. One way or another, customers didn't often get away with it in the Model Suits department.

Not that there were many customers anyhow, at least not the buying kind. There were the ones who were Just Looking, and a few who tried on – well good luck to them, they had more nerve than the majority. So expensive were the suits and so exclusive the alcove in which they condescended to hang, it was like a trap into which the unknowing would blunder now and then and snap, too late they'd realise where they were, as Misses Bacon, Dent and Blackburn bore down upon them. They'd panic like birds in a chapel, flapping against the rails, glancing this way and that for the way out, a flurry of battered hats and crumpled coats and last year's boots. If they were caught, which they usually were, they'd be forced to look at a rail of suits marked eighty and ninety guineas and when they came round it was remarked resentfully that "This is *Model* Suits, Modom." Some dared murmur feebly, "So expensive... didn't realise..." But the rest just crawled away to disintegrate in the exit.

Some bought. There were the very rich who spent money carelessly and were rather bored by what they bought, and the comfortably off who expected value for money and were genuinely thrilled when they got it; and sometimes the not at all well off who wanted something good but couldn't really afford it, except perhaps every five years. They'd save up about twenty-five pounds and plan with it months in advance and when they came in it was the Big Day and if they made a mistake it was the end of the world. Oh if they got Miss Blackburn, it was tragic. They'd trust her so and confide it all, the pathetic details about how they'd pinched and scraped and gone without – and should it be a coat or a dress? No, a suit, a really good one that would last, and they'd wear it for their niece's wedding. But they didn't quite know what they wanted and what did *she* think? And *she* thought it was about time to get rid of that petrol blue thing with the fringed cape back and she'd switch on her sweet, sincere smile.

"Oh but ..... isn't it rather extreme? Kingfisher blue? I've never quite thought...."

"But Madam, it looks so elegant on you! It's so becoming. Between you and me, this little suit is a real snip. I wouldn't tell everyone, but just between the two of us. The cut is quite beautiful – you can see that, can't you? Quite beautiful. A little more than you wanted to pay, just twenty-eight and a half guineas but it's worth it, isn't it when you find something unique. You'll have it? Oh good, you really won't regret it, believe me. Now would I try to sell you something I wasn't sure was right for you? Now really, would I? If only you could see yourself as others see you!"

Yes, I thought grimly, if only you could. It broke my heart. I thought I'd poison Miss Blackburn, I'd put something in her tea. But what was the use?

There couldn't just be one of her, bound to be others all waiting their chance to pop into her shoes.

I went to lunch with Pamela. She was a nice friendly girl, big and blonde and rosy-cheeked. She was a country girl, her father owned a farm and every day she travelled ten miles in from Cheshire.

"I don't know why I do it really," she said, "I'm bored by it and the money is chicken-feed and by the evening my feet are killing me. But what's the answer? I don't want to muck about with cows all my life. I thought I'd see a bit of life in Manchester, you know, the big, wicked city and all that. And what do I see? A lot of silly, sweaty women who don't know what they want, struggling into suits and out again. That's quite all right, Madam, no trouble. Cheerio."

We ate in the canteen. It was foul but very cheap. The floor was greasy, the tables clogged with stale food, and the smell of fried fish pervaded everything for hours afterwards, your clothes, your hair, your fingernails. But you got soup of a sort, meat and veg of a sort and a pud of a sort for one and seven.

"I've put on so much weight since I came here," said Pamela. "The trouble is there's so little to do and you get so bored you eat instead. I spend my whole time watching the clock. As soon as I arrive in the morning I'm thinking of the tea-break, and when that's over of lunch, and after lunch the tea-break in the afternoon. Sometimes I think the time will never pass."

"But what a way to spend your life."

"Oh I don't know – just think," she giggled, "If I'm a good girl I might end up like Mrs Dent."

After we came back to the department, while Miss Blackburn was obeying the call of nature and Mrs Dent was at lunch, I had my first customer. She was plump and had very pink cheeks and a mop of frizzy white hair like a nylon saucepan scourer.

"Miss!" she said to me, clutching the sleeve of a tweed suit the colour of bitter marmalade, "I'd like to try this one."

"Certainly, Madam," I said, all excited. "Is it your size?"

"I don't know, is it?" she asked coyly looking down at her generous hips. "It was the only one on the rail in this colour."

I was none too optimistic but I showed her into a fitting room and helped her out of her brown coat and brown dress, and underneath she was wearing coffee-coloured underwear with lots of bows and things scattered over it. She pulled the marmalade skirt over her head but it got stuck at her bosom, so we had to hoick it off again. She then stepped into it and overbalanced and fell against me, and her heel caught in the hem and ripped it. At last we got it on but it wouldn't meet round the waist. She tried to fasten the zip with no luck, and I tried and managed to move it half an inch. Then it stuck in a mound of coffee-coloured, nylon-covered flesh and wouldn't go either way, up or down.

"Can't you get it any further?" she asked, "I'll breathe in."

I tugged, but nothing happened.

"Oh do try harder, I so love myself in this colour," she said, trying to get a glimpse of her backside in the looking glass.

"It's no use, it seems to be jammed," I said.

"Oh try, try!"

"All right. Breathe in…"

"Ouch!" said the woman sharply. "What are you doing? Oh you careless girl, you've torn my petticoat. Oh dear, however did you do that? Leave it alone please or you'll make it worse. It's so caught up I don't know how I'm ever going to untangle myself. Oh it is a nuisance, how very careless of you!"

"Well I'm sorry," I said. Anyone would think I'd done it on purpose. Of course Miss Bacon had to choose that moment to come into the fitting room and say brightly, "Everything all right in here?" She could see at once that it wasn't.

"This assistant," said the customer, "made me try this suit and quite obviously it's not my size."

I was aghast. "*You* wanted to try it on," I said hotly, "Madam."

"That will do, Miss Despair," said Miss Bacon.

"Well I liked the colour but I thought it was too small. I asked her if it was my size and she didn't know."

"Honestly, can you beat that?" I said to the ceiling. I looked at her with the utmost dislike. We were terribly squashed in that hot little fitting room what with Miss Bacon and me and her and all her clothes lying around, so it was not surprising when Miss Bacon told me to leave. "And Miss Despair," she added, "I'd like to speak to you afterwards."

I went into the next fitting room so that I could listen to their conversation. It was not a good idea, as it turned out. I might have known, eavesdroppers never hear any good of themselves.

"I thought shop assistants were supposed to know about sizes," my customer was saying peevishly.

"Yes, indeed they are."

"Well she didn't seem to know anything. And she was so rough! Look, can you see where she's torn my petticoat? It's not an old one either, I've a good mind to claim. She just pulled the zip fastener, forcing it, not looking to see why it wouldn't pull. I should have thought it was common sense."

"I know Madam, and I'm so sorry. You see," said Miss Bacon confidentially, "She's one of our temporary staff that have been taken on to help out when the Sale starts next week. They're quite untrained though we do our best with them in the time that we have. They're never of a very high standard and this year for some reason they're worse than usual. Very poor quality on the whole, low IQ and no savoir faire."

"Well really!" I said indignantly. I went out of the fitting room and banged the door – except that it was a curtain and wouldn't bang. It was a savage blow to my morale, especially as it was probably true. And I was saddened to learn that I had no savoir faire. I determined to make a great effort in the future. There would be a new me, intelligent, witty and sophisticated. I would also not be a wimp any more about Lancashire. How dared I think it was not a good enough place for me to live in? Who did I think I was anyway? Why should my family think we were so damn superior? I resolved I would be a better person from now on, I had to be better for right now I was unworthy of Alec. He was a lovely man and I did not deserve him. But it was not too late to change. I hoped it was not too late.

On the following Monday the Sale started. At last we were busy. At nine o'clock prompt the doors opened and the queues of women of all shapes and sizes rushed in, thronging up and down the escalators and into the lifts, making their way to the bargains they had earmarked. It was a bitterly cold day and all the shoppers had red noses and lots of them just came in to get out of the cold – who could blame them? I wished I was on the Ground Floor instead of Model Suits which was not nearly so hectic and exciting. Yet we had our share of customers looking for bargains. I learnt a lot. In particular I learnt that most of the things said by assistants to customers can be translated quite differently. For instance:

Customer	Is this my size?
Assistant	Lets' see
Translation	*Shouldn't think so for a minute.*
Customer	I don't think it's really me somehow.
Assistant	Oh I think it's very elegant.

Translation	*No worse than what you came in.*
Customer	Do you think purple is my colour?
Assistant	Everyone is wearing purple this season.
Translation	*Quite hideous.*
Customer	It's rather loose at the waist isn't it?
Assistant	That's how it's meant to be, Madam.
Translation	*Clot!*
Customer	It is too extreme for my taste.
Assistant	But it is the very latest thing.
Translation	*Why on earth didn't you say so before you tried it on?*
Customer	It's not quite what I wanted.
Assistant	Just as you like.
Translation	*You don't know what you do want.*
Customer	I'd like to think about it if I may.
Assistant	Certainly, Madam.
Translation	*Can you?*
Customer	I'll come back this afternoon.
Assistant	Very well, Madam.
Translation	*Who do you think you're kidding?*

I learnt a lot about customers, too. Whether it was that they were in awe of the assistants or that they felt obliged to be polite to them I did not know but most of them would go to any lengths to avoid saying, "I don't like it." I myself had done the same many times, and saw myself again and again in their replies. I had not realised how easy it was to see through them:

"Yes, it's lovely and I'd have it if only it were orange with green spots. You're getting some in like that? Oh. (Damnation.) But when? When will you have them? Not till tomorrow morning, oh what a relie... pity, I'm afraid that's too late, I simply must have it by this afternoon or it's quite useless..."

Or: "You see the only trouble is –

My husband hates me in yellow/ My grandmother has one just like it/ It will clash with my purple hat/the dog's collar."

Every now and then a person said, "I think it's hideous." When they did the staff would draw themselves up most indignantly as though it were a reflection on their taste, although of course, as they hadn't chosen the things, it was nothing of the sort. Miss Bacon might well have been offended, but not the rest of them. It was a sort of misplaced loyalty to the shop, rather in the same way that you can say one of your relatives is round the bend but heaven help anyone else who says so.

Most of the people who came to the Sale were very different from the usual customers. They were on the whole bolder, greedier, more demanding. Some of them had the filthiest underwear imaginable, thick with grime. They would say, "You wouldn't think this was clean on this morning, would you?" and I would say, "No, I would not." One woman was wearing a fur coat and she came in with her mother. They made straight for the Big Reductions rail and grabbed at least eight suits which had been reduced from 100 to 50 and from 70 to 25 guineas.

"We'll try these, Miss. Is there a fitting room free?" they asked.

"I think so," I said, "This way please."

I went into the fitting room with them but they were too busy to notice me. The younger woman, who was no chicken, took off her fur coat and all she was wearing underneath was a deep shiny black satin bra and a black waist slip, revealing a roll of off-white flesh. She meant to do the Sales properly and it was too much fag to keep putting on all her clothes each time she left a shop. They tore their way in and out of the eight suits, flinging them on the floor inside out and higgledy-piggledy as they finished. "Hey Ma, I rather fancy meself in this – what d'you think?"

"It's lovely, Else. I've always said you suit lilac."

"Here, you try it. Give me that green when you've finished."

"Ugh, this is ghastly, let me get it off quick, I can't bear to look at meself in it."

I crept about them to retrieve the poor crumpled suits that were lying discarded on the floor.

"Hey, I haven't finished, *do* you mind?" said the daughter. "What d'you think you're doing? I'll have that turquoise one back. And the black lace."

"You're in a hurry, I must say! Where are your manners?" said her ma, and they had a second time round. Needless to say they didn't buy anything.

Sales manners were contagious. People who didn't normally misbehave pushed and shoved, grabbed and snatched, trampled and swore. They were frightened of missing the chance of buying something they would never wear that had been reduced from treble to double what it was worth.

Pamela got a large, overpowering woman who wanted to try on a lace cocktail dress and jacket in a shade of greyish blue that looked blue if you wanted grey and grey if you wanted blue, hence its vast reduction. "Oh dear," said Pamela in the next fitting room to mine, "You really need a strapless bra. Well never mind, we shall have some idea. Now you'll have to breathe in. Breathe… in. Hmm… could you just breathe in a little more, Madam? Oh dear. No, I'm afraid it's no good, it won't meet."

Oh Pamela, you're on dangerous ground, I thought. Next door I was serving a dear old lady who didn't give a damn what she looked like and was therefore easily pleased. She and I put our ears to the hardboard wall and listened avidly.

"Won't meet? I don't believe it. You must try a bit harder. These things are meant to be snug fitting after all."

"Yes Madam. But it doesn't go near you, Madam."

"Oh nonsense. How can you talk such nonsense? Here now, pull! Pull! PULL oh well of course, if you won't pull what can you expect?"

"Excuse me Madam, I think perhaps the size is wrong, Madam."

"Certainly not. I always take a size 18. This must be a smaller size. It's disgraceful the way they vary. In any case I don't like the jacket."

"Let's try the beige, shall we Madam?"

"Good gracious," said my customer. "What a lot you girls have to put up with."

"Oh but it's worth having ten like that just to have one like you," I said warmly. I thought afterwards it was the sort of sucking-up remark Miss Blackburn might have made and I hoped the dear old lady knew I really meant it.

On another occasion there was a tall, slim woman with silvery grey hair, as gracious as a duchess, who tried on one of the tweed suits reduced from £14 to £9 'Genuine Reduction.' It bore a label which I had sewn in not quite straight the week before.

"What do you think?" she asked when she had it on. "The skirt seems a bit skimpy to me."

"I think so too," I said.

"Do you really? Well that's honest of you."

"The material is horrid," I said, warming up. "Look how it creases?" and I screwed a bit of the skirt up in my hand.

"You're so right, it does crease. Tell me – are these reductions genuine, do you think?"

"Well – no, I don't think they are actually." (Traitor, traitor.)

"Isn't it amazing that a shop with a reputation like Kendal Milnes… ah well, I shall know in future. No, I won't have the suit. But I don't mind telling you, it's a nice change to find such an honest assistant, and in future I shall always come to you when I want something. I am most impressed."

So was I. I decided to make a cult of it. I would be the first truly honest salesgirl in the store. Thus for the next few days I was candid to the point of rudeness, believing people would prefer to know the truth than a load of flannel. When a customer said, "How do I look in this?" I would say, "Not too good," and when another customer said, "Shall I?" I said, "I shouldn't if I were you." I was lucky that the people to whom I spoke thus were too surprised to complain about me.

But one day when I was genuinely trying to be kind it didn't quite come off. There was one particular suit the assistants had been told to try and get rid of. It was a plaid suit with a pleated skirt in size 42 hips, made of some very thick material like a car rug. Pamela said it had been hanging around for months. A very short, fat girl of about thirty years old came up to me and insisted on trying on this suit, although I showed her lots of others. We went into a fitting room and she took off her own skirt and put the plaid one on, and it was so long and she was so short it reached way down below her boots, almost to the floor. It made her look vast, colossal, and she didn't seem to realise it. She put on the jacket and looked at her reflection and was quite pleased, excited even, with it. I felt I had to tell her.

"I don't think it's quite right for you, you know," I said gently.

"Oh, but why not?"

"The material is so bulky and thick, and with all those pleats from the waist it makes it thicker than ever."

"I see."

"And then that wide plaid pattern is all wrong for you. It makes you look larger than you are and you don't want to do that. If I were you I'd look for something very plain and straight, in a dark colour. It would make you look much slimmer, you know."

"Thank you for telling me. I suppose you're right – but how dull! I hate straight skirts." She took off the heavy plaid skirt and laid it wistfully on a chair, and struggled back into her own skirt again. I had not noticed before but now I saw that it was very plain and straight, in a dark colour. And now the girl's face was plain and straight too, for all the pleasure and excitement had died out of it. It struck me that I had spoilt the girl's day, unwittingly it was true, but nevertheless I had spoilt it. I had disillusioned her. I had not had the imagination to see that the girl really liked herself in the suit, and who was I to say it was wrong for her? Who was I to say what people who are fat or thin or short or tall should and should not wear? What does it matter as long as you are happy? I felt awful as I watched the girl walk away.

Then Miss Bacon, who seemed to have ears on stalks, appeared and said that wasn't the way to sell a suit and how dared I take it upon myself to criticise a customer.

"I'm afraid you'll never make a saleswoman, Miss Despair. Honesty doesn't pay — does it Miss Blackburn?" Whereupon Miss Blackburn, who had been listening nearby, smiled not quite as sweetly as usual.

After that I cut out the honesty cult. Instead I found myself becoming more diplomatic. It seemed to make a customer feel better if I identified her with myself, so I would say, "It's so difficult for us large-hipped people isn't it?" and vice versa if she was the skinny sort and looked like a sexless tube in everything, I would say "We thin ones always seem to lose out, don't we Madam?" and they would cheer up immediately. I began to pride myself on my handling of customers, until one day I said to a flat-chested matron, "Oh for a figure like Marilyn Monroe!" and the woman took it the wrong way and went white with rage. "How dare you say a thing like that to me! I shall report you to your Supervisor. I'll thank you to keep your cheek and your personal remarks to yourself."

"Oh, but I didn't mean…"

"I know what you meant and I think it very cheap and unkind. Quite uncalled for. Take me to your Supervisor."

My heart sank. I thought about what Miss Bacon had said of me in this very same fitting room two weeks ago, all that stuff about very poor quality and low IQ. "Please God, let her be at lunch," I thought. And by some merciful stroke on God's part, she was and I was able to take the irate lady to my old friend Mrs Harries instead. Mrs Harries looked much too nice to be a Supervisor or anyone in charge of anything but she listened sternly to the complaint and promised that the young lady would be reprimanded. "Whatever possessed you?" she asked when the woman had gone. "It's lucky Miss Bacon didn't hear of it."

I explained my new diplomatic approach, and Mrs Harries laughed and said I had better leave it alone in future or I would be in real trouble. The Sale went on for two weeks and then came my last day at Kendals. After lunch I was called to the office of the woman who had interviewed me right at the beginning and much to my amazement, was offered a job as a trainee buyer. It seemed that Miss Bacon had recommended me as a promising newcomer with good dress sense, which was unbelievable, as she had always given me the impression she thought me the lowest of the low.

I really didn't want to be a buyer, but I asked if it would be all right if I could come back if I couldn't get a job anywhere else. That was the most undiplomatic thing I could have said. The woman who had interviewed me said she didn't think so, that wasn't quite the right spirit of enthusiasm. It was an honour to have been chosen to be a trainee buyer, something no one ever turned down, but you had to be keen and clearly I was not. The offer was withdrawn, but I could not regret it for I felt I really wasn't cut out for that sort of job. All the same, I went back to my department full of warmth towards Miss Bacon who had said all those nice things about me. I worked very hard for the rest of the afternoon, moving suits about from one rail to another, helping check stock with Mrs Dent and being generally indispensable. At last it was half past five and I said goodbye to everyone. When I got to Miss Bacon I felt that confidence you have when you expect to be lavishly praised.

Miss Bacon, however, said: "So you're leaving us, Miss Despair? Well I can't say I'm sorry. I'd be a hypocrite if I didn't admit that with your talent for saying and doing the wrong thing, you'd never make a saleswoman!"

Thus ended my career as a shop assistant.

CHAPTER TWENTY

The following Monday I went into Manchester and took a shorthand/typing test, passing Grade I at an hourly rate of £6 15s. I was then sent to Messrs Graham Miller, a firm of loss adjusters, where I stayed for a week. It was deadly dull. The following week I went to an advertising firm called Bayard Publicity. There were some pretty rough sorts drifting in and out all the time, but I liked the regular staff and it was much more fun than the loss adjusters. Mr Dickin, the boss, who looked like Herbert Lom the film actor, was very kind. There was another man I nicknamed Big Mouth who was nice to me, though I thought he could be lecherous and felt sorry for his wife. There was a teenager like a young Elvis, and a woman I called the Bossy Old Bag, but really I liked them all. The snag was that they didn't have enough work for me to do.

Alec met me for lunch on the first day and we could not help laughing that I always seemed to be out of work and looking for a job. Yet it really wasn't funny at all. Other temping work was very scarce, and at the end of the week there was nothing and nowhere to go. Bayard Publicity were very decent and said I could go back the following Monday and possibly the Tuesday as well. In the end I stayed for the whole week. I wrote to the Manchester Guardian and to Preston for the Longridge job, and put an advertisement in a local Lancaster newspaper, but there were no replies. I bought the *World Press News* and the *Hotel and Caterer* and scanned the 'Situations Vacant' columns, but there was nothing.

There was, however, an advertisement for ground staff at Manchester Airport and that really appealed to me. The trouble was Ringway was quite a long way from Lancaster, so I had to ask Alec if he minded my applying for it. He agreed, albeit reluctantly, and I sent a letter of application with a photograph. I also applied for the post of assistant librarian at Preston, since he was so keen that I should, but they wrote to me subsequently to say I hadn't got it.

There was no temping work on the third Monday so that was a whole day without pay. I rang up Bayard's and they said "Chance it, and come in tomorrow." I did and Mr Dickin seemed really glad I was back, but I felt uncomfortable as there was no work for me all morning. Luckily they found something for me to do in the afternoon.

On the Wednesday I went to a firm of architects but it was only for one day and Bayards had told me to return on Thursday. They were so nice and Mr Dickin said I could give his name as a reference for anything else. I saw Alec on the last day of the week. We decided that if there were no jobs available in Lancashire, I would have to go back to London and get some temping there till something turned up. Alec was very upset at this thought but I needed a job and we had tried everything.

I rang BEA and asked if they would be holding interviews shortly and they said the recruitment was being held up and to go ahead and return to London till they notified me. So I packed my things and Alec took me to the railway station, and very sadly we said goodbye. My train was much delayed because of snow. I finally arrived at midnight. It was the 6th February 1958 and that night there was a terrible air crash at Munich. The BEA plane bound for Manchester was carrying the Manchester United football team and many were killed or injured. There was very much sorrow.

The next weeks were spent temping for me. I went to the Stella Fisher Bureau and after taking a test, they grudgingly gave me the top rate of £9.6s.4d an hour. I stayed for two lovely nights with Madge Harland in Beaufort Gardens where I was much spoilt, then to Badger and Peter's where it was agreed that in exchange for board and lodging I should get our breakfast in the morning, coffee in the evening and bath and feed Mark when I got home from work. This worked well. He was such a sweet little baby.

My first job was with the Invalid Children's Aid Association, in South Kensington. I did not at all like Miss Phillips-Williams, the woman who ran it, and found the work dull and the office dark and dreary with brown lino on the floor. The best part of this job was the very rich and beautiful debutantes who flitted in and out of the office on a purely voluntary basis. Some of them were friends of Princess Margaret. You would think such rich girls to be spoilt and not very nice but on the contrary, they were spunky and funny and interesting and immensely good company. I tried to work out why this should be, and decided it was because they had enough money to travel and do things that most young girls have no chance to do.

The next two weeks were at the East Midland Allied Press in Fetter Lane, which was a complete contrast. I was enchanted. The office was comfortable and newly decorated and I had never before – or since – encountered such a kind and considerate boss. His name was Mr Nuttall. The work was interesting and they seemed very pleased with me and to think I had picked it up very quickly. There was a nosy Yorkshire man there and I wrote that I supposed all Yorkshire men were nosy, the most foolishly sweeping statement imaginable. I had lunch at Jolly's, the café in Fleet Street where I had first fallen in love with custard tarts. I wrote an ecstatic letter to Alec. I felt very happy and thought life would be just perfect if I were only seeing him as well.

But my elation did not last. I received a very short letter from him which made me feel neglected and extremely downcast and despondent about our future. I wrote a sad letter back saying how much I hated us being apart, but Badger thought I should stay in London, and perhaps she was right. I desperately wanted him to try and get a transfer to a southern force or a job abroad, in the colonial police perhaps or anywhere away from Lancashire, but he had said he could not do this unless it was right, and he didn't want mere contract work but something with definite prospects. In any case he felt he should give Lancashire a chance first for it might be that his career in the police would be better there, and if he left he would never be able to go back. At the same time he was worried that if he didn't manage to get away I would give up on him. And I wasn't sure either how I would feel if we did not get away. What could we do? If only things could be different for us…

Poor Alec sounded so depressed and he asked me to write as often as possible. He said he needed my help just as much as I needed his. I wrote to him at once and tried to cheer him up.

Back at the East Midland Allied Press I was astonished by the concern of everyone for my welfare after an attack of Asian Flu. People don't usually bother about Temps, they are considered the lowest of the low. They are described as "Only the Temp" and are blamed for mistakes which were not their fault, but they can't defend themselves as they have probably left and gone somewhere else. It was quite different at the East Midland Allied Press. They could not have been kinder or more considerate. I was given luncheon vouchers, which was very decent of them and meant a big saving. It was certainly a super job, and they would have offered it on a permanent basis had

I not told them I wanted to go back north, so sadly Friday was my last day. Mr Nuttall got in touch with the Lancaster Guardian advertising department who said they wanted a shorthand typist, and he thought I should apply for it, but I was worried about doing this as I really wanted the job with BEA and preferred to wait until there was a definite Yes or No from them. After I left I received a letter from Mr Nuttall, thanking me for the work I had done. It was unheard of for a boss to write and thank someone who was Only a Temp but he was such a decent man and definitely the nicest boss I ever had.

On Monday I was depressed to find there was no work for me with the Stella Fisher Bureau. I phoned the Imperial Agency and was sent to Thomas Cooks, which was petrifying - a huge office with girls sitting shoulder to shoulder, face to face, back to back, in endless rows like hens in a battery farm. Luckily they didn't want me anyway. I rang up dozens of agencies and none of them had any work, but after lunch one called Burnetts had a job at Universal Sky Tours at 101 Piccadilly, starting the next day. It was only for a copy typist but at least I wouldn't have to go back and eat humble pie at the Stella Fisher Bureau.

Meanwhile I was delighted to get a letter from Alec saying he thought he might be able to come down at the weekend with Theo Yard, who was working in Preston on a temporary basis. Alec was trying desperately to save money and it made a huge difference that the two of them could share the cost of the petrol. He also sent me the addresses of airlines that had offices in Manchester, and I wrote to them all: Sabena, KLM, TWA, Air France and Canadian Pacific Airways. Of these, it transpired that neither TWA nor Canadian Pacific Airways operated out of Manchester, although TWA wrote a nice letter saying I could come in and see them. Air France was no good and Sabena only had something requiring fluent French in the reservations office in town. KLM offered me an interview, but from BEA on whom I had placed most hopes, there was nothing.

I started the job with Sky Tours. The office was pleasant, with large windows overlooking Green Park where I went in my lunch hour most days and had sandwiches. I shared the office with Peter who was gay and rather smug, and an Austrian woman who was a bit neurotic. They spent a lot of time complaining about each other but really they were fine and we got on all right. Sky Tours, being in the heart of the West End, was a good place to work and I stayed there for four weeks. Luckily no one seemed to care what we did, or to comment, in fact I can't remember there being anyone in charge at all. I know I abused it sadly, over-staying my lunch hour while I rushed around trying to fix up the holiday Alec and I were planning to take in October. My pay was quite good too, for although I was only a copy typist I received £9 6s 8d a week, the same as with the Stella Fisher Bureau.

When the weekend was over and Alec went back to Lancashire I was sad, but glowing inside with the memory of it. Life in London continued pleasantly. Michael Mott took me out to lunch at his Club and was immensely kind and encouraging about my short stories. Mark's christening took place and there was a very good party with lots of their friends. Susan Bayly came to stay and we shared a room and talked half the night. She was his godmother, and a most amusing person, one of those people you feel better just to see across a room. My uncle Tommy once said that about a man in a pub, a tall man with twinkly eyes and a beard, and Uncle Tommy said he felt better just to see him on the other side of the bar, and I thought that was the greatest compliment you could pay anyone. I felt like that about Susan Bayly, and was very sorry when she went.

Then I had a sudden invitation to stay for the weekend with Fuzz at Spitzbrook. Peter took me to the station and when I arrived we drove straight to a point to point on Romney Marsh, picking up her Uncle Willie en route. As always with the Day family the lunch was delicious, starting and finishing with cherry brandy, and as always there was a table laid with a white cloth and silver cutlery and chicken and ham and pate and pies and melon. They always knew how to do picnics, not like my efforts of soggy marmite sandwiches in a brown paper bag. Fuzz always backed horses on the tote and I did too, and luckily backed Uncle Willie's horse which won back all I had lost earlier.

That evening Fuzz's mother had a very serious talk with me, and it was fine till she said she would be heartbroken if Fuzz was to marry a porter from Billingsgate market, and went on about my mother and father and how upset they'd be if I went ahead and married Alec – and then I was lost, and wept bitterly. Who was right? I only knew I was unhappy without him.

In the afternoon we went for a drive in Mrs Day's new car and saw dozens of little cottages where I could have been happy with Alec. I thought, if only he could get a transfer to a Kent force. It was with regret that I left the luxury and well-being of Spitzbrook, but with the assurance that I could come again any time I liked.

So it was back to little Sky Tours and my two curious companions, both of whom had become very confiding in the other's absence, complaining endlessly about one another. Having heard nothing from BEA I took the plunge and telephoned them. I spoke to the recruitment officer's secretary and to my joy she said I could come up for an interview on the Thursday before Easter. At last I had something definite. In the evening I rang Alec, full of excitement telling him I had the interview and would come up for Easter, but to my disappointment he did not sound at all enthusiastic, and to make matters worse his next letters were slightly cool with no ardent declarations of love or signs of pleasure that I was coming to Lancashire for Easter.

How our relationship fluctuated all the time! One moment it was the most wonderful thing and the next it was like a damp squib. I was so short of confidence, and with the never-ending barrage of opposition, not only from the family, I needed constant reassurance that he loved me. It was not enough to be told a week ago, I needed it now, and if I did not get it, I was miserable. How stupid I was to doubt him, but I could not help it.

On getting the second cool letter with no word about whether he was pleased I was coming or not, I was nettled and wrote a very short note asking if he would have preferred me to leave it and not to come after all? Then I thought perhaps I had gone too far. It was stupid of me, I was asking for trouble but it was too late - I'd posted the letter and could not retract it. I wrote again and said how sad he'd made me and if this was the end, well at least I knew where I was.

My last day at Sky Tours came and went and then there were two days of wondering if it was over between us. I could hardly bear to wait to see him, but what if he no longer wanted me?

CHAPTER TWENTY-ONE

On Monday the 31ˢᵗ March I set off on the long coach journey to Joyce Hartley's house in Bury, where I was to stay until I'd had the interviews with KLM, TWA and BEA. The coach travelled via Oxford and Birmingham to Cheshire and on to Manchester, and all the time I was feeling wretched and wondering about Alec. What if he didn't come the next day, or if he sent me a wire to say, "Go back to London"? I thought I couldn't stand it, I had a physical pain with wanting to see him, but maybe I'd blown it. And at last, very tired, I got to Joyce's house.

On Tuesday he arrived just as we had planned and I could tell at once it was all right. He had missed me as much as I had missed him. But what I had suffered for no reason, the agony of being in love, the tricks the imagination plays – it was crazy, ridiculous, unnecessary, why on earth do we put ourselves through such hell? Instead we went to Southport, which was rather like Larnaca, and walked on the sand dunes. It was romantic. I called him silly little pet names, Christopher Columbus and Ali Baba. We laughed a lot and were blissfully happy.

The next day I had my interview with KLM but it was no good: stewardesses worked from nine to five and did mostly clerical work. Then I went to TWA, since they had suggested I should, and there felt I had made a botch of things, for the Manager said he would ring BEA about me and I was afraid this would put them off. I went back to Joyce's house. Her husband John had arrived and I found them faintly smug and irritating at times, but they were kind enough to put me up.

Thursday was the day of the interview with BEA. I dressed very carefully in a grey suit and a new pink beret and caught all the right trains and buses, but I was misinformed about the airport coach and had to take a taxi, costing an exorbitant fifteen shillings. Luckily I arrived on time, but felt very nervous. There were two interviewers, who were charming. They asked lots of general knowledge questions and seemed quite sure I could have a job if a vacancy arose. It was just the job I wanted and I felt very happy and excited but afterwards I talked to another applicant who told me that all applicants came away feeling confident and half of them didn't get in, so I had better watch out.

I caught a bus to Lancaster, where Alec met me and booked me in at a small hotel where it was only ten shillings a night, and I was able to stay there for the whole of Easter. On Saturday I bought a lovely Easter egg for Ali Baba but it cost me two days' rations, leaving only one shilling and five pence for the next three days. Luckily Alec had enough to pay for everything.

Over that Easter weekend we explored the Lake District, and it was a blissfully happy time. I remembered how I had hated it when I first went to boarding school and had two miserable terms in Keswick, and it was incredible to think back and dimly see that frightened white-faced child I had been, but now those memories were erased and I could fully appreciate the beauty of the Lake District and the grandeur of the mountains. And the best, the most exquisite part was being with Alec again. He said he had never felt so happy and I was the same. It was hard to believe how happy we could be when we were together and to remember how wretched I had felt when I thought it might be over.

All too soon it was Tuesday evening and time for me to return to London. The bill for my room came to £2 10s, which Alec paid, and once again he put me on the London train for what we hoped would be my last spell of temping.

The next day I was sent to the London Brick Company, which was very dreary. They all talked about the London Keeounty Keeouncil and theeousand peeound heeouses and their bricks were 'orrible. Luckily I managed to stay only to the end of the week and on Monday was sent to Saphir Shipping Company in the city. It was quite an easy journey there and though not a very nice building it was quite a pleasant job. Two very friendly girls invited me to go to lunch with them, which was unusual and unexpected. I was in a room with one rep, called Mr Stewart. Mr Saphir the boss who was a Pole, asked me to stay permanently and I told him my fiancé wanted me to go up to Manchester and he said he didn't blame him.

Alec had written to his old Cyprus boss, Chief Superintendent Dick Russell, asking for a reference and when it arrived he asked me to type out some copies. It was excellent. Amongst other things Dick Russell wrote, "*Throughout the time that he was with me, he worked extremely long hours under the most adverse conditions and with untiring enthusiasm, and with never a word of complaint. I found him an outstanding officer, extremely thorough, loyal, conscientious and willing. He has a pleasant disposition and was successful in getting the best from the men who worked under him and who were often untrained and very poor material. By his perseverance and his ability to lead, and by the force of his own example, he welded these men into a very useful band of workers. Sergeant Kay is a man of fine principles and of the highest integrity. I cannot speak too highly of the services he rendered to me and I am certain that he has it in him to go far in the Police Service, and I wish him success in his career.*"

My cousin Jean from Surbiton had got engaged and Badger and Peter invited her and Brian, her fiancé, to dinner. We could not decide whether we liked him or not. He was small and puny and didn't have much to say for himself, but he had a good speaking voice. That seemed the only thing in his favour and I could not help thinking how unfair that he was accepted socially because of this while Alec was not. Why should everything depend on the speaking voice? Alec was so obviously superior in every way, yet just because he was a police sergeant with a Lancashire accent he was considered beyond the pale.

Ridiculous as it may seem, this was how things were in those days – and how wrong it was, for in the event Brian turned out to be a total shit. He and Jean got married and emigrated to New Zealand, where he was not able to keep down a job and frittered away all their money. They moved constantly, always somewhere worse than before. In later years he was to join a strange religious sect and leave Jean for another woman in America, only to return like a leech and sponge on her again towards the end of her life, locking her money away where she could not get at it. Poor Jean by this time had diabetes and went blind. How lucky we do not know what is to happen in our lives – yet perhaps if we do know we could prevent such tragedies.

Back at work, Mr Saphir was again very insistent that I should stay permanently and I told him, No definitely. I thought he was likely to be flirtatious and from that point of view was glad I would be leaving. Mr Stewart, the rep in my room, however, was a charming man who resembled Trevor Howard. He had been in the Navy and his heart had never left it. He told me dreamy, nostalgic tales of the sea. But he was in rather a difficult position: he had a friend who worked at a crucial place on the Stock Exchange and every day Mr Saphir called him in to give a report on what stocks and shares to buy, and the information from his friend enabled Mr Saphir to make a fortune. Why didn't he make the money for himself? He didn't have the capital and besides he desperately needed the job at Saphir Shipping, for he felt in the current climate he was unlikely to get anything else. But he didn't like Mr Saphir and thought he was ruthless. If he didn't pass on the vital information from his friend, he felt sure he would be sacked. Any time I wanted such information in the future he said I should phone him, which was kind, but it was no good for I didn't have any capital either. I stayed with Saphir Shipping for two weeks and when I left they gave me a tremendous send-off with boxes of chocolates and flowers and lots of compliments - from Mr Saphir the Pole and of course Mr Stewart who I knew had liked me.

The next day I received what I had been waiting for: a letter of acceptance from BEA. I was surprised and delighted. It was a permanent position for a ground hostess and I was to start on Monday the 5th May, in ten days' time. It was so exciting. "Thank you God, it is so kind of you," I wrote in my diary. That same day I took a train to Wokingham, as Gillie had invited me for the weekend. She too was excited to have landed a job, with the World Health Organisation in Geneva, so we both had something to celebrate. I loved staying with her, the house was heavenly and the Glennie family was charming, her parents and her uncle Mac and her brother John Robert and sister Pat were all easy, friendly and entertaining. Her father called me Poppet all the time.

Her parents took us to a variety show in Reading which was a bit corny but fun. Gillie and I shared a room and she told me not to be surprised if I heard her father shout out in the night, for he had been shell shocked in the war and had nightmares. I did indeed hear him shouting and was sad for him, but in the morning he had forgotten all about it. That day Gillie and I sat in the garden and read the papers and took the dogs for a walk while her mother and father painted the kitchen pink and blue. Uncle Mac took us to the station on Monday morning. They were such a delightful family and I very much hoped I would stay in touch with them.

I had one more temping job in London with Tallon Limited, the pen people in Argyle Street, which was quite a decent placement for my last week. Alec wrote saying how pleased he was that I was coming back to Lancashire and that I'd got the job, and that, unlike me he'd always thought I would. The recruitment secretary at BEA had promised to let me have addresses where I might find accommodation, she said "Don't worry, we'll get you fixed up," which was friendly, and she gave me the address of a Miss Stewart, who lived in Gatley. Peter said he had to go north and he and Badger would drive me up there which was marvellous – they had been so good to me. I babysat for them and they went out to dinner and the theatre. Finally it was my last day. I finished my packing. I felt as if I were going away for years. I was now ready to go, and a new life lay ahead.

CHAPTER TWENTY-TWO

We drove up to Manchester and Badger and Peter dropped me off at Miss Stewart's house. She seemed very agreeable. Her house was in quite a pleasant road of similar semi-detached houses, and she showed me to a room with a bow window partially obscured by a dressing table with three mirrors. There was a bed with a shiny yellow counterpane, and a lot of large brown furniture covered with bright pink fringed mats. She said I could share the kitchen, and that we would sit in the lounge in the evenings and watch her television. I was a bit worried about this but said nothing. Alec rang up and said he would come down and see me on Wednesday when I finished work, then I unpacked some things and went to bed.

The next day was Sunday and I spent the day looking for flats. I went to Stockport, Bramhall, Wilmslow and Altrincham, looking at ads in shop windows. A woman in the newsagents was quite snooty and said, "This is a very expensive area, you know," and I was disappointed to discover she was right. They were all out of my league, so I decided I would have to forget about flats and stay with Miss Stewart for the time being. I wondered if perhaps in due course I could dispense with the pink-fringed mats. I went back to her house and we sat and watched a play. Alec rang again which was sweet, then I went to bed, excited at the thought of starting my new job the next day.

I went to the airport on the 64 bus. As soon as I went into the passenger section office, I knew I was going to love it. There was another new girl who started at the same time as me and she seemed really nice. Her name was Pauline Leigh, and like me, she was permanent. She told me she lived in Stalybridge with her mother. In the morning we were taken all over the airport and in the afternoon we had to take some passengers back and forth to aircraft. We both felt very excited but also self-conscious because we were the only girls not in uniform so we looked conspicuous, but we were told we would be going down to London to get this at the end of the week.

In the evening Badger rang up sounding delighted, but also Alec who sounded fed up and miserable. He still hadn't found new digs and was very unsettled, and although he was pleased for me to have this airport job, he really wanted me to be nearer to him in Lancaster and thought Ringway was too far away and the travelling would be too expensive. He didn't know how often we would be able to see each other and our days off might not coincide and it wasn't going to work. I was then depressed myself and kept worrying over his reaction. If he wasn't happy, I couldn't be either.

It rained all day on Tuesday and I was put on Gate 1, from where all the domestic flights came and went. It was very busy and all day we got drenched with rain as we took passengers back and forth to their aircraft. I didn't have a decent raincoat and even the soles of my shoes were soaked. In our office there was a blackboard on which our duties for the day were written up, and I asked who John Wild*goose* was. It was such a lovely name. Muriel and Brenda looked at one another and Muriel raised her eyes to the ceiling. I was told scornfully, it wasn't Wild*goose*, it was *Wild*goose. Then someone said to me, "I suppose you went to Roedean?" and stupidly I said, "How did you know?" Once again there was an exchange of derisory smiles and I realised I had made a faux pas. It seemed I had the wrong accent. I didn't really know what I was doing, I kept worrying about Alec and didn't enjoy the day. However, in the evening I found out he could get accommodation on Wednesday night at Mrs Craig's house next to Miss Stewart for only 7s 6d. I was so excited at the thought of seeing him again, and Miss Stewart kindly ordered groceries and greengroceries for me and said I could cook him a meal in her kitchen.

On the Wednesday I was on Gate 2, the international gate, and that was fun. I carried lots of babies out to aircraft and saw the actress Linda Christian, looking very glamorous in a fabulous leopard skin coat. I enjoyed the day very much and when the shift ended I rushed out and Alec was there to meet me. We were glad to see each other but it turned out to be a really stormy evening. He was very ardent, he took me in his arms and said he wished I would stop messing about and marry him, and I said I had promised the family to wait until I had spent time in Lancashire. He said he wanted to go abroad but what prospects were there, or indeed of moving to a southern force? And what was the point of his being in Lancaster and my being at Ringway? And I said I had tried hard enough to get a job in Lancaster, and there wasn't anything. He *knew* there wasn't anything. And he wanted me to be happy didn't he, and what was the point of my getting my dream job at long last if I had to give it up?

I cooked him a meal and he stayed the night next door, which was fine, and next day he drove me to Ringway. He would come down again next Tuesday and it would be better because I would finish at 3.30 and not be on again till 4 pm the next day, which would be perfect. I felt sure we would be able to see a lot of each other, even if we were quite far away and surely it was better than my being in London?

On the Friday Pauline and I were sent to London to get our uniforms. We travelled on a BEA Viscount and went to the BEA shop and collected two uniforms, one raincoat, one lining, one hood, and a pair of overshoes. I also bought three white blouses, another pair of high-heeled court shoes and five pairs of stockings, for which I paid £5. 6s. I stayed the night with Badger and Peter and next day went down to Brighton to get some summer dresses from the flat. I also destroyed Enid's letters and hid Alec's at the bottom of a locked trunk as my parents were soon returning home and I did not want my mother to read them. She would not be able to resist, just as she used to read my diary. When I found that out, I had switched to writing it in French, which gradually became more and more stilted, and eventually I'd bought a diary with a lock.

When I got back to Miss Stewart's I found rather a disturbing letter from Alec. He thanked me for mine and said I had written many sensible things which he appreciated, but he still felt he needed me to be near him. He said he knew how I felt about the airport job and would go along my way and hope that we could meet as often as possible, though the cost of travel was worrying him. His letter ended "I think the time has come when you and I should be straight with each other. Sometimes I feel that you are leading the way at present and whilst I will work with you, I will not be told what I have to do."

The next day I sat down to write to him and Miss Stewart kindly said I could go into her sunny front room and do it there. I wrote a tactful letter and hoped he could accept I was *not* telling him what to do. What would be the point when I knew he had always made the decisions and always would?

On Monday a whole lot of new girls arrived. One of them was really pretty, like Ava Gardner. They were all temporary, being employed until October, when their positions would be reassessed and some would be made permanent and some would be asked to leave. They didn't seem to realise Pauline and I were new too, so in our new uniforms we must have looked efficient, though neither of us were. We both wondered if people thought some

415

of them should have been made permanent instead of the two of us. We didn't feel confident and both knew we were making mistakes.

I made a really bad one at Gate One. I was on with Muriel Ayres, who scared me. While she was on tea break a call came over the box from Apron Control, which I misheard. I thought they said *"Take* the London," when in fact they said *"Gate* the London." All the London passengers, mostly tough, impatient businessmen, were sitting or standing around the Gate, waiting to board. So thinking I had been given the go-ahead, I announced the departure and led all fifty-five of them out to the aircraft.

There was immediate pandemonium. The aircraft was nowhere near ready, the cleaners were still on board and the man on the Apron told me to take them back. I had to go back down the aircraft steps and tell the passengers they could not board after all, and would they please go back into the waiting room?

They took no notice of me at all. They were all over the tarmac and Muriel rushed back from her meal break looking horrified and shouted to them to go back inside at once, whereupon they went like lambs. That was a very bad mistake on my part and earned me a lot of scorn not only from her and our supervisor, but the whole of Apron Control - and an immediate bad reputation for being thick. I was abashed and deeply ashamed.

But the day after that I was on Gate 1 with Biddy, who was good company and whom I liked very much. She kindly invited me to have lunch with her at the flat she shared with a flight clerk, and it was so much fun being with her. The day after that I was on Gate 2 and again, greatly enjoyed it. I tried very hard to be efficient and not to make mistakes, and when I was on with people like Pauline and Biddy it was so much easier. Biddy had a great sense of humour and later when we were on night duty together and I got to know her better, we christened ourselves Ethel and Edith, and one of the duty officers whom we thought excessively boring, we nicknamed Ernest. Another favourite of mine was Pauline who had started on the same day as me. She came up with a marvellous maxim which we decided we would follow:

"The secret of success, I've found,
Is in making mistakes when no one's around."

CHAPTER TWENTY-THREE

On the 13th June my old friend Glen Coats came to Cheadle and the next day we drove down to North Wales. I so much enjoyed seeing him again, he was such good company and one of the most original and charismatic people I had ever met. We found an old inn where we had lunch and he asked me lots of questions. He wanted to know all about Alec, and he was certainly very complimentary to me. Many years before I had even fancied I was a little in love with him, but that day wandering over the moors in North Wales I realised that though I was very fond of him and we would always be friends, it was Alec I was in love with, and only Alec.

I missed Alec very much over the following days and was overjoyed when he came again on the following Monday and stayed overnight. The next day we went for a long walk in the country, and afterwards I wrote in my diary: "*How I love him and how I fear his strength and admire his manliness and how I cherish his gentleness and his sincerity. We were fiercely happy in feeling so close to each another and I know I can never love anyone but him…*"

When we had days off at the same time he would either come down to see me or I would go up to Lancaster to see him. He was much more cheerful, as he had now found good digs with a really nice landlady called Mrs Hogg, a superintendent's widow. She lived in a smart bungalow in a pleasant part of Lancaster and she invited me to stay there when I came to see him. And when he came to Cheadle to see me, he could stay with Mrs Craig, who lived next door to Miss Stewart. In this way we managed to see quite a lot of one another, even though we were so far apart.

But all of a sudden, my landlady, Miss Stewart, stopped being nice and became bad-tempered and moody, as so often seems to happen with landladies. First she was annoyed when I wanted to have a bath, and refused to put the hot water on. The next day when Alec was coming down, she was very nasty and said we could not use her kitchen any more. Alec said it was no good my being there and I must leave.

In the next weeks the atmosphere was very cold, probably because I had used some of her lettuce and had left the front door unbolted. Eventually I gave notice and said I would be leaving in about a fortnight. I dreaded doing this but she did not seem too annoyed, in fact she was probably pleased. I realised I had proved a disappointment to her; what she had been looking for was a nice girl who did not have a boyfriend and who would be a companion for her and sit with her in her lounge and watch her television in the evenings. Also someone who would make sure the door was bolted and who would not eat her lettuce.

I started looking around for somewhere else, but could find nothing affordable in Gatley or Cheadle, and eventually decided on a bed-sitting room at 34 Lapwing Lane in Didsbury, where I was to some extent independent. However, it was very small and unsatisfactory, and the area was depressing. One day when I had been waiting all morning for the water to get even slightly warmer than tepid so that I could have a bath, I tripped over a pan of spinach and spilt it all over my face flannel. That was the last straw – I decided I must move out.

By a stroke of luck I was chatting to Pauline a couple of weeks later and she said she was prepared to share a flat with me. The very next day, the 25th July, Alec and I found a pleasant two-bedroom flat in Cheadle. We showed it to Pauline and she liked it too. We were very excited and took it at once.

The flat was a great success: Pauline and I got on well and were very happy there. It was light and bright and we were allowed to use the garden, where we would go and sunbathe on warm and sunny days. It was near enough to the airport for us to get there on the number 64 bus. I was now much more "into" my job and was loving it. I had made some good friends and when I was on the same shift as them it was very enjoyable.

Ringway seemed to attract some interesting people and there were a lot of real characters working there. One was Liz Rapallo, who was large with a very beautiful face, clever and extremely sophisticated. She had been married to an Italian from whom she was separated and she now lived in a wonderful isolated house at the end of a lane near the runway, where her lover, a married Captain, came to join her whenever he could. There were always parties at her house, to which we went. I liked her but at the same time was a little scared of her, because she didn't suffer fools gladly and was apt to talk about things of which you knew nothing. You didn't like to say you didn't know what she was talking about, as she took it for granted that you knew exactly. This was flattering, but half the time you hadn't a clue whether it was about a famous Russian ballet dancer or a horse race or an exotic pudding. She was the original person who, when someone came and banged on the check-in desk and said, "Do you know who I am?" put out an announcement on the tannoy that there was someone at the desk who didn't know who he was. She thought most PAPS (the code name for passengers) were stupid and most of them did seem to be. You could ask someone if they were on the flight to Geneva and they'd say No, they were going to Switzerland.

We saw the best and the worst of people passing through the airport. Aldermen and Mayors with chains of office around their necks were mostly self-important and tended to thump on the desk and say they were a friend of the chairman – that old chestnut. How they went down in our estimation! People who lost their luggage tended to be awful, especially MPs. I often wondered why they should be so horrible to the poor person taking down the details, for it was obviously not their fault, and being shouted at simply made you feel you didn't care if they lost their luggage or not, they deserved to. When an unidentified suitcase was brought into the office, it had to be opened by the supervisor, who would try to discover whose it was. One bag that came in was found to contain the most disgusting collection of porn. It belonged to a newscaster, quite a famous man, but I won't say who it was. We just thought how stupid people were to risk being shown up in that way.

We saw lots of celebrities, and I remember that Tommy Cooper was one of the most unpleasant. He was nasty not only to the ground staff but to his wife. He was just a bully and I never thought he was funny either. Kathy Kirby was also unpleasant and she couldn't really afford to be, for she wasn't that famous or that good a singer. The entire cast of *West Side Story* arrived from America and I was surprised they were so scruffy, but Alec and I went to the show and thought it wonderful. Other celebrities were Arthur Askey, who was sweet – he put his hand luggage on the scales and quipped, "Just my nightie," and James Mason and his wife were charming, and also Noel Coward whom I had met in Jamaica. These were people who did not want a lot of fuss made.

I once had to contact a duchess who was coming in from the Isle of Man. There were only three women on the flight and I spoke to each in turn. The Duchess turned out to be the most unlikely of the three: she was like a little brown mouse whom you would never notice, except for her charming smile.

There was a woman in a wheelchair who travelled frequently, she had been badly burnt and had a very scarred face. She tended to be nasty to the ground staff, and I think it was because she couldn't bear to see the pity in their faces, and if she was nasty to them the pity would change to anger, and she could cope with that.

Women with babies had to be boarded first, before the other passengers, and we always had to offer to carry the babies, who were then sick over our uniforms. Brenda Madden, the pretty girl who looked like Ava Gardner, was very funny about this. "A horrid big fat baby, I thought only tiny babies puked up all the time," she said bitterly. She was funny about other things too. Once coming out of the ladies' lavatory she remarked, "Why can't people aim straight?" and when a woman passenger bound for New York, complained, "What am I going to do, I was sick all the way over?" Brenda, at the end of her tether, having had a very hard day with diversions from fog-bound London, said, "You'll be sick all the way back."

There were lots of unaccompanied children, code-named 'SPMIN' which stood for Special Minor, and we had to stay with them every minute, whether they wanted us to or not. Often it was Not – little boys of perhaps nine years old whose parents worked abroad and who constantly travelled backwards and forwards for the holidays. They knew exactly what to do and where to go and would say, "I'm *quite* all right, thank you!" It must have been irritating for them but we just had to stick with them, for no unaccompanied child could be left alone for a moment.

Other code names for special passengers were SPBUS – special businessmen – and SPINV – special invalid. We had to look after these people and give them extra attention, for instance we had to board them ahead of the other passengers. Once the wrong information came in about a SPINV. I took a woman out to the aircraft and remarked I thought she was wonderful for ninety. "I'm not ninety!" she said indignantly, "I'm sixty."

"I would have taken you for sixty," I said – adding quickly, "in fact, no more than fifty-five." But it was too late - she was not appeased. This special attention was sometimes unwelcome, particularly with male SPINVs. Depending on where it was placed on the tarmac, it could be quite a long walk out to an aircraft and at check-in you would ask them if they wanted a wheelchair. Most of the women SPINVs would say gratefully, "Oh yes, please!" but not so the males, who often looked furious and said, "I most certainly do *not*." You wanted to say, "OK keep your hair on, it's no skin off my nose!" but of course you could say nothing – just smile.

We were forever just smiling. I was on Gate One - the domestic gate - one day with Biddy and when the London passengers arrived we decided to see how many of them we could get to smile back. They were usually quite grim-faced. On that occasion we were smiling so much, and our smiles were so genuine, unlike the switched-on smiles of the air hostesses, and we got nearly all of them to smile back. In the end we were laughing openly and they were laughing too. It was fun, it was always fun working with Biddy, and it was amazing to see the difference it made to us all.

Once when I was on Gate Two a Sabena flight came in from New York with thirty-two passengers in transit to Brussels. I was on duty with two young new girls and for a joke I handed out thirty-one green plastic transit cards and one red. The young man to whom I gave the red card wanted to know why his was red when everyone else had green ones. I told him he had been elected the handsomest man on the flight, and he said he felt very flattered, and then we were all laughing. It was childish, but harmless enough.

Pauline and I continued to make mistakes, especially in the early days when we were unsure what to do. There was a sort of hood in our office, with an outside telephone where you could take incoming calls and hear what was being said. Once Pauline was in the hood for about ten minutes and when she emerged I asked what was going on. "He's asked something and I've no idea what to say," she confessed.

"Is he still on?"

"Yes, I suppose so. I don't know what to say to him." So she just left him hanging on and never did give him an answer.

Pauline and I were both rather naïve and did not know that certain phrases had another meaning, so when she told someone in Apron Control to sod off, she had no idea it meant anything other than a clod of earth. And one day I was "on the box", which meant in control of all the passenger movements. It didn't happen often and you had to concentrate one hundred per cent and that day Roger was on the ticket desk and was being particularly pedantic and annoying and I told him to get knotted. He was furious. He came over afterwards and rebuked me. "That is not the sort of thing to say in front of passengers, Delia, it was very embarrassing." He then explained that the phrase was coarse and rude, of which I was totally unaware.

I once said something was a 'load of crap.' "Do you know what crap means?" said Bob, a senior three-ringer in Apron Control.

"Yes," I said, "it means rubbish."

He then enlightened me as to its true meaning. "You shouldn't use phrases you don't know the meaning of," he said.

"But I thought I did know – I thought it meant rubbish."

He was not impressed. Once on the tarmac he shouted something and I said, "What?"

"*What?*" he repeated, "Where were you dragged up? Don't you know you should say pardon?"

I didn't like to offend him by telling him my mother had told me never to say pardon.

One of the things we most dreaded was having to deal with passengers who were overbooked. This usually happened when travel agents made bookings for people and forgot to put their names down, so they would arrive for the flight with the ticket correctly endorsed for the flight but their names were not on our list and if the flight was full they could not travel and would have to be rebooked. This caused them heartache and us embarrassment. We would explain and apologise and then we would have to call the supervisor out to explain and apologise again, and these passengers - PAPS - would be put down as NAOs – Not Accommodated Overbooked. "Bloody travel agents," the supervisor Harry Dunn would say. He had the utmost contempt for travel agents.

I wrote a poem about it, called DILEMMA:

"Oh Lord Douglas, tell me true, what's a girl like me to do
When confronted with a PAP, ranting, raging, in a flap
Stamping, snorting, like a bull, when he hears the flight is full.
Angry, peevish, in a spin, simply cannot take it in
When I tell him so politely, "Though you made your booking rightly
Now alas the flight's complete: someone else has got your seat.
Yes indeed, it's very odd – I can't think, so help me God
How it happened – oh I know - it is vital that you go
Everybody on the flight simply must get there tonight.
I have heard it all before – please sir, spare me any more.
Yes sir, I can see you're harassed, as for me, I'm most embarrassed –
You can't travel BEA – there are no more flights today."
Still he stays – he cannot see, why he's told by such as me
"Sorry Sir, you cannot go. Frankly, you're an NAO."

The BEA magazine liked this poem and would have published it but could not as it was read not only by staff but by quite a lot of the general public, who would have been offended.

We had to make lots of announcements on the tannoy and we tried to whisper throatily down the microphone, hoping to sound seductive like Liz Repallo. One day Pauline was making an announcement about a Sabena flight, when someone came up behind her and tickled her in the ribs.

"Sabena, Sabena – OOH!" she gasped. This went all over the airport.

A lot of fooling around and joking went on, with people playing tricks on each other, especially when it was not very busy. When I was on night duty someone in Apron Control said he was sending me a toffee down the tube, a device whereby you could send messages from one department to another. The tube arrived with the toffee in and I unwrapped it and put it in my mouth. His voice came over on the box and said, "Did you get the toffee?"

"Yes, thank you."

"You're not eating it, are you?"

"Yes – why not?"

There were shouts of laughter. "It's for dogs," he said.

I thought it had a funny taste. I spat it out it and it was all red and frothy.

I caused unintentional amusement once in our lunch break, when I said to a crowd of my fellow workers: "I'm conducting a survey - do you play with your flannel in the bath?"

Everyone laughed and the men who were present said, "What do you think, Delia wants to know if we play with our ... in the bath!" But Louise was particularly amused by this as she knew I really meant 'flannel' and not something else.

When Pauline was on night duty she got a call from someone at two thirty in the morning who demanded to know who she was. She put on a silly voice and said, "I am a bird who flies by night..." I don't know if he was amused or not.

Once I took a phone call from a man who said he was the Superintendent of Strangeways Prison and he was bringing two prisoners to the airport for a flight to Belfast. I thought it was a joke and laughed. "Yes, I know – it's very funny – but I really *am* bringing two passengers for the Belfast flight."

It was always relaxed on night duty, for there weren't many flights and very little to do, except making out tickets and preparing the bays for the morning shift. It was good to be on with people you liked. Sometimes we played table tennis at three o'clock in the morning. My favourite supervisor was Alf Cooper, who came from Liverpool and had a wonderful sense of humour. Most of the Liverpudlians seemed to have a sense of humour. My least favourite supervisor was Jack Cannell, a little man who didn't approve of the way I spoke, nor of Biddy either, so as he always liked to do the duties for the next day we both found ourselves constantly on Gate One. You would get drenched to the skin, then dry off for half an hour, then get drenched again. Passengers complained about having to walk out to the aircraft.

The MP Walter Bromley-Davenport was always grumbling. "Why is the aircraft parked so far away from the Gate?" he grumbled.

"Never mind about that," I replied once. "What is the Government doing about Katanga?" He was speechless, and the people on the Apron loved it.

When Alf Cooper was on in the evening he let us go for the quarter to eleven 64 bus if there was nothing much to do, but Jack Cannell would make you stay on till the bitter end. Once, going out for the 11.15 pm bus, I remarked to Paul Ward, "If only Jack Cannell had let us go early we could have been in bed by now."

"Shh, Delia!" he said. "There are porters around." It was entirely innocently meant as he well knew, but the porters were a gossipy lot and could have taken it the wrong way.

One time the porters and baggage handlers went on strike. A porter was carrying a heavy suitcase for an elderly lady and he suddenly put it down in the middle of the tarmac and said, "It's three o'clock and we're on strike now."

"Don't be ridiculous," I said, "You can't just leave it there."

"I tell you, we're on strike."

I then picked the suitcase up myself. "All right then, I'll carry it."

"You put it down," he said. "It's against Union rules." He tried to wrestle the suitcase out of my grasp, but I pushed him away.

"I'll have the Union on to you!"

"Go ahead then, I don't care about your silly union rules," I said, and carried the case to the coach. The elderly lady was very grateful. I heard no more about it, but that porter remembered and was always awkward afterwards.

I particularly enjoyed being on with Biddy, Marna, Pauline, Louise Kane, Paul Ward, Peter Geary, Ralph Brown and Mo Felthouse, people with whom you could work well but still have fun. There were others, I liked – Puss Cat, Sheila Kletts, Estelle, Brenda Madden, Barbara, Joyce, Pam, Patsy – in fact too many to mention, for BEA tended to attract unusual and interesting people. I was very fond of Frances who worked for Sabena, but did not care for Peter of BOAC who went on to murder his wife (although we never knew that at the time, not until it was published in the *News of The World* some years later).

On night duty people came in from other departments, such as Ships' Papers or Cargo, and gave you soup they had heated up on a stove with photographic spirit. Liz and I went and chatted to some customs officers and we drank whisky with them - probably illegal stuff they had confiscated from passengers. I had breakfast with a captain whose hands were shaking. He told me he had lost his nerve and dreaded flying. I felt very sorry for him, but as he was due to fly in less than an hour, it was rather worrying and just as well the passengers didn't know.

Although I tried very hard to be efficient, I was still making mistakes, and not just when no one was around. Some of the mistakes were very visible – like when I boarded the Belfast passengers onto the Glasgow aircraft. Captain Hartley was *not* amused. "Not only did the receptionist take the passengers to the wrong aircraft but she was *laughing* about it," he complained to Mr Charlesworth, the senior supervisor, who called me to his office to give me a rap on the knuckles. "I know it was awful," I said, "But what else could I do but laugh? I'd made the mistake by then. And all the passengers were laughing, they thought it was a huge joke. In fact it was rather good public relations really."

"You could argue the hind leg off a donkey," he sighed.

In those days the air tickets had coupons inside for each leg of the journey and these had to be collected by the ground steward or stewardess who was processing the flight; thus if there were fifty-eight passengers there had to be fifty-eight coupons. This was of vital importance. If there was a mistake there would be a delay on the flight and a report had to be made and sent to Head Office. That meant trouble. A bad report reflected on our branch, right at the top. Questions would be asked and post mortems held.

Sometimes passengers would arrive late and would be accepted at the last moment, at Gate One. Then it was the job of the person on the Gate to extract the coupon and return it to Reception. One day there was a terrible row when it appeared there was one coupon missing. There was an inquest and a search made, but the coupon could not be found. I was on Gate One that day and I don't know what happened, but several hours later I discovered the coupon was attached to my clipboard. I was horrified – what should I do? It was much too late to confess that I had it all the time. I am surprised the suspicion did not fall on me but for some reason it did not. When we were on our lunch break I told Pauline and she was equally horrified. We knew there would be a terrible row if I confessed, so we dug a hole in the ground and buried it. That was one mistake that no one ever discovered.

Then two months later I was in trouble again and there I was back in Mr Charlesworth's office trying to explain my way out of something else. I was on a 9-7 shift which seemed to go on for ever, it was so tiring, and after the early shift went home at 3 pm there was still another four hours to go - but there was no excuse. In the evening I was processing BE 960, a flight to Glasgow, and Mr Moore, our most hated Station Traffic Officer, came to watch what I was doing, which threw me into a panic. The flight, a Viscount, was completely full and I could not add up the weights. I was not in Division 3 for Maths for nothing. Then Liz Rapallo came and sorted it out for me, but there was a terrible delay on the flight and it was all my fault. Flight delays for human error were considered unforgiveable.

I had to go and see tall Charlie and I loathed myself for going and crying about it. Thank goodness he was nice about it. In the afternoon the STO called me to his office for another telling off, this time for something that was not my fault. Surely I thought, no one has been to see Charlie and the STO so many times in so short a time. I felt very down-hearted.

It sounds as if we were constantly making mistakes or just having fun all the time, but in point of fact we often had to work very hard indeed, particularly when London Airport was fog-bound and all the flights were diverted into Manchester. At such times there was chaos, and you usually had to work a twelve-hour shift and not even stop for a cup of tea. We did our best to help all the displaced passengers, re-routeing them, getting them onto coaches for overnight hotel accommodation or accompanying them to train stations if there were suitable trains.

On one occasion I took a hundred people to Stockport station. I got home at ten past one and was up again next day for a 6 am start. There never seemed to be enough members of staff to deal with the hordes of passengers, many of whom were unhappy or difficult. I was doing my best for one man but it was not enough and he was quite impossible. Finally I said to him, "You are the rudest man I've ever met!" This remark really went home. He went up to a colleague and said "That girl says I'm the rudest man she's ever met!" It was a most successful remark as he could hardly complain about me without having egg on his face. Although dealing with diversions was by far the most difficult and tiring part of our job, it was also gratifying to know that in the end you had helped so many people, and that most of them had gone away satisfied.

I thought I was getting quite good at dealing with passengers but I had a shock on one occasion. I tried to be honest and told a group of businessmen that their flight was delayed for technical reasons, for which I apologised. One man, Mr Jack, who was always difficult, took the apology as a sign of weakness and he went for me and was so horrible that all the others took pity. One man apologised for the entire male sex, and another, an American, said he was so sure I was going to hit Mr Jack and get the sack, he was prepared to offer me a job in his company at double my salary.

CHAPTER TWENTY-FOUR

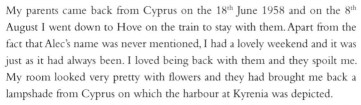

My parents came back from Cyprus on the 18th June 1958 and on the 8th August I went down to Hove on the train to stay with them. Apart from the fact that Alec's name was never mentioned, I had a lovely weekend and it was just as it had always been. I loved being back with them and they spoilt me. My room looked very pretty with flowers and they had brought me back a lampshade from Cyprus on which the harbour at Kyrenia was depicted.

We went to Jimmy's for lunch, shopping in East Street and to an Agatha Christie play on the Palace Pier in the evening. The next day we went on a speedboat on the pier, something I had always loved, and to Fairwarp in the afternoon for tea with Pauleen Lurcott and her father. In the evening we went to see *Vertigo* with James Stewart, and the next morning I got up early to catch my train back to Manchester.

The weekend had been fun, my parents were sweet and generous and I was happy – but I did miss Alec. He had missed me too. We went to Buxton and went up in the hills and sat on the grass and ate sandwiches. A sheep came nearby and stared at us with its funny yellow eyes. Alec told me how much he loved me and what it meant to him to have me. We felt that our love was very special and precious and we discussed getting engaged either before or after the holiday we had booked in Majorca in October.

But when I saw him again he was very depressed to have received a bad report from his Chief Superintendent, because "he was apparently worrying over the girl he has brought back from Cyprus, and would never go anywhere in his career as long as she was around." This was a bitter blow and we could think of little else. I was shocked that someone who had never even met me should think these things.

A month later Alec was told he was being transferred to Tyldesley, which was a town in a very depressing coal-mining area. We were both downcast when we saw the house we were to live in. It was wedged between a gasometer on one side and a coal pit on the other. It was as bad a posting as we could have imagined. The women of the town all looked older than their years, and all wore scarves over their heads, done up in turbans. They stood on the doorsteps of their terraced houses, looking right and left, and I imagined that would be me if I had to live there too.

On the 4th October we drove down to Blackbushe for our longed-for two weeks' holiday in Majorca. We were to travel with Danair, a company much despised by my colleagues at BEA, and not surprising really for Danair flights were always delayed, usually for technical reasons. They didn't have some vital piece of equipment or other. I remember seeing the Chinese Danair co-pilot getting off the incoming plane at Ringway and borrowing a spanner. Also at Ringway I had taken a crowd of passengers out to a delayed Danair aircraft and someone asked me if this happened often, to which I replied airily – and not very tactfully – "Oh yes – all the time." Our flight to Palma was no exception, we were delayed for five hours and could not help laughing inwardly. We were then fog-bound at Lyons, but at least we got to Palma eventually.

We stayed in Palma for the first week, and the first day we hired a boat to Palma Nova beach, where we lay in the sun hoping to acquire a tan. The next day we hired a little *biscuter* and drove to Formentor via Pollensa and the Hotel Illa D'Or, where there was a gorgeous sandy beach and we saw Princess Grace. Later we went along a very twisty road to Soller and Alec got quite sunburnt driving in the little open car. We laughed a lot and had fun. In the evenings we went to the Calypso Club, where we danced. I felt I could have danced all night. Alec said to me, "How happy you are! It shines out of your eyes. You bubble over with happiness." It was true – I was so happy: a little bit of sun and no thoughts of Lancashire and Tyldesley…

We spent our second week at the Hotel Brismar, Puerto Andraitx, arriving at night and waking up next day.. *and oh! How beautiful it was – a lake smooth as glass with mountains around covered with pine trees, and little fishing boats in the harbour.* We lay on the slab below our hotel and swam in and out of the sea between the jellyfish, trying to avoid the wicked black sea urchins with their sharp spines, suspended under the rocks. Andraitx was a dear little fishing village, picturesque with little cobbled streets, quite unspoilt and much nicer than Palma. We went for long walks, in the hills and around the lake exploring the countryside. One day we went to the Cave of Drach near Porto Cristo, which with all its stalactites and stalagmites was like fairyland, or even Aladdin's cave. I expected to see the genie with the lamp, instead of which I saw the gleaming teeth of the wide-mouthed manager of our hotel manager in Palma, who was delighted to see us again.

Also staying at our hotel in Puerto Andraitx was a very nice young German called Franz Scholl who was trying to avoid some awful Germans who were monopolising everything in the hotel including - of course - the sun-beds, so Franz attached himself to us quite a lot of the time. He had been in the German Navy during the war and Alec and he discovered they had been on opposite sides in the same sea battle, which was interesting. He was an Anglophile, he had a good sense of humour and we got on very well with him.

We felt very sad when our holiday was over, with the thoughts of Tyldesley hanging over us. Alec had to move there on 24th October. He disliked the place intensely but found the work much more interesting than Lancaster, where it had been mostly routine. Now there was serious crime for him to get his teeth into.

Then he saw a job advertised in Uganda. They wanted someone with experience of motor vehicles which would be right up his street. He decided to apply for it, and although he told me not to get my hopes up, I was delighted – I felt sure it would be the answer to all our problems.

We decided we would get officially engaged, and would get married the following year, when I was entitled to 90% free travel – if seats were available, that is. But I dreaded telling my parents, as I knew there would be continual rows, so I didn't say anything.

I told Badger first. She was still totally against the idea. I told her that my friends who had met Alec had all liked him very much and thought we should go ahead and not care what anyone else thought, and Badger said they were not true friends, because they were saying what they thought I wanted to hear, not what was the best thing for me. I said that was not true, Alec and I had gone to Hal's wedding in Hexham in April 1959 and she and Fuzz had met Alec for the first time. Afterwards Fuzz wrote and said how much they had both liked him; they had thought him utterly charming and that he had a very nice smile. Biddy said he was mature and capable, wouldn't hurt a fly, obviously adored me, and when he smiled he was good-looking in a very manly way. Sheila Kletts said she thought I was so lucky to have Alec, and that he was a man in a million. Pauline too, thought he was very sweet, unselfish, kind and thoughtful and how lucky I was.

I told Badger all these things but she was unconvinced, mainly, I think, because I would have to live in Tyldesley, which she knew I hated. She had hated South Lancashire as much as I had, and I could not deny it. I was upset that she was so against Alec, but I could not blame her, for I knew she only had my best interests at heart, and I found myself very much influenced by her reasoning.

Alec tried very hard to find an alternative, but nothing worked out. He wrote to Geoff White, the Commissioner of Police in Cyprus, and asked if he could have a transfer to Kent, Mr White's own force. Mr White wrote a nice letter back but said he did not think this a good idea. Alec wrote to the Colonial Office to find out what qualifications they would require for him to transfer into the Colonial Police. They wrote back to say his qualifications were all right but that he *must* submit his application through his Chief Constable, and this he felt reluctant to do, for he did not want to damage his chances in Lancashire. He decided he could not continue with his application for Uganda and though I was terribly disappointed I had to accept his decision. He then wrote to Tom Lockley, who had been his boss in Cyprus. Alec and he had got on very well and he had trusted Mr Lockley one hundred per cent, so he was really pleased to receive a wonderful and very sincere reply, saying he would be a referee and would help in every possible way. He said that pension rights were soon to be extended to colonial forces, and that he would personally see that Alec had a fair chance with any job that came along, however he thought that the job in Uganda was no good.

When a post came up for Nyasaland Alec consulted Mr Lockley, but the latter did not recommend that either. He had still not completely ruled the Uganda post out, but in January he received a letter from the Colonial Office saying that because of a fall in the prices of cotton, recruitment for Uganda had ceased, so that was that. I was disappointed as I had built up my hopes that we might be able to go there.

Alec begged me to think seriously about marrying him, even if it did mean living in Tyldesley and I promised I would, but I could not feel overjoyed at the thought of staying in that part of Lancashire. I would have felt the same way if it had been Prince Philip and not Alec asking me to live there. I realised I was a wimp – what made me turn my nose up at the idea? Thousands of other girls married policemen and lived contentedly in Lancashire, but they had been born and bred there and had nothing to compare it with. There was such a north-south divide, and I was not alone in finding the north depressing.

BEA crews from London who were diverted to Manchester because of fog told me what a dreary, awful place they found it.

I went down to Hove to stay with my parents, and Badger was there too. As usual it was a lovely weekend, they were all so sweet to me and for the first time I really dreaded going back to Lancashire. My diary entry: *I awoke at 5 am and cried and cried. Oh, why do I have to be so torn between my family and Alec? If I only didn't love him, how simple it would be. After the weekend I could scarcely wait to see him, but I had to tell him how I felt about coming back. He was very annoyed. Looking up at him I could not help loving him. Everything about him I love. I am really torn in two, for when I am at home I want to stay there but when I see him, it is him that I want.*

I decided I really did want to marry him, even if it meant living in Tyldesley. We had known each other for three years and were now more in love than ever. It seemed incredible, but it was true. However, Badger was still not happy about it, and I thought I would like to be married in Switzerland, away from the disapproval of both our families. In May 1959 we discussed the possibility of doing this. I had always loved Switzerland. I wrote to the British Consul and asked if it would be possible. He replied that it would, but I would have to establish residency in Switzerland. I would be able to stay with Gillie, who was now out there, working for the World Health Organisation, so we decided I should fly out to Geneva and try to make the necessary arrangements. I would go on the 30th June for four days, and I would be able to fly out on a concessionary staff ticket with 90% reduction. I told my parents I was going to Geneva, but not why. Badger said she would tell them, but she was sad and disapproving.

The trip went well. Gillie met me at the airport and took me back to her lovely flat, and it was so good to see her again. The next day I saw the British Consul and got the necessary certificates, which I took to the Ancienne Mairie. They were duly signed and our wedding fixed for the 21st September. I met Gillie for lunch right at the top of the beautiful United Nations building, from where we had a magnificent view. It was so much fun to be in Switzerland with Gillie, I adored the country, the city, Gillie's flat, the whole atmosphere.

That night we had a delicious fondue and I met Jean, her boyfriend and her friend Hilary. We got pleasantly tight and later I lost five francs at the Casino. The next day I went to the English church in Geneva and saw the Reverend Howells, who was fortunately just back from holiday. He said we could most certainly be married properly in the English church after the civil ceremony in the Mairie. He was such a sweet, lovely man.

On my last day we spent the time sunbathing. The girls were stunning, all in bikinis. Then Gillie took me to the airport and I managed to get on a Swissair flight to London. I felt very happy that the trip had been such a success: the arrangements made and everything worked out so well. I was to meet my family at Lords that day and dreaded seeing the parents, but was overjoyed to learn from Badger that they had at last accepted it. They even said they would come to the wedding. I marvelled at how kind and generous they were. We had lunch in Eton first and then went to Lords for the cricket match. Most of the family were there: Auntie Margaret and Uncle Cliff, Auntie Hazel and Uncle Teddy, Trevor Edmondson and his daughter Liz-Anne. It was a very hot day and I wore a hat and my new blue linen dress, which was much admired.

The next day I caught the flight to Manchester, where Alec met me. I was excited to see him and tell him all about my trip, and he was very pleased that it had gone so well. But then I had to tell him my parents were planning to come to the wedding, and at first he was furious and hurt. He immediately said he would have to ask his parents too. I had feared this might happen. Maybe I was as much of a snob as my parents, but I knew it would be disastrous for the four of them to meet. Yet he had to ask them, he could do nothing else. If it had just been his father it might have been all right, but I dreaded to think what they would make of his mother, and what she would make of them. They were such poles apart, and would never even be able to understand one another's language. What if she talked about 't'hills' or 'going oop pad'? It would be better really if she spoke Swahili, at least my father could cope with that.

I was sad that I had unwittingly hurt Alec, and I never did know if he asked them to come to the wedding, but if he did, they decided not to accept. It would not have been kind to insist, for in all their long lives they had never even been to Manchester. Anyway, we did not speak of it any more.

My friend Frances Walthew, who worked for Sabena, suggested I should meet her Italian friend Aina Pavolini, who was clever and sophisticated and a brilliant dressmaker. She lived in a beautiful Georgian house, but it was in a very slummy area of Manchester. Aina said you had to close your eyes as you drove through it, and then there you were in this very beautiful house. We arranged for her to make my wedding dress and my going away outfit, and Frances came with me to Manchester to choose the material. Afterwards I could not help thinking the material looked a bit like a tablecloth, but I was very pleased with all the things Aina made me. The going-away suit was in pale yellow linen. The skirt was narrow and the jacket had an enormous collar and a nipped in waist. It was really very elegant. She also made me a white night dress made of yards and yards of fine lawn trimmed with rows of broderie anglaise. I had bought some records, Ravel and Rimsky-Korsakov and Grieg and Aina laughed at me and said, "Ah, you like the romantic composers – but when you learn more about music, you will realise they are lightweight, compared with Mozart and Beethoven." I expect she was right, and I fear I am lightweight, for I have always preferred the romantic composers.

Alec took me to Manchester and bought me an engagement ring, an exquisite square-cut emerald surrounded by a cluster of diamonds. I loved it, and kept looking at it, and everyone at the airport admired it too, and thought it beautiful.

About this time my mother's favourite cousin, Tony Cooper, wrote a charming letter to me. He said he wanted to come up to Lancashire and meet Alec and take us out for a celebration dinner. It was so sweet of him – but I suspect it was prompted after speaking to my parents and hearing how depressed they were at the thoughts of my marriage to Alec. Although they had accepted it, they were still not happy and continued to hope they could make me change my mind.

On the 24th August they came up to Lancashire, and took a room at the lovely Bridge Hotel in Prestbury. Their plan was to see Tyldesley, where we would be living, to see Alec again, together with my friends, and to meet his parents. I really dreaded that meeting, and luckily, I don't know why, but it didn't happen. Maybe Alec could see how impossible it would have been.

On the 25th he drove us to Tyldesley and showed them the house we were to have. On one side there was a gasometer and on the other a coal pit. At first they said nothing. Then my father said, "Well Alec – I've been all over the world and I have to say I'd rather live in a mud hut in the middle of Africa." I couldn't help silently agreeing with him. A mud hut would have been lovely by comparison.

Everyone was very quiet on the journey back to Cheshire, and there was deep depression. My mother had always been affected by what she thought of as depressing places. She didn't even like Shoreham-by-Sea in Sussex, and never wanted to drive down the slummy hill by Brighton station, so poor old Lancashire didn't stand a chance. However it all went off splendidly with my friends, who were now Alec's friends as well. My parents liked and thoroughly approved of them all.

That evening we introduced them to Biddy and we all had a jolly meal at the Roebuck in Mobberley. The next day they met Louise and Jim and Pauline for lunch at the Bridge. Louise was very amused when my father appeared at the door wearing a mackintosh and carrying a brief case and my mother said, "Kenneth – you look like a commercial traveller!" In the evening we dined at the Bridge and were joined by Sheila Kletts, who was amusing and fun. In the past they had said I would lose my friends if I married Alec, but now they could see how well he got on with all of them.

Nevertheless, Tyldesley had been a shock and when he got home, my father wrote and said he thought it would be dreadful if I lived there, it would be hell on earth.

I am ashamed to see how much I was in thrall to my family. Practically at the last minute, with our marriage less than a month away, I phoned Alec and said I wasn't sure about us. Looking back I am ashamed of my behaviour, that I should have messed Alec around in that way was unforgiveable, one moment saying I would marry him, the next, even at this late stage, that I did not think I could go through with it. It was mainly because I was so deeply influenced by my family. All my life – until meeting Alec - I had obeyed their wishes, and now with the drip, drip, drip of family disapproval I kept having doubts. Badger, in particular, made me question what I should do, for she was the authoritative school prefect, so sensible, so reasonable, so wise and I had always allowed myself to be counselled by her and taken her advice.

Alec was very unhappy. Why he didn't give up on me I can't imagine. The day after this phone call I was meeting Badger and my mother in London. I flew down with BEA and the three of us were walking down Regent Street with me in floods of tears, I was so unhappy at the thought of parting from him, and then my mother said something to me which was extraordinary, yet I found it very comforting. She said, "Well, if you go ahead and you're not happy, there's always divorce."

Yes – there *was* a way out. I know you shouldn't go into marriage thinking you could divorce but I clutched at this thought as if it were a lifeline. The next day I met Alec and was shocked to see how unhappy he was. I said that I *would* marry him – if he still wanted me to – and that it was final, I wouldn't change my mind again.

Tony Cooper arrived at our flat late on the evening of the 12th September. The next day Alec came over to meet him and take him out for lunch. I was working, and they came to the airport to collect me and we went to tea at the White House in Prestbury. Then we drove him to Tyldesley and he was very depressed when he saw it.

"Oh Delia dear," he said, "I hate to think of you becoming like those women standing on the doorsteps of their terraced back-to-back houses with rollers in their hair!"

We came back to our flat and I gave him spaghetti bolognese, a foolproof recipe from my *Daily Telegraph* cookery book, but I was worried that the mince had gone off, as I had bought it the day before and we did not have a fridge. I'm sure it had gone off, but Tony was much too polite to say anything.

The next day Alec and I rushed into town to buy my wedding ring. Later we came back and picked up Pauline and then went to the Bridge Hotel, where Tony was waiting for us. We had dinner and talked for hours and it was a most enjoyable evening. Pauline was charmed by Tony, as we all were. Tony slept the night at our flat and the next morning after we had gone to work, Mrs Walker our landlady came to the door.

"What are *you* doing here?" she asked Tony accusingly. "Do you know that Miss Despair is engaged to be married?"

"I most certainly do," he said, drawing himself up to his full height. "I was having dinner with her fiancé last night. Perhaps *you* don't know that I happen to be Miss Despair's cousin."

I am not sure she believed him. The Walkers were not happy with Pauline and me as tenants, for they could not understand why we came and went at such odd hours, going off at half past five in the morning for six o'clock starts or arriving back in the middle of the night. It was beyond their understanding that we should work shift hours and they probably thought us no better than a couple of prostitutes.

I felt quite sad after Tony went home. I didn't know until afterwards that he had come prepared to try and dissuade me from marrying Alec, but when he met him he had liked him so much and been so charmed by him, he hadn't the heart to do it.

The 18th September was my last day at the airport as a single woman. Mo Felthouse and others presented me with a beautiful cut glass bowl as a wedding present, not only from Passenger Section but from Apron and Load Control as well. It was very sweet of them all and showed they must have liked me more than I had realised. I packed my case, then Lou and Jim drove me to Manchester railway station where Alec was waiting, for we had booked sleeper accommodation on the train to London. We all had coffee, then to the amazement of passers-by we stood on the platform and I made Alec try on a very beautiful but expensive paisley silk dressing gown which I was giving him as a wedding present. Lou was going to exchange it at Kendal Milnes if it didn't fit, but luckily it did. Then they waved us off on the first part of our journey.

I had never travelled in a railway sleeper before and thought it a wonderful and exciting way to travel. I still think so: the movement of the train rocks me most delightfully to sleep, especially if I have drunk lots of brandy, which I did that night to try and ward off a cold. Many years before I had travelled alone overnight to Switzerland and my father had been shocked to hear that my French companion and I had lain full length on opposite sides of the carriage (he would have been even more shocked had we lain on the same side) but being in a sleeper was infinitely more comfortable and cosy.

On arrival in London we went to the air terminus in Cromwell Road, where we met Badger, Peter and little Mark, and had breakfast together before going to the airport, then onto BE 250, the flight from London to Geneva. We were very happy and I was giggly with all the brandy. We dumped the luggage at Gillie's flat and Alec booked in at the hotel he was to stay at. The next day my parents arrived. Alec and I went to church and afterwards we met up with the Rev Howells, a dear old man with great charm who was so nice and who seemed to assess the position immediately. In the evening Gillie's boyfriend Jean cooked spaghetti for us four, then Jim and Lou arrived and I went to bed early in an attempt to get rid of my cold.

CHAPTER TWENTY-FIVE

And so on the 21ˢᵗ September 1959 in the beautiful English church in Geneva, Alec and I were finally married. First Gillie drove me to the ancient Mairie where Alec and Jim, his best man, were waiting. The civil ceremony was all in French, of which Alec did not understand or speak a word. Jim said "Say Oui," so he said "Oui". We were given a dark red book in which the marriage ceremony was recorded, with spaces for twelve children.

Then I changed into my bell-skirted wedding dress, made of white material that resembled a table cloth and in which I looked rather like a doll. My father took me up the aisle looking grim-faced and just could not bring himself to look happy for us, but my mother managed a weak little smile. Someone said I held my bouquet as if it were an ice cream cornet, but I didn't know how else to hold it. In any case I was too happy to care. That day Alec told me he was just as much in love with me then as when we first met, only more so. What more could I ask for than that?

The service was very simple and very lovely. It was an unusual and special wedding in that church and in that place. The Rev Howells was such a dear, sweet man. He said, "Alec, your only concern now is Delia's happiness and Delia, your whole concern is Alec's happiness." He said, "I want you to write to me from time to time. I shall always take a very great interest in what happens to you both." He said he thought I had married "a right one" and that Alec was good through and through. He was wise and discerning enough to see what my parents could not.

However they were kind enough to pay for our wedding breakfast. We all drove to Port Gitana, the most beautiful restaurant half way between Geneva and Lausanne, on the shores of Lake Geneva. There were fourteen of us: besides Alec and me, Rev Howells and my parents, there were Gillie, Jean and Hilary,

Madame Galland and Marie-Lise who had come over from Lausanne, and my airport friends, Louise and Jim, Biddy and Pauline. Afterwards my mother said she wished she had invited Mr Howells's wife, but she hadn't thought of it at the time. Jim read out telegrams of good wishes from Alec's parents, Badger and Peter, Tony, Fuzz, Mr Lockley, Peter Cooper and Les Girls. We ate rainbow trout, roast duck, a pudding, cheese, wedding cake and coffee, all washed down with red and white wine and champagne.

Then Alec and I drove to the Hotel de la Paix in Geneva, where we had a sumptuous suite with a balcony overlooking the lake. The bathroom was tiled with shades of blue mosaic tiles and there was a crystal chandelier hanging in the little hall. We wandered down to the lake and when we returned to our room we found some lovely flowers from Pauline and the others. We went to bed, and felt quite shy with each another. I put on the white nightgown trimmed with broderie anglaise that Aina had made for me. It was rather hot, for there was so much material in it, and I took it off. Alec said he was glad I had been a virgin when he married me.

That night I had the most vivid dream: that I had married someone else, a much older man, and that when we were about to go to bed I rushed out of the room and found Alec and said, "Please take me away, I can't bear to be touched by this man!" But he said, "It's too late, I can't, you're married now. It's too late." I woke up terrified, then remembered it was not true and I was indeed married to Alec. It was such an overwhelming relief. I lay in bed and gazed at the ceiling and tried to memorize everything about the room, so that I would never forget it.

After breakfast we went to my parents' hotel and looked at the photographs and saw them off for their holiday. Then we had a fondue and caught a train to Milan, and then on to Pallanza, but the hotel we had arranged to go to was on the wrong side of the road, commercial and horrible, and Alec was very angry. The next morning we moved out and found the Hotel Milano, a most delightful little family-run place built out onto the lake where we had a room with a balcony for 14 shillings and sixpence a night. There were grape vines beneath our window. I wore my tight-fitting cherry dress and the waitress was in raptures over it. She made us taste lots of liqueurs and endearingly poured our left-overs back into the bottle.

We stayed at the Hotel Milano for ten days – it was a dear romantic place and I loved it. We walked for miles all around Pallanza, looked longingly at the villas and wished we could live in one. We took a boat to Isola Bella and Isola

Madre, both of which were beautiful, but I liked Isola Madre best; it was less ornate, more natural and the gardens were wild but exotic. Alec loved to go anywhere by boat. At Stresa I was amused by the open plan gents' lavatories and while Alec was there I waved to him. We went to the Villa of Pallavicino and watched the Duke and Duchess of Milan leaving in their car and felt like a couple of children at another child's party. Alec said I was fun to be with. I'm sure I hadn't been much fun in Lancashire.

On our last day the chef at the little hotel took us out in his speed boat. We had noticed him speeding past us in his boat while we were sitting by the lake and Alec had thought he was showing off, but it turned out he was just lonely and longing to take us off with him for a long trip. We would have loved this but did not discover it until too late. We were very sad to leave the lakes and the Hotel Milano. All the staff came out to wave us goodbye and we took lots of photographs. Then we caught an early bus to Milan.

We spent our last night at the luxurious Grand Hotel Duomo, but it was not the best day: we were short tempered with each other and quarrelled. We both said hurtful things which we regretted afterwards. In the evening we talked about this and wondered why. I was to discover Alec had a quick temper, but luckily he did not sulk and it was always over quickly. And the making-up was sweet.

The next day we went to Malpensa Airport but had to wait for two flights before we could get on one to London, arriving at 1 am. We slept at the airport, had breakfast, then got on BE 580 to Manchester, where Pauline, Biddy and Marna met us and seemed really pleased to see us again. Our honeymoon was over.

CHAPTER TWENTY-SIX

Back to reality. Alec seemed very depressed, wondering where we would go and what would happen to us. He had been down to see his old boss Mr Lockley, now Chief Constable of Staffordshire, who had promised to help in any way he could. However he did not recommend the job in Nyasaland. My father too had made enquiries about the Colonial Police but it seemed to be in the doldrums with little or no recruitment, even for very senior officers. We had decided I should stay on at the airport, but I had to pass my driving test and we would be unable to live together until I had.

Alec had been teaching me to drive and I had also had some professional lessons till it was decided I was ready. My instructor took me into Manchester and parked the car in a little side street. I went to the driving centre and joined a group of people, all waiting to take their tests. A girl told me, "Beware of the tall thin man with glasses and a moustache, he's horrible. After you've taken your test he gives you a small piece of paper if you've passed, and a big sheet if you've failed. He nearly always gives you a big sheet."

"Oh dear," I said. It didn't sound very hopeful. At last it was my turn and who should come through the door but a tall thin man with glasses and a moustache. We went off together to find the car – but to my consternation I could not find it. All the mean little streets around the driving centre looked alike. As we passed each one I looked desperately to see if I could see it. There were lots of cars parked in each street but I could not see mine.

"How much further?" asked the examiner impatiently.

"Not much further," I said. (Please God!)

At last I found it, in the fifth little street. "It's there," I said in triumph. He was not amused. We got in and I set off. I think my undoing was that we came to a road where another learner driver was doing a three-point turn and I waited for him to do it. It seemed to take ages – should I try and drive round him? I decided to wait, though I could feel the examiner's irritation. He said very little and when the test was over he handed me a large sheet of paper. I burst into tears.

On October 23rd I had to go to Tyldesley to meet Inspector Bartholomew, who was Alec's boss there, and he made me feel I was walking into a trap. I was taken to see the house we were to live in and could not feel anything but despair. If I once agreed to go there we might be stuck for years. It seemed so awful that the police, unlike any other branch of society, had no choice in where they must live. It was like a prison sentence.

On 22nd October Badger gave birth to her second child, a baby boy to be called Adam. We were all delighted, and I went down to Hove to stay with my parents. Peter was very proud. He was staying there with little Mark. After the weekend I went to the Metropolitan Police HQ as Alec had thought he might be able to get a transfer. I spoke to a very nice and helpful policeman. He said that men in the Mets could live within an eight-mile radius of their police station, but that accommodation was hard to find.

Back in Cheadle Alec had bad news: he had seen the Chief Constable, who said he could *not* be transferred to the Mets, and furthermore he had to move into the house in Tyldesley. Alec seemed very disillusioned with Lancashire. He said, "At least I have you – they can't take that away from me."

But the following days were difficult. We quarrelled a lot and said harsh and horrible things to one another, then we'd make up, but the thought of Tyldesley loomed like a black cloud. My parents wrote to me with an awful suggestion: that Alec should drop his rank and go to the Mets as an ordinary constable and try and work his way up again from there. When I told Alec this he was very angry, as I knew he would be. Then he said I had to choose between two alternatives, either to go and live with him in Tyldesley or to be separated. If we went to Tyldesley I would have to give up my lovely job at the airport and our marriage might not survive, whereas if we were separated I could continue with my job but we would only be able to see one another once a week. I hated the thought of either of the alternatives. It was horrible. I had to remember that I was to blame for the bad report Alec had received from the Chief Superintendent in Lancaster who had said, "As long as Alec Kay associates with the girl he has brought back from Cyprus, he will never do any good in this force." I was despondent. Perhaps it would be best if I were to get out of Alec's life altogether? He would be better without me.

But he said he was very sorry he had hurt me. He said, "I love everything about you. You're such a funny little creature. If you do anything to yourself, you'll break my heart." And he said, "I love you far, far more than you love me, far more than you'll ever know."

On the 5th November he said he was going to see the Deputy Chief at Preston HQ that afternoon, and asked me to go round to Jim and Lou's and wait there till he telephoned with the result. I went – and at ten o'clock he rang with wonderful news. The Deputy had been very nice. He said Alec could be transferred to Urmston. It seemed Tom Lockley had intervened and said he knew me and I was a girl from a very different background and that Tyldesley was not the place for us to start our married life. That blessed man had worked the miracle for us and we were overwhelmed with gratitude for him and delight.

I passed my driving test at the second attempt – the examiner was entirely different from the thin man with glasses and a moustache and somehow I knew he would pass me as soon as I got into the car.

CHAPTER TWENTY-SEVEN

The police house at Urmston was attached to the police station, which was on the corner of a road. It was enormous, quite old-fashioned and badly in need of decorating and none of the other policemen and their wives had wanted to live there, but we could see its potential immediately, for it was a fine Georgian house which, if it had been set in its own grounds in a country setting, would have been really beautiful. It had no garden, just a walled yard at the back, but Alec said he would put tubs there and paint them and fill them with geraniums. The front faced directly onto the road so that everyone could see exactly what was going on inside. People suggested we should get net curtains, but I hated those and we got Venetian blinds instead.

We started to decorate and the Inspector came in to see how we were getting on. "You won't have to bother with the lounge," he said, "that's been newly decorated already."

"Yes, but such terrible paper," I said, "Can you imagine anyone choosing that?"

Alec kicked me under the table, for the Inspector had chosen it himself. Would I never learn not to open my big mouth?

We put a black and white paper in the hall, depicting maps of old London with the Thames running through it, and we chose a Regency grey and white striped paper for the landing and stairs. It took nineteen rolls for that alone. Alec stood at the top of the ladder and let down the roll of paper. "Is it straight?"

I standing at the bottom said uncertainly, "Yes I think so….."

But it wasn't straight after all, or not straight enough and he had to take it off. He would get quite cross with me and I would grumble and say, "I'm fed up with always being the assistant."

"But a pretty awful assistant," he said, and it was true. I was. Once when we were painting a bedroom we were having an argument and he said, "If you say another word I'll throw this at the wall." He was holding a tin of glossy white paint at the time. I did say another word and he threw the tin of paint all over the wall.

That first year our marriage was not all sweetness and light. We were both very independent people and it was quite a volatile relationship. Not for nothing my father had said I was the most argumentative person he had ever known and Alec had a quick temper and was always the Boss.

On one occasion we were sitting in the kitchen eating our supper and we had a silly argument in which he said some Hollywood actress in a well-known film was Joan Crawford and I said, "No, it was Joan Fontaine."

"No it wasn't," he said.

"Yes it was," I insisted.

"If you say that again, I'll throw my dinner at the wall."

"But honestly, Alec, it *was* Joan Fontaine."

With that he threw his plate at the wall. It was cottage pie, which had taken me ages to make. It went all over our newly-painted kitchen wall. We both leapt to our feet at once and started clearing it up. It was a lesson to me, not to have to always prove that I was right. A bit irritating if I was, but what did it matter? It didn't help to prove it. Once after an argument he put me outside the front door. It was cold and I ran away and sheltered in the church in the middle of Urmston, where he found me. He was very sorry and so was I and we made it up.

Another time I was fed up about something or other and I thought I'd teach him a lesson. I took a suitcase with our dirty washing to the launderette because we didn't have a washing machine, and I wrote a note saying, "I have gone away, please don't try and find me," and left it propped up on the mantelpiece. I was in the launderette for hours reading a book, and people kept saying, "Your washing's stopped," and I said, "Yes I know," and carried on reading. Eventually I went home. He would be very upset by now, I thought.

But the joke was on me: there was no sign of Alec and the note was still propped up on the mantelpiece. He had gone to the cinema. We managed to laugh about that.

Our first furniture was a blue kitchen table and two chairs with blue plastic seats. We ordered a beautiful bedroom suite from Kendal Milne consisting of a bed, a dressing table, a wardrobe and a chest of drawers which we paid for out of Alec's savings account. I had no savings of my own. My mother had two beds sent up to us by Carter Paterson for our spare room, and I bought green candy striped sheets and green candlewick bedspreads, and the curtains were glazed chintz with green candy stripes. I was really into candy stripes, I thought they looked so fresh, and bought blue candy striped sheets for our bed, and forget-me-not blue woollen blankets trimmed with blue satin. Our kitchen was enormous with an old fashioned cooker and a stone sink with a wooden draining board. There was a walk-in larder, but we had no fridge and once I left half a cottage pie in the cooker. The next day I found it was covered with maggots, for a bluebottle had got in at the bottom and laid its eggs on it. We kept milk cool by standing the bottle in a bowl of cold water. We used orange boxes covered with a cloth for bedside tables. Our bathroom was so large you could have held a dance in it. We put some lino down and I painted it bright pink. We only ever had hot water when the back boiler was lit, and I longed desperately for an immersion heater but it was a long time before we could afford it.

I bought some very beautiful Sanderson material and gave it to a little woman to have it made up into long curtains, ice blue with sprays of roses for our bedroom, and grey with bunches of scarlet flowers for our sitting room, but she had never made lined curtains before and they were never quite right. We had a moss green sofa and two armchairs and I bought cushions in sweet pea colours to go with them, and a red rug for the hearth.

I went to a gallery and ordered a Renoir print of a little girl with a watering can on her head. When it was ready I went to collect it and put it in our bedroom but Alec said he couldn't bear to look at this spotty-faced little girl for the rest of his life, so I had to take it back. But he was mostly very good about letting me choose the things for our house. And besides, I thought I had such wonderful taste. I exchanged it for a Picasso from his blue period, of a child with a dove. For our sitting room I ordered a very large Gauguin print of five Tahiti women sitting on a bench.

One day there was a police dance and the Chief Superintendent spoke to each of us wives in turn. "Do you work?"

"No."

"That's good," he said approvingly. "Do *you* work?"

"No."

"And you?"

"No."

"That's good. A woman's place is in the home."

Then it was my turn. "Do you work?"

"Yes. I work at Ringway Airport."

It was not the right answer. He turned away in disgust.

I never really fitted in with police people. I tried very hard but the wives did not accept me and their husbands probably thought I was a snooty bitch. Partly, I think, because I was a southerner and I talked differently. In the canteen at the airport I had once asked for a glass of water, and the girl behind the counter said nastily, "We don't have glarses of water here, only glasses". There my friends had rushed to my defence and five of them standing in the queue behind me, including John Ellis, the supervisor immediately asked for "a glarse of water." They had rallied round to protect me, but here in the police circles there was no one to rally round. I was on my own.

Once I was trying to open a drawer in one of our built-in cupboards and I couldn't do it, it was stuck, so I went down the passage leading to the police station and spoke to the duty constable. He was a man in his fifties, coming up for retirement. "D'you think you could help me?" I said, "I've got my drawer stuck." He came in at once and we went upstairs and he managed to open the drawer, but I could see he was laughing to himself and I didn't know why. Later Alec explained he'd been telling everyone the sergeant's wife had got her drawers stuck. It had never struck me as funny, for to me, drawers were drawers, I had never thought of them as knickers. I was embarrassed.

The wife of a police inspector told me that she had moved house twenty-two times and she had it down to a fine art. She could do it in two hours flat. When she went on holiday, she said, she got up at five o'clock and put all her washing in the twin tub washing machine and had it dried and ironed before they left at eight. This was deeply depressing. How could I ever match up to that? I was inefficient and always had been.

My parents came up to stay with us, and they slept in the spare room with the beds with the green candy striped sheets. In the morning my mother said she had heard a lot of banging and what was it? I said their room was above the cells in the police station and the noise she had heard was the prisoners banging on the cell door. She was shocked. One of the other police wives told me she would hate to live in our house because once one of the prisoners had escaped and come into the kitchen and confronted the sergeant's wife who was living there at the time. I wouldn't have liked that either. I wondered what I would do if it happened to me.

At night I would be sitting reading and Alec would tap on the window as he went by, which was a signal that he was ready to come in for his evening meal. But one day there was a tap on the window and I rushed to greet him, but when I raised the Venetian blind it wasn't him at all, it was a horrible man leering in at me.

There is not much more to tell, for I stopped writing my diary soon after we were married. I saw no point in going on with it.

I often thought about that dream I had, that I had married someone else – well it was a nightmare, really. And I thought how very nearly my parents had prevailed upon me to do as they wanted, and how difficult it had been to go against them, and to go against all the people who thought they knew better.

For how lucky I was that I did marry him, and I so nearly might not have done. I was weak and kept having doubts and had shilly-shallied and made a huge fuss about not wanting to live in the grim north, which wasn't so grim after all. It was enough to make anyone change their minds. How lucky, how very lucky I was that he did not change his mind and give up on me.

INDEX OF CHARACTERS

(IN ORDER OF APPEARANCE)

EARLY DAYS - Hove

Mrs Priestley (A.J./Auntie Joan Priestley – who looked after us – I called her my Red Mummy)

Bretton Priestley (her son and my honorary brother)

Mrs Edwards (her mother - Granny Hove)

Badger (my sister)

Susie Roberts (first best friend)

Auntie Barbara (her mother)

Uncle Bruce (her father)

Tim and Richard Roberts (her brothers)

Richard and James Van den Bergh (other lodgers)

SURBITON

My Mother, when in England (my Blue Mummy)

There was also a Violet Mummy and a White Mummy (friends of AJ)

Auntie Winnie Cooper (Winks)

Macfee (Winks's Scottie dog who disappeared in the war)

Granny Cooper

Grandpa Cooper

Auntie Joan Moodey (sister to Winks and my mother)

Audrey and Jean Moodey (my cousins)

My Father (who I don't remember before age 6)

Maud (a maid)

Granny's Gardener at Fownhope, Surbiton

Edith (much disliked nurse-maid)

Great Uncle Harry & Aunt Elaina (who lived next door)

Guy, Valerie, Peter and Tony Cooper (their children, cousins to my mother)

Great Aunt Charlotte Sterry (Aunt Chattie – Wimbledon champion)

Great Uncle Alfred (her husband who spent the family fortune)

Great Uncle Archie and Aunt Maud Cooper

Nina (their daughter) and Bill Carr, her husband

YORKSHIRE

Auntie Margaret Scott-Hopkins (my father's sister)

Uncle Cliff (her husband)

Elizabeth and Clive (their children, & my cousins)

Nanny Scott-Hopkins (who disapproved of me)

Madge Harland (her best friend, later my landlady)

Mrs Reeves (first landlady in Kirbymoorside)

Mrs Jackson (second landlady, farmer's wife)

Our Jack (her son)

Mary-Ann, Whitey, Greybird (her cats)

Miss Adams (our first governess who was sacked)

Miss Taylor (second governess)

Margot K-Smith (my second best friend)

Metcalf and Baker (soldiers billeted at Town Farm)

Major Enderby, Mrs Enderby, Jonathan and Jasper

Wendy Peto (to whom I was unkind)

DITCHLING - SUSSEX

Mrs Macrae (first landlady)

Miss Dampier (Damps –second & most beloved landlady)

Mountenay Welcome (her ward)

Sir Henry Welcome and Syrie Maugham (his absentee mother)

Twopence and Pops (her cat and Pekinese dog)

Herbert and Eleanor Fargeon (writers, lived next door to Damps)

Josephine Phillips (my next best friend)

Misses Edith and Mary Dumbrell (who ran the school)

Miss Knowles (my form teacher)

Margaret Vixen (who was unkind to me)

HOVE

Mrs Marshall (our beloved daily)

Our grumpy gardener

Maureen Glen (& Esme her mother)

Pauleen Lurcott (daughter of good friends Capt & Mrs Lurcott)

Marigold Westle (best friend at the Convent)

Barbara Leek, Pamela Philpott, Betty Veil (convent girls)

Mother Lilley (a strong influence on me at the Convent)

Reverend Mother

Dr Dorothea Hunt (family doctor and Mother's friend)

Silly Jilly Willy (daughter of opposite neighbours)

Sir Seymour Howard (next door neighbour & Lord Mayor of London)

Edith (his fat wife)

Twinkle (my tabby cat) & Mr Chips (our dachshund)

Granny and Grandpa Despair (we didn't love her as much as our other Granny, she gave us *plain* chocolate, didn't take hints and was always in a hurry – for us to go)

Auntie Hazel (my father's sister) and Uncle Teddy

Uncle Tommy (father's brother) and Aunt Liesl

Grace Cox-Ife (Editor of 'Cats and Kittens' magazine, and my friend)

ROEDEAN SCHOOL

Miss Leigh (Tilda – house-mistress of the Prep)

Judy Harris (niece of Mother's friend Lilian Sparks)

Miss Holroyd (later Mrs Hart, my piano teacher)

Rosemary Day (Fuzz, my best friend at school & ever after)

Mr & Mrs Day (Fuzz's parents) & Edward (her brother)

Soppy Sid & Jealous Joyce (Fuzz's uncle & aunt)

Margaret Highwood (her cousin) and brother Tony

Miss Walters (Wallie – dreaded school matron at Keswick)

Jane Bowman (who ran away from school at Keswick)

Hilary and Pamela (unkind room-mates)

Mrs Taylor (the cook)

Mrs Postlethwaite (Possy) her assistant

Miss Cook (Matron, Junior School, Brighton)

Christine, Valerie, Lizzie Whitehouse, (Girls)

Elaine Cameron, Melanie Harmsworth, Daphne Pecker,

Miss Mortimer (favourite red-haired English teacher)

Miss Will (house-mistress of Number Three House)

Miss McCulloch, Matron (the Muck) her sister (the Mess)

Miss Trower & Miss Groves under-matrons

Mr Palmer (disappointing hospital physio who treated me for water on the knee)

Mlle Lavauden (the Lav) French teacher

Miss Woodcock (Peahen) English teacher

Anne Hall (Hal) and Elizabeth Davies (Felix)

Veronica Chevalier (Wonk) Pam and Gill

Colleen, Jill P, Jackie, Joyce, Pat Smouha

Sue Pettman (Soup) Lizzie Grant, Curry, Lodgy, Hamish, Cocky

Juliet, Sashby, Jean Pentreath, Libs, Grant, Lizzie Ham, Jean Carr,

Eileen, Rachel Nickerson, Joan, Stella, Sheila, Fiona, Sabo, Cherry,

Jos, Phillida, Nina Wingate, Gill Richards (Gordon) Pat Illingworth

Susan Grigor-Taylor (Grigor) & Tatiana

Martha Hamilton, Head Girl & friend of Badger

School Staff, Miss Bacon Music, Minnie Ha-ha English, Miss Middleton (Tiddle) Geography, Miss Bingham, Singing, Miss Mason

Miss Horobin Headmistress (the Horror) Miss Tanner (former Headmistress)

Miss Russell History, Miss Shipley Gym, Miss Ratcliffe and Patmac Latin,

Miss O'Kelly (Nokey) Maths, Miss Dunlop & Miss Mason, Piano, Miss

Lloyd Williams, Chemistry & Head of No.2 House

SURBITON

Mr Johnson (tennis coach)

Second Cousin Betty Filmer, sons John and Bill

Mrs Joy Rossiter & Mary H

Cousin Belmont

Richard Angeloni, Marietta, Richard Adams (friends of Badger from Nigeria, also Toby Lewis and wife Jean)

Michael Gould & sister Gill (friends of Badger)

Christine and Lionel Lawrence (Canadians who stayed with us at 28 St Matthews Avenue, Surbiton)

NIGERIA

Naomi Trevor-Williams

Kano: Diana and Desmond Milling, (Police) & son John

'Hydes and Skins'

Bill Sherley

Elizabeth Walls, Rachel and Edward

Steven and Fuhru (butler and cook at The Residency, Onitsha)

John and Isla Mann (formerly Isla White)

Dorothy Perkins (coached me in Maths, said I was hopeless)

Jimmy Jackson (Forestry)

Phyllis and Bud Savory

Dennis Gibbs (first love)

Hilary and Ray Bridges and son Robert

Mother Bernard and Sister Patrick Mack

Lonely Frenchman

HOVE

Susan Bayly (great friend of our family)

John Harland & Michael Pope (boyfriends of Badger)

Mary Reid (my friend who went to Kenya)

Mrs Langton and Mrs Gilling (friends of my mother)

Dear old Vicar of Poynings

Mr Middleborough (our dentist)

CUCKFIELD PARK

Miss Black and Miss France (Principals)

Staff: Mrs Hilder Dressmaking, Miss Thornton Sewing, Miss Wilson (Willie) Cookery, Laundry and Housework, Miss Eyre, Piano, Miss Dengate

Cuckfield girls: Sally Pearson, Pat Pears, Pam Malthouse, Phil Fox, Flick, Judy Gay, Lily Sansom daughter of Odette Churchill, Liz Aglionby, Ann Herbert, Molly Roe, Jean Paterson, Evelyn Aspinall, Christine Lennad, Elspeth Hardy

SWITZERLAND (I thought if there was just *one* thing in the world I would have liked, it was to stay on in Switzerland after my five months were up – but my father wouldn't pay for me any longer)

Paul, the Frenchman on the train

Mrs Smith who introduced me to:

Madame Galland

Bertil Galland, her son

Ariane Galland, her daughter

Christina, a Swedish girl

Ion Collas, son of the Greek Ambassador in Lausanne

Olivier, young French boy

Delphina, maid at 10 Chemin du Grand Praz

Victor Kravchenco (Ion and I were reading a book about him)

Claudia (a German girl who arrived after me)

Gillian (an English girl ditto)

Joyce (an American, pupil of Segovia whose room I inherited)

Harriet and Jenny two English girls who were not happy in digs

Hardy Regli, Swiss friend of Margaret Smith who took me to France

Ninine (German friend of Claudia, in my Class at school)

Hensley Nankeville who joined us at Madame Galland's

Bruna (maid who came after Delphina left)

Somerset Maugham whom Gillian and I visited in hospital

Marie-Lise Rossat, friend of Ariane who gave me French lessons

Bertil's friends: Francois, Alec, Danny, Luc and 2 Jacques

THE TRIANGLE, LONDON AND SOCIAL LIFE

Miss Jones (who taught us at the Triangle)

Miss Jenkins, Principal

Josephine Phillips

Pat Pears (whom I'd met at Cuckfield Park)

Jill Massey friend at Triangle, also Jane, Joanna & Brenda

Dr C a doctor at the Boltons and Mrs C for whom I worked while Val his secretary was on holiday – half way through my course, I was hopeless, he must have wished I hadn't.

Guy Aziz, first real boy-friend (who broke my heart)

Bunny Aziz, his brother

Other boyfriends, Tim, Leonard the Pole, Steve a dance partner

Mick who took me to a Cambridge ball also Paddy and Bob Pearch

Glen Coats most loved friend – we wrote to one another constantly till his death in a helicopter accident

Pets: Pym my Siamese cat – and Mr Chips

Susan Sparks, Auntie Lilian and Uncle Cedric

Nigel and Adele

FIRST JOB, SIMKIN MARSHALLS

Mr Harwood

Doreen and Nina

Mr MacKenzie

Mrs Minet

Dr Bloch

DAILY TELEGRAPH

Evelyn Garrett – the Editor

Rosemary, her secretary

Winefride Jackson, Fashion Editor

Beryl Thomson, Features

Claire Butler, Cookery

Alice Hope, Features

Wendy Peterson, Features

Felicity Brown, Reporter

Judy, second secretary to Miss Garrett

Margaret, my assistant

Hyacinth, Fashion illustrator

Michael Goode, News Room

Fanny Cradock, TV Cookery presenter

Johnnie Cradock, her husband

BEAUFORT GARDENS

Mrs Harland, friend of Auntie Margaret and best loved landlady

Glen Coats, dearly loved friend, we corresponded regularly till his death in a helicopter accident

Coila Coats, his elder sister

Camilla Coats, his younger sister

Commander Coats, his father, and Mrs Coats his mother

John and Rosamund, his cousins

Marigold, my friend

JAMAICA – (And before)

Holly (aged 6, my charge)

Lois Lynn, her mother

Chester Lynn, her stepfather

Peter R, her father (& page at my parents' wedding) & Elaine, his wife

Auntie Ailsa, her granny and my mother's best friend

Uncle Dick, her grandpa

Sister, her former carer who left as I arrived

Miranda and Merle, Holly's older sisters

Madame Morell, Lois's dressmaker

Monsieur Rene, the hairdresser

Buffy, the dog

S.S. ANTILLES

Marion and Frank – passengers

Peggy and Maureen

Paul Berger

Maureen (and Kenzie McCool)

Robert Lake, solicitor

CAPE CLEAR, JAMAICA

Harold, the butler, (and Beverley, his daughter)

Ethline, the house-keeper (Mrs Danvers who frightened me at first)

William, under butler

Stella, our maid

Mildred and Jean, other maids

Hilda, the cook

Beris, the chauffeur

Morgan, the cow-man

Roy, the groom

Captain Ellis, neighbour & estate manager

Denis S-Bingham & June, his partner

Major Vaughan, a neighbour

Victoria and David Vaughan, his children

Mary, governess to his children

Horses: Tina, Trigger, Calypso & October

Mrs Lynch, dressmaker

Mrs Kavanagh, mother of Lois

Mrs Lynn senior, mother of Chester

Arthur Prothero, solicitor and friend

Maurice Cargill, Editor of the Gleaner

Phoebe and Herbert Hart, friends of Maurice Cargill

Sir Harold Mitchell

Donald Pringle, Charlie and Marjorie (neighbours)

Patricia (Patsy) their niece and my friend

Ian Something-Brown and his friend Roy

Mr and Mrs Brindsley (American neighbours)

John Brindsley (their son)

Mr Macrae (Mac) friend

Mr and Mrs Ronald Graham

Sir Hugh Foot (Governor) & Lady Foot

Mrs Sharpe (friend of Lady Foot)

Noel Coward

John Gielgud

Princess Margaret

Douglas Williams of the Daily Telegraph

David Johnson of the Sketch

Jean-Pierre of a French paper

Errol Flynn

Driver Cox

Father Gary

Mr Wint (who gave Chester massage)

Colonel Veasey

Mrs Johnson, grandmother of Patsy Pringle

Meryl Leicester

Lady Leicester, her mother

Penny Kavanagh, (Auntie Penny, sister-in-law of Lois)

Supt Charles Howell and his wife Maureen

Mr Jarrett (friend of Mac)

S.S. PATRICIA (Swedish ship on return to UK)

Chief Deck Steward

First Officer At my dinner table)

Chief Engineer (Uncle Andy)

The Purser (Big Bully)

Mrs Margie Ching (a passenger) "

The Captain

Susan Bishop

IRELAND

Mrs K's family:

Cherie (her sister) Robey (her brother) & wife Molly

Denyse and Rosemary (nieces) Avril & Tom, Mary & Lynette, Frances and Ossie, Charlie and June, Alex Mitchell

Ken Freeman (son of Cherie) my boyfriend

The Cobbler's wife

WALES

Mr & Mrs George (caretaker of our Welsh cottage)

SPAIN

Bretton

Julian (his friend)

Marguerite (his girlfriend)

HOVE

Geoffrey & Roger H, sons of my landlady

Mr & Mrs Gilling (friends of my mother)

Mrs Langton (friend of my mother)

Eve Fyffe (my mother's best friend in Hove)

The Websters, the Herberts, the Kirkleys

Leonard the Pole (lodging with the Kirkleys opposite)

GRAND HOTEL, BRIGHTON

Mr Billington (Manager)

Mr Howard (Assistant Manager – 'Fancy Pants')

Miss Kyle (Head Recptionist)

Eunice (receptionist)

Vera (receptionist)

Alma (head of Bookkeeping) and Doreen

William the cheeky page

Jock the barman

Mr Ward, Head Waiter

Dizzy (my friend)

Old Daisy (chambermaid)

Carol (young chambermaid & my friend)

Guests: Mr W.H. Harper, Mr A. White

Doctor Ryder

Graham Wimbolt (took me out)

Mr Brown (met and married Vera)

ZERMATT

In our party: Martin

Colin

Virginia

Valerie

Bill

CYPRUS

S.S. Grimani – Salvo Italian 1st Officer who took me out

Maria (Greek girl who showed me round Athens)

Archbishop Makarios (deported to Seychelles the day we arrived at Athens, causing widespread riots)

Joy (my father's secretary)

Kasmaris (Greek Cypriot, worked in my father's office)

Tex (worked in my father's office)

Lottie (proprietor of the Octopus)

Paddy Rooney (first UK policeman to be shot)

Colonel Anstis proprietor of the Country Club, Kyrenia

Sally Anstis his daughter

Wing Commander Furzeman

POLICE HQ, PAPHOS GATE, NICOSIA

Joe Mounsey (UK Police, captured EOKA terrorists)

Margaret Mounsey (his wife, worked at Police HQ)

Enid (Confidential Assistant – recuited in UK)

Gillian (Confidential Assistant – recruited in UK)

Edwina (Secret Registry)

Macklouzarides (Head of the Secret Registry) Uncle Mac

Selma (Turkish lady at Paphos Gate)

Mr Robbins (Head of Colonial Police)

Phiippa Knox (his secretary)

Mr Biles (Assistant Head – for whom we worked)

Monty Rich (Head of Admin. Colonial Police)

Frank Woolnough (Colonial Police)

'Precious' (Colonial Police)

Chief Supt Tom Lockley (UK Police - Staffordshire)

Mr Dick Russell (Head of Transport (UK Police - Kent)

Tom Watkinson (Lancashire Police - Transport)

Alec Kay (Lancashire Police – Transport)

Sir John Harding (Governor of Cyprus)

Mayor of Lapithos (Greek-Cypriot)

Colonel Hunter (Wiltshire Regiment)

Superintendent Philip Atfield (Colonial Police, murdered by EOKA)

Michael Caraolis (EOKA terrorist, subsequently hanged for murder)

Sir Harry Luke (eminent traveller & author)

Fred Maxie (his friend)

Batchie Brown (took me out)

Eve (my friend in Kyrenia)

Trevor & Edward Edmondson (cousins of my mother)

Evelyn (their sister) & husband Don 'Fish Tarbet'

Tony & John RAF (my tennis partners at Nicosia Club)

Teddy and Ray (UK Police, friends of Alec)

Janet Gooch (took me to Nicosia from Kyrenia)

Colonel Prince (from Hove) who took me sailing

Tim B (Blues and Royals)

John H (Wiltshire Regt, stationed at the Castle)

Mike and Judy C (Wiltshire Regiment)

Vivian R (Wiltshire Regt)

Bill T (Wiltshire Regt)

Richard O (Wiltshire Regt)

Dim R & his wife Mary (Wiltshire Regt)

Sergeant Reginald Tipple (UK Police, murdered by EOKA)

Mr & Mrs Kaberry (shot by EOKA)

Yorgadjis (EOKA terrorist)

Sgt Eden and Sgt Demman (UK Police) shot by EOKA

Colonel Geoffrey White (UK Police Chief) took over from Robbins

Mr Webster (UK Leicester) 2nd in command, my boss after Biles

Mr Saunders (UK Police, Asst to Mr Webster)

Bill A (Wiltshire Regt, later transferred to Guards)

Brigadier Pickthorne

Paul (fiancé of Gillie's sister, took me to Cape Kormakiti)

Mr Ramsay (Admin boss, Secretariat, Nicosia)

Bob Browning (his assistant and my later boss)

Jean Yard (p.a. to Mr Ramsay)

Mrs Davies (secretary)

General Kendrew

Brigadier Balfour

McKendrick (worked at the Secretariat)

Ted and Vera Morgan (Police friends)

Maxie Ball (Lancs Police)

Ingrid Lushington & fiancé Rex

Peter Wildebloode, Lord Montagu & Michael Pitt Rivers (on trial and defended by Peter Rawlinson; their solicitor was Arthur Prothero)

EDINBURGH

Mr Gibson-Kerr (friend of Vera & Bill who purported to help with job)

June (friend at first hotel in Edinburgh)

Mr Allen (North British Hotel)

Shona (office worker)

Miss French (office manager)

Pat (secretary and my friend thereafter)

Frank (Restaurant Manager who drove us to the Trossachs)

Magdalene & Jean (in car for Trossachs excursion)

Will, Ian and Charlie (others on excursion)

Mr Berry (Manager of the North British Hotel)

LANCASHIRE

Mr & Mrs Kay

Mrs Platten

Harold Taylor (the butcher) and his wife

Peter and Norah

Margaret

Cousin Alice and husband Jim

John Wren (Police Supt)

Muriel (Chief Constable's secretary)

John and Joyce Hartley

KENDAL MILNE, MANCHESTER

Miss Bacon (head of my department, Model Suits)

Mrs Harries, Mrs Dent, Miss Blackburn (assistants in dept)

Pamela (my friend at Kendals)

BAYARD PUBLICITY

Mr Dickin (Managing Director)

'Big Mouth'

'Bossy Old Bag'

'Young Elvis'

INVALID CHILDREN'S AID ASSN

Miss Phillips-Williams

EAST MIDLAND ALLIED PRESS

Mr Nuttall (CEO)

UNIVERSAL SKY TOURS

In my office, Peter and Austrian woman

SAPHIR SHIPPING

Mr Saphir (CEO)

Mr Stewart

MANCHESTER AIRPORT

Miss Stewart (1st landlady) & Mrs Craig (neighbour)

Pauline Leigh (started at the same time and remained friends)

Roger C, Paul Ward, John Wildgoose

Muriel, Brenda B, Liz Rapallo

Supervisors: Alf Cooper, John Ellis, Harry Dunn, Jack Cannell

Mr Charlesworth (Admin Supervisor)

Mr Moore (much hated Senior Traffic Officer)

Louise and Jim Kane

Favourites at Ringway: Pauline, Biddy, Marna, Louise, Paul, Peter G, Ralph, Mo, Pusscat, Sheila K, Estelle, Brenda, Joyce, Pam, Patsy

Frances of Sabena, and Raye

Captain Hartley (ticked me off)

Mr Jack (unpleasant passenger)

Mrs Walker (our landlady at flat in Cheadle)

Aina Pavolini, (brilliant Italian dressmaker & designer)

Franz Scholl (German we met in Majorca who became a friend)

Gill Glennie's family

Rev Howells (Geneva)